Transboundary Heritage and Intellectual Property Law

Since the Intangible Heritage Convention was adopted by UNESCO in 2003, intangible cultural heritage has increasingly been an important subject of debate in international forums. As more countries implement the Intangible Heritage Convention, national policymakers and communities of practice have been exploring the use of intellectual property protection to achieve intangible cultural heritage safeguarding outcomes.

This book examines diverse cultural heritage case studies from Indigenous communities and local communities in developing and industrialised countries to offer an interdisciplinary examination of topics at the intersection between heritage and property which present cross-border challenges. Analysing a range of case studies which provide examples of traditional knowledge, traditional cultural expressions, and genetic resources by a mixture of practitioners and scholars from different fields, the book addresses guidelines and legislation as well as recent developments about shared heritage to identify a progressive trend that improves the understanding of intangible cultural heritage.

Considering all forms of intellectual property, including patents, copyright, design rights, trade marks, geographical indications, and sui generis rights, the book explores problems and challenges for intangible cultural heritage in cross-border situations, as well as highlighting positive relationships and collaborations among communities across geographical boundaries. *Transboundary Heritage and Intellectual Property Law: Safeguarding Intangible Cultural Heritage* will be an important resource for practitioners, scholars, and students engaged in studying intangible cultural heritage, intellectual property law, heritage studies, and anthropology.

Patricia Covarrubia is a Reader of Law at the University of Buckingham, Law School, UK. She is an intellectual property consultant at the Latin America IPR SME Helpdesk, co-funded by the EU Commission, and a member of the Comité Scientifique at Centre de coopération internationale en recherche (CIRAD), working for the sustainable development of tropical and Mediterranean regions. Patricia is manager and blogger at IPTango (Intellectual Property weblog – Latin America).

Cultural Heritage and International Law

Regulating Transnational Cultural Heritage
Diversity, Memory and Identity
Merima Bruncevic

Transboundary Heritage and Intellectual Property Law
Safeguarding Intangible Cultural Heritage
Patricia Covarrubia

Transboundary Heritage and Intellectual Property Law

Safeguarding Intangible Cultural Heritage

Edited by
Patricia Covarrubia

Routledge
Taylor & Francis Group
LONDON AND NEW YORK

First published 2023
by Routledge
4 Park Square, Milton Park, Abingdon, Oxon OX14 4RN

and by Routledge
605 Third Avenue, New York, NY 10158

Routledge is an imprint of the Taylor & Francis Group, an informa business

British Library Cataloguing-in-Publication Data
A catalogue record for this book is available from the British Library

Library of Congress Cataloging-in-Publication Data
A catalog record has been requested for this book

ISBN: 978-0-367-52077-9 (hbk)
ISBN: 978-1-032-38472-6 (pbk)
ISBN: 978-1-003-34523-7 (ebk)

DOI: 10.4324/9781003345237

Typeset in Times New Roman
by Deanta Global Publishing Services, Chennai, India

For my Gordito,
Joseita and Chewy,
Mamá Coro

Contents

Figures

Contributors

Bernardo Alarcón Porflidtt is a qualified Chilean lawyer currently doing PhD research at the Université Catholique de Louvain, Brussels, Belgium funded by the Chilean 'Programa de Formación de Capital Humano Avanzado (BECAS)'. His current research focuses on the interaction between intellectual property rights and the protection of Indigenous traditional knowledge in Chile. Until recently, he worked at the European Magazine Media Association in Brussels where he analysed European public policy on copyright law. He was also a teaching assistant at the renowned Universidad Austral de Chile where he taught public law.

Pamela Andanda is Professor of Law at the University of the Witwatersrand, Johannesburg, South Africa. She previously practised as an advocate and conveyancer and was a policy research and analysis consultant before joining the School of Law. She is the Chairperson of Wits University's advisory committee on ethics, has acted as an expert for the World Intellectual Property Organization's Standing Committee on the Law of Patents (WIPO/SCP), and was an external expert reviewer of the World Health Organization's Guidance Document on the Ethics and Governance of Artificial Intelligence for Health, 2021. Her research interests are in the areas of intellectual property, data protection, research integrity and ethics, biotechnology, health law, and governance of research.

Christoph Antons is Professor of Law at Macquarie Law School, Macquarie University, Sydney, Australia; Affiliated Research Fellow at the Max Planck Institute for Innovation and Competition; Senior Fellow at the Centre for Development Research, University of Bonn; and Associate Researcher at the German Development Institute. His research focuses on intellectual property law, and law and society in Asia. He is currently project leader of the ARC Discovery project 'Food Security and the Governance of Local Knowledge in India and Indonesia' and sole investigator of the ACR Discovery project 'Building an Intellectual Property System: The Indonesian Experience'.

Peter Harrison has a BSc (Hons) degree in Physiology and earned a PhD in Pharmacology. He practised law for 20 years with a particular interest in enforcing and exploiting intellectual property rights in the pharmaceuticals, biotechnology, and chemicals sectors. He has litigated in high-profile cases in the English High Court and Court of Appeal, Trial and Appeal Divisions of the Federal Court of Canada, the Court of Justice of the European Union, and the European Patent Office. On his return to academia, he received a PhD in Law for his work on the protection of Indigenous peoples' right to control genetic resources and related traditional knowledge. He is currently Assistant Professor in Law at the University of York, UK, and Programme Director for the LLM in International Corporate and Commercial Law.

Gyooho Lee is Professor of Law at the Chung-Ang University, Seoul, Republic of Korea. He has taught several classes at the WIPO summer school opened in Daejon, South Korea, since 2008. Currently, he is the president of the International Cultural Heritage Law Association under the auspices of the Korea Private International Law Association. He is a serving member of the Association of Critical Heritage Studies ICH Network Committee, and of the International Law Association's Committee on Intellectual Property and Private International Law (Standing Committee Geographical Indications). For his contribution to public service, he has won official commendations from the Ministry of Culture, Sports and Tourism of Korea, from the Small and Medium Business Administration of Korea, and from the Prime Minister of Korea.

Raúl Matta is a research fellow at the Institute of Cultural Anthropology/European Ethnology, Georg-August-Universität Göttingen, Germany, and at the Paris Institute for Advanced Study. He conducts research at the intersection of the anthropology of food, heritage, and cultural studies, with an emphasis on the cultural, social, and political uses of food and cooking by different actors and stakeholders. He has held research and teaching appointments in France, Peru, Germany, Mexico, and Malaysia, and taken leading roles in projects funded by the German Research Foundation (DFG), the French National Research Agency (ANR), and the European Commission (HERA JRP/ Horizon 2020).

Benedetta Ubertazzi is a practising attorney in the field of intellectual property and EU law. She is Aggregate Professor at the University of Milan-Bicocca, Italy, and involved in numerous research positions. She was the co-principal researcher in the project titled 'At the UNESCO Feast: Foodways across Global Heritage Governance', and researcher and trainer of the project 'EU Judiciary Training on Brussels IIa Regulation: From South to East'. She was the legal expert for the project 'AlpFoodway – A Cross-Disciplinary, Transnational and Participative Approach to Alpine Food Cultural Heritage'. She was also the legal expert representing the Italian Ministry of Foreign Affairs in the United Nation's negotiations, Ad Hoc Open-Ended Informal Working Group on Genetic Resources and Biodiversity.

Florelia Vallejo-Trujillo is Professor of Law at the University of Tolima, Ibague, Colombia. She is a council member of the Departmental Cultural Heritage

Council of Tolima. As a qualified lawyer, she previously litigated in a law firm specialising in intellectual property and competition law. She was also a patent examiner at the Colombian Superintendence of Industry and Commerce. Vallejo-Trujillo acquired her research experience at the National University of Colombia and at the Alexander von Humboldt Institute, where she had the opportunity to work closely with the Indigenous communities living in the Amazon rainforest.

Introduction

Patricia Covarrubia

Since the Intangible Heritage Convention was adopted by UNESCO in 2003 (the 2003 Convention),[1] intangible cultural heritage and its parallel concepts such as traditional knowledge and traditional cultural expressions have been increasingly important subjects of debate in several other international forums, e.g., the World Intellectual Property Organization (WIPO), the Convention on Biological Diversity (including its Nagoya Protocol), the World Health Organization, and the World Trade Organization. To the degree that more countries implement the 2003 Convention, national policymakers and local communities have been exploring the use of intellectual property protection to achieve intangible cultural heritage safeguarding outcomes (as well as political and economic goals). For example, the inscription of ways to make food and create handicraft products on the Lists of the Convention is often associated with efforts to register geographical indications to protect the use of the names of those products. Although international treaties are invoked to 'protect' cultural heritage, they lack enforcement mechanisms.[2] Moreover, while the inscription of intangible cultural heritage on the UNESCO list gives global recognition, thus making it visible to a wider audience, it does not necessarily safeguard it.

Additionally, the intersection between intangible cultural heritage safeguarding and intellectual property protection raises questions about the nature of ownership or stewardship of intangible cultural heritage, the appropriate nature of any kind of intellectual property protection, and its likely effects. Furthermore, plenty of scholarly work has warned of the difficulty of fitting traditional knowledge and traditional cultural expressions within mainstream and formalised intellectual property regimes. To date, many of these issues have been and continue to be discussed in the context of the WIPO Intergovernmental Committee on Genetic Resources, Traditional Knowledge, and Traditional Cultural Expressions, but there has been relatively little debate about protecting intangible cultural heritage

1 Convention for the Safeguarding of the Intangible Cultural Heritage, 17 October 2003, 2368 UNTS 3 (entered into force 20 April 2006).

2 Andrea Durbach and Lucas Lixinski (eds), *Heritage, Culture and Rights: Challenging Legal Discourses* (Hart 2017) 3.

DOI: 10.4324/9781003345237-1

in transboundary and diaspora heritage.[3] That said, intangible cultural heritage is generally linked to a community rather than a place; in contrast, intellectual property is connected to a place, a geographical area, and/or a jurisdiction. Intangible cultural heritage might be shared across borders; 'inspired by', or taken from a source, it may evolve in different places over time. This poses challenges for protecting intangible heritage as a form of intellectual property across borders and jurisdictions, especially in the absence of widely ratified international agreements. As there is limited if any scholarly analysis on transboundary intangible heritage,[4] the primary focus of the volume is to examine practices and strategies (intellectual property or related rights and norms) of safeguarding intangible cultural heritage that is shared in different countries.

Drawing examples from around the world, from both developing and industrialised countries, the book identifies several normative perspectives that explore the relationships between intangible cultural heritage and intellectual property. Identifying a progressive trend that improves the understanding of intangible cultural heritage, it combines perspectives that perceive intangible cultural heritage pragmatically (how communities approach it) and avoids framing intangible cultural heritage. Additionally, some chapters provide original suggestions or examples of the way communities shape norms and practices. Therefore, the focus of the book triggers distinct types of standpoints, namely protecting traditional knowledge and traditional cultural expressions under current legislation, environmental/cultural consequentialist arguments and distributive justice, ownership and management including cultural economy, protection and safeguarding, community participation, and rights enforceability. The book also covers key themes such as legal certainty, community rights, the principles of free and prior informed consent, and the inalienable nature of traditional knowledge among others. Exploring these, scholars and current practitioners in the areas of law and cultural and urban heritage, a pharmacologist, history and cultural anthropologists, and sociologists bring together interdisciplinary expertise and personal cultural interactions. Additionally, the contributors bring wide geographic coverage as the chapters cover the Americas, Europe, Africa, and Asia, providing a unique insight into different cultural/regional backgrounds.

In addition to offering a range of legal tools for safeguarding intangible cultural heritage in transboundary settings, the book provides the reader with a rich

3 The term transboundary is explained in Chapter 1. One of the common meanings is that of involuntary mass migration. See Aníbal Arregui, Gesa Mackenthun, Stephanie Wodianka, 'Introduction Decolonial Heritage: Natures, Cultures, and the Asymmetries of Memory' in Aníbal Arregui, Gesa Mackenthun, Stephanie Wodianka (eds), *DEcolonial Heritage Natures, Cultures, and the Asymmetries of Memory* (Waxmann Verlag 2018) 11. For 'transnational heritage' see Merima Bruncevic, *Regulating Transnational Heritage* (Routledge 2021).

4 But see Diane Sabenacio Nititham and Rebecca Boyd (eds), *Heritage, Diaspora and the Consumption of Culture: Movements in Irish Landscapes* (Routledge 2014); Alexandra Dellios, Eureka Henrich (eds), *Migrant, Multicultural and Diasporic Heritage: Beyond and between Borders* (Routledge 2020).

multidisciplinary frame of analysis that interconnects a variety of multifaceted thematic areas: on the one hand, the protection of collective and sometimes vague and widespread rights in favour of a community, and on the other hand, the regulation of industrial or intellectual rights, which as a rule are usually identified as territorial and individual rights. In this context, when it comes to recognising protected rights, that is, legal rights in transboundary situations, the book aims to guide the reader to understand (legal or common) practices and to appreciate national and international conventions, to guarantee the full exercise of these rights. To do so, some chapters give suggestions and/or describe what is done by examining the operational reality of what different legal systems deliver in practice; nevertheless, the majority of them do have a prescriptive approach that can be taken as supportive guidance for what governments, non-governmental organisations (NGOs), and communities can and should do. Consequently, the intended legacy of the book is to bring about development on cultural and/or legal strategies and practices by suggesting ways to protect and safeguard transboundary intangible cultural heritage. However, these are examined under the understanding that such practices and approaches should be adaptable to every country's peculiarities and/or circumstances.

The book discusses local case studies, examples, and practices, by bringing together field research and scholars' viewpoints. While states have a duty to be observant of international conventions and treaties, the book highlights good practices and guidelines that other nations and communities are applying in implementing their treaty commitments. For a broad overview, the study includes references to all forms of intellectual property, including patents, copyright, design rights, trade marks (certification marks and collective marks), geographical indications, and *sui generis* rights. It extends to the problems and challenges of the business of intangible cultural heritage in cross-border situations as well as positive relationships and collaborations among communities across geographical boundaries.

The book proceeds as follows. *Chapter 1* starts by detangling concepts and definitions. The title 'Enredados' (tangled in Spanish) is taken after the network of policymakers, academics, and practitioners in the fields of intellectual property and intangible cultural heritage.[5] The network aims to encourage debate on the relationship between intellectual property and intangible cultural heritage safeguarding, the intersections between intellectual property and intangible cultural heritage-related policy, and how intellectual property protection might be used as a tool for safeguarding intangible cultural heritage. All the book's contributors are part of this network and note the need to detangle the language and terms commonly used in heritage discourse which may have different meanings in different settings. Therefore, the chapter introduces the reader to common terms, what they

5 The *Enredados* Network was established in London, UK, during summer 2017, by Charlotte Waelde, Chair in Intellectual Property Law at Coventry University, and Harriet Deacon, Visiting Research Fellow at Coventry University

mean and how they are defined, what they cover, and why they can (not) be used interchangeably. This is a crucial introductory chapter especially as the book is aimed at an interdisciplinary readership.

Chapters 2 and 3 aim to map the broad intellectual property regime and the relationship with intangible cultural heritage. Specifically, *Chapter 2* notes the importance of understanding the concept of 'cultural property' and its relationship with intellectual property from the point of view of UNESCO and WIPO as well as national governments promoting development. *Chapter 3* follows with a debate on intellectual property and intangible cultural heritage using a topic that touches us all, that of food. It highlights the synergies of food in culture, traditions, and history but notes that the heritagisation of food is transboundary in character and, therefore, acknowledges a disjuncture between global and local perspectives.

As Chapters 2 and 3 highlight the existing inadequacies and limitations of the intellectual property regime in governing shared intangible cultural heritage, Chapters 4, 5, and 6 bring the discussion onto these matters. *Chapter 4* examines the normative justifications for protecting traditional knowledge and traditional cultural expressions using as a primary example genetic resources and drug discoveries. *Chapter 5* examines the legal framework safeguarding Korean intangible cultural heritage and addresses the question of whether such protection is consistent with intellectual property laws. *Chapter 6* considers the issues brought by protected geographical indications and trade marks.

While the previous chapters constitute the platform for discussing the complex interplay between intangible cultural heritage and intellectual property also from a cross-border perspective, Chapters 7 and 8 examine the commercial and business approaches from which heritage originates. Coombe asserts that there has been a 'cultural turn in development policies' in regard to cultural heritage,[6] and this may be due to intangible cultural heritage having different values, whether social, economic, political, or social.[7] On one hand, WIPO focuses on intangible cultural heritage as a tool for job creation, skill development, tourism, and revenue, and on the other hand, UNESCO uses the tool of inscriptions as makers of authenticity, which serve as attractions. Overall, both can be used as commercial tools supporting economic opportunities, which prompt conflicts of ownership that become even more problematic in regions with much shared cultural heritage. Therefore, two cases in Latin America are examined: *Chapter 7* examines the *Kuna* people and the creation of *molas*, and *Chapter 8* discusses the famous spirit drink *Pisco* a cultural staple for both Chile and Peru.

The use of intangible cultural heritage in promoting either tourism, traditional medicine, or creative industry, for example, has seen tension between neighbouring countries or regions that share cultural heritage. Therefore, Chapters 9, 10,

6 Rosemary Coombe, 'The Expanding Purview of Cultural Properties and Their Politics' (2009) 5 *Annu Rev Law Soc Sci* 393.

7 Christoph Antons and William Logan (eds), *Intellectual Property, Cultural Property and Intangible Cultural Heritage* (Routledge 2018) 68.

and 11 look at the challenges and conflicts brought by transboundary heritage *per se*. *Chapter 9* discusses the challenges associated with the misappropriation of intangible cultural heritage, and the contest ensuing from cross-border litigation and enforcement. Due to shared geo-political history, while disputes around intangible cultural heritage may occur in cross-border situations, the participation of communities is also observed. Together, governments, NGOs, and communities are starting to establish better working relationships by avoiding the term 'ownership'. Therefore, the final chapters of this book focus on the notion of 'community participation'. *Chapter 10* covers codes and protocols, which can be used strategically to protect transboundary intangible cultural heritage. *Chapter 11* emphasises the importance of cooperation as an effective regime for the safeguarding of shared intangible cultural heritage and notes the disputes over territorialisation and the importance of working together. It reflects on the UNESCO guidance and WIPO law and returns to the essence of them: to protect/safeguard.

By studying cultural and legal strategies as well as local case studies, the book develops perspectives and experiences by examining legislative provisions, traditional practices, local protocols, guidelines, and recommendations to establish and protect what is believed under Western views to be an intellectual property right over intangible cultural heritage in transboundary contexts. It is against this background that the idea to write this book emerged, providing a framework to explore the role of intellectual property in safeguarding intangible cultural heritage and the transboundary issues presented in local communities. The idea of the book emerged at the Fourth Biennial Conference of the Association of Critical Heritage Studies (ACHS) in a session organised by the *Enredados* Network. Therefore, drafts of some chapters collected in this volume were delivered in September 2018 in Hangzhou, China.

1 *Enredados* – detangling definitions and strengthening views

A lexicon of relevant terms, institutions, and legislations

Patricia Covarrubia

Introduction

As the edited collection is dedicated to a vast audience and its contributors come from different disciplines, cultures, and regions, it seems appropriate to explain the terms used throughout the book. Therefore, the aim of this chapter is to clarify the terminology used in the book by identifying common terminology, discussing its relevance, and assessing the practical and legal consequences of interchanging terms from a field to another in a sort of cross-pollination. For instance, remarkably simple terms such as 'safeguard', which is common in cultural heritage law and not used in the intellectual property system, can co-exist in both legal frameworks, if one aims to reach the same goal, that of protecting and safeguarding intangible heritage. In other words, meanings can be successfully entangled to promote policy coherence across regimes.

The book is the outcome of several multidisciplinary meetings of the *Enredados* ('tangled' in Spanish), a network of policymakers, academics, and practitioners in the fields of intellectual property and intangible cultural heritage. The network aims to encourage debates on the relationship between intellectual property protection and intangible cultural heritage safeguarding; the intersections between intellectual property and intangible cultural heritage-related respective policies; and how intellectual property protection might be used as a tool for safeguarding intangible cultural heritage. All the contributors to this book are members of this network led and coordinated by Charlotte Walde (Professor at Coventry University, Chair in Intellectual Property Law), Harriet Deacon (Heritage Consultant and Visiting Research Fellow at Coventry University), and Patricia Covarrubia (Reader at Buckingham University).

The book thus relies on varied and multidisciplinary expertise. Experts from different fields, cultures, and regions have worked together to discuss key issues of transboundary intangible heritage. The following sections will elucidate the key terms used in this multidisciplinary work. The chapter unfolds as follows: the first section elucidates the notion of intangible cultural heritage. The second section zooms in on the notion of transboundary heritage. The third section concludes by briefly discussing additional notions and relevant institutions and legal instruments. While the chapter illuminates key terms used throughout the book,

DOI: 10.4324/9781003345237-2

and provides a minimum common denominator, the definitions it provides are not exhaustive and each chapter may provide additional views.

Intangible cultural heritage: what you see is not what you get

In the era of globalisation, intangible cultural heritage is becoming a common topic discussed by diverse groups. Globalisation has built opportunities and opened minds; it has also provided societies with a willingness to meet different cultures. This has also resulted in the attempt to enhance domestic cultures and the use of 'nation brands' to increase advertising revenues, opportunities for development, and distinction in a world where thirst for cultural identification persists. States have adopted development strategies based on their cultural capital, in the form of tangible heritage such as monuments and sites, and intangible cultural heritage, such as festivals, traditions, food preparation practices, etc.

Intangible cultural heritage reflects culture that cannot be 'touched' and has no 'physical presence'.[1] In intellectual property law, intangible resources are reckoned as assets, like any other property, e.g., land and equipment in general. While intellectual property was traditionally excluded from measured GDP,[2] nowadays, it is becoming an important power tool of modern economic growth and development.[3] As part of intangible capital, skills, knowledge, technology, processes, and culture are included.[4] Cultural intangibles are usually inseparable from tangibles, as the non-tangibility is used to create tradable tangible goods.[5] For instance, art, handicraft, food, and medicines among others are referred to as tangible products and objects; however, the book discusses the skills, knowledge, and the intangible elements that are transmitted when producing them. Therefore, as Luzen suggests, the distinction between tangible and intangible appears to be artificial,[6] as they are not two separate things.[7] Moreover, as Shand observes, Indigenous peoples do not accept this separation between tangible and intangible heritage, rather conceptualising heritage in a holistic way due to their 'interconnectedness of things'.[8]

1 *Concise Oxford English Dictionary* (12th edn, OUP 2011).

2 Carol Corrado, Charler Hultern and Daniel Sichel, 'Intangible Capital and U.S. Economic Growth' (2009) 55 *Rev Income Wealth* 661.

3 Kamil Idris, *Intellectual Property: A Power Tool for Economic Growth* (WIPO 2003).

4 Corrado, Hultern and Sichel (n 2). Erik Brynjolfsson, Lorin M Hitt and Shinkyu Yang, 'Intangible Assets: Computers and Organizational Capital' (2002) 1 *Brookings Papers on Economic Activity* 137.

5 Sudipta Basu and Gregory Waymire, 'Has the Importance of Intangibles Really Grown? And If So, Why?' (2008) 38 *Account Bus Res* 171.

6 Jean-Louis Luzen, *UNESCO 2000 Report of the Bureau of the World Heritage Committee* (24th session 26 June–1 July).

7 Laurajane Smith, *Uses of Heritage* (Routledge 2006) 56; Harriet Deacon, Luvuyo Dondolo, Mbulelo Mrubata and Sandra Prosalendis, *The Subtle Power of Intangible Heritage, South Africa* (HSRC Publishers 2004) 10.

8 Peter Shand, 'Scenes from the Colonial Catwalk: Cultural Appropriation, Intellectual Property Rights, and Fashion' (2002) 3 *CultAnalysis* 47, 60.

All the contributors use the term *intangible cultural heritage*, taking as a starting point the 2003 UNESCO Convention for the Safeguarding of the Intangible Cultural Heritage (the 2003 Convention).[9] While the discussion within and including other disciplines has developed through years, today's discussion has departed from the philosophical rationale of the 2003 Convention.[10] In general terms, however, any notion of intangible cultural heritage should not be taken as written in stone. Rather, intangible cultural heritage is the 'living' culture of peoples and, as such, not static.[11]

The definition of *intangible cultural heritage* is found in the 2003 Convention, Article 2(1) as

> practices, representations, expressions, knowledge, skills – as well as the instruments, objects, artefacts, and cultural spaces associated therewith – that communities, groups and, in some cases, individuals recognize as part of their cultural heritage. This intangible cultural heritage, transmitted from generation to generation, is constantly recreated by communities and groups in response to their environment, their interaction with nature and their history, and provides them with a sense of identity and continuity, thus promoting respect for cultural diversity and human creativity.

Other conventions and legal instruments use similar wording. For instance, the Convention on Biological Diversity refers to cultural (tangible and intangible) heritage including a list similar to that under Article 2(2) of the 2003 Convention. Moreover, the World Intellectual Property Organization (WIPO) is aiming to finalise an international legal instrument for the protection of traditional knowledge, traditional cultural expressions, and genetic resources that refers to the 2003 Convention and thus harmonise definitions.[12]

Transboundary: beyond the pale

After having defined the notion of intangible heritage, this section briefly explores the concept of transboundary heritage. Traditionally, cultural heritage, be it tangible or intangible, has a linkage with identities. Yet, cultural interactions transcend boundaries, triggering a complex set of political, economic, and social matters. In fact, boundary lines do not circumscribe cultural heritage. Hence, the book attempts to evaluate the approaches adopted by states and the international community when intangible cultural heritage is shared by more than one state.

9 Convention for the Safeguarding of the Intangible Cultural Heritage (CSICH), 17 October 2003, 2368 UNTS 3 (entered into force 20 April 2006).

10 Federico Lenzerini, 'Intangible Cultural Heritage: The Living Culture of Peoples' (2011) 22 *EJIL* 101.

11 ibid.

12 WIPO, *Glossary of Key Terms* (WIPO/GRTKF/IC/41/INF/7).

In the book, the term *transboundary* heritage refers to heritage that extends across international political borders and transcends boundaries. The term includes cases of 'diasporic' heritage, namely, that form of intangible heritage that accompanies people in their (mostly involuntary mass) migration from one part of the world to another. It also includes instances in which borders are drawn between populations that have not moved anywhere for centuries.[13] Transboundary heritage can also include cases of Indigenous cultural heritage, as 'first nations' have their own concepts of territory within and across larger nation states.

Let's tango [I mean … tangle]

This section aims to clarify and explain some key verbs, adjectives, words, and expressions that are used by scholars, policymakers, and practitioners of different fields when discussing intangible cultural heritage. While the intention is to *detangle* and explain the meaning of such terms, there is awareness that, in some cases, a common word may not be found that would satisfy all disciplines involved and that there are variations across different fields of study.

In particular, this section discusses the meaning of *safeguarding* and *protecting cultural heritage*. The verb 'safeguarding' is often used in conjunction with, or in lieu of, other verbs such as 'preserving', 'protecting', and 'conserving'. The question is: what do these terms mean? Do they have identical meaning across disciplines? Cultural heritage law generally requires states to *safeguard* or protect cultural heritage.

Article 1 of the 2003 Convention sets up as one of its main purposes to 'safeguard' intangible cultural heritage while Article 2(3) describes activities of 'safeguarding'. The latter is explained as

> measures aimed at ensuring the viability of the intangible cultural heritage, including the identification, documentation, research, *preservation*, *protection*, *promotion*, *enhancement*, transmission, particularly through formal and non-formal education, as well as the revitalization of the various aspects of such heritage.
>
> [emphasis added]

It is submitted that all the expressions used are consequential of one another. For example, by documenting heritage, one is *preserving* it, by *promoting* heritage, one is *enhancing* it. Twarog explains that countries may focus on different objectives in accordance with their priorities and their own circumstances. For instance, one country may attempt to *preserve* its intangible cultural heritage to prevent rapid loss; others may focus on *protection* to *prevent* misappropriation; and others may focus on *promoting* heritage thus enhancing its potential by dissemination

13 See, e.g., Makau W Mutua, 'Why Redraw the Map of Africa: A Moral and Legal Inquiry' (1995) 16 *Michigan Journal of International Law* 1113.

and integration into governmental projects.[14] While such terms are not easily exchangeable, scholars tend to shift from one word to another swiftly.

The word 'safeguard' is usually found in cultural heritage law, while the word 'protection' is used in other legal instruments. For instance, the intellectual property system uses the terms 'defensive protection' and 'positive protection' to distinguish the protection of commercial rights. Yet, WIPO's Intergovernmental Committee on Intellectual Property and Genetic Resources, Traditional Knowledge and Folklore (WIPO IGC) has acknowledged that the 'protection of traditional knowledge' goes further than legal protection, and accordingly, extends to practical conservation, thus *safeguarding* such knowledge against loss.[15] The 2003 Convention aims to 'safeguard' intangible cultural heritage, while the Convention for the Protection of Cultural Property in the Event of Armed Conflict (the Hague Convention)[16] focuses on the *protection* of cultural property from damage and *misappropriation*. Nonetheless, the Hague Convention requires states to *protect* cultural property by adopting 'safeguarding measures such as the preparation of inventories'. Consequently, one can conclude that in the latter context, the verbs 'safeguard', 'protect', and 'preserve' can be interchanged.

The 2003 Convention calls for communities at large to take responsibility in safeguarding intangible cultural heritage and consequently, helping 'to enrich cultural diversity and human creativity'.[17] On the other hand, the Hague Convention calls for public and cultural heritage professionals, the military, and law-enforcement agencies with a view to sparing cultural heritage from consequences of possible armed conflicts, the rationale being protecting cultural heritage from damage and misappropriation. Both instruments aim to protect cultural heritage; nonetheless, the Hague Convention focuses on 'keeping the possession of' cultural property while the 2003 Convention focuses on the 'transmission' and 'revitalisation' of cultural heritage. That said, the Hague Convention focuses on 'keeping possession of' cultural property for the future transmission of the same to future generations.[18] The different priorities of the examined legal instruments explain the use of slightly different terms.

Finally, the International Labour Organization (ILO) Convention 169 on Indigenous and Tribal Peoples requires states to adopt special measures 'for safeguarding the persons, institutions, property, labour, cultures and environment of

14 Sophia Twarog, 'Protecting and Promoting Traditional Knowledge: Systems, National Experiences and International Dimension' in Sophia Twarog and Promila Kapoor (eds), *Protecting and Promoting Traditional Knowledge: Systems, National Experiences and International Dimensions* (United Nations Conference on Trade and Development 2004) 63–64 and 66.

15 WIPO, *Intergovernmental Committee on Intellectual Property and Genetic Resources, Traditional Knowledge and Folklore* (37th session Geneva, 27–31 August 2018 WIPO/GRTKF/IC/37/6).

16 Convention for the Protection of Cultural Property in the Event of Armed Conflict (Hague Convention), 14 May 1954, in force 7 August 1956, 249 UNTS 240.

17 Henrietta Marrie, 'The UNESCO Convention for the Safeguarding of the Intangible Cultural Heritage and the Protection and Maintenance of the Intangible Cultural Heritage of Indigenous Peoples' in Laurajane Smith and Natsuko Akagawa (eds), *Intangible Heritage* (Routledge 2009) 174.

18 Deacon, Dondolo, Mrubata and Prosalendis (n 7).

the peoples concerned'.[19] In other words, the International Labour Organization protects intangible cultural heritage by focusing on the rights of Indigenous peoples. The United Nations Declaration on the Rights of Indigenous Peoples (UNDRIP) adopts a similar approach.[20] Alternatively, the Convention on Biological Diversity (CBD) and its Nagoya Protocol both protect intangible cultural heritage by regulating access to and use of genetic resources. In conclusion, different legal instruments adopt diverse approaches and varied terminologies depending on their special focus, intended aim, and objectives.

The concept of *preservation* is also common in the context of cultural heritage law. Preservation can be 'in situ' and 'ex situ'.[21] Preservation in situ refers to the preservation of an archaeological asset in its original location. Preservation ex situ indicates the preservation of artifacts outside their original/natural contexts/habitats. Preservation generally refers to protection from damage; it also indicates maintaining something in its original state by protecting its uniqueness. However, such a literal meaning cannot be taken because culture is fluid. Yet, when referring to documentation and inventories, then the literal meaning applies. On the other hand, the rationale of preservation is to support the continuation of transmission, and this goes beyond securing the interest of state parties. Finally, preservation of intangible cultural heritage means avoiding the dissolution of such culture by safeguarding and indeed protecting it. By preserving, one protects tradition and a way of life.[22] For instance, the WIPO IGC Secretariat aims to 'preserve' cultures.[23] For Gervais, by preserving, one contributes to safeguarding traditional cultures.[24] In conclusion, it is impossible to provide a universal definition of the term 'preservation' that may be satisfactory to use in a variety of contexts; this is because the definition may not fulfil all the expectations or needs in such complex and varied settings.

(Mis)appropriation: thou shalt not steal

Paterson and Karjala note that the term *appropriation* is used to narrate the sense of cultural loss that Indigenous peoples experience due to ongoing societal

19 C169 – Indigenous and Tribal Peoples Convention, 1989 (No. 169), Article 4.

20 United Nations Declaration on the Rights of Indigenous Peoples (UNDRIP) GA Res. 61/295, UN Doc. A/RES/61/295, in force 13 September 2007.

21 Twarog (n 14) 64.

22 Russel Staiff and Somyot Ongkhluap, 'Tourism and the Perceptions of Local Communities: Case Study of the World Heritage Site of the Historic City of Ayutthaya' in Marie-Theres Albert, M Richon, Maria Jose Vinals and Andrea Witcomb (eds), *Community Development through World Heritage* (UNESCO 2012) 50.

23 WIPO IGC Secretariat, The Protection of Traditional Cultural Expressions, Draft Articles, WIPO Doc WIPO/GRTKF/IC/18/4 9 (2011).

24 Daniel Gervais, 'Traditional Innovation and the Ongoing Debate on the Protection of Geographical Indications' in Peter Drahos and Susy Frankel (eds), *Indigenous Peoples' Innovation: Intellectual Property Pathways to Development* (ANU Press 2021) 140.

practices.[25] The cultural appropriation of Indigenous heritage (explained by Antons in Chapter 2 as 'the taking of culture') by non-Indigenous people entails a loss that goes beyond economic deprivation. Such taking can be of secret and/or sacred culture and thus, not only of economic value but also cultural and even spiritual value. Rogers defines appropriation as 'the use of one's culture's symbols, artefacts, genres, rituals, or technologies by members of another culture – regardless of intent, ethics, function, or outcome'.[26] Due to the right of Indigenous peoples to maintain the control of their cultural heritage, Shand considers the cultural appropriation of Indigenous heritage as a new type of colonisation.[27]

In parallel, the term *misappropriation* was developed by common lawyers to indicate a form of unfair competition, which involves free-riding and direct competition.[28] It is therefore a legal term that adds responsibility to the wrong user as it focuses on the tort of misappropriation. Nonetheless, such legal misappropriation provides economic rights and remedies to affected individuals that appear not to be adequate in the cases of appropriation of cultural heritage. It is understandable that any type of cultural reproduction breaches cultural integrity and consequently, intellectual property rights. Nonetheless, Rebecca Tsosie, of Yaqui heritage, warns against a restrictive and limited view focusing just on economic harm due to the 'profound cultural harm' that could happen due to misuse of cultural heritage.[29] Expanding intellectual property rights to protect intangible cultural heritage can address some abuses. Yet, while some scholars believe that the system is inadequate and unsuitable to safeguard Indigenous heritage,[30] other scholars consider the use of moral rights in copyright, e.g., unlimited in time, inalienable, and imprescriptible, as better suited to protect such heritage. There are two types of intellectual property protection, one which is called 'defensive protection', that prevents third parties from seeking rights over one's rights; and the other, called 'positive protection', that establishes intellectual property rights over one's rights. However, the intellectual property legal system is designed to protect the economic interest of the parties rather than 'safeguarding' heritage.[31] As a result, intellectual property is widely ignored as a tool for protecting Indigenous

25 Robert Patterson and Dennis Karjala, 'Looking beyond Intellectual Property in Resolving Protection of the Intangible Cultural Heritage of Indigenous Peoples' (2003) 11 *Cardozo J of Int'l & Com Law* 657.

26 Richard Rogers, 'From Cultural Exchange to Transculturation: A Review and Reconceptualization of Cultural Appropriation' (2006) 16 *Commun Theory* 4, 474–503.

27 Shand (n 8) 47–88.

28 Patterson and Karjala (n 25) 659.

29 Rebecca Tsosie, *Intergovernmental Committee on Intellectual Property and Genetic Resources, Traditional Knowledge and Folklore* (33rd session Geneva, 27 February–3 March 2017 WIPO/GRTKF/IC/33).

30 See Shand (n 8) referring to this thought, 61.

31 Marrie (n 17) 181.

heritage because it is a negative right, that is, a right to exclude others from use, rather than enabling opportunities to safeguard Indigenous heritage.[32]

When local communities and Indigenous peoples design the means to safeguard intangible heritage, Coomber urges them to consider 'a wide range of social objectives', including community security and environmental sustainability.[33] Additionally, Correa recommends a regime to prevent misappropriation by following a step-by-step approach, covering documentation, proof of origin, and free prior informed consent.[34] Nevertheless, there is still no development of such a regime. Domestic efforts exist in the form of *sui generis* systems, but which lack an extra-territorial effect. In a world that is becoming more culturally uniform rather than culturally knowledgeable due to globalisation, it is imperative that we prevent (mis)appropriation by building a regime that focuses on respect and liability, rather than purely acknowledging entitlement and ownership, and thus empowering communities with the right to control their culture.[35]

Indigenous peoples, local communities, minorities, and groups: adding a label

As governments often require people to be defined for ease of governing them, legal definitions have legal consequences.[36] Therefore, this section briefly discusses key terms used in the book such as Indigenous peoples, local communities, minorities, and groups. Some of the terms used in the book are connected and can overlap. Once again, it is important to acknowledge that terms may mean more than their ordinary meaning and that terminology keeps evolving over time.[37]

No officially accepted definition of Indigenous peoples is adopted in the book. Some countries refer to tribes, nomads, and aboriginals, among others; others use a different terminology.[38] Because international conventions and organisations

32 Roya Ghafele, 'How Developing Countries Can Benefit from Intellectual Property: The Role of Collective Marks in Tourism' (2011) Munich Personal RePEc Archive, Paper No. 32762.

33 Rosemary J Coombe, Sarha Ives and Daniel Huizenga, 'Geographical Indications: The Promise, Perils and Politics of Protecting Place Based Products' in Matthew David and Debora J Halbert (eds), *The SAGE Handbook of Intellectual Property* (Blackwell 2014).

34 Carlos Correa, 'Traditional Knowledge and Intellectual Property: Issues and Option Surrounding the Protection of Traditional Knowledge' (2001) *Quaker United Nations Office Discussion Paper* 18. See also Shand (n 8) 67–69.

35 Reichman advocates for a liability regime rather than a property-based system. Jerome Reichman, 'Using Liability Rules to Stimulate Local Innovation in Developing Countries' in K Maskus and J Reichman (eds), *International Public Goods and Transfer of Technology under a Globalized Intellectual Property Regime* (Cambridge University Press 2005).

36 Urike Barten, 'What's in a Name? Peoples, Minorities, Indigenous Peoples, Tribal Groups and Nations' (2015) 14 *JEMIE* 1.

37 'Things are never gonna be the same now. I mean, look at this. You got aliens. You got big green guys tearing down buildings. When I was kid, I used to draw cowboys and Indians'.

'Um actually, it's Native American but whatever'. Adrian Toomes and Phineas Mason in *Spider-Man: Homecoming* (Marvel Comics 2017).

38 See Indigenous Corporate Training Inc in Canada.

refer to one term or several terms, or even different terminology, the contributors adopt the terms that are generally used in their field of study in line with the subject matter. In addition, in referring to peoples, groups, communities, etc., the contributors gave due consideration to how such peoples, groups, and/or communities prefer to be acknowledged.

That said, the two most prominent instruments that deal with Indigenous peoples, that of the United Nations Declaration on the Rights of Indigenous Peoples (UNDRIP) and the International Labour Organization Convention (No 169) concerning Indigenous and tribal peoples in independent countries (aka ILO Convention 169), shall be the standard point of reference when dealing with Indigenous peoples and their cultural heritage.

Human rights instruments approach the term *Indigenous peoples* based on self-identification, rather than providing a definition. In that regard, self-identification and consent of the group is required.[39] UNESCO also refers to a description rather than a definition when mentioning Indigenous peoples.[40] The ILO Convention 169 refers to self-identification as a fundamental criterion and so does UNDRIP. The United Nations has developed a modern understanding of this term based on:

> self-identification as indigenous peoples at the individual level and accepted by the community as their member; historical continuity with pre-colonial and/or pre-settler societies; strong link to territories and surrounding natural resources; distinct social, economic or political systems; distinct language, culture and beliefs; from non-dominant groups of society; and, resolve to maintain and reproduce their ancestral environments and systems as distinctive peoples and communities.[41]

The United Nations often uses the terms 'Indigenous' and 'tribal' based on differences that have little practical relevance in this book.[42] However, ILO Convention 169 differentiates 'Indigenous peoples' from 'tribal people'. While the former refers to groups that existed before colonisation retaining their social system and institutions, the latter indicates groups that are based on self-regulation found on customs.[43] The 2003 Convention refers to 'communities', and 'groups' to indicate non-Indigenous peoples. Communities, as asserted by Deacon, are 'fluid entities'.[44] The Convention on Biological Diversity refers to the terms 'Indigenous peoples' and 'local communities' but it does so, as explained by Marrin, in geo-

39 Barten (n 36).

40 UNESCO, *International Meeting of Experts on Further Study of the Concept of the Rights of Peoples* (1989 SHS.89/CONF.602/7) para 22.

41 United Nations, *Who Are Indigenous Peoples?* (United Nations 5th session Factsheet No 1).

42 Barten (n 36) 13.

43 Peter Drahos and Susy Frankel, 'Indigenous Peoples' Innovation and Intellectual Property: The Issues' in Peter Drahos and Susy Frankel (eds), *Indigenous Peoples' Innovation: Intellectual Property Pathways to Development* (ANU 2012) 10.

44 Deacon, Dondolo, Mrubata and Prosalendis (n 7).

political terms.[45] It refers to Indigenous peoples to indicate peoples of the new world who were colonised,[46] while the term 'local communities' is preferred by countries like Russia, China, and India and widely used in Africa to identify their own ethically and culturally diverse populations.[47]

Minorities is another term that sometimes appears in the literature. Minorities are not recognised as a 'people' in international law and have no right to self-determination. Barten claims that the purpose of such categorisation is to keep their distinctiveness while being included in the state rather than enabling their autonomous development.[48]

Traditional knowledge, traditional cultural expressions, folklore, traditional medicine, and genetic resources

The word 'culture' is the main protagonist of the book. Within such a notion, reference is made to the intangible part of it that includes 'tradition'. *Traditional knowledge* refers to the way knowledge is acquired and used, rather than merely indicating 'antique' or 'ancient' knowledge. The book avoids adopting a dogmatic idea of what is to be regarded as traditional knowledge, rather adopting different approaches depending on context. In fact, traditional knowledge is valuable to its holders in diverse ways, from their livelihoods and well-being to economic and social management; from exploitation of local ecosystems to facing cultural extinction; from preserving knowledge to land rights, among others. Therefore, a range of definitions exists, and there is not yet an accepted international meaning. As the book interlinks culture with intellectual property, its starting point is the definition adopted by the WIPO IGC. This text-based negotiation aims to reach an agreement on an international legal instrument for the protection of traditional knowledge, traditional cultural expressions, and genetic resources. However, 20 years on, the debate continues.[49]

The WIPO IGC distinguishes traditional knowledge in the broad sense from traditional knowledge in the strict sense. The broad description of traditional knowledge embraces the content of knowledge itself that is included in practices and knowledge and that considers Indigenous and local communities alike.[50] Traditional knowledge in the narrow sense refers to knowledge that results from intellectual activity in a 'traditional context'. This is eligible if it has an objective link with the community of origin, forming part of the community's own self-identity.

45 Marrie (n 17) 184.

46 Barten distinguishes three categories of Indigenous peoples: groups subjected to colonialism; groups not subjected to colonialism; and groups in which settlers occupied the land. Barten (n 36) 12.

47 Marrie (n 17) 184.

48 Barten (n 36) 11.

49 WIPO IGC was established in September 2000, and it began its deliberation in 2001.

50 WIPO, *Glossary of Key Terms* (n 12).

The term *traditional medicine* is also used in the chapters. The World Health Organization has defined traditional medicine as

> the sum total of the knowledge, skills and practices based on the theories, beliefs and experiences Indigenous to different cultures, whether explicable or not, used in the maintenance of health, as well as in the prevention, diagnosis, improvement or treatment of physical and mental illnesses.[51]

Regarding *traditional cultural expressions*, as the WIPO has not reached a consensus on the term, it thus refers to it with examples such as traditional music, performances, and narratives, among others. Traditional cultural expressions can be in either 'tangible or intangible forms'. Other terms are used in national or regional forums and therefore, the chapters reflect this variety. Moreover, as indicated by the WIPO IGC, 'expressions of folklore' are synonyms with traditional cultural expressions and as such are used as an alternative.

Finally, when examining the term *genetic resources*, the WIPO IGC covers different regimes such as the Convention on Biological Diversity, and the Decision 391 on Access to Genetic Resources of Andean Community; it also refers to the Food and Agriculture Organization (FAO) Glossary for Fisheries. It adds other terms that are used in other legislations that touch upon genetic resources such as the FAO International Treaty on Plant Genetic Resources for Food and Agriculture, the FAO International Code of Conduct for Plant Germplasm Collecting and Transfer, and the FAO International Undertaking on Plant Genetic Resources. All of them give the reader a wealthy and wide evaluation of what such a term entails. In summary, all definitions refer to genetic and biological material.

UNDRIP, WIPO, WTO

The book refers to several international conventions, agreements, and treaties relating to culture. However, there exist cultural differences among states and their international obligations differ, depending on their ratification of such international legal instruments, and the existence of customary law and general principles of international law. Moreover, while some international legal instruments are binding, others constitute soft law. This section briefly discusses the most relevant instruments and international organisations pertaining to intangible cultural heritage detailing their aim and objectives, scope, membership, and current use.

Adopted by the United Nations General Assembly in 2007, the United Nations Declaration on the Rights of Indigenous Peoples (UNDRIP) has no legal binding effect. Some scholars nonetheless argue that it already reflects binding norms

51 World Health Organization, *Traditional Medicine* (*World Health Organization*) <www.who.int/health-topics/traditional-complementary-and-integrative-medicine#tab=tab_1> accessed 17 December 2021.

of customary law or that some of its parts can achieve the status of customary norms.[52] It is the most comprehensive international instrument setting out the rights of Indigenous peoples. It amounts to 'the minimum standards for the survival, dignity and well-being of the Indigenous Peoples of the world'. The Declaration protects the collective and individual rights of Indigenous peoples concerning self-government, culture, land, education, employment, health, and other areas. Its Article 31 interlinks the culture and intellectual property rights of Indigenous peoples by setting out the rights that they do have over their cultures and traditions.

The Convention on Biological Diversity (CBD) is an international legally binding treaty.[53] It has three main objectives: conserving biological diversity, promoting its sustainable use, and ensuring the fair and equitable sharing of benefits arising from genetic resources. The CBD recognises the contribution of Indigenous peoples and local communities in conserving biological diversity.[54] Under Article 8(j) of the Convention, states parties commit to respect, preserve, and maintain the knowledge, innovations, and practices of Indigenous peoples and local communities relevant for the conservation of biological diversity and to encourage equitable sharing of benefits arising out of the use of biological diversity.[55] By May 2022, the CBD had 196 parties (168 signatures). While it reaffirms national sovereignty, it is also concerned with communal control of genetic resources. Most of its parties have adopted the Cartagena Protocol on Biosafety (173 members, 103 signatures) and the Nagoya Protocol on Access to Genetic Resources and Benefit Sharing (137 ratifications). In addition, parties to the CBD have established a permanent 'Open-Ended Working Group on Traditional Knowledge'.[56]

Established in 1967 as an agency of the United Nations, the WIPO is the international forum for intellectual property. By May 2022, it had 193 member states. It leads the development of the international intellectual property system encouraging innovation and creativity by developing cooperation among states and setting out negotiating bodies. It offers training and raises global awareness. It also administers the international patent system, the international trade mark system, the international design system, the international system of geographical indication, and the international microorganism deposit system. It offers a time- and cost-efficient alternative dispute resolution option that 'enables private parties to

52 Mauro Barelli, *Seeking Justice in International Law: The Significance and Implications of the UN Declaration on the Rights of Indigenous Peoples* (Routledge 2016).

53 Convention on Biological Diversity of 5 June 1992, 1760 UNTS 69.

54 CBD preamble.

55 Johanna Gibson, 'Traditional Knowledge and the International Context for Protection' (2004) 1*SCRIPT-ed* 1.

56 Braulio F S Dias, 'The Slow but Steady Progress in the Implementation of the Biodiversity Agenda' (*IUCN World Conservation Congress* 31 July 2020) <www.iucn.org/news/world-commission-environmental-law/202007/slow-steady-progress-implementation-biodiversity-agenda> accessed 1 December 2021.

settle domestic or cross border commercial disputes'.[57] The WIPO IGC provides a good starting point to reach a legal consensus on the interplay between intangible cultural heritage and intellectual property. In theory, it intends to be an influential international instrument that has formal understanding and commitments and, in practice, will only be as effective as the parties make them, as they need national implementation and compliance.

The Trade-Related Aspects of Intellectual Property Rights (TRIPS) Agreement is an international legal agreement between all the member states of the WTO.[58] It is binding and subject to compulsory dispute settlement. The TRIPS Agreement sets out the minimum intellectual property standards of protection to be provided by each member. It allows members to provide more extensive protection if they so wish. Disputes between governments about compliance are subject to the dispute settlement system of the WTO. The dispute settlement is a major feature of the WTO legal system and one of the most active international dispute settlement mechanisms, despite the recent paralysis of the Appellate Body.[59]

Several WTO members advocate governing aspects of cultural heritage at the WTO, while others consider public international law in general and human rights law to be the proper legal framework governing cultural entitlements.[60] Accordingly, if culture were included in the WTO agenda, it would be seen as 'solely' having a commercial value. While the 2003 Convention does not intend to have legal repercussions in international trade because it does not mandate any specific action with legal consequences, Broude argues that some intangible cultural heritage may have commercial aspects with commercial interest that, consequently, has trade law implications.[61] Consistently, Lixinski asserts that 'by offering legal protection to heritage, one necessarily exposes it to the market'.[62]

The TRIPS Agreement is in line with the International Covenant on Economic, Social and Cultural Rights (ICESCR) as Article 15.1 ICESCR recognises the right to benefit from the protection of the moral and material interest resulting from any scientific, literary, and artistic production of which a person is the author.[63] The 2003 Convention, Article 3(b) notes that the convention does not affect states parties' rights and obligations under international intellectual property instruments.

57 WIPO, *Alternative Dispute Resolution* (WIPO IP Services).

58 Agreement on Trade-Related Aspects of Intellectual Property Rights, Apr. 15, 1994, Marrakesh Agreement Establishing the World Trade Organization, Annex 1C, 1869 UNTS 299, 33 ILM 1197 (1994).

59 Antony Taubman, Hannu Wager and Jayashree Watal, *A Handbook on the WTO TRIPS Agreement* (Cambridge University Press 2012).

60 Tania Voon, 'Culture, Human Rights and the WTO' in Ana Filipa Vrdoljak (ed), *The Cultural Dimension of Human Rights Law* (OUP 2013).

61 Tomer Broude, 'Taking "Trade and Culture" Seriously: Geographical Indications and Cultural Protection in WTO Law' (2014) *U Pa J Int'l L* 623–692.

62 Lucas Lixinski, *Intangible Cultural Heritage in International Law* (Oxford University Press 2013), Introduction.

63 Voon (n 60).

In conclusion, international organisations and bodies have their own agenda; even if the guidelines and rules they produce touch upon matters which are interdisciplinary, their aims and priorities do differ. Therefore, to conclude, whether terminologies are tangled or working in parallel, the reality is that we, as a society, do benefit from the discussion. By opening forums, discussing the interplay between intangible cultural heritage and intellectual property and culture, we can all contribute to the safeguarding and protection of intangible cultural expressions.

References

Barten U, 'What's in a Name? Peoples, Minorities, Indigenous Peoples, Tribal Groups and Nations' (2015) 14 *JEMIE* 1

Basu S and Waymire G, 'Has the Importance of Intangibles Really Grown? And If So, Why?' (2008) 38 *Account Bus Res* 171

Broude T, 'Taking "Trade and Culture" Seriously: Geographical Indications and Cultural Protection in WTO Law' (2014) *U Pa J Int'l L* 623

Brynjolfsson E, Hitt L M and Yang S, 'Intangible Assets: Computers and Organizational Capital' (2002) 1 *Brookings Papers on Economic Activity* 137

Concise Oxford English Dictionary (12th edn, OUP 2011)

Coombe R, Ives S and Huizenga D, 'Geographical Indications: The Promise, Perils and Politics of Protecting Place Based Products' in M David and D J Halbert (eds), *The SAGE Handbook of Intellectual Property* (Blackwell 2014)

Corrado C, Hultern C and Sichel D, 'Intangible Capital and U.S. Economic Growth' (2009) 55 *Rev Income Wealth* 661

Correa C, 'Traditional Knowledge and Intellectual Property: Issues and Option Surrounding the Protection of Traditional Knowledge' (2001) *Quaker United Nations Office Discussion Paper* 18

Deacon H, Dondolo L, Mrubata M and Prosalendis S, *The Subtle Power of Intangible Heritage, South Africa* (HSRC Publishers 2004)

Dias B, 'The Slow but Steady Progress in the Implementation of the Biodiversity Agenda' (IUCN World Conservation Congress 31 July 2020) <www.iucn.org/news/world-commission-environmental-law/202007/slow-steady-progress-implementation-biodiversity-agenda>

Drahos P and Frankel S, 'Indigenous Peoples' Innovation and Intellectual Property: The Issues' in P Drahos and S Frankel (eds), *Indigenous Peoples' Innovation Intellectual Property Pathways to Development* (ANU 2012)

Ghafele R, 'How Developing Countries Can Benefit from Intellectual Property: The Role of Collective Marks in Tourism' (2011) *Munich Personal RePEc Archive*, Paper No. 32762

Gibson J, 'Traditional Knowledge and the International Context for Protection' (2004) 1 *SCRIPT-ed* 1

Idris K, *Intellectual Property A Power Tool for Economic Growth* (WIPO 2003)

Lenzerini F, 'Intangible Cultural Heritage: The Living Culture of Peoples' (2011) 22 *EJIL* 101

Lixinski L, *Intangible Cultural Heritage in International Law* (OUP 2013)

Luzen J L, 'UNESCO 2000 Report of the Bureau of the World Heritage Committee' (24th session 26 June-1 July Paris)

Reichman J, 'Using Liability Rules to Stimulate Local Innovation in Developing Countries' in K Maskus and J Reichman (eds), *International Public Goods and Transfer of Technology Under a Globalized Intellectual Property Regime* (Cambridge University Press 2005)

Shand P, 'Scenes from the Colonial Catwalk: Cultural Appropriation, Intellectual Property Rights, and Fashion' (2002) 3 *Cult Analysis* 47

Smith L, *Uses of Heritage* (Routledge 2006)

Twarog S, 'Protecting and Promoting Traditional Knowledge: Systems, National Experiences and International Dimension' in S Twarog and P Kapoor (eds), *Protecting and Promoting Traditional Knowledge: Systems, National Experiences and International Dimensions* (United Nations Conference on Trade and Development 2004)

Marrie H, 'The UNESCO Convention for the Safeguarding of the Intangible Cultural Heritage and the Protection and Maintenance of the Intangible Cultural Heritage of Indigenous Peoples' in L Smith and N Akagawa (eds), *Intangible Heritage* (Routledge 2009)

Taubman A, Wager H and Watal J, *A Handbook on the WTO TRIPS Agreement* (Cambridge University Press 2012)

UNESCO, *International Meeting of Experts on Further Study of the Concept of the Rights of Peoples* (1989, SHS.89/CONF.602/7)

United Nations, *Who Are Indigenous Peoples?* (United Nations 5th session Factsheet No 1)

Voon T, 'Culture, Human Rights and the WTO' in A F Vrdoljak (ed), *The Cultural Dimension of Human Rights Law* (OUP 2013)

WIPO, *Intergovernmental Committee on Intellectual Property and Genetic Resources, Traditional Knowledge and Folklore* (Thirty-Seventh Session Geneva, August 27 to 31, 2018 WIPO/GRTKF/IC/37/6)

——— *Alternative Dispute Resolution* (WIPO IP Services)

——— *Glossary of Key Terms* (WIPO/GRTKF/IC/41/INF/7)

World Health Organization, *Traditional Medicine* (World Health Organization) <www.who.int/health-topics/traditional-complementary-and-integrative-medicine#tab=tab_1>

2 Intangible cultural heritage, intellectual property, and the politics of development in Southeast Asia

Christoph Antons[1]

Introduction

Social scientists such as lawyer and anthropologist Coombe have noted a 'cultural turn' in development policies.[2] The marketing of local and/or national culture has become a tool for corporations and development-oriented governments alike.[3] Attempts at establishing exclusivity using legal and non-legal mechanisms raise questions about the territorial scope and control over culture – whether there are borders or boundaries of cultural realms and if so, how they relate to the borders of national legal systems.[4] It will be submitted that countries in Southeast Asia have introduced European concepts of law, but that heritage relates to national history and founding myths, which are based on older concepts of space and legal

1 This research was supported under the Australian Research Council's Discovery Projects funding scheme (project number DP160104402). The chapter was written while the author was a Fellow at the Käte Hamburger Center for Advanced Study in the Humanities 'Law as Culture' in Bonn, Germany (October 2020 to March 2021). The author would like to thank the editor, Dr Patricia Covarrubia, and an anonymous reviewer for helpful comments on an earlier draft of this chapter.

2 Rosemary Coombe, 'The Expanding Purview of Cultural Properties and Their Politics' (2009) 5 *Annu Rev Law Soc Sci* 393–412.

3 This is particularly true in tourism. See for the long history on the island of Bali Adrian Vickers, *Bali: A Paradise Created* (2nd edn, Tuttle Publishing 2012). See also the contributions in Michel Picard and Robert E Wood (eds), *Tourism, Ethnicity, and the State in Asian and Pacific Societies* (University of Hawai'i Press 1997) and in Michael Hitchcock, Victor T King and Michael Parnwell (eds), *Heritage Tourism in Southeast Asia* (NIAS Press 2010). For the intellectual property tool of the geographical indication, see contributions in Irene Calboli and Wee Loon Ng-Loy (eds), *Geographical Indications at the Crossroads of Trade, Development and Culture: Focus on Asia-Pacific* (Cambridge University Press 2017). Regulation No. 13 of 2017 of the Indonesian Ministry of Law and Human Rights on Communal Intellectual Property Data states in the preamble that 'Indonesian cultural diversity and natural wealth in the form of traditional knowledge, traditional cultural expressions, genetic resources and the potential of geographical indications constitute the basic capital of national development'.

4 See, e.g., Christoph Antons, 'Asian Borderlands and the Legal Protection of Traditional Knowledge and Traditional Cultural Expressions' (2013) 47 *Mod Asian Stud* 1403; Christoph Antons, 'Legal and Cultural Landscapes: Cultural and Intellectual Property Concepts, and the "Safeguarding" of Intangible Cultural Heritage in Southeast Asia' in Christoph Antons (ed), *The Routledge Handbook of Asian Law* (Routledge 2017).

DOI: 10.4324/9781003345237-3

and political control. The chapter discusses this in the context of the politics of development and shows the standardising and often coercive tendencies of development policies. In the context of heritage, they can lead to national governments taking local culture to create a sanitised and standardised version of national heritage. The chapter looks at the use of the concept of cultural property as it is expressed in UNESCO Conventions and of intellectual property related to heritage, traditional knowledge, and traditional cultural expressions, developed by the World Intellectual Property Organization (WIPO) and UNESCO model laws and in WIPO discussions about an international treaty in this field. The activities in these various international forums and their adaptations in national laws lead to overlaps between cultural and intellectual property related to heritage in some national and regional laws in Southeast Asia and problematic claims made by national and regional governments on this basis. Cultural and intellectual property terminology is also influential in media and public discourse. The chapter will provide examples for such developments and discourses.

The chapter will attempt to answer the following questions:

1. It is clear that there is a cultural property in tangible heritage, but does the concept also extend to intangible cultural heritage?
2. Is it possible to claim intellectual property for such material?
3. If the answer to both questions is yes, what about the overlap between these concepts and what does it mean for the claims to such heritage described below? In this context, the chapter will provide examples of contested forms of heritage and heritage administration.

The marketing of culture, development policies, and cross-border competition

Political scientist James C Scott has referred to development schemes as 'transformative state simplifications', an administrative ordering of society and nature using a high modernist ideology. Such simplifications can turn oppressive and trigger resistance when they are applied by governments with little or no attention to the views of civil society.[5] In heritage, such developmental attitudes can manifest themselves in the construction of national and/or regional heritage for development purposes, frequently using simplified and/or decontextualised local elements. Such state simplifications of heritage can lead to conflicts with neighbouring countries, in which the same heritage is practised, or with local communities from which the simplified national heritage is taken. As for the authoritarian nature of the governments, there has been a struggle in Southeast Asian countries since independence between authoritarian and sometimes military-backed governments that practice paternalistic and top-down development policies and

5 James C Scott, *Seeing Like a State: How Certain Schemes to Improve the Human Condition Have Failed* (Yale University Press 1998) 4–6.

reform movements fighting for democracy, decentralisation, and human rights.[6] However, even in countries where reform movements have been relatively successful, as in Indonesia, older laws from earlier periods can still create problems and political forces from the past are not simply disappearing.[7]

One of the most famous and successful examples of the use of culture for marketing in the pursuit of economic development in Southeast Asia is the 'Singapore Girl' marketing campaign of Singapore Airlines. Marketed to an international audience in this case is the Peranakan or Nyonya culture of the Chinese population in Singapore, the culture of the Straits Chinese whose presence in Southeast Asia goes back a long time.[8] The costumes of Singapore Airlines flight attendants use a modern version of a traditional kebaya dress, redesigned for the company in the 1960s by French fashion designer Balmain.[9] More recently, Singapore's hawker (street) food, prepared at the many food stalls in the city, was inscribed in 2020 in the UNESCO Representative List of the Intangible Cultural Heritage of Humanity.[10] However, both cultures, the Nyonya Straits Chinese culture and the hawker food culture, exist also in Singapore's neighbouring countries, in particular in Malaysia. Not surprisingly then, the hawker food nomination has attracted criticism in Malaysia,[11] and the Malaysian state of Penang suggested a joint nomination by Singapore and Malaysia.[12] The tourism industry is of course a major commercial user of culture. As in the case of Singapore and Malaysia, this may lead to controversies when several countries want to offer the same or a similar cultural experience to their visitors. Further examples include the Malaysian use for a tourism campaign of the folksong 'Rasa Sayang', in Indonesia regarded as a folk song from the Moluccan islands, and the use of a Balinese dance for another Malaysian tourism promotion. In both cases, there were serious diplomatic tensions between the two countries and a group of eminent persons had to be formed to mediate.[13]

6 Richard Robison, 'Interpreting the Politics of Southeast Asia: Debates in Parallel Universes' in Richard Robison (ed), *Routledge Handbook of Southeast Asian Politics* (Routledge 2011).

7 Christoph Antons and Roman Tomasic, 'Introduction: Law Reform and Legal Change in East Asia' in Christoph Antons and Roman Tomasic (eds), *Law and Society in East Asia* (Ashgate 2013) xi–xxxiii; Christoph Antons, 'Law Reform in the "Developmental States" of East and Southeast Asia: From the Asian Crisis to September 11, 2001 and beyond' in Christoph Antons and Volkmar Gessner (eds), *Globalisation and Resistance: Law Reform in Asia since the Crisis* (Hart Publishing 2007).

8 See, e.g., Felix Chia, *The Babas* (Landmark Books 2015).

9 See the website of Singapore Airlines: <www.singaporeair.com/en_UK/sg/flying-withus/our-story/singapore-girl/> accessed 1 December 2021.

10 Decision of the Intergovernmental Committee: 15.COM 8.b.6.

11 Mike Ives, 'Singapore's Claim as a Street-Food Hub Riles Malaysians' *The New York Times* (New York, 5 November 2018) <www.nytimes.com/2018/11/05/world/asia/singapore-malaysia-street-food-unesco.html> accessed 1 December 2021.

12 Audrey Dermawan, 'Malaysia, Singapore Could Vie for Joint UNESCO Listing on Hawker Culture' *New Straits Times* (Kuala Lumpur, 2 May 2019).

13 Ho Ying Chan, *Special Relationship in the Malay World: Indonesia and Malaysia* (ISEAS Publishing 2018) 356–360; Antons, 'Legal and Cultural Landscapes' (n 4) 251.

Conflicts erupted also between Thailand and Cambodia when Cambodia in 2008 inscribed the Royal Ballet of Cambodia and Sbek Thom, the Khmer shadow theatre, in the UNESCO Representative List of the Intangible Cultural Heritage of Humanity. Thai officials raised objections over hand gestures that were part of the inscriptions and used in Thai dance.[14] Yet further disputes were triggered by intellectual property registrations. Malaysia in collaboration with the Massachusetts Institute of Technology (MIT) in the United States registered a patent for a traditional herbal remedy known in Malaysia as *Tongkat Ali* and in Indonesia as *Pasak Bumi*.[15] Communities in both Malaysia and Indonesia registered geographical indications for organic highland rice from the interior of Borneo, known in Indonesia as Adan Krayan rice and in Malaysia as Bario rice.[16] While there are different geographical indication rights and names for what anthropologists describe as varieties of the same rice, their research has pointed out that the communities on both sides of the border are in fact related, use similar methods of growing it, and help each other during harvests.[17] This research, carried out in 2003 and 2004, further explains that, due to geographical isolation and prohibitive transportation costs, the Adan Krayan rice growers are selling much of their rice on the Malaysian side of the border and thus in an area where the Malaysian geographical indication is promoted for varieties of the same rice. Such difficulties notwithstanding, some of the lessons from earlier cross-border disputes meanwhile seem to have been learnt. The recent UNESCO inscription of *pantun*, Malay poetry, by Malaysia and Indonesia jointly, demonstrates this.[18]

Borders and cultures in Southeast Asia history

When considering how borders in the region came into being, the practice of cultures across such borders is easy to understand. Historian Thongchai Winichakul highlights the historical existence of different ways of conveying geographical information and conceptualising power.[19] When the French arrived in Southeast Asia towards the end of the 17th century, they produced maps that showed European style 'royaumes' or kingdoms, with the kingdom of Siam stretching across the entire Malayan peninsula except for Malacca, at that time held by the

14 Lindsay Murdoch, 'Simple Hand Gesture Has Two Countries up in Arms', *Sydney Morning Herald* (Sydney, 15 August 2011) <www.smh.com.au/entertainment/dance/simple-hand-gesture-has-two-countries-up-in-arms-20110814-1it5o.html> accessed 3 December 2021.

15 Antons, 'Asian Borderlands and the Legal Protection of Traditional Knowledge and Traditional Cultural Expressions' (n 4) 1427–1429.

16 Christoph Antons, 'Geographical Indications, Heritage, and Decentralization Policies: The Case of Indonesia', in Calboli and Ng-Loy (n 3) 501–505.

17 Iketut Ardhana, Jayl Langub and Daniel Chew, 'Borders of Kinship and Ethnicity: Cross-Border Relations between the Kelalan Valley, Sarawak, and the Bawan Valley, East Kalimantan' (2004) 35 *Borneo Research Bulletin* 144.

18 Decision of the Intergovernmental Committee: 15.COM 8.b.30.

19 Thongchai Winichakul, *Siam Mapped: A History of the Geo-Body of a Nation* (University of Hawai'i Press 1994).

Dutch.[20] Southeast Asian maps looked different. A Siamese map from the early 19th century shows details of houses, temples, rivers, and mountains and even historical facts, such as the burning house of a disloyal local ruler during a military campaign.[21]

Of course, traditional kingdoms in the region were aware of their borders, but the difference in comparison to early modern Europe lay in the significance of these borders. When the British became the colonial rulers of Burma and neighbours of the Kingdom of Siam, they entered into prolonged negotiations with the Siamese about border regions important for tin mining. During these negotiations, British officials wanted clearly marked borders and to know on which side areas rich in raw materials were. Their Siamese counterparts were thinking about borders more in terms of relationships with tribute-paying local rulers in the region. Rather than a precisely demarcated line, the border of Siam was, in their view, where the last loyal ruler paying tribute to the King of Siam was to be found.[22] Wolters has called such tributary networks of governance in Southeast Asia 'mandalas'.[23]

European concepts of power were based on territorial conquest, not on multilayered hierarchical relationships. For pre-colonial Asian kingdoms, a decentralised administration of law was not a problem, but such a loose system could not be used for the much tighter legal administration and clearly defined property relationships that the Europeans wanted to apply. Thus, with the arrival of the colonial powers, territorial borders finally did become more strictly defined, and they often cut through the cultural realms of communities living along these borders.[24]

This background knowledge is important to understand discussions in Southeast Asia about cultural realms, heritage, and cultural and intellectual property related to it. As for the marketing and promotion of Malaysian and Indonesian heritage, different historical empires inspire current concepts and explain the connection to the respective culture. In the case of Malaysia, the concept of the 'Malay world' is used,[25] centred on Malacca and its historical predecessor Srivijaya in Sumatra. In the case of Indonesia, it is the Majapahit Empire, centred on Java and extending at the height of its power to Malaysia and other parts of Southeast Asia.[26]

20 See the 1686 map of le Père Placide in Thomas Suárez, *Early Mapping of Southeast Asia* (Periplus Editions 1999) 213.

21 Santanee Phasuk and Philip Stott, *Royal Siamese Maps: War and Trade in Nineteenth Century Thailand* (River Books 2004) 64–65.

22 Winichakul (n 19) chapter 3.

23 Oliver William Wolters, *History, Culture and Region in Southeast Asian Perspectives* (Southeast Asia Program Publications, Cornell University/Institute of Southeast Asian Studies, Singapore 1999) chapter 2.

24 See, e.g., Janet C Sturgeon, *Border Landscapes: The Politics of Akha Land Use in China and Thailand* (Silkworm Books 2005).

25 Joseph Chinyong Liow, *The Politics of Indonesia-Malaysia Relations: One Kin, Two Nations* (Routledge 2005) 46–48.

26 ibid 30–31, 37–38.

Heritage promotion at national level

Another example of the shared heritage of Malaysia and Indonesia is *batik*, which both countries produce, but which Indonesia inscribed on the Representative List of the Intangible Cultural Heritage of Humanity in 2009.[27] Both countries are promoting the batik industry and requiring government officials to wear batik once a week to work.[28] Within Indonesia, batik is traditionally associated with the island of Java.[29] However, Indonesia's first President Sukarno encouraged the development of what became called *Batik Indonesia* (Indonesian batik), which drew on designs from across Java and incorporated Balinese motifs.[30] Nowadays, the production of batik takes place across the entire country, including in regions where it was not traditionally produced. These regions do have traditional textiles, but production is based on weaving.[31] In the new Indonesian batik, motives from such woven cloth are often used to produce batik clothing. Examples are batik from the Batak region in North Sumatra, which uses motifs from the traditional *ulos* cloth of this region.[32] An Indonesian media report on the new nationwide batik industry quotes a Papuan batik designer in Jayapura that people from various tribes are happy to share their traditional patterns for his Papuan batik designs. A woman working for his company explains how she learned batik making skills from a teacher from Java in a course organised by the local government.[33]

While in many countries, the use of traditional motifs and symbols for a new industry could be regarded as problematic, much will depend on the support of heritage bearing communities for development and job creation policies that often spark such industries based on traditional culture. Parts of the Papuan communities, who live in two provinces on the western side of the island of Papua New Guinea, have in the past been amongst the most critical of Indonesian government policies towards this part of the country. As part of the former Dutch India, the

27 Decision of the Intergovernmental Committee: 4.COM 13.44. The decision explains that Indonesian Batik refers to hand-dyed cotton and silk garments. They are produced by craftspeople who draw designs on fabric using dots and lines of hot wax. The hot wax resists vegetable end other dyes and allows the artisan to colour selectively by soaking the cloth in one colour, removing the wax with boiling water and repeating if multiple colours are desired. Malaysian batik making evolved using Indian derived tie-and-dye techniques, wooden and metal printing blocks, and, more recently, hand painting. Some batik making using wax was introduced in Malaysia in the 20th century, see Muzium Tekstil Negara – National Textile Museum (Department of Museums Malaysia 2012) 63–65. For further details see Pepin van Roojen, *Batik Design* (The Pepin Press 1994) 169–183.

28 Chan (n 13) 360.

29 Kusnin Asa, *Mosaic of Indonesian Batik* (Red & White Publishing 2014) 13–16.

30 Inger McCabe Elliott, *Batik: Fabled Cloth of Java* (Periplus 2004) 186.

31 Anne Richter, *Arts and Crafts in Indonesia* (Chronicle Books 1993) 92–95.

32 Fatimah Rahmawati, 'Pesona Gorga Batak, Motif Batik Kebanggaan Medan yang Mirip Ulos' (*Merdeka.com*, 3 August 2020) <www.merdeka.com/sumut/pesona-gorga-batak-motif-batik-kebanggaan-medan-yang-mirip-ulos.html> accessed 1 December 2021.

33 'Batik beyond Java' (*Tempo*, 11 October 2016) <https://magz.tempo.co/read/outreach/32256/batiks-beyond-java> accessed 1 December 2021.

western part of Papua New Guinea became part of Indonesia after the 1963 New York Agreement between Indonesia and the Netherlands and a controversial referendum in 1969.[34] Since then, a militant separatist group has been fighting for independence, and the government has granted autonomy status to the province.[35] Papuan heritage under such circumstances takes on a special sensitivity and symbolic significance. Among the 92 national and international geographical indications that have so far been registered in Indonesia are two from the Papuan provinces.[36] The Papuan weaving technique *noken* was also inscribed by Indonesia in 2012 in the UNESCO List of Intangible Cultural Heritage in Need of Urgent Safeguarding.[37]

Looking at the UNESCO Representative List of the Intangible Cultural Heritage of Humanity, one finds further examples of heritage from areas in Asia, in which the rule of the central government is to some extent contested. Examples are traditional Tibetan medicinal practices[38] and Uighur heritage[39] in China and Muslim heritage in the Southern Philippines.[40]

Intellectual and cultural property in intangible cultural heritage

The language of property has been much used in recent debates about heritage. Politicians, the media, and academics like to speak of a country's intellectual property in culture or cultural property. The language is often emotional and legal details are disregarded.[41] However, commercial, or international laws seem not well suited to deal with the rather elusive concept of culture. Although always concerned with cultural products, intellectual property, for example, did not initially pay attention to non-European cultures. Early international agreements in intellectual property law were concluded at the height of imperial expansion almost exclusively by European nations, which indeed had similar approaches when it came to rewarding creative endeavours. Tunisia, then a French protector-

34 Richard Chauvel, 'Papua and Indonesia: Where Contending Nationalisms Meet' in Damien Kingsbury and Harry Aveling (eds), *Autonomy and Disintegration in Indonesia* (RoutledgeCurzon 2003) 119.

35 ibid 122–127; Jacques Bertrand, *Nationalism and Ethnic Conflict in Indonesia* (Cambridge University Press 2004) 144–160.

36 Nutmeg from the town and regency of Fakfak in West Papua and Baliem Wamena Arabika coffee from the Baliem Valley in Papua, see the website of the Directorate General for Intellectual Property <http://ig.dgip.go.id/> accessed 1 December 2021.

37 Decision of the Intergovernmental Committee: 7.COM 8.3.

38 Lum medicinal bathing of Sowa Rigpa, knowledge and practices concerning life, health, and illness prevention and treatment among the Tibetan people in China. Decision of the Intergovernmental Committee: 13.COM 10.b.8.

39 Meshrep. Decision of the Intergovernmental Committee: 3.COM 1.

40 Darangen epic of the Maranao people of Lake Lanao. Decision of the Intergovernmental Committee: 3.COM 1.

41 See, e.g., 'Malaysia Urges Indonesia to Drop Plans to Sue over Folk Song' *Jakarta Post* (Jakarta, 8 October 2007); 'Indonesian Outrage over a Dance' *Asia Sentinel* (25 August 2009); H Susilo, 'Beras Adan Resmi Dipatenkan' *Kompas* (15 January 2012).

ate, was the only non-European country among the initial signatory states of the Berne Convention for the Protection of Literary and Artistic Works of 1886. The only non-European country among the initial signatories of the Paris Convention for the Protection of Industrial Property was Brazil. Few independent countries from outside Europe joined the international IP system before World War II. The significant expansion of the system occurred with the decolonisation process after the end of the war and with the conclusion of the World Trade Organization (WTO)'s Agreement on Trade-Related Aspects of Intellectual Property Rights (TRIPS). As more newly independent countries joined the international intellectual property system, it became clear that they brought with them some forms of knowledge and artistic expressions that European-derived intellectual property systems found difficult to accommodate.

'Folklore', as 'traditional cultural expressions' were then called, turned up on the agenda of Berne Convention revision meetings and other WIPO and UNESCO meetings during the 1960s and 1970s. A newly introduced Article in the Berne Convention concerned 'unpublished works where the identity of the author is unknown'. It allowed for the creation of a 'competent authority' to represent the author and 'to protect and enforce his rights'. Although many developing countries at the time adopted a similar formula in their copyright acts, only one country (India) actually designated such a 'competent authority'.[42]

The folklore provisions of the Tunis Model Law on Copyright for Developing Countries were drafted in 1976. They again saw rights exercised by a 'competent authority' with regards to 'works of national folklore'. The nationalist focus of the Tunis Model Law was probably following the spirit of the time when governments of young countries were shaping a national identity.[43] The difficulties in putting such policies into practice led to the joint drafting by UNESCO and WIPO of the Model Provisions for National Laws on the Protection of Expressions of Folklore against Illicit Exploitation and Other Prejudicial Actions. The Model Provisions shifted the focus from copyright to *sui generis* (specialised) protection. For authorisation and collection of fees, they leave a choice between a 'competent authority' at a national level and authorisation by the communities themselves.[44]

Negotiations about an international instrument in the WIPO Intergovernmental Committee on Intellectual Property, Traditional Knowledge and Folklore (IGC) began in 2001. A provision on traditional knowledge in the Convention on Biological Diversity had renewed the interest in relevant intellectual property rules. The negotiations have meanwhile produced draft texts for the three subject

42 Antons, 'Asian Borderlands and the Legal Protection of Traditional Knowledge and Traditional Cultural Expressions' (n 4) 1408.

43 Christoph Antons, 'Intellectual Property Rights in Indigenous Cultural Heritage: Basic Concepts and Continuing Controversies', in Christoph B Graber, Karolina Kuprecht and Jessica C Lai (eds), *International Trade in Indigenous Cultural Heritage: Legal and Policy Issues* (Edward Elgar 2012) 147–148.

44 ibid 149–151.

areas under negotiation of genetic resources, traditional knowledge, and expressions of folklore or traditional cultural expressions.[45]

Without an international agreement, claims of intellectual property with regards to culture raised against foreign parties or countries have no legal basis. Those seeking exclusive rights to culture then often turn to international law and to cultural property. This term has its origins at the Vienna Congress of 1815 when the nations of Europe were discussing the restitution of artwork plundered by the Napoleonic army in various parts of Europe.[46] The discussion flared up again at the end of World War II, and it led to the conclusion of the 1954 Hague Convention for the Protection of Cultural Property in the Event of Armed Conflict. The notion of national repatriation and cultural property was carried further in the UNESCO 1970 Convention on the Means of Prohibiting and Preventing the Illicit Import, Export and Transfer of Ownership of Cultural Property, which listed categories of cultural property consisting exclusively of tangible objects.[47]

The World Heritage Convention of 1972 brought together the previously separate spheres of cultural and natural heritage and included 'cultural landscapes'.[48] However, the Convention and the accompanying guidelines make extensive reference to cultural property, and it is clear that both cultural and natural heritage remain firmly under the control of sovereign nation-states.[49] The UNESCO Recommendation on the Safeguarding of Traditional Culture and Folklore of 1989 proved equally disappointing for communities seeking greater control.[50] In the Recommendation, the concept of 'cultural heritage' was expanded to include intangible subject matter, such as Indigenous and local knowledge. This was carried further in the UNESCO 2003 Convention for the Safeguarding of the Intangible Cultural Heritage (the 2003 Convention), giving 'communities, in particular Indigenous communities, groups and, in some cases, individuals' an 'important role in the production, safeguarding, maintenance and recreation of the intangible heritage'. Furthermore, 'intangible cultural heritage' now also includes

45 For a recent analysis of the negotiations see Chidi Oguamanam, *Tiered or Differentiated Approach to Traditional Knowledge and Traditional Cultural Expressions: The Evolution of a Concept* (Centre for International Governance Innovation 2018).

46 Ana Vrdoljak, *International Law, Museums and the Return of Cultural Objects* (Cambridge University Press 2008) 22–29.

47 Barbara T Hoffman, 'Exploring and Establishing Links for a Balanced Art and Cultural Heritage Policy' in Barbara T Hoffman (ed), *Art and Cultural Heritage: Law, Policy and Practice* (Cambridge University Press 2006) 11.

48 Aurélie Elisa Gfeller, 'Negotiating the Meaning of Global Heritage: "Cultural Landscapes" in the UNESCO World Heritage Convention, 1972–1992' (2013) 8(3) *J Glob Hist* (2013) 483.

49 Ben Boer, 'Article 3 Identification and Delineation of World Heritage Properties' in Francesco Francioni (ed) *The 1972 World Heritage Convention: A Commentary* (Oxford University Press 2008) 85–87.

50 For details see Christoph Antons, 'Epistemic Communities and the "People without History": The Contribution of Intellectual Property Law to the "Safeguarding" of Intangible Cultural Heritage' in Irene Calboli and Srividhya Ragavan (eds), *Diversity in Intellectual Property: Identities, Interests and Intersections* (Cambridge University Press 2015) 464.

practices, knowledge, and skills, especially 'knowledge and practices concerning nature and the universe'. While the tangible heritage of the previous convention was either non-movable cultural property (heritage protected buildings and other sites) or movable tangible cultural property that could only be in one place at a time (such as handicrafts or other cultural expressions), 'intangible cultural heritage' in the form of knowledge can now be held simultaneously by many people on both sides of borders.[51] Interestingly, the 2003 Convention negotiations triggered intensive debates about the phrase 'communities, groups and individuals'[52] very similar to debates in the WIPO IGC about the beneficiaries of protection.[53]

State control of heritage in Asia

Although the 2003 Convention leaves intellectual property outside of its scope[54] and only obliges countries to take measures for the conservation of intangible cultural heritage, UNESCO listings have achieved powerful symbolic value. Such listings do not prevent neighbouring countries from practising the tradition, but they are nevertheless seen as an important advantage in the competitive marketing of tourism and local products.

In view of large-scale cultural diffusion, one should approach claims to exclusive 'ownership' of cultural material with caution. Scholars interested in the legal protection of cultural heritage have long advocated a move away from the language of property.[55] In the 2003 Convention the term 'cultural property' is no longer used. Hence, it covers a wider range of material and emphasises international cooperation and assistance.[56] There is also the possibility of a joint request to the Intergovernmental Committee for the Safeguarding of the Intangible Cultural Heritage by two or more parties related to intangible cultural heritage present in their territories.[57] Malaysia has recently made use of this option for *pantun* poetry, jointly inscribed with Indonesia,[58] and for the *Wangkang* ceremony, a barge festival of the Chinese community in Malaysia, jointly inscribed with China. It must be hoped that such joint initiatives become more frequent and replace attempts to monopolise and claim ownership to culture.

An overlap of intellectual and cultural property concepts remains, however, visible in many national laws. This overlap creates a potential for conflict, where

51 Antons, 'Asian Borderlands and the Legal Protection of Traditional Knowledge and Traditional Cultural Expressions' (n 4) 1425.

52 Janet Blake, *Commentary on the UNESCO 2003 Convention on the Safeguarding of the Intangible Cultural Heritage* (Institute of Art & Law 2006) 29.

53 Antons, 'Intellectual Property Rights in Indigenous Cultural Heritage: Basic Concepts and Continuing Controversies' (n 43) 164–170.

54 Article 3(b) of the 2003 Convention.

55 Lyndel V Prott and Patrick J O'Keefe, '"Cultural Heritage" or "Cultural Property"?' (1992) 1(2) *IntJ Cult Prop* 307.

56 Article 19 of the 2003 Convention.

57 Article 23 of the 2003 Convention.

58 See n 18.

laws continue to use the language of cultural property and where intellectual property laws incorporate elements of heritage protection or vice versa. The Philippines' National Cultural Heritage Act of 2009,[59] for example, uses the terms 'cultural heritage' and 'cultural property' side by side, whereby 'cultural property' extends to intangible cultural heritage.[60] Section 3 (y) defines 'intangible cultural property' as 'peoples' learned processes along with the knowledge, skills and creativity that inform and are developed by them, the products they create and the resources, spaces and other aspects of social and natural context necessary for their sustainability'. Gallardo points to the overlaps with the Indigenous Peoples' Rights Act (IPRA) of 1998.[61] This landmark legislation defined 'community intellectual rights' as Indigenous Cultural Communities'/Indigenous Peoples' (ICCs'/IPs') 'right to practice and revitalise their own cultural traditions and customs'. It obliges the state to 'preserve, protect and develop' manifestations of their cultures and the right to restitution of cultural, intellectual, religious, and spiritual property taken without consent or in violations of their laws, traditions, and customs.[62] It also entitles ICCS/IPs to 'the recognition of the full ownership and control and protection of their cultural and intellectual rights and to special measures to control, develop and protect their sciences, technologies and cultural manifestations'.[63] While the IPRA asks for measures to protect ownership in 'community intellectual rights', it avoids using the term 'intellectual property'. A Community Intellectual Rights Protection Bill was introduced into the Senate in 2001 but has not been approved.[64] A Joint Administrative Order of 2016 of the Intellectual Property Office of the Philippines and the National Commission on Indigenous Peoples (NCIP) is mainly concerned with disclosure in intellectual property applications and registry of Indigenous knowledge systems and practices.[65]

While both the IPRA and a recent administrative order of the NCIP stress Indigenous self-determination, the goal of the Heritage Acts and their implementing rules and regulations is to 'preserve and protect for the nation'.[66] Section 21 determines that the 'appropriate cultural agency' in consultation with

59 Republic Act No. 10066 of 2009 – an Act Providing for the Protection and Conservation of the National Cultural Heritage, Strengthening the National Commission for Culture and the Arts (NCCA) and its Affiliated Cultural Agencies, and for Other Purposes.

60 See the definition in s3(o): 'Cultural Property' shall refer to all products of human creativity by which a people and a nation reveal their identity … whether public or privately owned, movable or immovable, and tangible or intangible.

61 Leilene Marie C Gallardo, 'Comparative Case Analysis of FPIC Processes for Community Intellectual Property Rights in the Philippines', in Christoph Antons and William Logan (eds), *Intellectual Property, Cultural Property and Intangible Cultural Heritage* (Routledge 2018) 184.

62 IPRA s32.

63 ibid s34.

64 Christoph Antons, '*Sui Generis* Protection for Plant Varieties and Traditional Knowledge in Biodiversity and Agriculture: The International Framework and National Approaches in the Philippines and India' (2010) 6 *Indian J Law Technol* 89, 120.

65 Joint IPOPHL-NCIP Administrative Order No 1, 2016.

66 Gallardo (n 61).

the NCIP shall 'establish a program and promote regulations to assist Indigenous people in preserving their particular cultural and historical properties'.[67] It appears that the national cultural agencies listed in Section 34.2 of the Implementing Rules and Regulations would be the lead agencies in such collaborations with the NCIP.

Intangible cultural heritage in Laos falls under the Law on National Heritage of 2005 either as cultural or historical heritage.[68] The state asserts copyright ownership to Lao national cultural and historical heritage outside of Laos, in the illegitimate possession of other countries or in respect of which foreign countries have illegitimately asserted copyright.[69] The state will also 'consider' copyright registration 'in the name of the nation with international organisations' in 'national heritage items at national level which have high value, are rare and are of unique national character'.[70] Meant here is presumably heritage listing with UNESCO, despite the copyright language.[71]

A further example of a regulation mixing copyright and heritage protection comes from Indonesia. The title of Part Three of the 2002 Indonesian Copyright Act was 'Copyright to Works of Unknown Authors'. Provisions in this part mixed elements from Article 15.4 of the Berne Convention with the 'national folklore' approach of the Tunis Model Law. Article 10(1) declared the state to be the holder of copyright in prehistoric and historic relics and 'other national cultural objects'. According to Article 10(2), the state also held the copyright to various expressions of folklore and 'products of popular culture'. Foreigners needed a licence to use such material.[72] In 2014, a new Copyright Act deleted the reference to prehistorical and historical works but retained the role of the state regarding copyright and traditional cultural expressions.[73] The influence of the 2003 Convention can be seen in the obligation of the state to safeguard and create an inventory. Concerning is that an explanatory note of the government to the provision extends 'traditional cultural expressions' to *adat* rituals.[74] *Adat*, a word derived from Arabic, refers in Indonesia to the customs and customary principles of ethnic communities.[75] Adat often has religious connotations and is intimately related to a community's cultural and religious identity.[76] Giving copyright to aspects of this identity to the state is a potentially controversial move.

The wide interpretation of 'traditional cultural expressions' is in accordance, however, with Regulation No. 106 of 2013 Concerning Indonesian Intangible

67 Implementing Rules and Regulations s24.
68 Articles 9 and 12 Law on National Heritage No. 08/NA.
69 Article 27 Law on National Heritage No. 08/NA.
70 Article 28 Law on National Heritage No. 08/NA.
71 Antons, 'Legal and Cultural Landscapes: Cultural and Intellectual Property Concepts, and the "Safeguarding" of Intangible Cultural Heritage in Southeast Asia' (n 4) 254.
72 Article 10(3) Law No. 19 of 2002 on Copyright.
73 Law No 28 of 2014 on Copyright, Article 38.
74 See the explanatory memorandum of the government to Article 38(2) Copyright Act.
75 *Adat* law, on the other hand, is regarded as a Dutch colonial creation, see Daniel S Lev, *Legal Evolution and Political Authority in Indonesia: Selected Essays* (Kluwer Law International 2000) 20.
76 Franz von Benda-Beckmann, *Property in Social Continuity: Continuity and Change in the Maintenance of Property Relationships through Time in Minangkabau, West Sumatra* (Martinus Nijhoff 1979) 113–114.

Cultural Heritage of the Ministry of Education and Culture, in which 'intangible cultural heritage' extends to 'belief systems' (*sistem kepercayaan*) and adat ceremonies (*adat istiadat*).[77] More recently, Law No. 5 of 2017 on the Promotion of Culture introduced a registration and licensing process for 'Promotion of Culture Objects', which appears to overlap to some extent with the 'traditional cultural expression' provision of the Copyright Act. 'Promotion of culture objects' includes, among other things, oral traditions, adat ceremonies, rites, traditional knowledge, traditional technology, and art.[78] 'Large industries' and 'foreign parties' need to obtain a licence from the Minister of Education and Culture to use any such material for commercial purposes.[79] Conditions for the granting of a licence include prior informed consent, benefit sharing, and source indication for the material.[80] Benefit sharing income must be used by the central government to liven up and protect the ecosystem of the 'promotion of culture object'.[81] The implementing government regulation foresees a coordination between the Ministries of Education and Culture, Law and Foreign Affairs in the defence of the material against foreign intellectual property claims,[82] while obliging various levels of government to facilitate intellectual property registrations by Indonesians.[83]

The Indonesian Plant Variety Protection Act also states that local plant varieties, developed by farming communities over longer periods, are 'owned by the community' but 'controlled by the state'.[84] An implementing decree empowers government agencies to register the traditional variety on the community's behalf.[85] Any individual or legal entity that wants to use the variety for further breeding then needs to conclude a licensing agreement with this agency.[86] While compensation for the community 'may' be included in the agreement, this is not compulsory.[87] If compensation is included, government authorities have the discretion to use it for broadly worded public interest considerations such as raising the prosperity of the community and conservation of genetic resources in the locality of the variety.[88]

77 Article 1 No. 1 Regulation of the Ministry of Education and Culture of the Republic of Indonesia No. 106 of 2013 Concerning Indonesian Intangible Cultural Heritage.

78 See Article 5 Law No. 5 of 2017 on the Promotion of Culture.

79 Article 37(1) Law No. 5 of 2017 on the Promotion of Culture.

80 Article 37(2) Law No. 5 of 2017 on the Promotion of Culture.

81 Article 37(3) Law No. 5 of 2017 on the Promotion of Culture.

82 Article 40(1) Government Regulation No. 87 of 2021 Concerning Implementing Provisions of Law No. 5 of 2017 on the Promotion of Culture.

83 Article 79 Government Regulation No. 87 of 2021 Concerning Implementing Provisions of Law No. 5 of 2017 on the Promotion of Culture.

84 Law No. 29 of 2000 on Plant Variety Protection Article 7.

85 Government Regulation No. 13 of 2004 on the naming, registration, and use of the initial variety for the making of essentially derived varieties, Articles 5 and 7.

86 ibid Article 9.

87 ibid Articles 9(4) and 10.

88 ibid Article 10.

Decentralisation and heritage: the example of Indonesia

The questions regarding the role of communities and minorities in heritage in Indonesia can be linked to the national motto. It is derived from Sanskrit and can be found in the country's coat of arms: 'Binneka Tunggal Ika', meaning 'unity in diversity'. Most Indonesians would agree that this is an important motto in a multi-ethnic country, but there are differences in interpretation with the emphasis more on 'unity' or on 'diversity'. During the period of military-backed rule by former President Suharto, the emphasis was on 'unity' and the centralisation of resources and decision-making in Jakarta. After the end of his rule and with democratisation, the Constitution was amended to give stronger powers to regional governments and to recognise customary law or adat communities.[89] The cultural identity and rights of so-called 'traditional communities' are now also guaranteed in a human rights chapter of the Constitution.[90]

Decentralisation and democratisation have created a three-tier structure of governance with somewhat different goals at each level. This brings the potential for conflicts between the central and regional governments and communities about which part of the governance structure is entitled to exploit natural and other resources, such as cultural resources.[91] There is further potential for conflicts between the central government and communities about the impact of transmigration of the population from more densely populated to less densely populated parts of Indonesia. While controlled trans-migration is a typical goal of the central government, the local population can be frustrated by its impact on their socio-economic conditions.[92] Conflicts in cultural tourism between and within regions can emerge, if, for example, there is competition for tour guide jobs between locals and outsiders, flight schedules benefit competing attractions, and cultural tourism is controlled in a centralised manner rather than at the local level.[93]

The new democratic openness has enabled communities and NGOs to test the strength of constitutional guarantees in public interest litigation in which the rights

89 Article 18B(2) of the Constitution of 1945.

90 Article 28I(3) of the Constitution of 1945.

91 For examples of such conflicts in Indonesia see Tania Murray Li, *The Will to Improve: Governmentality, Development, and the Practice of Politics* (Duke University Press 2007) 256–266; Roem Topatimasang, 'Mapping as a Tool for Community Organizing against Power: A Moluccas Experience' in J Peter Brosius, Anna Lowenhaupt Tsing, and Charles Zerner (eds), *Communities and Conservation: Histories and Politics of Community Based Natural Resource Management* (AltaMira Press 2005).

92 Mary Hawkins, 'Violence and the Construction of Identity: Conflict between the Dayak and Madurese in Kalimantan, Indonesia', in Minako Sakai, Glenn Banks and J H Walker (eds), *The Politics of the Periphery in Indonesia: Social and Geographical Perspectives* (NUS Press 2009) 167 (dating the beginning of transmigration processes in Indonesia to 1905 during the period of Dutch colonial rule).

93 Kathleen M Adams, 'Touting Touristic "Primadonas": Tourism, Ethnicity, and National Integration in Sulawesi, Indonesia' in Picard and Wood (eds) (n 3).

of farming communities and Indigenous peoples are invoked.[94] Decentralisation has further allowed regional governments to draft local intellectual property laws. The autonomous Province of Papua was the first to draft in 2008 a special regional regulation on the protection of intellectual property rights of Indigenous Papuans.[95] The Regional Intellectual Property Regulation protects only Indigenous Papuans or people recognised as such by Papuan customary communities.[96] In contrast to the national Copyright Act, in Papua the government of the Province holds the copyright to works of archaeological remains and cultural objects, as long as the customary community does not claim them.[97] However, the provincial government also holds the customary community rights to all sorts of communally owned traditional cultural expressions,[98] which suggests that communities themselves may not have much to claim after all.

Other provinces have followed the trend towards regional intellectual property laws particularly for traditional knowledge and traditional cultural expressions. A West Javanese Provincial Regulation for a while declared the regional government of West Java as holder of the copyright to traditional cultural expressions and traditional knowledge and entitled to collect royalties from foreign users.[99] The Regulation was replaced in 2018 with one that no longer conflicts with the national Copyright Act.[100] A regulation reportedly in preparation in the province of East Nusa Tenggara wants to specifically protect the copyright of female weavers in the local Tenun Ikat weavings.[101] While frequently in conflict with national legislation, such regional regulation of intellectual property related to cultural expressions, in theory, has the advantage of greater proximity of the regulators to the producers of the material. However, how precisely royalties will be distributed after they have been collected mostly remains as vaguely regulated as in national laws. A concern is that communities would need to deal with a variety of regulators and administrators, whose relationships and responsibilities may not always be clear.

94 On the Constitutional Court decisions of 2013 and 2016 related to farmers see Christoph Antons, Yunita T Winarto and Adlinanur F Prihandiani, 'Farmer-Plant-Breeders and the Law on Java, Indonesia' (2020) 52(4) *Crit Asian Stud* 589; on the Constitutional Court decision of 2013 related to Indigenous peoples see Noer Fauzi Rachman and Mia Siscawati, 'Forestry Law, *masyarakat adat* and Struggles for Inclusive Citizenship in Indonesia' in Christoph Antons (ed), *The Routledge Handbook of Asian Law* (Routledge 2017).

95 Special Regional Regulation of the Province of Papua No 19 of 2008 on the Protection of Intellectual Property Rights of Indigenous Papuans.

96 ibid Article 1.

97 ibid Article 11(3).

98 ibid Article 16.

99 Regional Regulation of the Province of West Java No. 5 of 2012 Regarding the Protection of Intellectual Property, Article 26.

100 Regional Regulation No 10 of 2018 on Management of Intellectual Property.

101 'NTT akan Jadi Provinsi Pertama Jika Perda Perlindungan Hak Cipta Tenun Ikat Disahkan' *Suara NTT* (7 September 2020).

Finally, geographical indications (GIs) have been introduced to protect forms of heritage at the community level. GIs are supposed to guarantee the quality of regional products. They have been promoted in European Union Free Trade Agreements in particular[102] and are often recommended to boost the agricultural and creative industries sectors of developing countries.[103] Ninety-two GIs have been registered in Indonesia so far, with 9 of them foreign and 83 for local products.[104]

GIs could present an opportunity for communities to market their traditional products and heritage because organisations representing local producer communities are the main rights holders and applicants. Such communities call themselves usually 'Community for the protection of…' and in rarer cases 'Association of adat (customary) communities for the protection of…'.[105] Their composition indicates, however, that they are not traditional representative bodies. The initiative to set up such associations often comes from the local government, and local government leaders are involved as senior members, advisors, or supervisors. Other members not immediately involved in the production or trading can be lawyers, university experts, or members of institutions for skills training.[106] The local government also forms by decree the executive committee of such associations. The executive committee drafts the description of the GI with all details about the good, the territory that the GI relates to and its borders, and the logo for it. However, the ultimate decision about the appropriateness of such local regulations rests with an Expert Team in Jakarta, appointed by the Minister of Justice with representatives from various Ministries, supervisory and quality assurance bodies, and other experts.[107]

In short, the promotion of GIs is an important development policy sponsored by national and local governments and as such administered top-down rather than bottom-up. Whether the hopes placed in GIs will materialise depends on the circumstances of every single case. Given the extensive documentation and collaboration with authorities that are required, GI protection could be a difficult tool for the most marginalised communities. However, many local and Indigenous communities are organising themselves with the support of NGOs and may consider

102 Michael Blakeney, 'The Pacific Solution: The European Union's Intellectual Property Rights Activism in Australia's and New Zealand's Sphere of Influence' in Peter Drahos and Susy Frankel (eds), *Indigenous Peoples' Innovation: Intellectual Property Pathways to Development* (ANU E Press 2012) 165, 187–188.

103 For a brief discussion of relevant literature, see Antons, 'Geographical Indications, Heritage and Decentralization Policies', in Calboli and Ng-Loy (n 16) 485–486.

104 See the website of the Directorate General for Intellectual Property <www.ig.dgip.go.id> accessed 1 December 2021.

105 For an example of a Customary Community Association, see Antons, 'Geographical Indications, Heritage, and Decentralization Policies: The Case of Indonesia' in Calboli and Ng-Loy (n 16) 501.

106 ibid 499.

107 ibid 500–501.

GI protection, if they have suitable products. Effective community representation on the executive committees will then be decisive for its impact.

Conclusion

Governments in Southeast Asia have merged cultural and intellectual property concepts into powerful claims for national culture, which they use vis-à-vis neighbouring countries and to make originally 'regional' and locally specific cultural products 'national'. Batik in Indonesia is a good example. It was vigorously defended against Malaysia as Indonesian. At the same time, batik making with local motives has been encouraged in regions with no batik tradition. Batik thus has become a nationwide practice rather than being associated predominantly with Java. As a reaction to the shift of heritage to the national level, regional governments have introduced their own intellectual property laws, which are meant to bring more benefits to the regions, but sometimes contradict the national laws.

The examples in this chapter show how cultural material has been diffused across borders through processes of migration and the division of communities by colonial borders. The 2003 Convention urges international collaboration rather than competition. Some of this collaboration is now beginning to develop, but many countries over the past few years have combined cultural and intellectual property concepts in attempts to control the use of material derived from heritage. At an international level, the overlaps between heritage and intellectual property approaches remain unresolved, as WIPO and UNESCO activities in this field are no longer coordinated as they were during the drafting of the Tunis model law and the WIPO/UNESCO model provisions. Both intellectual property with its focus on individual rights holders and international law with its focus on nation-states continue to have difficulties accommodating the collective rights of communities. This suggests that the progress of the discussions at the international level requires some re-thinking of international law or treaty negotiations with a less general and more diversified focus. In the meantime, the best-organised communities with clear goals may be able to gain sufficient control over carefully selected intellectual property tools such as GIs to benefit from them.

References

Adams K M, 'Touting Touristic "Primadonas": Tourism, Ethnicity, and National Integration in Sulawesi, Indonesia' in M Picard and R E Wood (eds), *Tourism, Ethnicity and the State in Asian and Pacific Societies* (University of Hawai'i Press 1997)

Antons C, 'Law Reform in the "Developmental States" of East and Southeast Asia: From the Asian Crisis to September 11, 2001 and Beyond' in C Antons and V Gessner (eds), *Globalisation and Resistance: Law Reform in Asia since the Crisis* (Hart Publishing 2007)

——— '*Sui Generis* Protection for Plant Varieties and Traditional Knowledge in Biodiversity and Agriculture: The International Framework and National Approaches in the Philippines and India' (2010) 6 *Indian J Law Technol* 89

——— 'Intellectual Property Rights in Indigenous Cultural Heritage: Basic Concepts and Continuing Controversies' in C B Graber, K Kuprecht and J C Lai (eds), *International Trade in Indigenous Cultural Heritage: Legal and Policy Issues* (Edward Elgar 2012)

——— 'Asian Borderlands and the Legal Protection of Traditional Knowledge and Traditional Cultural Expressions' (2013) 47 *Mod Asian Stud* 1403

——— 'Epistemic Communities and the "People without History": The Contribution of Intellectual Property Law to the "Safeguarding" of Intangible Cultural Heritage' in I Calboli and S Ragavan (eds), *Diversity in Intellectual Property: Identities, Interests and Intersections* (Cambridge University Press 2015)

——— 'Legal and Cultural Landscapes: Cultural and Intellectual Property Concepts, and the "Safeguarding" of Intangible Cultural Heritage in Southeast Asia' in C Antons (ed), *The Routledge Handbook of Asian Law* (Routledge 2017a)

——— 'Geographical Indications, Heritage, and Decentralization Policies: The Case of Indonesia' in I Calboli and W L Ng-Loy (eds), *Geographical Indications at the Crossroads of Trade, Development and Culture: Focus on Asia-Pacific* (Cambridge University Press 2017b)

Antons C and Tomasic R, 'Introduction: Law Reform and Legal Change in East Asia' in C Antons and R Tomasic (eds), *Law and Society in East Asia* (Ashgate 2013)

Antons C, Winarto Y T and Prihandiani A F, 'Farmer-Plant-Breeders and the Law on Java, Indonesia' (2020) 52 *Crit Asian Stud* 589

Ardhana I, Langub J and Chew D, 'Borders of Kinship and Ethnicity: Cross-Border Relations Between the Kelalan Valley, Sarawak, and the Bawan Valley, East Kalimantan' (2004) 35 *Borneo Research Bulletin* 144

Asa K, *Mosaic of Indonesian Batik* (Red & White Publishing 2014)

Benda-Beckmann F von, *Property in Social Continuity: Continuity and Change in the Maintenance of Property Relationships Through Time in Minangkabau, West Sumatra* (Martinus Nijhoff 1979)

Bertrand J, *Nationalism and Ethnic Conflict in Indonesia* (Cambridge University Press 2004)

Blake J, *Commentary on the UNESCO 2003 Convention on the Safeguarding of the Intangible Cultural Heritage* (Institute of Art & Law 2006)

Blakeney M, 'The Pacific Solution: The European Union's Intellectual Property Rights Activism in Australia's and New Zealand's Sphere of Influence' in P Drahos and S Frankel (eds), *Indigenous Peoples' Innovation: Intellectual Property Pathways to Development* (ANU E Press 2012)

Boer B, 'Article 3 Identification and Delineation of World Heritage Properties' in F Francioni (ed), *The 1972 World Heritage Convention: A Commentary* (Oxford University Press 2008)

Calboli I and Ng-Loy W L (eds), *Geographical Indications at the Crossroads of Trade, Development and Culture: Focus on Asia-Pacific* (Cambridge University Press 2017)

Chauvel R, 'Papua and Indonesia: Where Contending Nationalisms Meet' in D Kingsbury and H Aveling (eds), *Autonomy and Disintegration in Indonesia* (Routledge Curzon 2003)

Chia F, *The Babas* (Landmark Books 2015)

Coombe R, 'The Expanding Purview of Cultural Properties and their Politics' (2009) 5 *Annu Rev Law Soc Sci* 393

Dermawan A, 'Malaysia, Singapore Could Vie for Joint UNESCO Listing on Hawker Culture' *New Straits Times* (May 2, 2019)

Gallardo L M C, 'Comparative Case Analysis of FPIC Processes for Community Intellectual Property Rights in the Philippines' in C Antons and W Logan (eds), *Intellectual Property, Cultural Property and Intangible Cultural Heritage* (Routledge 2018)

Gfeller A E, 'Negotiating the Meaning of Global Heritage: 'Cultural Landscapes' in the UNESCO World Heritage Convention, 1972–1992' (2013) 8 *J Glob Hist* 484

Hawkins M, 'Violence and the Construction of Identity: Conflict between the Dayak and Madurese in Kalimantan, Indonesia' in M Sakai, G Banks and J H Walker (eds), *The Politics of the Periphery in Indonesia: Social and Geographical Perspectives* (NUS Press 2009)

Hitchcock M, King V T and Parnwell M (eds), *Heritage Tourism in Southeast Asia* (NIAS Press 2010)

Ho Y C, *Special Relationship in the Malay World: Indonesia and Malaysia* (ISEAS Publishing 2018)

Hoffman B T, 'Exploring and Establishing Links for a Balanced Art and Cultural Heritage Policy' in B T Hoffman (eds), *Art and Cultural Heritage: Law, Policy and Practice* (Cambridge University Press 2006)

Ives M, 'Singapore's Claim as a Street-Food Hub Riles Malaysians' *The New York Times* (New York, 5 November 2018) <www.nytimes.com/2018/11/05/world/asia/singapore-malaysia-street-food-unesco.html> accessed 1 December 2021

Lev D S, *Legal Evolution and Political Authority in Indonesia: Selected Essays* (Kluwer Law International 2000)

Li T M, *The Will to Improve: Governmentality, Development, and the Practice of Politics* (Duke University Press 2007)

Liow J C, *The Politics of Indonesia-Malaysia Relations: One Kin, Two Nations* (Routledge 2005)

McCabe Elliott I, *Batik – Fabled Cloth of Java* (Periplus 2004)

Murdoch L, 'Simple Hand Gesture has Two Countries up in Arms' *Sydney Morning Herald* (Sydney, 15 August 2011) <www.smh.com.au/entertainment/dance/simple-hand-gesture-has-two-countries-up-in-arms-20110814-1it5o.html> accessed 1 December 2021

Muzium Tekstil Negara – National Textile Museum (Department of Museums Malaysia 2012)

Oguamanam C, *Tiered or Differentiated Approach to Traditional Knowledge and Traditional Cultural Expressions: The Evolution of a Concept* (Centre for International Governance Innovation 2018)

Picard M and Wood R E (eds), *Tourism, Ethnicity, and the State in Asian and Pacific Societies* (University of Hawai'i Press 1997)

Phasuk S and Stott P, *Royal Siamese Maps: War and Trade in Nineteenth Century Thailand* (River Books 2004)

Prott L V and O'Keefe P J, '"Cultural Heritage" or "Cultural Property"?' (1992) 1(2) *Int J Cult Prop* 307

Rachman N F and Siscawati M, 'Forestry Law, *masyarakat adat* and Struggles for Inclusive Citizenship in Indonesia' in C Antons (ed), *The Routledge Handbook of Asian Law* (Routledge 2017)

Rahmawati F, 'Pesona Gorga Batak, Motif Batik Kebanggaan Medan yang Mirip Ulos' (*Merdeka.com*, 3 August 2020) <www.merdeka.com/sumut/pesona-gorga-batak-motif-batik-kebanggaan-medan-yang-mirip-ulos.html> accessed 1 December 2021

Richter A, *Arts and Crafts in Indonesia* (Chronicle Books 1993)

Robison R, 'Interpreting the Politics of Southeast Asia: Debates in Parallel Universes' in R Robison (ed), *Routledge Handbook of Southeast Asian Politics* (Routledge 2011)

Roojen P van, *Batik Design* (revised edn, The Pepin Press 1994)

Scott J C, *Seeing Like a State: How Certain Schemes to Improve the Human Condition Have Failed* (Yale University Press 1998)

Susilo H, 'Beras Adan Resmi Dipatenkan' *Kompas* (Jakarta, 15 January 2012)
Sturgeon J C, *Border Landscapes: The Politics of Akha Land Use in China and Thailand* (Silkworm Books 2005)
Suárez T, *Early Mapping of Southeast Asia* (Periplus Editions 1999)
Topatimasang R, 'Mapping as a Tool for Community Organizing against Power: A Moluccas Experience' in J P Brosius, A L Tsing and C Zerner (eds), *Communities and Conservation: Histories and Politics of Community-Based Natural Resource Management* (AltaMira Press 2005)
Vickers A, *Bali – A Paradise Created* (2nd edn, Tuttle Publishing 2012)
Vrdoljak A, *International Law, Museums and the Return of Cultural Objects* (Cambridge University Press 2008)
Winichakul T, *Siam Mapped – A History of the Geo-Body of a Nation* (University of Hawai'i Press 1994)
Wolters O W, *History, Culture and Region in Southeast Asian Perspectives* (Southeast Asia Program Publications, Cornell University/Institute of Southeast Asian Studies, Singapore 1999)

3 Scaling up and down the edible heritage

Food and foodways as terrains of cultural friction

Raúl Matta

Introduction

Food and foodways are crucial to debates on intellectual property and cultural heritage as they involve visceral and deep effects, on the one hand, and encompass central concerns for rural populations, ranging from biocultural knowledge to food security, strategic territorialisation, and market participation, on the other hand. This sets the ground for a contentious heritage arena wherein various actors participate in the adoption, rejection, and selective appropriation of elements of food cultures by implicitly or explicitly deploying notions of authenticity, identity, and tradition. These processes prompt tensions and controversies within and between societies but are most often concealed by accounts of smooth consensus-making contained in official discourses about heritage.

The local controversies on food heritagisation explored in this chapter are embedded in larger political-economic contexts with outside actors who have dissimilar conceptions of local foodways. There is one major thread running through these controversies (as well as through several cultural works related to food) that needs to be briefly mentioned before addressing them from the point of view of scales. This thread can be summed up as appropriation. Here, appropriation means the deliberate redefinition of food cultures by outsiders according to objectives and criteria independent of local needs and interests. While there is no refuting the significance and necessity of attending to issues of biological and cultural diversity, nutrition, and economic development, it is important to remember that it is outsiders (politicians, firms, researchers, and other non-rural actors) who largely establish priorities and define food agendas that directly affect the lives of insiders. Several examples across the world point to external forces engaging in social, economic, and political activities that manipulate food with the intention to make changes in the food itself or in the rules and boundaries that shape public perceptions and the meanings of food.[1] In most of these examples, the voices of

1 John Brett, 'Conclusions: Culture, Tradition and Political Economy' in Elizabeth Finnis (ed), *Reimagining Marginalized Foods* (University of Arizona Press 2012).

DOI: 10.4324/9781003345237-4

local communities concerned with or impacted by these activities are little heard or not at all.

Colonial settler societies and developing countries are negatively affected by the above-mentioned dynamics. Central to this is the lens outsiders use to define the scope of their intervention within and across the territories and socio-cultural environments to which they have gained access. Usually, the scope of intervention of outsiders extends beyond and often runs counter to the social, political, and cognitive assemblages that local actors and communities have built throughout their history. For instance, the increasing demand for agricultural products and the uncertainty of international food markets has led governments and firms to invest in agricultural lands in the developing world. This land-grabbing has raised concerns because the foods produced in those lands are generally exported at higher prices and become inaccessible to the people who work and inhabit these spaces.[2] In addition, attempts to develop markets for marginalised, native, or Indigenous foods for the sake of preserving agricultural and biological diversity often result in an appropriation of these foods in the process of redefining their new use and value.[3]

Food heritagisation is not exempt from these dynamics. On the contrary, the entry of food and culinary cultures into heritage frameworks and into the UNESCO 2003 Convention for the Safeguarding of the Intangible Cultural Heritage (the 2003 Convention) in particular has unveiled and prompted food's potential to convey national and private interests within the fields of entrepreneurship and public diplomacy. Governments' competing enthusiasm for obtaining rewards from UNESCO encourages reductionist views of food cultures, evolving towards materiality and accumulation rather than towards immateriality and transmission. Indeed, food-related intangible cultural heritage nominations have usually been supported by backstage policymaking aimed at marketing valuable versions of 'national' cuisines and 'ethnic' food products within and beyond boundaries. This leaves the local populations to respond as best they can to a range of opportunities and constraints.

This troubling scenario is caused by a series of clashing scales. The heritagisation of food taking place within frameworks established by national governments and international organisations is inherently large scale and transboundary in character as its effects are never expected to be dealt with at the local level only. Such heritagisation of food thus puts pressure on local populations (the supposed beneficiaries of heritage) who see themselves at risk of being marginalised by heritage policies. A vast amount of literature has addressed local participatory

2 Maria Cristina Rulli and Paolo D'Odorico, 'Food Appropriation through Large Scale Land Acquisitions' (2014) 9(064030) *Environmental Research Letters* 1.

3 See generally Elizabeth Finnis (ed), *Reimagining Marginalized Foods* (University of Arizona Press 2012); Emma McDonell and Richard Wilk (eds), *Critical Approaches to Superfoods* (Bloomsbury 2020).

approaches to heritage management as a potential solution to this contradiction.[4] However, these approaches will have little effect if there is no prior local participation in providing clear and straightforward answers to fundamental and historical questions: why (food) heritage? By whom? For whom? To what end? By focusing on recent controversies in Brazil and Mexico, the next sections argue that an approach in terms of scales might shed new light on these old questions.

Exploring the heritagisation of food through the lens of (clashing) scales

Since food and foodways extend to numerous domains and agendas including agricultural biodiversity, human and non-human relationships, health and nutrition, environmental ethics, tourism, and critiques of the Anthropocene, the analysis of their framing as cultural heritage has to pay attention to the interplay and friction between actors' specific views, 'lenses', and 'scopes', to elucidate motivations and the consequences these motivations engender. To acknowledge the diversity of the living entities involved in the heritagisation of food and the disjuncture this process might entail, this chapter proposes to examine food heritage-making under the conceptual prism of 'scales'. Anthropologists Thomas H Eriksen and Anna Tsing note that the notion of scale refers to a combination of the size and the complexity of a particular phenomenon.[5]

Eriksen distinguishes four types of scale between which there is no necessary congruence: the social scale, the physical scale, the temporal scale, and the cognitive scale. The social scale denotes the amount and reach of the networks a system is made of. Large-scale systems depend on the contributions of many persons, while small-scale systems depend on fewer persons. In the context of this chapter, the social scale of heritage-making (composed of individuals, groups, and private and public entities) determines whether a heritage goal is to be significant either at the local, national, or global level. The physical scale encompasses the infrastructure that makes it possible for people within systems to coordinate, monitor, and reproduce their actions. Government bodies, universities, museums, and a diversity of landscapes, sites, and repositories comprise the cultural heritage infrastructure. The temporal scale is the time horizon imagined for the system. Time scales concern both individual and collective horizons; both are crucial to the governance of cultural resources, even more when they are communicated as shared or common goods to be preserved. The cognitive scale refers to cultural and individual

4 Emma Waterton and Steve Watson (eds), *Heritage and Community Engagement: Collaboration or Contestation?* (Routledge 2013); Cath Neal, 'Heritage and Participation' in Emma Waterton and Steve Watson (eds), *The Palgrave Handbook of Contemporary Heritage Research* (Palgrave 2015).

5 Thomas Eriksen, *Overheating: An Anthropology of Accelerated Change* (Pluto Press 2016); Anna Tsing, 'On Nonscalability: The Living World Is Not Amenable to Precision-Nested Scales' (2012) 18(3) *Common Knowl* 505. International lawyers and historians have also used the notions of scale, see Valentina Vadi, 'Perspective and Scale in the Architecture of International Legal History' (2019) 30(1) *European Journal of International Law* 53.

representations of society, the world, or the cosmos. In other words, it refers to the size of one's perceived world. Since the examples in this chapter involve populations and communities rooted in tradition, one equates 'cognitive scales' with the concept of *cosmovision*, here understood as the underlying culture-specific view of the world, encompassing the structure of the universe and ideas about its origin or development.[6]

A clash of scales occurs when the intersection of two or more levels of scale leads to a contradiction, a conflict, or a friction. For example, most environmental policies are decided and implemented at the national level, whereas climate change is a global concern, and all countries are connected through international trade, mobility, and communication networks.[7] Heritage decisions taken both at the state and transnational levels can lead to local resistance if populations feel dispossessed or excluded from the changes generated around them. This brings into consideration the potential of cultural heritage to generate economic profits through standardisation, reproducibility, and extrapolation, and how different actors benefit or are negatively affected by these processes. Whereas some material objects (e.g., certain traditional crafts and souvenirs) successfully portray cultural heritage to the extent of becoming cultural commodities, other objects will not enter market relations beyond local or national boundaries without objections by actors voicing perspectives on 'loss'[8] – such as loss of authenticity, loss of substance, loss of meaning, loss of aesthetic and spiritual integrity, and loss of emotional intensity. In such contexts, the concepts of 'scalability' and 'non-scalability' coined by Tsing may prove to be a useful tool to grasp actual and potential controversies related to heritage diffusion and marketability.

Scalability refers to 'the ability to expand (and expand and expand) without rethinking basic elements'.[9] The term characterises any enterprise proceeding in a way that can be reproduced at all scales, its extension making no relevant difference.[10] When small projects can become big without changing the nature of the project, it means they are 'scalable'. Tsing uses the example of the colonial mode of production of monoculture plantations, the first-ever scalable enterprise. Conceived for sugarcane in the middle of the 16th century by the Portuguese colonies in Brazil, it meant eradicating local inhabitants, animals, and plants and introducing in this 'clean' environment both sugarcanes and slaves. Cloning sugarcane, transplanting it to a new environment where it has few interspecies relations, and building a system of slave labour where humans are severed from

6 Johanna Broda, 'Astronomy, Cosmovisión, and Ideology in Pre-Hispanic Mesoamerica' (1982) 385(1) *Ann NY AcadSci* 81.

7 Eriksen (n 5).

8 Keisuke Yamada, 'Shamisen Skin on the Verge of Extinction: Musical Sustainability and Non-Scalability of Cultural Loss' (2017) 26(3) *Ethnomusicology Forum* 373.

9 Anna Tsing, 'On Nonscalability: The Living World Is Not Amenable to Precision-Nested Scales' (2012) 18(3) *Common Knowl* 505, 505.

10 Martin Savransky and Isabelle Stengers, 'Relearning the Art of Paying Attention: A Conversation' (2018) 47(1) *SubStance* 130.

past social relations provided a model that was replicated in the Caribbean by the Spanish, the English, the French, and the Dutch.[11] Scalability characterises the triumph of 'precision design' and any enterprise that aims at establishing manners of functioning impermeable to encounters, eventuality, and conjunctures. Tsing's concern is in 'the exclusion of biological and cultural diversity from scalable designs'. Scalable projects, she argues, undermine complexity as they 'banish meaningful diversity, which is to say, the diversity that might change things'.[12]

Studying *shamisen*, a three-stringed traditional Japanese musical instrument, ethnomusicologist Yamada offers an insightful depiction of two competing approaches to scalability in the context of a project of cultural preservation.[13] Shamisen is similar to a guitar or a banjo, with a neck and strings stretched across a resonating body. The materials used in its traditional fabrication include animal skin (dog, cat, or snake) and elephant ivory. This fact has raised controversy between two camps of practitioners: those who support the cultural preservation of shamisen but suggest replacing the animal materials with synthetic ones to facilitate the large-scale dissemination of the shamisen and related cultural practices, and those who support a traditionalist viewpoint that argues that such replacement would threaten the existence of the remaining traditional shamisen manufacturers, long-standing cultural traditions related to the instrument, and the sensory knowledge related to its animal materials. While the former sees the preservation of shamisen as a scalable project, that can expand in size and scale and allow for new spaces for diffusion and replication beyond Japan, the latter see cultural preservation as non-scalable, as it runs against the concerns of local practitioners that have different perspectives on life. Similarly to shamisen, the examples in the next sections use scaling, scalability, and non-scalability to show how the heritagisation of food and foodways brings about notable disjuncture between global and local perspectives on gain and loss.

A scalar analysis also offers a framework with which to examine notions of boundaries in the context of cultural movement, societal evolution, and state, sub-state, and supra-state policies. A distinction between boundaries and borders is applied here, wherein boundary broadly 'refers to any type of division whether it is a semantic divider between categories or a line-on-the-ground political division', while border refers specifically to the case of territorialised line-on-the-ground political borders.[14] Boundaries are malleable; they are not achieved processes but rather ongoing, never finished or fixed (even if they appear to be), and need to be rewritten and renegotiated.[15] By adopting such an approach, the examples in this chapter also address 'bounding', namely, how groups determine spatial, political,

11 Michael Fakhri, *Sugar and the Making of International Trade Law* (Cambridge University Press 2014); Sidney Mintz, *Sweetness and Power* (Penguin Books 1986).

12 Tsing (n 9) 507.

13 Yamada (n 8).

14 Reece Jones, 'Categories, Borders and Boundaries' (2009) 33(2) *Prog in Hum Geogr* 174, 180.

15 ibid.

and cognitive bounds to organise cultural diversity in ways that are consistent with their expectations and/or beliefs.

Impacts and responses to the heritagisation of Amerindian foods

This section builds on the views and experiences of the Amerindian cook and food activist Tainá Marajoara. Since 2014, she has run the association called Iacitatá, which means 'fertile place' in the Tupi language. Located in Belém do Pará, Brazil's Amazonian metropolis, Iacitatá is both a restaurant and a 'centre for food culture', which hosts meetings, debates, and events on topics related to agroecology, food security, and food sovereignty. As one of Brazil's representatives of Slow Food International, Iacitatá dissents from the dominant food system. It shares goals with organisations, activists, and institutions that can be grouped under the designation of Alternative Food Movements.[16] It aims at promoting the consumption of organic food, which is produced without pesticides, chemical inputs, and additives, and illuminating the linkages between food production on the one hand and social justice and sustainability on the other. On a local level, Iacitatá creates awareness about possibilities of fair trade that could counter the exploitative relationships generated by industrial and monoculture food production, sparks reflection on the political ecology of Amazonian development, and supports the struggles for environmental justice of Brazil's landless peasant movement. Concerning culinary culture, the association focuses on conservation efforts to tackle the decrease of food biodiversity and the loss of significance of native Amazonian ingredients among young generations. Central to this is to highlight and expose the processes that make invisible culinary knowledge rooted in local communities. These processes are reflective of what Marajoara calls 'a colonisation of taste', which she links to the prevalence in the food system of actors, private and public, who adhere to neoliberal values and interests. Interesting for this chapter is the fact that Marajoara depicts the heritagisation of food as playing a central role in the colonisation of taste. This leads to asking in what contexts (or through which lenses) cultural heritage, originally conceived to enhance people's sense of identity, can be seen as a threat to cultural diversity. Marajoara's view is taken from two interviews she gave to sociologists Laurence Granchamp[17] and Carlos Alberto Dória[18] and appearances she made over recent years in various

16 Liz Grauerholz and Nicole Owens, 'Alternative Food Movements' in James Wright, *International Encyclopedia of the Social & Behavioral Sciences* (2nd edn, Routledge 2015).

17 Laurence Granchamp, 'Penser l'Alimentation d'un Point de Vue Décolonial. Entretien avec Tainá Marajoara (Bélém, Brésil)' (2019) 61(2) *Revue des Sciences Sociales* <https://journals.openedition.org/revss/3611> accessed 8 December 2021.

18 Carlos Alberto Dória, 'Uma Garota do Barulho quer Roubar Cena da Gastronomía' (*São Paulo São*, 29 June 2016) <https://saopaulosao.com.br/conteudos/colunistas/1735-uma-garota-do-barulho-quer-roubar-cena-da-gastronomia.html> accessed 8 December 2021.

forums.[19] In these, she engages with events that stem from a surge of cultural and policy work whose goal is to promote the city of Belém as a major cultural and tourist destination, with Amazonian food as one of its pillars.

Belém saw itself recently under the culinary spotlight. In September 2011, the Legislative Assembly of the State of Pará recognised six typical Amerindian dishes as part of the intangible cultural heritage of the state: 'pato no tucupi', 'maniçoba', 'caruru', 'tacacá', and 'vatapá'.[20] In 2013, the *tacacazeiras*, the street vendors of tacacá, were also included in the same register. That same year, the city hosted the first Conference on Amazonian Gastronomy, which resulted in a request to the federal authorities to recognise gastronomy in all public policies related to culture. In 2015, Belém became a UNESCO City of Gastronomy and a member of the Creative Cities Network, with the commitment of developing programmes on food technology and innovation that contribute to sustainable agri-food systems.[21] In 2016, the plan of Sao Paulo's star chef Alex Atala to create an Amazonian gastronomic hub on the premises of the city's Museum of Contemporary Art prompted heated tensions and debates that led to the project's withdrawal.[22] In the meantime, food activism and alternative food networks grew significantly in the region. These events take on a special meaning in a state like Pará, where the Amerindian population is most numerous and which has experienced internal colonisation since the 1960s.[23] The establishment of externally driven but domestic cattle ranches and soybean farms, the exploitation of forest wood, and the extraction of mineral resources have disenfranchised and disempowered Indigenous populations, a typical outcome of colonial relationships in Latin America (and elsewhere). Multicultural policies implemented in the 1990s have created possibilities for Indigenous groups to express claims in terms of ethnic identity while raising awareness among both Amerindian and non-Amerindian populations that ethnicity is something that can be valued, commoditised, and commercialised.

Marajoara criticises the processes of value-making for Pará's food by non-Paraenses with high discursive and financial means. In her view, internal colonisation,

19 Berlin Brazil Dialogue | Urban-Rural Relations between Agroexport and Food Sovereignty, 19 January 2021, organised by Lateinamerika-Institut der FreienUniversität Berlin and Mecila, Maria Sibylla Merian Centre Conviviality-Inequality in Latin America and partners.
<www.youtube.com/watch?v=srAekuJ13Rg&list=LL&index=4&t=151s> accessed 8 December 2021; see also <www.youtube.com/watch?v=-wNJwKsXj7o&feature=emb_logo> accessed 8 December 2021.

20 Ana Paula Caetano Jacques, 'Patrimônio Cultural e Atrativo Turístico Gastronômico en Belém do Pará, Brasil' (Master thesis, Universidade de Brasília 2015).

21 See <https://en.unesco.org/creative-cities/node/324> accessed 8 December 2021.

22 PARÁ, 'Chef Alex Atala Desiste de Participar de Polo Gastronômicoem Belém' (PARÁ Rede Liberal 01 July 2016) <http://g1.globo.com/pa/para/noticia/2016/07/chef-alex-atala-desiste-de-participar-de-polo-gastronomico-em-belem.html>accessed 8 December 2021.

23 What we see in internal colonialism, in a broader sense, is an in-country region-to-region subordination.

the surge of 'gastronomisation'[24] in Brazil,[25] and the global enthusiasm for 'ethnic fine-dining'[26] are changing the status and role of Pará's food in ways that benefit external players, namely, male 'white' chefs of fine-dining restaurants and members of the tourist industry. For instance, tacacá, formerly only known as humble street food, can be found today as 'tacacá chic' in fancy restaurants located both inside and outside the region, or as 'mini tacacá' among the appetisers (*petits fours*) in official receptions.[27] Ironically, the increasing visibility of Amerindian foods throughout the country takes place at the expense of the culinary knowledge and taste of Amerindian communities, which are said to be non-refined or simply wrong. For instance, as Marajoara explains, while the *tucupi*, a cassava juice used as seasoning, is locally consumed sour, some chefs argue that its new, sweet variation is the 'corrected' version. It is these contexts where Amerindian food is honoured but Amerindian identity downplayed that Marajoara calls the colonisation of taste. Such culinary imperialism takes place 'when I am told that my taste, which has been shaped by my culture, is not a refined or sophisticated taste, and that for it to be civilised, I would have to forget it!'[28] Who tells her to forget her food culture, Marajoara explains, is the mainstream media, which conveys simplified and sometimes inaccurate knowledge on Para's food and foodways.

> TV was broadcasting reports about Pará's gastronomy. And what you saw in those reports made it look as if the food popped up itself on the table. Those marvellous *cupuaçu*, those marvellous *jambus*, those marvellous *filhotes*! It always made me uncomfortable because I come from an Indigenous group, the Marajoara. But here in Pará, everything goes through food! The food-gift,

24 By gastronomisation, Barbosa means the process of valorisation, recognition, learning, and enjoyment of the pleasures of the table in all its extension. Gastronomisation includes sub-processes such as the recovery and ennoblement of traditional or ethnic culinary practices and knowledge and the extension of the notion of gastronomy to all kinds of culinary expressions.

25 Livia Barbosa, 'A Ética e a Estética na Alimentaçaõ Contemporânea' in Fabiana Thomé da Cruz, Alessandra Matte and Sergio Schneider (eds), *Producão, Consumo e Abastecimiento de Alimentos: Desafios e Novas Estratégias* (UFGRS 2016) 104.

26 Lisa Markowitz, 'Highland Haute Cuisine: The Transformation of Alpaca Meat' in Elizabeth Finnis (ed), *Reimagining Marginalized Foods* (University of Arizona Press 2012); Raúl Matta, 'Recipes for Crossing Boundaries: Peruvian Fusion' in Steffan Igor Ayora-Díaz (ed), *Cooking Technology: Transformations in Culinary Practice in Mexico and Latin America* (Bloomsbury 2016); Clare Sammells, 'Haute Traditional Cuisines: How UNESCO's List of Intangible Heritage Links the Cosmopolitan to the Local' in Ronda Brulotte and Michael Di Giovine (eds), *Edible Identities: Food as Cultural Heritage* (Ashgate 2014); Tainá Zaneti and Sérgio Schneider, 'Ingredientes Singulares à la Carte: Implicações do Uso de Produtos Diferenciados na Gastronomia Contemporânea' [2016] *Anthropol Food* 1 <https://journals.openedition.org/aof/8111> accessed 8 December 2021.

27 Pascale de Robert P and Lucia van Velthem, 'L'Heure du Tacacá. Consommation et Valorisation d'Aliments Traditionnels Amazoniens en Zone Urbaine (Brésil)' [2008] *Anthropol Food* S4 <https://journals.openedition.org/aof/3533> accessed 8 December 2021.

28 Granchamp (n 17). Note that quotations from Tainá Marajoara are this author's own translation from Portuguese and French languages.

> the food-pleasure, the food-spice, the food-medicine, the same leaves we use to prepare a dish we also use in purification rituals … what we use to spice up the dishes also serves us as a remedy to cure pneumonia, or to release from a spell … Now, chefs take our spices and our food by extracting them from their symbolic universe and including them in a kind of gastronomic spectacularisation that dispossesses us and serves them to dominate us. And that has always bothered me enormously.[29]

In the same line

> When a chef talks about a certain food, it's as if he absolutely knows what he's talking about. And often he forgets that that food represents a people, a culture, that there is a language behind it. Take the example of the *canhapira*, as it happened. A chef from Pará presented the *canhapira* in São Paulo. But the press in São Paulo uses indistinctly 'canhapira, quinhampira or cunhapira'. I was surprised, because, first, the chef spoke of 'a kind of feijoada-paraense', when the *canhapira* is not a *feijoada*; it is a preparation that can be done with game, with fish, with reptile, with anything.[30]

Marajoara seeks to challenge how 'white' chefs make Indigenous foodways invisible either by omitting knowledge or by diffusing imprecise knowledge in a move that serves to legitimate their culinary achievements. To do so, she breaks with the conventional discourse conveyed by the national media in a sharply pointed way and condemns the fact that several chefs from the south of Brazil (the whitest and richest part of the country) come to the north to proclaim themselves both defenders of the Amazon and ambassadors of Amazonian cuisine; '[b]ut how can they claim to be ambassadors when they don't represent any people here?'[31] Marajoara further argues that large companies that appropriate the Amazon's land and water resources, thus threatening the survival and reproduction of Amerindian populations, sponsor chefs' endeavours.[32]

Marajoara can develop sophisticated criticism by stressing her Indigenous roots, by being a member of international activist networks such as Slow Food, but also by building on the ideas of Portuguese sociologist Boaventura de Sousa Santos, of whom she attended the lectures addressed to Latin American grassroots leaders in the framework of the Popular University of the Social Movements, in which she participated actively.[33] Santos' thesis is a critique of Western epistemology, which

29 ibid.
30 Dória (n 18).
31 Granchamp (n 17).
32 ibid.
33 Tainá Marajoara, '2015_UPMS_Oficina do Rio de Janeiro – Cultura Alimentar' (*YouTube*, 11 January 2016) <www.youtube.com/watch?app=desktop&v=-wNJwKsXj7o&feature=emb_title> accessed 8 December 2021.

he characterises as a methodology for dividing the world between regions of order (civilised and lawful) and regions of chaos (savage and lawless).

Modern Western thinking is abyssal thinking. It consists of a system of visible and invisible distinctions, the invisible ones being the foundation of the visible ones. The invisible distinctions are established through radical lines that divide social reality into two realms, the realm of 'this side of the line' and the realm of 'the other side of the line'. The division is such that 'the other side of the line' vanishes as reality, becomes non-existent, and is produced as non-existent. Non-existent means not existing in any relevant or comprehensible way of being. What most fundamentally characterises abyssal thinking is thus the impossibility of the co-presence of the two sides of the line. To the extent that it prevails, this side of the line only prevails by exhausting the field of relevant reality. Beyond it, there is only non-existence, invisibility, non-dialectical absence.[34]

Modern Western thinking, according to Santos, is 'abyssal' in that it is based on the invisibility of everything positioned 'on the other side of the line'. This argument can adopt a more nuanced form under the light of Eriksen's conceptualisation of scales, which instead of building on the idea of irreconcilable epistemological differences, seeks to illuminate contradictions of diverse nature in the global system. One of the most fundamental contradictions, Eriksen argues, consists in the chronic tension between the universalising forces of global modernity and the desire for autonomy in local communities. He affirms[35] that processes on the large scale that shape '[t]he drive to standardisation, simplification and universalization', as exemplified by Marajoara in terms of the whitening and spectacularisation of Amerindian foods, are always countered by processes on the small scale characterised 'by a defence of local values, practices and relations'. The heritagisation and valorisation of Amerindian foodways illustrate a situation in which large-scale decisions made by powerful actors (those located on 'one side of the line', that of 'civilisation' in de Santos' terms) clash with the tangibly lived live at the small, community-scale (that of lawlessness). Marajoara's defence thus takes the form of a 'post-abyssal' discourse. On the one hand, her discourse denounces the appropriation of local foods by external actors who redefine these foods' roles and values to match the expectations of other outsiders. On the other hand, Marajoara's discourse seeks to reinstall pride and urgency in Amazonian populations for local cognitive forms that support the provision of a varied and diverse diet.

> [o]ur identity has become a commodity as if it were reduced to placing a product in a market that would give it its so-called 'added value', while we [peoples] of the Amazon are experiencing a serious situation in terms of food security and sovereignty because our food is being transformed into

34 Boaventura de Sousa Santos, 'Beyond Abyssal Thinking: From Global Lines to Ecologies of Knowledges' (2007) 30(1) *Review* 45, 45–46.

35 Thomas Eriksen, *Overheating: An Anthropology of Accelerated Change* (Pluto Press 2016) 7.

> commodities. And all this poses another problem: the market is cruelly cutting back! We only eat [these market-integrated foods], filhote, jambú, açaí or cupuaçu, as if there was nothing else in Pará, and we forget to consume the food that comes from the biodiversity of the forest![36]

Advertisement material by the tourism office of Belém provides an example of how the commercialisation of Amerindian food for outsiders can be a drawback in terms of identity for local populations.[37] The example concerns a poster showing the dish 'pato no tucupi' (duck in tucupi) in an aestheticised fashion. Traditionally, 'pato no tucupi' contains three main ingredients: duck, tucupi, and jambu. The duck is roasted, cut into pieces, and boiled in the tucupi. The jambu covers the pieces of duck. Manioc flour (farinha de mandioca) and rice are served on the dish as accompaniment. The promotional image presents the dish with changes, additions, and removals. The duck is served in larger pieces, jambu is placed around the duck, and the rice is decorated with chilli pepper. Manioc flour, the symbol of Paraense, is excluded from the dish. This could be perceived as a charge against the identity of people who acknowledge themselves as 'comedoresde farinha' (farinha eaters).[38] Marajoara has also expressed concern in relation to the açaí, a fruit that in recent years turned into a global 'superfood'.[39]

> [A]çaí is the blood of the forest in the cosmovision of several peoples. It is the food that supplies all needs, that brings life. Açaí in Pará differs from the rest of Brazil because it is at the mouth of the Amazon, where everything the river brings flows, and this becomes one of the best açaí, with the most peculiar flavour. The growing demand for açaí, especially for export, has started to interfere directly with the local economy. Açaí has become a commodity. Before there was a funny expression: a thick person was an 'açaí of three' ('Fulano é grossoigualaçaí de três') because it refers to the thick açaí, which costs three reais. Today to make a litre of thick açaí, I have to pay 25 reais! And açaí, which has had all that significance to both ancestral and contemporary food cultures is now leaving the Paraense table and being replaced by industrial products.[40]

Marajoara's combat results from clashing scales: *cosmovision* clashes with economic growth and expansion. The notions of scalability and non-scalability offer an additional reading of this tension. While renowned chefs scale up economic

36 Granchamp (n 17).

37 Ana Paula Caetano Jacques, 'Patrimônio Cultural e Atrativo Turístico Gastronômico en Belém do Pará, Brasil' (Master thesis, Universidade de Brasília 2015).

38 Raul Lody (ed), *Farinha de Mandioca: O Sabor Brasileiro e a Receitas da Bahia* (Senac 2019).

39 Eduardo Brondizio, 'The Global Açaí: A Chronicle of Possibilities and Predicaments of an Amazonian Superfood' in Emma McDonell and Richard Wilk (eds), *Critical Approaches to Superfoods* (Bloomsbury 2020).

40 Dória (n 18).

projects based on 'spectacular' Amerindian foodways, Marajoara scales down by re-territorialising Amerindian foods in their social, ecological, and cultural contexts. While external interpretations of Amerindian foods expand beyond local, regional, and even national boundaries thus eradicating knowledge rooted in Amerindian *cosmovision*, Marajoara constructs a response that seeks to avoid cultural loss. The misappropriation of food does not just entail a loss of specific foods or culinary techniques; it also entails a loss of cognitive forms that are crucial to the cultural reproduction and survival of local communities but mean very little, if anything, to capitalist modes of intervention.

Mexico's culinary heritage and the 2010 Intangible Cultural Heritage UNESCO nomination

This section draws on recent discussions around the commemoration of the tenth anniversary of the declaration of 'Traditional Mexican Cuisine – Ancestral, Ongoing Community Culture, the Michoacán Paradigm' as intangible cultural heritage by UNESCO. It was the second of two attempts by Mexico to make it into the Representative List with food-related practices. The first unsuccessful try took place in 2005 with a dossier called 'People of Maize. The Ancestral Cuisine of Mexico', whose strong focus on maize as a symbol of national identity failed for being easily available for commodification and provoking the opposition of neighbouring Guatemala, which considered itself entitled to claim a similar relationship to the crop.[41] The 2010 nomination inscribed the 'comprehensive cultural model comprising farming, ritual practices, age-old skills, culinary techniques and ancestral community customs and manners'.[42] The document was prepared by a group of specialists gathered under the initiative of the *Conservatorio de la Cultura Gastronómica Mexicana* (Conservatory of Mexican Gastronomic Culture, hereinafter the Conservatorio), a powerful civil association committed to the 'preservation, rescue, safeguarding and promotion of habits, customs, products, cultural practices and knowledge that constitute the common core that defines traditional Mexican cuisine' and 'the expression of innovative trends … to ensure its transmission to future generations'. Including traditional Mexican cuisine in the intangible cultural heritage list is Conservatorio's major achievement.

The nomination sought to counter processes that threaten livelihoods in impoverished rural areas such as environmental and cultural degradation, lack of incentives for agriculture, chronic emigration, and broken families. The safeguarding measures meant to make this happen combine awareness of traditional food knowledge and the integration of new knowledge to gradually build up economic

41 Albert Moncusí and Beatriz Santamarina, 'Bueno para Comer, bueno para Patrimonializar: La Propuesta de la Cocina Mexicana como Patrimonio Cultural de la Humanidad' in Marcelo Álvarez and F Xazier Medina (eds), *Identidades en el Plato* (Icaria 2008).

42 UNESCO inscribed in 2010 on the Representative List of Intangible Cultural Heritage of Humanity. Decision of the Intergovernmental Committee: 5.COM 6.30.

circuits that ensure local development. The nomination form mentions efforts to meet tourist demand but that do not modify the cultural framework within which traditional cuisine evolves, which is characterised by attachment to customs, rituality, and collective work. As such, they would comply with the soft approach to the commercialisation of intangible cultural heritage contained in the 2003 Convention and recently endorsed by UNESCO through the concept of 'commercialisation without over-commercialisation'.[43] Since the nomination, the Conservatorio reports to UNESCO on the measures implemented, organises food events throughout the country and beyond, and encourages Indigenous women from rural villages to present their food in ways that can be appreciated by tourists and to present themselves as *cocineras tradicionales* (traditional female cooks), a figure that the association has a major role in promoting.[44] The work done by the Conservatorio has been further supported by government institutions (the Mexican Ministry of Tourism (SECTUR)), and contributed to an increased interest in traditional foods and culinary practices all over the country.

On 16 November 2020, the Conservatorio and its allies celebrated and assessed the work done over ten years. Due to the COVID-19 pandemic, the meeting, called 'Día Nacional de la Gastronomía Mexicana y el 10° aniversario de la Declaratoria de la Cocina Tradicional Mexicana como Patrimonio Cultural Inmaterial de la Humanidad por la UNESCO' (hereinafter the National Day meeting), was hosted online by the Mexican Ministry of Tourism and made publicly available through its social media accounts.[45] Participating in the event were members of the Conservatorio, government and international organisations' representatives (e.g., UNESCO and the UN World Tourism Organization), cocineras tradicionales, and a diverse group of stakeholders of the restaurant and hospitality industry. In November 2020, a series of seminars hosted by the Coordinación Nacional de Antropología and titled 'Miradas críticas y propositivas a diez años del nombramiento de la comida Mexicana en la UNESCO'[46] (hereinafter the Critical Views meeting) were held to provide a more nuanced view on the nomination and its impact on society. Attending the event were scholars, village cooks, and NGO representatives. These events lend themselves as an instructive touchstone for arguing for scaling as an appropriate tool to grasp the conflicting nature of

43 Chiara Bortolotto, 'Commercialization without Over-Commercialization: Normative Conundrums across Heritage Rationalities' (2021) 27(9) *IJHS* 857.

44 Raúl Matta, 'Mexico's Culinary Heritage and Cocineras Tradicionales (Traditional Female Cooks)' (2019) 27(3) *Food and Foodways* 211; Raúl Matta, 'Documenting the UNESCO Feast: Stories of Women's "Empowerment" and Programmatic Cooking' (2021) 29(1) *SocAnthropol* 188.

45 Secretaria de Turismo de México, 'Día Nacional de la Gastronomía Mexicana y el 10° aniversario de la Declaratoria de la Cocina Tradicional Mexicana como Patrimonio Cultural Inmaterial de la Humanidad por la UNESCO' (*Facebook*, 16 November 2020) <https://m.facebook.com/SECTUR.MX/videos/425208665146969?_rdr> accessed 8 December 2021.

46 Coordinación Nacional de Antropología, 'Miradas Críticas y Propositivas a Diez Años del Nombramiento de la Comida Mexicana en la UNESCO' (*YouTube*, 3 November 2020) <www.youtube.com/playlist?list=PLMjBEEGSmdaBtDj5wnIDRo2qMIIkoP8-Ek> accessed 8 December 2021.

heritage, as they show how different heritage looks when one moves it up and down the scales.

The overall tone in the National Day meeting was positive and congratulatory. The speakers emphasised the possibilities provided by the UNESCO nomination to boost the local and the national economy through entrepreneurship across the food value chain, with tourism signalled as the main engine. They stressed the role of Mexico as one of the states parties that instigated the debates that led food cultures and practices to be considered as intangible cultural heritage. The meeting was also the occasion to recall that the stakeholders' work is still unfinished, as the potentialities of food and cuisine seem, at least for the participants in the meeting, to be unlimited.

The Minister of Culture praised Mexico's cultural diversity and traditional foodways and emphasised 'gastronomy' as 'important not only for being a factor of local economic and social development' but also as 'an added value, a differential element, recognised both at the national level and beyond our borders'.[47] He elaborated by stating that tourists increasingly look for authentic cultural experiences such as those offered by 'cuisines', and that Mexico's food has conquered palates and hearts around the world 'either in its traditional version or through the sophisticated contemporary dishes'. He then called for promoting entrepreneurship in the gastronomic sector, designing and implementing technical and educational schemes, certifying culinary skills, supporting state programs that promote traditional cuisine, stimulating competitiveness among all agents involved in tourism, and developing geographical indications and collective marks. The Mexican Ministry of Tourism emphasised how Mexican 'gastronomy' or 'cuisine' could contribute to larger national goals including tourism. Bounding the culinary heritage to a community or a region is of no interest or even detrimental to this stakeholder's plans.[48]

A similar view can be found in the speech by the director of the Conservatorio and a former official at UNESCO and the Mexican Ministry of Culture. Her address paralleled that of the Minister of Culture on the recognition of 'cuisine' both as an element of the value chain and as a 'powerful and irreplaceable engine' that drives toward sustainable development. However, her point was to highlight the role she and the Conservatorio played in the UNESCO nomination. A diplomat, she emphasised the decade-long effort to inscribe 'Mexican cuisine on the representative list'; an effort made of 'diplomatic twists and turns that need to be handled to bring together the interests of a member state [state party] with those of an international community'. The Director of the Conservatorio also noted that 'Mexico has known how to move very well, searching for coincidences and agreements that have allowed it to place itself among the leading countries in the recognition of their cultural heritage'. These remarks place 'cuisine' (and not

47 Secretaria de Turismo de México (n 45). Do note that the quotations from the participants in each of these meetings are this author's own translation from the Spanish language.

48 ibid.

traditional Mexican cuisine) within the order of scale of the national effort to move the domestic relevance of Mexican cuisine to the international realm. But more intriguing and puzzling in this intervention was the view of cultural heritage as 'power that generates power' and on Mexican cuisine as 'a true amulet, as a true Aladdin's lamp to which one asks for gifts and gets granted'.[49] The format in which the meeting was held did not allow questions or requests for clarification from the audience. However, one can infer from this account dimensions of reproducibility and expansion that posit the UNESCO nomination of traditional Mexican food as a scalable project linked to capitalist development.[50]

Vice-versa, in that same event, the representative of UNESCO in Mexico opted for scaling down. He began by recognising the work of Mexico as a pioneer in food-related UNESCO inscriptions and applauded the fact that traditional Mexican cuisine shares a place in the intangible cultural heritage list with other expressions of food cultures of other states parties. However, aware of the impetuses of Mexican stakeholders when it comes to food, he reminded that

> the UNESCO recognition to traditional Mexican cuisine is for representing a comprehensive cultural model that comprises the entire traditional food chain, from planting and harvesting to cooking and eating … Those of us who are here know this well, but I believe that this first ten-year anniversary could encourage us to strengthen [the] dissemination [of this idea] among people.[51]

By saying this, he remoulded the idea of Mexico's culinary heritage as a project that aims at exploiting all the potentialities of the country's foodways – as expressed by his Mexican counterparts – into one that builds on localised, specific elements. He then listed these elements, which include a variety of foods (maize, beans, chilli, and wild herbs and greens), traditional farming methods such as milpas (rotating swidden plots) and chinampas (man-made farming islets in lake areas), cooking processes such as nixtamalisation (lime-hulling maize), singular utensils (including grinding stones and stone mortars), and food sociability that strengthens community ties. In other words, the UNESCO representative scaled down Mexico's culinary heritage from an object seeking national and global appraisal (Mexican cuisine) to an object that reinforces 'the values and traditional knowledge that these [rural] populations possess and strengthens the local networks of [food] production and consumption' (traditional Mexican cuisine).[52]

The latter perspective was shared and developed by the participants of the Critical Views meeting. Unfolded in three panels over three days, the event aimed at making space for voices that were not heard throughout both the process of

49 ibid.
50 ibid.
51 ibid.
52 ibid.

inscription and the results of it. The first panel, titled 'Views from Academia' was composed of anthropologists and culinary researchers, while the other two, titled 'Views from the Kitchen', gathered village cooks and members of civil society such as independent researchers and members of NGOs.

In the first panel,[53] anthropologists Yuriria Iturriaga and Catharine Good agreed that the UNESCO nomination could serve economic projects by powerful actors in the tourism and hospitality sectors. Good perceived this as a deviation from the nomination's original intended goal. Although she did not oppose combining heritage and commercialisation, she expressed concern about the use of local cultures to serve projects with capitalist means and ends. Good criticised the spirit that reigned after the nomination, which favours the marketability of Mexican cuisine at the international level over development models based on fair trade that do not undermine food security in rural areas. Iturriaga particularly criticised the establishment of a competency standard aimed at certifying the practices, ingredients, and technologies used by individuals who produce traditional cuisine. This involves training on and compliance with specific customer contact and self-presentation protocols, hygienic food-handling practices, and marketing techniques. The overall goal of such endeavours is, as expressed by the Secretary of Tourism of the state of Michoacán at the National Day meeting, to integrate the village cooks into the tourism sector 'by training them in the knowledge and complex practices and dynamics of tourism as well as in the different trades that compose the gastronomic service' and help them to 'perfect their knowledge' and promote their businesses. Iturriaga asked why, if UNESCO considers traditional cultural practices as cultural wealth, 'there should be someone who has to guide, organise, supervise and control' (one may ask why there is a need 'to perfect' traditional knowledge). For Iturriaga, the better view is to disseminate information about what the UNESCO nomination means among the cultural heritage bearers for them to decide if they want to make something of it or not, rather than imposing knowledge that is external to communities.[54]

In the second panel,[55] village cook María Elena Castillo from the state of Querétaro affirmed that the information regarding the UNESCO nomination did not reach her and other fellow cooks while admitting she did not make any particular effort to be acquainted with the concept of heritage. Castillo said that news and invitations to events displaying *cocineras tradicionales* reached and circulated within groups composed of scholars and entrepreneurs (local cooks that own restaurants). The fact that people possessing higher status and influence benefit the most from a culinary heritage of which she and other village cooks regard

53 Coordinación Nacional de Antropología (1st Panel), '16 de Noviembre de 2020. Miradas Críticas y Propositivas a Diez Años del Nombramiento de la Comida' (*YouTube*, 16 November 2020) <www.youtube.com/watch?v=foAG7lCZk24&t=310s> accessed 8 December 2021.

54 ibid.

55 Coordinación Nacional de Antropología (2nd Panel), '18 de Noviembre de 2020. Miradas Críticas y Propositivas a Diez años del Nombramiento de la Comida' (*YouTube*, 18 November 2020) <www.youtube.com/watch?v=JjucNceGBr4&t=5038s> accessed 8 December 2021.

themselves as being the bearers is something that makes her feel frustrated and powerless, she said. The next speech by village cook Reyna Mendoza from the state of Oaxaca supported Castillo's remarks by saying that, although there are undoubtedly benefits to be gained from participation in the events organised by the Conservatorio and the Ministry of Tourism, the benefits remain elusive as they always 'go to other people'. Mendoza also recalled that she was not allowed to become part of the group of *cocineras tradicionales* of Oaxaca, organised and run by delegates of the Conservatorio, who told her that she was 'on another level'.[56]

> But I do not understand this part that there are levels to become *cocinera tradicional*. I know what my level is: I am traditional, I was born with my culture, and I thank my grandmother, my mom, my family that instil in me the tradition, my culture, how to transmit it, how to bring it to the table. Here we try to explain to the people that we serve food that is seasonal.[57]

The latter remark on food seasonality, voiced by other cooks participating in the second and third[58] panels, is important to the analysis in terms of scales. By emphasising the seasonality of food as essential to the cuisine practised in rural areas, village cooks scale down to the smaller traditional Mexican cuisine, which contrasts to Mexican cuisine framed as a scalable project oriented to tourism and gastronomes. In addition, in the view of many village cooks and scholars participating in the panels, traditional Mexican cuisine is not scalable: chefs and restaurateurs whose activities depend on the influx of tourist dollars will not be able to (re)produce traditional cuisine for two reasons. First, because the regular sourcing of local, native ingredients is extremely difficult if not impossible and, second, because the cuisine they practice seeks to impress customers looking for ethnic culinary experiences rather than cuisine rooted in Indigenous knowledge. The account of Mexico City's chef Azari Cuenca at the National Day meeting is an example of this.

> I feel very fortunate to be able to transform my country with my ingredients, the farmers, the traditional cuisines … I have to unite the gastronomies of the country, respect them, take care of them, teach them [to others], but above all, give them this small touch of a mixture of Spanish and French [cultures], parts of our history, so we can also be proud of the traditional part … I've learned how to use an ingredient to dignify it, to respect it; to shift an ordinary ingredient into an extraordinary one to surprise in gastronomy … We cook using the traditional Mexican basis; we transform it a little; we give it some

56 ibid.

57 ibid.

58 Coordinación Nacional de Antropología (3rd Panel), '20 de Noviembre de 2020. Miradas Críticas y Propositivas a Diez Años del Nombramiento de la Comida' (*YouTube*, 20 November 2020) <www.youtube.com/watch?v=3VM3XWbD8-o&list=PLMjBEEGSmdaBtDj5wnIBRo2qMHkoP8-Ek&index=3> accessed 8 December 2021.

> detail, some twists, something that comes from our minds, but we don't lose the basis. That's what I'm proud about. The goal is to dignify Mexico, to take the ingredients out of our borders, be proud and feel all Mexican.[59]

Furthermore, it is also possible to read in this excerpt a tendency to exclude, by performing twists and shifts and highlighting European influences, features of tradition that chefs consider as having no appeal for cosmopolitan customers (or not worthy enough). This is in line with Tsing's view that scalable designs banish biological and cultural diversity that is meaningful to many.

Against this background, village cooks and food activists are uniting forces under associations to create new bounds that work within a scope limited to communities, as expressed in the third panel of the Critical Views meeting. These are scaling-down initiatives that grow outside of the universalistic pretensions of global heritage governance and in opposition to the scalable projects by stakeholders committed to economic priorities. Their objective is to make sense of local food cultures and allow people to live following their cultural and spiritual values as noted by cook Castillo, relating traditional cuisine to 'our connection to the cosmos'.

Conclusion

This chapter has proposed to add the perspectives of scale and scalability to the study of heritage-making to bring into the equation the diversity of knowledge and living entities involved and affected by heritagisation. Local foods and food cultures make for a compelling case, as their entry into the heritage arena is particularly contentious and characterised by agendas imposed by outsiders who appropriate and shape the meanings of food in ways that extend beyond local cultures and territories. As the controversies in Brazil and Mexico have shown, the heritagisation of food cultures cannot be illustrated through a single narrative, but rather generates multiple narratives and diverging viewpoints. This is likely due to the nature of food and foodways themselves, which are probably one of most, if not the most, commodifiable cultural features, creating a divide between the expectations held by powerful stakeholders and less powerful local populations. The analyses in terms of scales, scalability, and non-scalability provided here offer analytical benefits to critical approaches to food heritage governance and, more generally, to studies dealing with the heritagisation of any kind of living forms. The scalable dimension in food heritage projects by official stakeholders suggests perspectives on cultural preservation based on capitalist expansion and production processes that lead to an eradication of life forms (crops, plants, ingredients, techniques, and knowledge) that are hardly scalable and, consequently, seen by powerful stakeholders as undermining their projects. The non-scalability addressed by critical local actors emphasises, in contrast, the

59 Secretaria de Turismo de México (n 45).

complexity and diversity of human perceptions and perspectives. Be it through the denunciation of a 'colonialisation of taste' as in the case of Brazil or by emphasising rooted tradition and food seasonality as in the case of Mexico, non-scalable approaches assemble heterogeneous sets of claims, ethical orientations and conceptions of life expressed in terms of *cosmovision*. Although the divergent viewpoints presented here appear through scaling up and down *a posteriori*, that is, after the consequences of the implemented heritage policies emerge and manifest differently for different groups and populations, it is also possible to apply a perspective on scales, scalability, and non-scalability *a priori*, so we can think carefully and critically about problems and potential risks inherent in heritage-making projects, as well as pursue a critical inquiry into the nature and origin of cultural loss.

References

Barbosa L, 'A Ética e a Estética na Alimentaçaõ Contemporânea' in F Thomé da Cruz, A Matte and S Schneider (eds), *Producão, Consumo e Abastecimiento de Alimentos: Desafios e novas Estratégias* (UFGRS 2016)

Bortolotto C, 'Commercialization without Over-Commercialization: Normative Conundrums across Heritage Rationalities' (2021) 27(9) *IJHS* 857

Brett J, 'Conclusions: Culture, Tradition and Political Economy' in E Finnis (ed), *Reimagining Marginalized Foods* (University of Arizona Press 2012)

Broda J, 'Astronomy, Cosmovisión, and Ideology in Pre-Hispanic Mesoamerica' (1982) 385(1) *Ann NY AcadSci* 81

Brondizio E, 'The Global Açaí: A Chronicle of Possibilities and Predicaments of an Amazonian Superfood' in E McDonell and R Wilk (eds), *Critical Approaches to Superfoods* (Bloomsbury 2020)

de Robert P and van Velthem L, 'L'Heure du Tacacá. Consommation et Valorisation d'Aliments Traditionnels Amazoniensen Zone Urbaine (Brésil)' [2008] *Anthropol Food S4* <https://journals.openedition.org/aof/3533> accessed 8 December 2021

Dória C, 'Umagarota do Barulhoquerroubar cena da Gastronomía' (*São Paulo São*, 29 June 2016) <https://saopaulosao.com.br/conteudos/colunistas/1735-uma-garota-do-barulho-quer-roubar-cena-da-gastronomia.html> accessed 8 December 2021

Eriksen T H, *Overheating: An Anthropology of Accelerated Change* (Pluto Press 2016)

Fakhri M, *Sugar and the Making of International Trade Law* (Cambridge University Press 2014)

Finnis E (ed), *Reimagining Marginalized Foods* (University of Arizona Press 2012)

Granchamp L, 'Penser l'Alimentation d'un Point de vue Décolonial. Entretien avec Tainá Marajoara (Bélém, Brésil)' (2019) 61(2) *Revue des Sciences Sociales* <https://journals.openedition.org/revss/3611> accessed 8 December 2021

Grauerholz L and Owens N, 'Alternative Food Movements' in J Wright (ed), *International Encyclopedia of the Social & Behavioral Sciences* (2nd edn, Routledge 2015)

Jacques A, 'Patrimônio Cultural e Atrativo Turístico Gastronômico en Belém do Pará, Brasil' (Master thesis, Universidade de Brasília 2015)

Jones R, 'Categories, Borders and Boundaries' (2009) 33(2) *Prog Hum Geogr* 174

Lody R (ed), *Farinha de Mandioca: O Sabor Brasileiro e a Receitas da Bahia* (Senac 2019)

Markowitz L, 'Highland Haute Cuisine: The Transformation of Alpaca Meat' in E Finnis (ed), *Reimagining Marginalized Foods* (University of Arizona Press 2012)

Matta R, 'Recipes for Crossing Boundaries: Peruvian Fusion' in S Ayora-Díaz (ed), *Cooking Technology: Transformations in Culinary Practice in Mexico and Latin America* (Bloomsbury 2016)

——— 'Mexico's Culinary Heritage and Cocineras Tradicionales (Traditional Female Cooks)' (2019) 27(3) *Food and Foodways* 211

——— 'Documenting the UNESCO Feast: Stories of Women's "Empowerment" and Programmatic Cooking' (2021) 29(1) *Soc Anthropol* 188

McDonell E and Wilk R (eds), *Critical Approaches to Superfoods* (Bloomsbury 2020)

Mintz S, *Sweetness and Power* (Penguin Books 1986)

Moncusí A and Santamarina B, 'Bueno para Comer, Bueno para Patrimonializar: La Propuesta de la Cocina Mexicana como Patrimonio Cultural de la Humanidad' in M Álvarez and F Medina (eds), *Identidades en el Plato* (Icaria 2008)

Neal C, 'Heritage and Participation' in E Waterton and S Watson (eds), *The Palgrave Handbook of Contemporary Heritage Research* (Palgrave 2015)

Rulli M and D'Odorico P, 'Food Appropriation through Large Scale Land Acquisitions' (2014) 9(064030) *Environmental Research Letters* 1

Sammells C, 'Haute Traditional Cuisines: How UNESCO's List of Intangible Heritage Links the Cosmopolitan to the Local' in R Brulotte and M Di Giovine (eds), *Edible Identities: Food as Cultural Heritage* (Ashgate 2014)

Santos B, 'Beyond Abyssal Thinking: From Global Lines to Ecologies of Knowledges' (2007) 30(1) *Review* 45

Savransky M and Stengers I, 'Relearning the Art of Paying Attention: A Conversation' (2018) 47(1) *SubStance* 130

Tsing A, 'On Nonscalability: The Living World is Not Amenable to Precision-Nested Scales' (2012) 18(3) *Common Knowl* 505

Vadi V, 'Perspective and Scale in the Architecture of International Legal History' (2019) 30(1) *European Journal of International Law* 53

Waterton E and Watson S (eds), *Heritage and Community Engagement: Collaboration or Contestation?* (Routledge 2013)

Yamada K, 'Shamisen Skin on the Verge of Extinction: Musical Sustainability and Non-Scalability of Cultural Loss' (2017) 26(3) *Ethnomusicology Forum* 373

Zaneti T and Schneider S, 'Ingredientes Singulares à la Carte: Implicações do Uso de Produtos Diferenciados na Gastronomia Contemporânea' [2016] *Anthropol Food* 1 <https://journals.openedition.org/aof/8111> accessed 8 December 2021

4 Tangled webs and remote paths

Transboundary consent and justifiable downstream limits in the protection of traditional knowledge associated with genetic resources within the context of drug discovery – the problems of a consequentialist account

Peter Harrison

Introduction

Highlighting the origins of the concept of prior informed consent within the field of medical ethics, Dutfield suggests that the 'stretching' of that concept from medical ethics into the area of misappropriation of genetic resources and traditional knowledge associated with genetic resources has been done 'without sufficiently thinking through the practicalities, without much theoretical reflection and without necessary consideration of political economy'.[1] He goes on to cite Burns' warning on the probability of unintended outcomes that the best laid schemes of mice and men go often awry ('The best-laid schemes o' mice an' men, Gang aft agley').[2]

The aim of the current work is to investigate two practicalities with regard to the workings of the right for Indigenous people to control traditional knowledge associated with genetic resources within the Nagoya Protocol on Access to Genetic Resources and the Fair and Equitable Sharing of Benefits Arising from Their Utilization to the Convention on Biological Diversity. These are, first, the scope of this *sui generis* positive right to control downstream use of traditional knowledge associated with genetic resources within the context of drug discovery; and second, from whom consent is required to use such controlled traditional

1 Graham Dutfield, 'Protecting the Rights of Indigenous Peoples: Can Prior Informed Consent Help?' in Rachel Wynberg, Doris Schroeder and Roger Chenells (eds), *Indigenous Peoples, Consent and Benefit Sharing: Lessons from the San-Hoodia Case* (Springer 2009) 53, 66.

2 Robert Burns from 'To a Moose, on Turning Her up in Her Nest with the Plough November, 1785' in *The Poems of Robert Burns, Introduction by James MacKenna* (Collins 1945) 116. To which me may well reply with the next stanza that such schemes leave us nothing but grief and pain, instead of promised joy! ('An' lea'e us nought but grief an' pain, For promis'd joy!')

DOI: 10.4324/9781003345237-5

knowledge associated with genetic resources within the context of drug discovery (particularly within transboundary situations).

These questions may appear at first sight to be quite different. However, the answers to both may be found in the underlying justifications of these rights; furthermore, seeking an answer to the first question may well inform the answer to the second, and vice versa. This chapter focusses on the broadly consequentialist (and in some cases more narrowly utilitarian) justifications for the protection of traditional knowledge associated with genetic resources within the Nagoya Protocol and uncovers significant problems with that approach.

Claims of misappropriation of traditional knowledge associated with genetic resources

Many compounds that have pharmacological effects in humans are derived from living organisms.[3] To a significant degree, the understanding of Western science that a particular organism contained a compound of potential therapeutic benefit has arisen out of the knowledge of folk-healers or traditional medicine systems.[4] Western ethnobotanists and scientists accessing and using traditional knowledge associated with genetic resources have often treated the originators of this knowledge as being undeserving of recognition or reward for its subsequent use.[5] Since the late 1980s, the interface between genetic resources, traditional knowledge associated with genetic resources, and Western pharmacology has become an area of high emotions and political activism.[6]

The history of claimed misappropriation eventually led to a movement to secure legal mechanisms by which Indigenous peoples would gain control over genetic resources and traditional knowledge associated with genetic resources such that misappropriation should no longer occur.[7] However, the particular nature of it is such that its protection is not easily achieved by what might be termed 'established' intellectual property rights.[8] Attempts to protect traditional knowledge

3 Norman R Farnsworth, 'The Role of Ethnopharmacology in Drug Development' in *Bioactive Compounds from Plants* (John Wiley & Sons 1994) (Ciba Foundation Symp 154) 2.

4 Londa Schiebinger, *Plants and Empire, Colonial Bioprospecting in the Atlantic World* (Harvard University Press 2004); Bill Laws, *Fifty Plants that Changed the Course of History* (David and Charles 2010); Michael J Balick and Paul A Cox, *Plants, People, and Culture: The Science of Ethnobotany* (Scientific American Library 1997); and CM Cotton, *Ethnobotany: Principles and Applications* (John Wiley & Sons 1996) 234.

5 Philip Schuler, 'Biopiracy and Commercialization of Ethnobotanical Knowledge' in J Michael Finger and Philip Schuler (eds), *Poor People's Knowledge* (World Bank and OUP 2004).

6 For a review of the history of this debate, see Graham Dutfield, 'Traditional Knowledge, Intellectual Property and Pharmaceutical Innovation: What's Left to Discuss?' in Matthew David and Debora Halbert (eds), *The Sage Handbook of Intellectual Property* (Sage 2014) 649.

7 Rosemary Coombe, 'The Recognition of Indigenous Peoples' and Community Traditional Knowledge in International Law' (2002) 14 *St Thomas L Rev* 275.

8 Graham Dutfield, *Intellectual Property Rights, Biogenetic Resources and Traditional Knowledge* (Earthscan Publications 2004) 101.

associated with genetic resources have therefore focussed on the creation of a set of *sui generis* rights which, independent of currently established intellectual property rights, would ensure that those originally holding the information could only control such traditional knowledge associated with genetic resources. The drive to prevent 'misappropriation' of genetic resources and traditional knowledge associated with genetic resources has taken place with differing rates of progress, in several international fora.[9] By far the most developed amongst these international approaches is the October 2010 Nagoya Protocol.

The Nagoya Protocol

The United Nations Convention on Biological Diversity came into force on 29 December 1993 and has been ratified by 196 members of the United Nations.[10] This Convention looks to protect the biodiversity of the planet,[11] whilst ensuring sustainable use and fair and equitable sharing of the exploitation of biodiversity.[12] However, it does not contain detail as to how its 'access and benefit sharing' aims should be met, and the bringing into *binding* effect of those aims had to await the adoption of the Nagoya Protocol, which came into force on 12 October 2014 and has 132 parties.[13] It looks to apply two obligations (*access* subject only to prior informed consent and *use* subject to benefit sharing) on the users of two separate, but closely related, resources: genetic resources and traditional knowledge associated with genetic resources. The key operative provisions are summarised in Table 4.1.

Originating from the Convention of Biological Diversity, the Nagoya Protocol is deliberately limited in its scope: its focus is on the misappropriation of genetic resources (and the misuse of traditional knowledge associated with genetic resources), rather than attempting to create any sort of broader positive right in traditional knowledge *per se*, or in Indigenous cultural expression.

The dilution of traditional knowledge associated with genetic resources within drug discovery

The development 'trails' within drug discovery are often long and complicated.[14] A piece of traditional knowledge associated with genetic resources which 'inspires' drug discovery can take many routes within the drug discovery process

9 A history of the development of protection of traditional knowledge associated with genetic resources can be found in Frantzeska Papadopoulou, *The Protection of Traditional Knowledge on Genetic Resources* (Edward Elgar 2018).

10 <www.cbd.int/information/parties.shtml> accessed 06 December 2021.

11 Tobias Kiene, *The Legal Protection of Traditional Knowledge in the Pharmaceutical Field: An Intercultural Problem on the International Agenda* (Waxmann 2012) 198.

12 Convention on Biological Diversity, Article 8(j).

13 <www.cbd.int/abs/nagoya-protocol/signatories/> accessed 06 December 2021.

14 Graham Dutfield, 'A Critical Analysis of the Debate on Traditional Knowledge, Drug Discovery and Patent-Based Biopiracy' (2011) 33(4) *EIPR* 238.

Table 4.1 Key elements of the Nagoya Protocol articles giving rise to positive rights

Article	*Right holder*	*Subject matter*	*Controlled activity*	*Condition*
5(1)	Party	Genetic resources	Utilisation (including 'subsequent applications and commercialisation')	Fair and equitable sharing upon mutually agreed terms
5(2)	Indigenous and local communities	Genetic resources	Utilisation	Fair and equitable sharing based on mutually agreed terms
5(5)	Indigenous and local communities	Traditional knowledge associated with genetic resources	Utilisation	Fair and equitable sharing upon mutually agreed terms
6(1)	Party	Genetic resources	Access for utilisation	Prior informed consent
6(2)	Indigenous and local communities	Genetic resources	Access	Prior informed consent or 'approval and involvement'
7	Indigenous and local communities	Traditional knowledge associated with genetic resources	Access	Prior informed consent or 'approval and involvement' and establishment of mutually agreed terms

throughout which the original information may be 'diluted' or 'attenuated' by an admixture to a greater body of known, and newly developed, information.

Figure 4.1 shows a much-simplified schematic displaying some of the potential steps that a genetic resource/piece of traditional knowledge associated with genetic resources may take within a drug discovery process.

Figure 4.1 suggests that the steps are fairly linear. However, the 'real life' drug discovery trail for a particular drug, or family of drugs, will rarely show such linearity. The science of pharmacology is full of the use of relatively simple plant extracts (or compounds directly purified from such extracts) to give a therapeutic benefit. However, the extraction and testing a biochemical constituent of a genetic resource are, within modern drug discovery, usually merely the *beginning*, rather than the end, of a process of finding a safe and efficacious drug.[15] Chemical modification of

15 DG Grahame-Smith and JK Aronson, *Oxford Textbook of Clinical Pharmacology and Drug Therapy* (OUP 1992) 3; John Hall, 'The Drug Development Process' in Ignazio Di Giovanna and Gareth Hayes (eds), *Principles of Clinical Research* (Wrightson Biomedical Publishing 2001) 1.

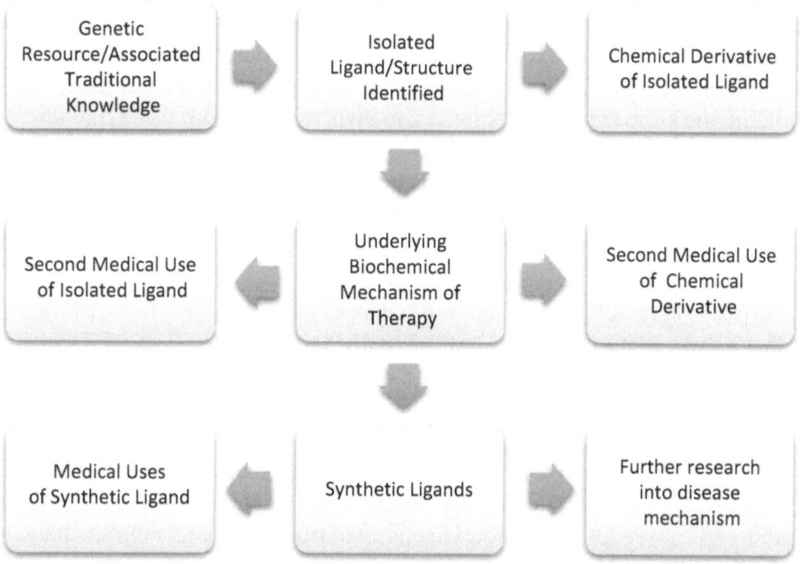

Figure 4.1 Simplified schematic of path taken by a genetic resource/piece of traditional knowledge associated with genetic resources within the drug discovery process.

such biological constituents can produce enhanced pharmacological entities, but such modification of compounds is but one element of the drug discovery process. The finding of a new pharmacologically active compound within a genetic resource may uncover a yet unknown biological mechanism within humans (or at least previously unknown ways of affecting known systems) which can give rise to further lines of research, both in terms of new chemical entities and new therapeutic benefits. In this way, it is highly likely that the scientific (and commercial) benefits of using a piece of traditional knowledge associated with genetics resources will be significantly distal to a complex process of mixing and dilution of the original information.

However, the Nagoya Protocol is not orientated towards dealing with the problem of distal downstream use within drug discovery. What seems to be missing from the positive rights in relation to traditional knowledge associated with genetic resources under the Nagoya Protocol is any principle or guidance for determining a balance, which combines fair protection for the rights holders with a reasonable degree of legal certainty for third parties. Where such knowledge serves as a research 'lead' for further development, the Nagoya Protocol gives no clear guidance as to how far that knowledge can have a 'reach through effect' into new scientific discoveries, or at what stage a downstream researcher would be considered 'free' of the traditional knowledge associated with genetic resources right.[16]

16 Peter Harrison, 'Grasping Frankenstein's Monster: Uncertainty in the Downstream Scope of the Nagoya Protocol' (2019) 1 *IPQ* 61.

The question of consent

Article 7 of the Nagoya Protocol is not drafted in what one might consider to be a 'classic' way to create a positive intellectual property right to veto use by others. It *either* requires prior informed consent from Indigenous and local communities holding the knowledge *or* 'approval and involvement' from those Indigenous and local communities with, in either case, a further requirement that 'mutually agreed terms' should be established. It is not clear how, if at all, such 'approval and involvement' is materially different from 'prior informed consent'.[17] It seems difficult to argue that the operative effect of 'consent' should be any different from 'approval' considering the overall context of the Nagoya Protocol.[18] This is particularly true where both 'approval' and 'consent' are allied to a further requirement that access should be subject to 'mutually agreed terms'. Indeed, Decision V/16 of the Convention on Biological Diversity Conference of the Parties of 2000 states that:

> Access to traditional knowledge, innovations and practices of Indigenous and local communities embodying traditional lifestyles should be subject to prior informed consent or prior informed approval from the holders of such knowledge, innovations and practices.

While this Decision is not legally binding, it does appear to amount to agreement within the Convention on Biological Diversity parties that 'consent' and 'approval' both represent an acceptable interpretation of original access language of the Convention on Biological Diversity in relation to traditional knowledge.[19]

Article 5(5) of the Nagoya Protocol is perhaps even less clear in creating positive veto rights. It requires that the benefits arising out of *use* should be shared in a 'fair and equitable' way and that such sharing should be on 'mutually agreed terms'. A requirement for 'fair and equitable' sharing arguably does not, in itself, create a *veto* right – one might imagine that a third-party user of a resource may simply continue to use the resource without hindrance, provided that a 'fair and equitable' share is provided to the right holder. One might further imagine that this fair and equitable share could be determined *ex post facto* by a binding determination (whether by a court, tribunal, binding mediator, or arbitrator). In many ways, such an approach would mirror the compulsory licensing regimes seen in

17 Elisa Morgera et al., *Unravelling the Protocol: A Commentary on the Protocol on Access and Benefit Sharing to the Convention on Biological Diversity* (Brill/Nijhoff 2014) 152 and 175; Annalisa Savaresi, 'The International Human Rights Law Implications of the Protocol' in Elisa Morgera, Matthias Buck, and Elsa Tsioumani (eds), *The 2010 Protocol on Access and Benefit-Sharing in Perspective: Implications for International Law and Implementation Challenges* (Martinus Nijhoff Publishers 2012) 53, 70.

18 Morgera (n 17) 153; Gurdial Singh Nijar, *The Protocol on ABS: An Analysis* (CEBLAW 2011) 26.

19 See Grahame-Smith and Aronson (n 15); Convention on Biological Diversity, Article 8(j).

numerous intellectual property systems.[20] Crucially, however, such an approach would not, of itself, allow for an *absolute* veto on use.

The requirement that 'benefit sharing' is on *mutually agreed terms* is difficult to interpret in the light of the 'fair and equitable' requirement. If the mutual agreement is not on 'fair and equitable' terms, is the agreement rescindable/voidable? Who is to say what is fair and equitable? Regarding consent, Article 5 of the Nagoya Protocol seems to imply that, even if the terms of the potential agreement are perfectly 'fair and equitable', the party having the right to impose sharing must have a right to refuse to agree; if this were not the case it could not be a truly free, *mutual* agreement. If this is correct, the right to refuse to agree (even on what would appear to an external observer to be objectively fair terms) should be seen as a right to refuse consent (that is, a veto right) similar to that (perhaps more clearly and expressly) set out in Article 7.

Assuming that both Articles, 5(5) and 7 create a veto right over the use of traditional knowledge associated with genetic resources, we need to go on to ask ourselves to *whom* should a person seeking to access or utilise a particular piece of traditional knowledge associated with genetic resources contact? We should note that this could cause considerable transboundary issues. The Nagoya Protocol is brought into effect through the national laws of each party. Even though it is conceivable that a single Indigenous group who are the holders of a piece of traditional knowledge associated with genetic resources could reside solely within a nation state, it is equally conceivable that such traditional knowledge can be distributed between Indigenous groups who reside across an area which is (from their perspective) arbitrarily divided between many nation states. National laws concerning consent could arbitrarily exclude Indigenous peoples residing in neighbouring nation states from partaking in the ability to consent and/or receive economic reward.[21]

Two case studies

The two case studies presented here have been chosen from among the numerous cases of (mis)use of traditional knowledge associated with genetic resources[22] as they both stimulate a few difficult questions concerning both the justifiable scope

20 See for example sections 48, 48A, 48B, 49, and 50 UK Patents Act 1977 (as amended).

21 Note that Article 10 of the Nagoya Protocol envisages that the parties may need in the future to establish 'a global multilateral benefit-sharing mechanism to address in transboundary situations' – though to date nothing binding has been created.

22 See Margo Bagley and Frederic Perron-Welch, 'Study to Identify Specific Cases of Genetic Resources and Traditional Knowledge Associated with Genetic Resources that Occur in Transboundary Situations or for Which It Is Not Possible to Grant or Obtain Prior Informed Consent' March 2020 <www.cbd.int/abs/Art-10/study-art10-peer-review-revd.pdf> accessed 08 December 2021; Dutfield, 'Traditional Knowledge, Intellectual Property and Pharmaceutical Innovation: What's Left to Discuss?' (n 6) 653.

of protection and transboundary problems concerning the identity of those who should have the right to grant consent.

Case study 1: the quinaquina tree: quinine, mauveine, sulphonamides, quinolineand pyrazoles

Quinine derived from bark of the *quinaquina* tree (of the *Cinchona* species) has been one of the most important tools in the fight against malaria.[23] The *quina quina* tree has a native range across Costa Rica, Panama, Colombia, Venezuela, Ecuador, Peru, and Bolivia. The mechanism by which the Indigenous understanding of the anti-malarial properties of the bark of the *quinaquina* tree entered Western science is uncertain. On one account, in 1638, in Lima the physician to the Countess of Chinchón (1576–1639), the wife of the Viceroy of Peru, successfully treated her malarial fever using the bark of the *quinaquina* tree, this therapy having long been used by the Indigenous peoples of Andes. After the Countess recovered, reportedly she brought the bark of the *quinaquina* tree back to Spain. It also appears that Jesuit missionaries, having been informed of the properties of the bark of the *quinaquina* by the Indigenous peoples of what is now Ecuador, began to use the *quinaquina* bark for the prophylaxis and treatment of malaria in Europe.[24]

In 1820, the French chemists Pierre-Joseph Pelletier (1788–1842) and Joseph Bienaimé Caventou (1795–1877) isolated an alkaloid compound from the bark of the yellow *Cinchona* that they called quinine.[25] Purified quinine had great advantages in terms of patient compliance and control of side effects over the bark. However, quinine itself could not be synthesised, and its only source remained purification from *quinaquina* bark. Demand for the bark led to substantial supply problems and denudation of the native *Cinchona* species in the Andes.[26] In early 1856, the British chemist and entrepreneur William Henry Perkin (1838–1907), working on a project to synthesise quinine, accidentally synthesised a vibrant purple aniline dye (eventually known as *mauveine*).[27] Perkin's use of aniline as a starting point for the manufacture of vibrant, colourfast dyes was very rapidly taken up from the mid-19th century onwards.[28] The first systemically used antimicrobial drug, the sulphonamide Prontosil, was developed from an analine dye

23 Jane Achan et al., 'Quinine, an Old Anti-Malarial Drug in a Modern World: Role in the Treatment of Malaria' (2011) 10 *Malar J* 144.

24 Laws (n 4) 42.

25 Walter Sneader, *Drug Discovery: The Evolution of Modern Medicines* (John Wiley & Sons 1985) 9 and 13; Enrique Raviña, *The Evolution of Drug Discovery: From Traditional Medicines to Modern Drugs* (Wiley-VCH 2011) 128.

26 Balick and Cox (n 4) 28; Raviña (n 25) 129.

27 Roy Porter (ed), *The Hutchinson Dictionary of Scientific Biography* (Helicon 1994) 545; S Garfield, *Mauve: How One Man Invented a Colour Which Changed the World* (Faber & Faber 2000).

28 Anthony S Travis, 'Perkin's Mauve: Ancestor of the Organic Chemical Industry' (1990) 31(1) *Technology and Culture* 51.

within the laboratories of Bayer AG.[29] This stimulated further development of anti-microbial drugs based on dyes.[30] The structure of quinine was eventually determined by the German chemist Paul Rabe (1869–1952) in 1918[31] and, in 1944, the American chemists Robert Burns Woodward (1917–1979) and William Doering (1917–2011) finally published details of a *de novo* route for quinine synthesis.[32] The quinoline ring structure (seen in quinine) has formed the core of a number anti-parasitic compounds (including chloroquine and mefloquine).[33] Quinine also served as the initiator of another research trail in 1887 when the German chemist Ludwig Knorr (1859–1921) made an antipyretic and analgesic called antipyrine whilst seeking to make a quinoline derivative. Antipyrine became the basis of a family of pyrazole drugs, which are very widely used in pain relief.[34]

Case study 2: the Madagascar periwinkle: vinca alkaloids

The Madagascar or rosy *periwinkle* (*Catharanthus roseus*) is a plant which, though originally Indigenous to Madagascar, has long been cultivated as an ornamental species across the tropics and sub-tropics.[35] Working at the University of Western Ontario in 1949, Canadian endocrinologist Ralph Noble sought to examine the effect of extracts of the Madagascar *periwinkle* on rat blood glucose. Noble was inspired to begin this work after he had heard of the folk use in the Caribbean of the Madagascar *periwinkle* in the treatment of diabetes. Noble prepared an extract from samples of the plant (sourced from Jamaica) but found no effect on blood glucose levels. However, when injecting the animals with extract, Noble found that the rats seemed to suffer from an enhanced level of infection and greatly reduced leucocyte levels (which seemed to be the result of damage to the bone marrow of the animals). Given that similar effects were seen with then current anti-tumour drugs, Noble wondered whether the extract might contain an anti-cancer agent. Working with organic chemist, Charles Beer, Noble isolated

29 H Otten, 'Domagk and the Development of the Sulphonamides' (1986) 17(6) *J Antimicrobial Chemotherapy* 689.

30 Ernst Bäumler, *In Search of the Magic Bullet: Great Adventures in Modern Drug Research* (Thames and Hudson 1965) 15.

31 Paul Rabe and Karl Kindler, 'Uber die partielleSynthese des Chinins. ZurKenntnis der China-Alkaloide XIX' (1918) 51 *BerDtschChemGes* 466.

32 Robert B Woodward and William E Doering, 'The Total Synthesis of Quinine' (1944) 66(5) *J Am ChemSoc* 849; Raviña (n 25) 129.

33 Satyavan Sharma and Nitya Anand, 'Approaches to Design and Synthesis of Antiparasitic Drugs' (1997) 24 *Pharmacochemistry Library* 393; Stan K Bardal et al., *Applied Pharmacology* (Elsevier 2011) 233.

34 Raviña (n 25) 26.

35 M A van Bergen, 'Revision of *Catharanthus* G. Don Series of Revisions of Apocynaceae XLI' (1996) 96(3) *Wageningen Agricultural University Papers* 1–45; and W Snoeijer, 'Catharanthus Roseus, the Madagascar Periwinkle, a Review of Its Cultivars' (1996) 96(3) *Wageningen Agricultural University Papers* 47.

an active alkaloid, vincristine, from the *periwinkle* extract, which was found to have an inhibitory effect on transplanted tumours. This work was reported at a New York Academy of Sciences meeting in 1958.[36] At that meeting, a representative from Eli Lilly & Co announced that a team at the pharmaceutical company (similarly stimulated by reports of folk use of Madagascar *periwinkle* against diabetes – but this time in the Philippines) had similarly found that extract of the plant (obtained from within the United States) showed no anti-diabetic efficacy. However, Eli Lilly had a general pharmacological screening programme, and an extract from the plant was put through it. This resulted in a beneficial effect when it was used against transplanted acute lymphocyte leukaemia in mice.[37] This work led to the use of vinblastine against lung and breast cancer.[38] Synthetic chemistry and screening studies at the Institut de Chimie des Substances Naturelles at Gif-sur-Yvette, Paris, have since led to the development of two semi-synthetic analogues of the naturally occurring vinca alkaloids – vindesine and vinorelbine – which have anti-tumour activity.[39]

Questions stimulated by the case studies

Question 1: what is the downstream limit to the right to control traditional knowledge associated with genetic resources?

Before beginning the analysis, it is noted that whilst the Nagoya Protocol itself has no *retrospective* effect, historic examples are helpful when analysing the Nagoya Protocol rights as they identify equivalent problems that could easily arise in the future.[40]

If there were a right to control traditional knowledge associated with genetic recourses related to the *quinaquina* tree, would that have extended to control over quinine, or even over chloroquine and mefloquine? But for a recognition of the effects of quinine, Perkin would not have accidentally discovered mauveine and the discovery of the sulphonamide drugs would likely have been significantly delayed. Is the right to control *quinaquina* traditional knowledge associated with

36 R L Noble et al., 'Role of Chance Observations in Chemotherapy' (1958) 76 *Ann NY AcadSci* 882.

37 Sneader (n 25) 356; Walter Sneader, *Drug Discovery, A History* (John Wiley & Sons 2005) 102; Dutfield, 'Protecting the Rights of Indigenous Peoples' (n 1) 63; Raviña (n 25)157.

38 N Neuss et al., 'Vinca Alkaloids. III. 1. Characterisation of Leurosine and Vincaleukoblastine, New Alkaloids from *Vincarosea* Linn' (1959) 81 *J Am Chem Soc* 4754; Bagley and Perron-Welch (n 22) 10.

39 Sneader, *Drug Discovery, A History* (n 37) 103; Raviña (n 25) 158.

40 The lack of retrospective effect within the Nagoya Protocol does not erase existing Indigenous claims based on inherent rights outwith the Nagoya Protocol. Under the Nagoya Protocol traditional knowledge associated with genetic resources' rights has no temporal limit so new benefits arising out of prior (or ongoing) uses of a piece of traditional knowledge associated with genetic resources could give rise to new benefit sharing obligations. See Thomas Greiber et al., *IUCN Explanatory Guide to the Protocol on Access and Benefit-Sharing* (IUCN Environmental Policy and Law Paper No.83, 2012) 219.

genetic resources? If that seems too remote, why is it too remote? Knorr's discovery of antipyrine analgesic (whilst seeking to make a quinoline derivative) may seem more proximal in a chain of causation to the original *quinaquina* traditional knowledge associated with genetic resources than are the sulphonamides, but again it required an accidental discovery of a compound whose therapeutic area is unrelated to that of quinine.

Noble's work was stimulated by folk knowledge of the anti-diabetic effects of the Madagascar *periwinkle*, but the anti-cancer effect he found was biologically unrelated to an anti-diabetic therapy. Again, if there were a right to control traditional knowledge associated with genetic resources related with Madagascar *periwinkle*, would that have extended to the anti-cancer effects of vincristine (and derivatives thereof)? This may seem too remote for some, but there is a chain of causation between knowledge of *some* therapeutic benefit and the successful treatment of cancers by vinca alkaloids.

Question 2: who gets to control the traditional knowledge associated with genetics resources?

If we accept that the anti-fever effects of the bark of the *quinaquina* tree have been well known to the Indigenous peoples of central and south America for a very long time, and a new downstream user of that knowledge was to look to find someone from whom they could ask for consent to use, who would they ask? If it was well known across the region in the 17th century, which Indigenous peoples knew of the effect of *quinaquina*? Where are their ancestors today? Does the putative user have to ask *all* the different groups who are inheritors/current holders of that knowledge? Does that consent have to be unanimous? Do the (right) holders have to, in some way, prove their inheritance/current right?

The Madagascar *periwinkle* case throws up a further challenge. The Madagascar *periwinkle* seems to show no anti-diabetic efficacy, but it is believed to be a folk-remedy against diabetes in Jamaica and the Philippines. Did that belief arise separately in each or was it transferred from one to the other and, if so, in which direction? If transferred, does the originator/transferor alone have a right to control the traditional knowledge associated with genetic resources, or does the transferee also have a right?

How are we to decide? Causation in fact/causation in law and underlying justifications

The first approach to *Question 1* may be to say that it has a simple answer based upon a simple causation analysis: did the downstream use in question *in fact* derive from the original piece of traditional knowledge associated with genetic resources? If so, consent is required. *In fact*, if we broadly look at the application of a causation test to the situation in which a new drug has been developed on the basis of a piece of traditional knowledge associated with genetic resources, we will find that *but for* the original piece of traditional knowledge, one would never have arrived at the final drug in the way in which it was arrived at. Of course, one may have eventually arrived at that drug by other (path-independent) means, for example through random screening, but possibly less simply, quickly, or cheaply as by the path-dependent means. However, the path-independent means does not concern us in this respect – it is, by definition, not dependent *in fact* upon the original information.

If causation in fact *alone* is sufficient to create liability (no matter how distal or remote, and no matter how changed, diluted, and widely dissipated the original 'inspiration' has become) it might be successfully argued that *any* downstream use can be subject to control from the original holder of the traditional knowledge associated with genetic resources. However, the limitations of 'but for' tests in relation to determination of legal responsibility have given rise to much serious scholarship.[41] Simply put, a 'pure' *in fact* test encounters extreme difficulty when applied to legal problems. Hart and Honoré[42] argue the merits of a bifurcated analysis in which an initial causation *in fact* test is subject to a second stage (causation *in law*) analysis which examines whether there is any reason which precludes treating a cause as a cause for policy purposes. If there *is* to be a difference in outcome between a strict causation *in fact* analysis and causation *in law* analysis on a particular set of facts, that difference must reflect the original justifications, which underpin the right which the putative claimant is seeking to assert.

The key high-level philosophical justifications for the existence of intellectual property rights protecting knowledge (or its expression) are most often divided into *consequentialist* claims and *deontological* approaches.[43] In ethics, consequentialism is a theory that says whether something is good or bad depends on its outcomes. Consequentialist or utilitarian theories thus entail a sort of cost/benefit analysis and justify intellectual property based on the social welfare it produces. The deontological approaches, by contrast, justify intellectual property based on natural rights, human rights, or other matters of 'duty'. The 'classic' natural rights justifications essentially fall into two main camps. First, creators and inventors have a right to their creations and inventions respectively because they have a right to the fruits of their labour. In other words, by mixing our labour with the world we gain ownership in that with which we have mixed our labour.[44] Second, intellectual property is justified as it constitutes the extension of individual

41 For example, see HLA Hart and Tony Honoré, *Causation in the Law* (OUP 1985); Richard W Wright, 'Causation in Tort Law' (1985) 73 *Cal L Rev* 1735; Michael S Moore, *Causation and Responsibility: An Essay in Law, Morals and Metaphysics* (OUP 2009); Richard Goldberg, *Perspectives on Causation* (Hart Publishing 2011).

42 Hart and Honoré (n 41) 110.

43 Peter Drahos, *A Philosophy of Intellectual Property* (Dartmouth Publishing 1996); Graham Dutfield and Uma Suthersanen, *Global Intellectual Property Law* (Edward Elgar 2008) 47; Estelle Derclaye, 'Patent Law's Role in the Protection of the Environment: Re-Assessing Patent Law and Its Justifications in the 21st Century' (2009) 40(3) *IIC* 249; *Stanford Encyclopedia of Philosophy* <http://plato.staford.edu/enties/intellectual-property> accessed 08 December 2021.

44 Robert P Merges, *Justifying Intellectual Property* (Harvard University Press 2011) 31.

personality.[45] Although generally not among these 'classic' justifications for intellectual property, ideas based on the concept of *communitarianism* – that communities are entitled to rights based on their being a distinct community – have been used as a justification for rights in traditional knowledge.[46] More recently, Munzer has discussed ideas of restorative/corrective justice to justify rights in traditional knowledge.[47] In Munzer's view, there are compelling arguments for recognising intellectual property rights in traditional knowledge as a matter of corrective justice for past harms by governments, corporations, and other actors. Recognising such rights would be a part of an effort to restore justice to the Indigenous people who have been harmed in the past.

The way traditional knowledge is conceived and respected by Indigenous peoples is not necessarily founded upon Western notions of the self and (particularly) of property.[48] Notwithstanding this, we should consider the positive rights to control genetic resources (and traditional knowledge associated with genetic resources) established within the Nagoya Protocol as a function of *positive law* created within a Western legal philosophical framework. Critics of the protection of traditional knowledge associated with genetic resources (perhaps at some time hence a pharmaceutical company seeking to avoid a veto over downstream use) are likely to root their arguments in the Western philosophical tradition and such criticisms are likely to be most easily countered using the same philosophical paradigm.

The aim of this chapter is to examine only the competing *consequentialist claims* (encompassing in some cases narrower utilitarian claims) relating to the protection of traditional knowledge associated with genetic resources and how they might help to answer *Questions 1* and *2* noted above. This is in no way to deny the importance of deontological (or other non-consequentialist) approaches. However, examining consequentialist claims alone has the advantage that the competing arguments (though by no means straightforward) at least arise out of the same philosophical foundations. There has long been significant debate about the tenability of 'mixing' philosophical justifications for intellectual property rights which we cannot realistically cover here, save to say that any such mixing

45 ibid 68.

46 Johanna Gibson, *Community Resources: Intellectual Property, International Trade and Protection of Traditional Knowledge* (Ashgate 2005).

47 Stephen R Munzer, 'Corrective Justice and Intellectual Property Rights in Traditional Knowledge' in Annabelle Lever (ed), *New Frontiers in the Philosophy of Intellectual Property* (Cambridge University Press) 58.

48 Joseph Githaiga, 'Intellectual Property Law and the Protection of Indigenous Folklore and Knowledge' (1998) 5(2) *E Law: Murdoch University Electronic Journal of Law* para 18 <www.murdoch.edu.au/elaw/issues/v5n2/githaiga52.html> accessed June 2021; Johanna Gibson, 'Community and the Exhaustion of Culture: Creative Territories in Creative Cultural Expressions' in Fiona Macmillan and Kathy Bowrey (eds), *New Directions in Copyright Law* Volume 3 (Edward Elgar Publishing 2006) 21; Gibson, *Community Resources* (n 46) 82; Andreas Rahmatian, 'Neo-Colonial Aspects of Global Intellectual Property Protection' (2009) 12(1) *J World Intellect Prop* 40.

needs to be done with a full appreciation of the potential problems.[49] An analysis of the competing consequentialist claims allows for a certain scoping of the main elements in *Questions 1* and *2* noted above, and where competing consequentialist arguments fail to provide solutions this may potentially offer a structure for the future application of deontological (or other non-consequentialist) claims.

Consequentialist arguments for, and against, a positive right in traditional knowledge associated with genetic resources under the Protocol

Enhancing the preservation of biological diversity and cultural diversity by creating value in traditional knowledge

Even if not deliberately seeking to destroy Indigenous society, the approach of many Western governments (and of some governments in the global South) has often been to discount the utility provided by Indigenous ways of life, at the expense of the utility provided by a Western-style economy. Consequently, many examples of traditional activity are in decline, and many modes of traditional cultural expression are being lost.[50]

Providing a positive right in traditional knowledge associated with genetic resources allows the holders to (potentially) make a current economic gain from such existing traditional knowledge. This may create an *incentive* to retain knowledge that would otherwise not be apportioned economic value and would potentially be lost in wake of the spread of 'Western' cultural and scientific norms and a market economy where 'money talks'.

Biological diversity

The conservation of the environment from which traditional knowledge originates is put forward as a key consequentialist justification for providing a positive right to traditional knowledge associated with genetic resources.[51] Actually, one of the aims of the Nagoya Protocol is contributing to the conservation of biological diversity (and the sustainable use of its components) through achieving the fair and appropriate access to genetic resources and by appropriate transfer of relevant technologies.[52] Of course, the preservation of biological diversity is a key aim of the Convention on Biological Diversity itself.[53] However, it would be naive to assume that giving Indigenous peoples rights to control traditional knowledge associated with genetic resources will, simply *of itself*, preserve the biodiversity

49 Merges (n 44) 10.
50 Dutfield and Suthersanen (n 43) 329; Dutfield, *Intellectual Property, Biogenetic Resources and Traditional Knowledge* (n 8) 97.
51 ibid 99.
52 Nagoya Protocol, Article 1.
53 Convention on Biological Diversity, Article 1.

of the area from which such traditional knowledge originates. What then is the mechanism by which the creation of these rights would achieve environmental preservation? More broadly, intellectual property rights or other rights which restrict use can create enhanced value (or at least a perception of value) in those 'things' whose use they restrict due the creation of artificial scarcity – at least where there is a market that wants to use those 'things'. Is creating a perception of *value* in traditional knowledge associated with genetic resources the mechanism by which rights over it achieve environmental preservation? The next section will show that there are many problems with this approach.

Problems with value approaches

Western-style economic theory is predicated on the value of economic development *today* over long-term values such as the preservation of something (whether traditional knowledge or a biodiverse environment) for the future (even where an allocation of value could be made).[54] One may be sceptical of the ability of enhanced value of genetic resources and traditional knowledge associated with them to successfully counter such immediate economic drivers. In addition, one might imagine scenarios where there is a significant disconnection between the value of genetic resources and traditional knowledge associated with genetic resources on the one hand, and preservation of the biodiverse environment on the other. Profiting from Western use of genetic resources and traditional knowledge associated with that resource could conceivably occur in the absence of the environment from which it originated. It could happen that the genetic resource has already been collected (and could be propagated elsewhere) and/or the relevant traditional knowledge has already been 'collected' and preserved, thereby leaving the land upon which the genetic resource originated free for other uses to generate monetary profit. This admittedly extreme case highlights that the linkage between genetic resource and/or traditional knowledge associated with genetic resources value in general and the preservation of biodiversity is in good part based on the *promise* of yet unknown (and yet potentially valuable) genetic resource and/or traditional knowledge combinations.

Unfortunately, much of the promise of genetic resources (and traditional knowledge associated with genetic resources) 'in the bush' is just that, a promise. Some genetic benefits may be entirely unknown, others may be directed through Indigenous knowledge; however full realisation of their true value to Western science/commerce may appear a relatively distant probability compared to the near certainty of the return to be made from, say, clear-cutting a forest to create animal pasture to produce hamburger meat.

Notwithstanding this scepticism in overall efficacy, the perception amongst all the concerned actors of *some* value in genetic resources and in traditional knowledge associated with those resources (created through the existence of a right to

54 Peter Singer, *Practical Ethics* (Cambridge University Press 1999) 270.

control use) must be better than *no* perceived value whatsoever (created through the absence of a right to control use). Evidently, where Indigenous peoples are not of their own free will destroying local genetic resources or abandoning their traditional knowledge, it would appear to follow that they are assigning some value to their genetic resources and traditional knowledge associated with genetic resources' existence. It is to that (likely a very different kind of 'value' from commercial value that would be readily recognised by a corporate accountant) which the chapter will now turn.

Direct utility through 'control' of information

This right to exclusively consent to the use of traditional knowledge associated with genetic resources may, of itself, *directly* contribute to the 'well-being' of Indigenous peoples. It may create spiritual fulfilment of Indigenous peoples; for example, if their traditional religious beliefs and/or customary norms direct that sacred or special information should be maintained within the Indigenous group, or it 'might confer a very real and cultural/spiritual sense of independence and self-reliance where that knowledge is used to the benefit of the community'.[55]

Although this may be an entirely justifiable basis for having a right to control access, its applicability will be case-dependent rather than the general applicability which applies to the valorisation of traditional knowledge. We need to note that the 'utility through control' goal is reliant, in the long term at least, on the broader preservation of the culture and environment that supports the appropriate traditional religious beliefs and/or customary norms. Actually, a piece of traditional knowledge associated with genetic resources along with the understanding of how that information is related to the broader ecosystem, and ecosystem management and stewardship, is often rolled-up into a web of cultural heritage, spiritual belief, and community identity which confounds classical 'Western' attempts at atomisation and categorisation.[56] Note that the absolute exercise of a veto over use of traditional knowledge associated with genetic resources in achievement of a 'utility through control' goal may in certain cases play against the creation of value in that knowledge which might otherwise be achieved through consensual commercial exploitation.[57]

A conflicting utilitarian goal: freedom to develop and global health?

If one is seeking an enhancement in the *greater* utility of the *greatest* number, might not that broad utility be better served in the present case by allowing those

55 Djims Milius, 'Justifying Intellectual Property in Traditional Knowledge' [2009] *IPQ* 184, 198.

56 See Darrell Addison Posey, 'Culture and Nature: The Inextricable Link' in Darrell Addison Posey (ed), *Cultural and Spiritual Values of Biodiversity* (Intermediate Technology Publications 1999) 1.

57 On this point, and on how to balance access to traditional medicine and the safeguard of Indigenous peoples' rights, see Valentina Vadi, 'Intangible Heritage, Traditional Medicine and Knowledge Governance' (2007) 2(10) *JIPLP* 682.

with the better skill and financial resources untrammelled access to traditional knowledge associated with genetic resources? If a pharmaceutical company (with those skills and resources) can take a piece of traditional knowledge (with the related genetic resource) and develop it into a product, which successfully removes or alleviates a disease state (or its symptoms) in a broad population of people that would otherwise not have access to that drug, is that not a greater utility for the greater number of persons than its use being restricted to groups of Indigenous peoples – notwithstanding that the pharmaceutical company will be compensated for its own investment?

In contrast, allowing a veto on downstream use of traditional knowledge associated with genetic resources would mean that the development of a therapy which could benefit all (or a large part) of humanity could potentially be prevented by the decision of a small group of Indigenous people. Here the existence of the veto right, which is supposed to bring about one set of utilitarian goals (preservation of the environment and traditional knowledge *per se*) through the creation of value in the traditional knowledge associated with genetic resources, arguably directly counters another type of utility (that of wider human health and life).

As we have seen the causal link between the impositions of veto rights, the valorisation of traditional knowledge associated with genetic resources, and the preservation of the environment and Indigenous lifestyles is reliant on an uncertain idea of 'perception of value' in traditional knowledge associated with genetic resources. In contrast, the causal link between a piece of traditional knowledge serving as stimulus for drug development, and the final product may arguably be more concrete. Looking at 'utility through control', we can see a *direct* link between the creation of a positive right and a utilitarian goal. However, such a goal is still subject to questions of competing utilities, namely: is the happiness of a small group of Indigenous peoples more important than wider human health and life?

Application of consequentialist arguments to Questions 1 and 2

This section examines to what extent (if at all) these consequentialist justifications can help answer *Questions 1* and *2* noted above and which were raised by the *quinaquina* and Madagascar *periwinkle* case studies.

Question 1: what is the downstream limit to the right to control traditional knowledge associated with genetic resources?

VALORISATION APPROACHES

If the creation of a positive right in traditional knowledge associated with genetic resources has its consequentialist effect on the preservation of biodiversity and Indigenous culture through the creation of a perception of value in such traditional knowledge, one might argue that any attempt to restrict the downstream scope of protection may diminish the perceived value of a piece of traditional knowledge associated with genetic resources and the utilitarian effect of the positive right. This seems an overly simplistic approach.

The 'indirect' utilitarian effect through creating value makes concrete linkages inherently difficult. Does the perception of value really require that *all* downstream use can be controlled – even accidental discoveries? It seems unlikely. In contrast, if an immediate downstream user could easily evade a positive right in traditional knowledge associated with genetic resources through (say) minor derivatisation of an extracted compound, that would clearly undermine the perception of value in a particular piece of such traditional knowledge and, indeed, the overall concept of its value as it could be damaged. Therefore, attempting to find the *exact* point at which downstream scope of protection should end cannot be achieved solely through the lens of diminution of value.

Of course, providing for any absolute veto over downstream use would run contrary to the freedom to develop life-saving medicines discussed above. Any such conflict could potentially be ameliorated if one were to allow for a degree of compulsory licensing of certain downstream uses. It is submitted that the presence of any compulsory licensing regime would still further complicate any assessment performed solely through a diminution of value lens.

DIRECT UTILITY THROUGH 'CONTROL' OF INFORMATION APPROACH

Simply put, the question we need to ask here is, would the utility gained by an Indigenous group through control of information be reduced/destroyed if certain downstream uses of traditional knowledge associated with genetic resources were excluded from that control? The potential advantage of this approach is that we do not have the problem of *indirect* effect, which we saw when looking at a diminution of value approach; an Indigenous group would potentially be able to tell us whether a particular downstream use was offensive to their traditional religious beliefs and/or customary norms.

As an external observer, one might intuitively assume that control over new 'accessing' of elements of traditional knowledge associated with genetic resources which are of cultural or religious importance may be responsible for greater utility for a group holding that knowledge than a new accessing of something which (though *causally* connected with the original traditional knowledge) is very distal to the cultural or religious concerns of the holders. First, in the case of the Madagascar *periwinkle*, the accidental discovery of entirely new therapeutic use of a plant (anti-cancer) was unrelated to original understanding of the traditional knowledge associated with genetic resources holders (anti-diabetes). Second and even more distally, in the case of the sulphonamide anti-microbials, the chain of causation even passed through a non-therapeutic stage (i.e., mauvine). However, as stated above, the degree to which control over traditional knowledge associated with genetic resources provides a degree of social utility is determined on a case-by-case basis, subject to the traditional religious beliefs and/or customary norms of the group in question – it is not reliant upon an external observers' intuition.

Therefore, creating a more generally applicable, rule utilitarian, structure on this justification alone would be difficult.

Evidently, where direct utility is created through an absolute veto on downstream use, this would immediately run contrary to the freedom to develop/worldwide health care utility discussed above. As mentioned in relation to the diminution of value approach, such conflict could potentially be ameliorated if one were to allow for a degree of compulsory licensing of certain downstream uses. However, the introduction of a compulsory licensing scheme would seem likely to be much more destructive to the goal of 'utility through control' than it would be to the goals achieved through creating a perception of value of traditional knowledge associated with genetic resources.

Question 2: who gets to control the traditional knowledge associated with genetic resources?

VALORISATION APPROACHES

As noted, the valorisation approaches suffer from an indirect link between creation of a positive right in traditional knowledge associated with genetic resources and preservation of a biodiverse environment and Indigenous culture (or a conflation of the two). However, to a degree, the valorisation approach may be a more helpful tool in relation to answering *Question 2* than *Question 1*. Where something is wanted in the first place, value is created (or a least maintained) through exclusivity; if my neighbour is giving something away that I also have, then the value of that item to third parties will likely be diminished. Consequently, enhancing the value of traditional knowledge associated with genetic resources would be served by ensuring that consent needs to be obtained from *all* right holders,[58] wherever those holders may be and regardless of which side of a national boundary they find themselves on. There is an acute transboundary problem here – national laws would ideally be required to ensure that consent was gained from Indigenous groups who were subject to the laws of neighbouring jurisdictions (or even in the case of the Madagascar *periwinkle*, jurisdictions on different continents).[59]

However, can the valorisation approach assist us with determining *who* those rights holders should be in the first place? Arguably Indigenous groups would most strongly see an *incentive* to retain knowledge that would otherwise not be valued, where it was clear that those groups who maintained knowledge were those that benefitted (or potentially benefitted) from a positive right over that knowledge. If others were to wrongly benefit, that might serve to 'dilute' the incentivisation. However, beyond that sense of 'fairness', it is hard to see that the valorisation approach can easily assist us with deciding the rules governing

58 Although all proven holders would need to be free to use traditional knowledge associated with genetic resources for their own 'traditional' purposes.

59 See note 21 re Nagoya Protocol Article 10.

how putative holders of the right should demonstrate/prove their inheritance/current right.

DIRECT UTILITY THROUGH 'CONTROL' OF INFORMATION APPROACH

What types of factors will be governing the degree of social utility gained through control over traditional knowledge associated with genetic resources? Understandably, we may consider the following: first, how closely aligned a group feels to information that is widely dispersed across a geographical area and/or amongst similar (or even different) groups?; and second, to what extent would utility gained through control be undermined were another group (say in the Philippines) to give their consent without involving the first group (say in Jamaica)? Instinctively, we might believe that the more narrowly a piece of knowledge is held (and the more tightly it is controlled) the stronger sense of ownership is felt in it and the stronger the utility gained through control.

However, we encounter a major problem. As noted, the utility gained through control is not (through this lens) determined by external observers' intuition; it is subject to the *traditional* religious beliefs and/or customary norms of the group in question. Reliance on this justification alone makes it difficult to create a generally applicable, rule utilitarian, structure. It also makes it difficult to determine questions of priority about 'ownership' in knowledge between groups (in say Jamaica and the Philippines) – the justification is simply not equipped to answer the question. The inability to easily arrive at an objective sense of utility for a given degree of control again makes it difficult to balance this justification in the light of the competing worldwide health utility derived through the freedom to develop pharmaceuticals.

Conclusion

This chapter has focussed on the *consequentialist* (including in some cases more narrowly *utilitarian*) justifications for the protection of traditional knowledge associated with genetic resources within the Nagoya Protocol. In particular, the chapter examines the degree to which the 'direct' utility, which is created when Indigenous peoples are able to exercise control over traditional knowledge associated with genetic resources, may assist in understanding: first, the justifiable scope of this *sui generis* positive right to control downstream use of traditional knowledge associated with genetic resources within the context of drug discovery; and second, from whom consent is required to use such controlled traditional knowledge associated with genetic resources within the context of drug discovery (particularly within transboundary situations).

Although this direct *utility* justification (focussing as it does on the particular traditional religious beliefs and/or customary norms of the group in question) might be said to be closer in spirit to broader arguments for the preservation of intangible cultural heritage, the chapter concludes that a *consequentialist* analysis alone (though perhaps of some use in framing the problems at hand) is insufficient to effectively answer these questions. It seems that other, deontological philosophical tools – notably those which are more usually deemed to be the basis for moral rights and those used more broadly in examining ownership in other areas of intangible cultural heritage – are required. However, even in bringing those justifications into play we need to be mindful of not being too reductionist; traditional knowledge associated with genetic resources needs to be seen in a broader landscape of rights. As stated by Dutfield:

> What use is ecological knowledge without land rights? How can traditional medicinal knowledge stay in use if the lands where the plants grew have been ploughed over? Why do decisions affecting Indigenous peoples continue to be made by urban educated elites, well-meaning as they so often are?[60]

References

Achan J et al., 'Quinine, an Old Anti-malarial Drug in a Modern World: Role in the Treatment of Malaria' (2011) 10 *Malar J* 144

Bagley M and Perron-Welch F, 'Study to Identify Specific Cases of Genetic Resources and Traditional Knowledge Associated with Genetic Resources that Occur in Transboundary Situations or for Which it is not Possible to Grant or Obtain Prior Informed Consent' March 2020 <www.cbd.int/abs/Art-10/study-art10-peer-review-revd.pdf>

Balick M J and Cox P A, *Plants, People, and Culture: The Science of Ethnobotany* (Scientific American Library 1997)

Bardal S K et al., *Applied Pharmacology* (Elsevier 2011)

Bäumler E, *In Search of the Magic Bullet: Great Adventures in Modern Drug Research* (Thames and Hudson 1965)

Coombe R, 'The Recognition of Indigenous Peoples' and Community Traditional Knowledge in International Law' (2002) 14 *St Thomas L Rev* 275

Cotton, C M, *Ethnobotany: Principles and Applications* (John Wiley & Sons 1996)

Derclaye, 'Patent Law's Role in the Protection of the Environment – Re-assessing Patent Law and its Justifications in the 21st Century' (2009) 40(3) *IIC* 249

Dutfield G, *Intellectual Property Rights, Biogenetic Resources and Traditional Knowledge* (Earthscan Publications 2004)

——— 'Protecting the Rights of Indigenous Peoples: Can Prior Informed Consent Help?' in R Wynberg, D Schroeder and R Chenells (eds), *Indigenous Peoples, Consent and Benefit Sharing: Lessons from the San-Hoodia Case* (Springer 2009)

——— 'A Critical Analysis of the Debate on Traditional Knowledge, Drug Discovery and Patent-based Biopiracy' (2011) 33(4) *EIPR* 238

——— 'Traditional Knowledge, Intellectual Property and Pharmaceutical Innovation: What's Left to Discuss?' in M David and D Halbert (eds), *The Sage Handbook of Intellectual Property* (Sage 2014)

Dutfield G and Suthersanen U, *Global Intellectual Property Law* (Edward Elgar 2008)

Drahos P, *A Philosophy of Intellectual Property* (Dartmouth Publishing 1996)

60 Dutfield, 'Traditional Knowledge, Intellectual Property and Pharmaceutical Innovation: What's Left to Discuss?' (n 6) 649.

Farnsworth N R, 'The Role of Ethnopharmacology in Drug Development' in *Bioactive Compounds from Plants* (John Wiley & Sons 1994) (Ciba Foundation Symp 154)

Garfield S, *Mauve: How One Man Invented a Colour which Changed the World* (Faber & Faber 2000)

Gibson J, *Community Resources: Intellectual Property, International Trade and Protection of Traditional Knowledge* (Ashgate 2005)

——— 'Community and the Exhaustion of Culture: Creative Territories in Creative Cultural Expressions' in F Macmillan and K Bowrey (eds), *New Directions in Copyright Law Volume 3* (Edward Elgar Publishing 2006)

Githaiga J, 'Intellectual Property Law and the Protection of Indigenous Folklore and Knowledge' (1998) 5(2) *E Law: Murdoch University Electronic Journal of Law* <www.murdoch.edu.au/elaw/issues/v5n2/githaiga52.html>

Grahame-Smith D G and Aronson J K, *Oxford Textbook of Clinical Pharmacology and Drug Therapy* (OUP 1992)

Greiber T et al., *IUCN Explanatory Guide to the Protocol on Access and Benefit-Sharing* (IUCN Environmental Policy and Law Paper No. 83, 2012)

Goldberg R, *Perspectives on Causation* (Hart Publishing 2011)

Hall J, 'The Drug Development Process' in I Di Giovanna and G Hayes (eds), *Principles of Clinical Research* (Wrightson Biomedical Publishing UK 2001)

Harrison P, 'Grasping Frankenstein's Monster: Uncertainty in the Downstream Scope of the Nagoya Protocol' (2019) 1 *IPQ* 61

Hart H L A and Honoré T, *Causation in the Law* (OUP 1985)

Kiene T, *The Legal Protection of Traditional Knowledge in the Pharmaceutical Field. An Intercultural Problem on the International Agenda* (Waxmann 2012)

Laws B, *Fifty Plants that Changed the Course of History* (David and Charles 2010)

Merges R P, *Justifying Intellectual Property* (Harvard University Press 2011)

Milius D, 'Justifying Intellectual Property in Traditional Knowledge' [2009] *IPQ* 184

Moore M S, *Causation and Responsibility, An Essay in Law, Morals and Metaphysics* (OUP 2009)

Morgera E et al., *Unravelling the Protocol: A Commentary on the Protocol on Access and Benefit Sharing to the Convention on Biological Diversity* (Brill/Nijhoff 2014)

Munzer S R, 'Corrective Justice and Intellectual Property Rights in Traditional Knowledge' in A Lever (ed), *New Frontiers in the Philosophy of Intellectual Property* (Cambridge University Press 2012)

Neuss N et al., 'Vinca Alkaloids. III. 1. Characterisation of Leurosine and Vincaleukoblastine, New Alkaloids from *Vincarosea* Linn' (1959) 81 *J Am ChemSoc* 4754

Nijar G S, *The Protocol on ABS: An Analysis* (CEBLAW 2011)

Noble R L et al., '*Role of Chance Observations in Chemotherapy*' (1958) 76 *Ann NY AcadSci* 882

Otten H, 'Domagk and the Development of the Sulphonamides' (1986) 17(6) *J Antimicrob Chemother* 689

Papadopoulou F, *The Protection of Traditional Knowledge on Genetic Resources* (Edward Elgar 2018)

Porter R (ed), *The Hutchinson Dictionary of Scientific Biography* (Helicon 1994)

Posey D A, 'Culture and Nature – The Inextricable Link' in D A Posey (ed), *Cultural and Spiritual Values of Biodiversity* (Intermediate Technology Publications 1999)

Rabe P and Kindler K, 'Uber die partielleSynthese des Chinins. ZurKenntnis der China-Alkaloide XIX' (1918) 51 *BerDtschChemGes* 466

Rahmatian A, 'Neo-Colonial Aspects of Global Intellectual Property Protection' (2009) 12(1) *J World Intellect Prop* 40
Raviña E, *The Evolution of Drug Discovery: From Traditional Medicines to Modern Drugs* (Wiley-VCH 2011)
Savaresi A, 'The International Human Rights Law Implications of the Protocol' in E Morgera, M Buck and T Elsa (eds), *The 2010 Protocol on Access and Benefit-Sharing in Perspective: Implications for International Law and Implementation Challenges* (Martinus Nijhoff Publishers 2012)
Schiebinger L, *Plants and Empire, Colonial Bioprospecting in the Atlantic World* (Harvard University Press 2004)
Schuler P, 'Biopiracy and Commercialization of Ethnobotanical Knowledge' in J M Finger and P Schuler (eds), *Poor People's Knowledge* (World Bank and OUP 2004)
Sharma S and Anand N, 'Approaches to Design and Synthesis of Antiparasitic Drugs' (1997) 24 Pharmacochemistry *Library* 393
Singer P, *Practical Ethics* (Cambridge University Press 1999)
Sneader W, *Drug Discovery: The Evolution of Modern Medicines* (John Wiley & Sons 1985)
——— *Drug Discovery, A History* (John Wiley & Sons 2005)
Snoeijer W, 'Catharanthus Roseus, the Madagascar Periwinkle, a Review of its Cultivars' (1996) 96(3) *Wageningen Agricultural University Papers* 47
Travis A S, 'Perkin's Mauve: Ancestor of the Organic Chemical Industry' (1990) 31(1) *Technology and Culture* 51
Vadi V, 'Intangible Heritage, Traditional Medicine and Knowledge Governance' (2007) 2(10) *Journal of Intellectual Property Law and Practice* 682
van Bergen M A, 'Revision of Catharanthus G Don Series of Revisions of Apocynaceae XLI' (1996) 96(3) *Wageningen Agricultural University Papers* 1
Woodward R B and Doering W E, 'The Total Synthesis of Quinine' (1944) 66(5) *J Am ChemSoc* 849
Wright R, 'Causation in Tort Law' (1985) 73 *Cal L Rev* 1735

5 The legal protection of intangible cultural heritage

The inadequacy of intellectual property in the Republic of Korea

Gyooho Lee

Introduction

When it comes to intangible cultural heritage, 'more than one community makes similar use of the same resources, sometimes even using the same processes'.[1] Hence, taking into account lack of originality, novelty, or distinctiveness in character, some common law scholars argue that pre-existing intellectual property laws are deficient and generally inappropriate for protecting the intangible cultural heritage of Indigenous peoples and local communities.[2] Therefore, they propose the use of traditional concepts of contract, privacy, trade secret, and trade mark to afford better protection to such intangible cultural heritage.[3]

From the perspective of civil law scholars, trade secrets and trade marks can be categorised as types of intellectual property. Hence, trade secrets, certification marks,[4] collective marks, geographical indications (GIs), certification marks,[5] and collective marks can all contribute to the promotion of intangible cultural heritage. At the international level, the World Intellectual Property Organization (WIPO) has tried to complete a couple of treaties that would protect the intangible cultural heritage of Indigenous peoples.[6] The global campaign has been initiated

1 Naomi Roht-Arriaza, 'Of Seeds and Shamans: The Appropriation of the Scientific and Technical Knowledge of Indigenous and Local Communities' (1996) 17 *Mich J Int'l L* 919.

2 Robert K Paterson and Dennis S Karjala, 'Looking beyond Intellectual Property in Resolving Protection of the Intangible Cultural Heritage of Indigenous Peoples' (2003) 11 *Cardozo J Int'l & Comp L* 633.

3 ibid 669.

4 ibid 666–667.

5 Peter K Yu states that '[o]ne can also explore the use of certification marks and geographical indications, rewards that are based on stewardship and local innovation, moral rights-type protection, and open source and collaborative models' in Peter K Yu, 'Cultural Relics, Intellectual Property, and Intangible Heritage' (2008) *Temp L Rev* 433; Emanuela Arezzo discusses use of open source and collaborative models in connection with traditional knowledge in Emanuela Arezzo, 'Struggling around the "Natural" Divide: The Protection of Tangible and Intangible Indigenous Property' (2007) 25 *Cardozo Arts & Ent L J* 367, 410–412.

6 See generally WIPO, 'The Protection of Traditional Cultural Expressions: Draft Articles' 28th session WIPO/GRTK/IC/28/6 (June 2, 2014).

DOI: 10.4324/9781003345237-6

under the umbrella of 'traditional knowledge' rights covering cultural expression, and Indigenous technologies, know-how, and bio-resources,[7] among others.

Traditional knowledge rights can be justified under cultural integrity and economic justice rationales.[8] However, Korea has yet to enact a law which recognises traditional knowledge rights, so that the holders of this type of intangible cultural heritage can rely on pre-existing intellectual property laws and cultural heritage regimes. This chapter investigates whether and to what extent the current Korean intellectual property laws can contribute to the preservation and promotion of intangible cultural heritage and thus, makes several proposals to better preserve and promote intangible cultural heritage, including transboundary heritage, mainly in terms of intellectual property law.

Clarification of terminology

The term intangible cultural heritage refers to 'the part of culture that cannot be touched or interacted with, such as annual festivals, skills, song, dance, and cuisine'.[9] UNESCO defines intangible cultural heritage as '(a) oral traditions and expressions, including language as a vehicle of the intangible cultural heritage; (b) performing arts; (c) social practices, rituals and festive events; (d) knowledge and practices concerning nature and the universe; (e) traditional craftsmanship'.[10]

In Korea, the term intangible cultural heritage is defined in both the Korean Act on the Safeguarding and Promotion of Intangible Cultural Heritage and the Korean Cultural Heritage Protection Act (hereinafter CHPA). It includes:

> Traditional performances and traditional arts; traditional skills concerning crafts, art, etc.; traditional knowledge concerning Korean medicine, agriculture, fishery, etc.; oral traditions and oral expressions; traditional ways of life concerning food, cloth, shelter, etc.; social rituals such as folk religion; traditional games, festivals, and practical and martial arts.[11]

The term *holder* under the Korean Intangible Cultural Heritage Act means a person recognised as an individual holder of national or municipal/provincial intangible

7 Emily Marden, 'The Neem Tree Patent: International Conflict over the Commodification of Life' (1999) 22 *B C Int'l Comp L Rev* 279, 283–86; WIPO, 'Protection of Traditional Knowledge and Genetic Resources: A Bottom-up Approach to Development' [2003] *WIPO Magazine* Nov–Dec 18, 20.

8 Sean A Pager, 'Traditional Knowledge Rights and Wrongs' (2016) 20 *Va J L & Tech* 82, 92.

9 UNESCO 2003 Convention for the Safeguarding of Intangible Cultural Heritage Article 2.

10 ibid.

11 See CHPA (Act No 17586) revised on 8 December 2020 and effective since 9 June 2021, Article 2(1) 2. The definition of the term intangible cultural heritage under the Korean Intangible Cultural Heritage Act is followed by the one defined in Article 2 (1) 2 of the CHPA. See Korean Intangible Cultural Heritage Act (Act No 17708) revised on 22 December 2020 and effective since 23 June 2021, Article 2(1).

cultural heritage,[12] who is 'able to master and practice technical skills, artistic skills, etc., of [intangible cultural heritage] as the archetype of that [intangible cultural heritage], as prescribed by Presidential Decree'.[13] The term *group holder* means a group recognised as a group holder of national or municipal/provincial intangible cultural heritage,[14] that is 'able to master and practice technical skills, artistic skills, etc., of [intangible cultural heritage] as the archetype of that [intangible cultural heritage], as prescribed by Presidential Decree'.[15] Transmission of archetype is the key factor for the Korean central or local government to designate a certain cultural heritage as intangible cultural heritage. Hence, the Korean Intangible Cultural Heritage Act does not grant its ownership to a holder of intangible cultural heritage.

Continuing with the meaning of terms, *archetype* refers to 'intrinsic features prescribed by Presidential Decree, which constitute the value of specific [intangible cultural heritage]'. According to the Korean Intangible Cultural Heritage Enforcement Decree, *archetype* means 'intrinsic techniques, forms, and knowledge that should be transmitted, maintained, and practiced throughout several generations'.[16] In this regard, an intangible cultural heritage *successor* means as follows: (i) a person who is able to master and practice technical skills, artistic skills, etc., of intangible cultural heritage as the archetype of that intangible cultural heritage, as prescribed by Presidential Decree; (ii) a group that is able to master and practice technical skills, artistic skills, etc., of intangible cultural heritage as the archetype of that intangible cultural heritage, as prescribed by Presidential Decree; (iii) an assistant instructor for successor training, recognised from certified trainees[17] to assist holder or group of holders in transmitting intangible cultural heritage; or (iv) a certified trainee, a person issued with a certificate of completion of successor training.[18] As far as intangible cultural heritage is concerned, the Korean Intangible Cultural Heritage Act takes precedence over the Cultural Property Protection Act.[19]

When it comes to the Framework Act on intellectual property,

> [t]he term 'intellectual property' means knowledge, information, technology, the expression of ideas or emotions, the indication of business or goods, varieties of organism or genetic resources and other intangibles created or

12 Intangible Cultural Heritage Act, Articles 17(1) and 32(2).
13 ibid Article 2(3).
14 ibid Articles 17(1) and 32(2).
15 ibid Article 2(4).
16 Article 2(1) of the Enforcement Decree of the Act on the Safeguarding and Promotion of Intangible Cultural Heritage (Presidential Decree No 31138) (Intangible Cultural Heritage Enforcement Decree).
17 Intangible Cultural Heritage Act, Article 19(1).
18 ibid Articles 26 (1) and 2(6).
19 Cultural Heritage Protection Act (Act No 17711), Article 5.

> discovered by creative activities, experience, etc., of human beings, the value of property of which may be realised.[20]

Also, 'the term "intellectual property right" means any right relating to intellectual property recognised or protected according to Acts and subordinate statutes, treaties, etc.'[21]

Basic principles and policy considerations

The Intangible Cultural Heritage Act aims

> to maintain the archetype of [intangible cultural heritage], giving due consideration to the following:
>
> 1. Cultivation of the national identity;
> 2. Transmission and development of traditional culture;
> 3. Realisation and enhancement of the value of [intangible cultural heritage].[22]

Article 4 of the Intangible Cultural Heritage Act notes the responsibilities of the state to 'formulate and implement a comprehensive policy to safeguard and promote [intangible cultural heritage]'.[23] It also provides that '[e]ach local government shall formulate and implement a policy to safeguard and promote [intangible cultural heritage], giving due consideration to regional characteristics, in compliance with the State's policy'.[24]

Traditional foodways such as *Kimjang*, the making and sharing process of the spicy dish kimchi that has been widely spread by Korean communities throughout the globe, constitute a form of intangible cultural heritage. Such foodways constitute a type of intangible cultural heritage because they encapsulate traditional knowledge concerning Korean medicine, agriculture, fishery, and so on; traditional ways of life concerning food; social rituals; and/or traditional festivals. The transmission of the archetype of intangible cultural heritage is one of the pivotal factors in order for the Korean government to approve cultural heritage as intangible cultural heritage.[25] This is because the term *archetype* refers to intrinsic features constituting the value of specific intangible cultural heritage.[26] In order for the Korean central and local governments to formulate and implement a policy

20 Framework Act on Intellectual Property (Act No 15245), Article 3(1).
21 ibid Article 3(3).
22 Intangible Cultural Heritage Act, Article 3.
23 ibid Article 4(1).
24 ibid Article 4(2).
25 Gyooho Lee, 'How to Protect Traditional Food and Foodways Effectively in Terms of Intangible Cultural Heritage and Intellectual Property Laws in the Republic of Korea' (2018) 24 *Int'l J Cult Prop* (4) 565, 569.
26 Intangible Cultural Heritage Act, Article 2(2).

to safeguard and promote intangible cultural heritage, they 'shall secure a budget necessary' for such policies.[27]

Criteria to designate a national intangible cultural heritage and to recognise its holder

Legal sources

In accordance with Article 12(1) of the Intangible Cultural Heritage Act, the 'Administrator of the Cultural Heritage Administration may designate significant [intangible cultural heritage] as national [intangible cultural heritage] following deliberation by the Committee'.[28] The criteria and procedures for the designation of national intangible cultural heritage are set by the Intangible Cultural Heritage Enforcement Decree.[29]

Upon designating national intangible cultural heritage or national intangible cultural heritage in need of urgent safeguarding, the Administrator of the Cultural Heritage Administration shall give public notice of the objectives and details of such designation in the official gazette,[30] having effect on the date on which the designation is publicised in such gazette.[31] The Administrator of the Cultural Heritage Administration prescribes and announces the 'detailed indicators regarding the criteria for the designation of national [intangible cultural heritage], the awarding of points, and other relevant matters'.[32] When designating national intangible cultural heritage, the Administrator of the Cultural Heritage Administration shall recognise a holder of group holder of that national intangible cultural heritage unless it is impracticable to do so by the nature of such national intangible cultural heritage as prescribed by the Intangible Cultural Heritage Enforcement Decree.[33] Hence, the Administrator of the Cultural Heritage Administration will not recognise a holder or group holder of national intangible cultural heritage

> where it is impracticable to recognise that only a specific person or specific group is able to master, safeguard, and practice the relevant national [intangible cultural heritage] just like the archetype of that national intangible cultural heritage, because the technical skill, artistic skill, or knowledge of such national [intangible cultural heritage], is part of the public domain or has become a custom.[34]

27 ibid Article 4(3).
28 ibid Article 12(1).
29 ibid Article 12(2). The Intangible Cultural Heritage Enforcement Decree is the specific name of the 'Presidential Decree', see n 16.
30 ibid Article 14(1).
31 ibid Article 14(2).
32 Intangible Cultural Heritage Enforcement Decree, Article 14(5).
33 Intangible Cultural Heritage Act, Article 17(1).
34 Intangible Cultural Heritage Enforcement Decree, Article 16(3).

Article 16(1) of the Intangible Cultural Heritage Enforcement Decree sets up that the Administrator of Cultural Heritage Administration may recognise a person or group as a holder or group holder of national intangible cultural heritage in circumstances such as having the ability and means to transmit the relevant national intangible cultural heritage; showing outstanding performance in transmitting the relevant national intangible cultural heritage and having a strong commitment to the transmission thereof; the person or group shall have contributed to transmitting the relevant national intangible cultural heritage. In this context, the group holder has to fall under any of the following: intangible cultural heritage can be practised only by a group due to the nature of the technical skill, artistic skill, or knowledge of that intangible cultural heritage; several persons are eligible to be recognised as a holder of the relevant intangible cultural heritage; a number of residents practice technical skill, artistic skill, or knowledge of intangible cultural heritage, by forming a group or community where that relevant intangible cultural heritage is transmitted.[35] A group holder of intangible cultural heritage which has been recognised by the Administrator of the Cultural Heritage Administration shall be a non-profit legal person incorporated with the permission of the Administrator of the Cultural Heritage Administration.[36] The Administrator of the Cultural Heritage Administration may recognise *another* holder or group holder of national intangible cultural heritage, in addition to the holder or group holder of that intangible cultural heritage recognised as national intangible cultural heritage.[37] In regard to matters which are necessary for criteria, such procedures shall be prescribed by the Presidential Decree.[38] In regard to criteria for the recognition of (groups of) holders of national intangible cultural heritage, as well as the awarding of points, and other relevant matters, the Administrator of Cultural Heritage Administration shall set these.[39] The designation of national intangible cultural heritage is governed by the Public Notification of Cultural Heritage Administration (No 2019-149).[40]

Criteria to designate national intangible cultural heritage and to recognise an individual holder or group holder as its holder

Criteria to designate the subject-matter of national intangible cultural heritage

This consists of transmittable value (70 pts) and environment for transmission (30 pts). Transmittable value is composed of the following factors: (i) historical features (20 pts); (ii) academic features (15 pts); (iii) artistry or technical features (15

35 ibid Article 16(2).
36 Civil Act, Article 32; Intangible Cultural Heritage Act, Article 17(2).
37 ibid Article 17(3).
38 ibid Article 17(4).
39 Intangible Cultural Heritage Enforcement Decree, Article 16(5).
40 ibid Articles 14(5) and 16(5).

pts); (iv) representativeness (20 pts). On the other hand, environment for transmission (30 pts) consists of social and cultural value (20 pts) and sustainability (10 pts).

Criteria to recognise a holder of intangible cultural heritage as a group holder of national intangible cultural heritage

This consists of ability for transmission (75 pts), environment for transmission (20 pts), and the level of participation in transmitting activities (5 pts).

UNESCO Intangible Cultural Heritage of Humanity list in South Korea

The Convention for the Safeguarding of the Intangible Cultural Heritage was adopted by UNESCO on 17 December 2003 (the 2003 Convention). South Korea became the 11th signatory on 9 February 2005. Since then, 21 items of South Korea have been inscribed on the UNESCO Intangible Cultural Heritage of Humanity list.[41] As of December 2021, those are as follows: Royal Ancestral Rite and Ritual Music of *Jongmyo Jerye* (Royal ancestral ritual in the Jongmyo shrine and its music);[42] *Pansori* (epic chant);[43] *Gangneung Danoje* festival;[44]*Ganggangsullae* (women's circle dance);[45]*Namsadang* (the all-male vagabond clown theatre);[46] *Yeongsanjae* (re-enactment of Buddha's delivery of the Lotus Sutra on the Vulture Peak in India);[47] *Jeju Chilmeoridang Yeongdeunggut* (Yeongdeungrites for the Goddess of wind);[48] *Cheoyongmu* (a court dance of Cheoyong);[49] *Gagok* (lyric song cycles accompanied by an

41 Cultural Heritage Administration, 'Korea's Intangible Human Heritage' (Cultural Heritage Administration 2000) <www.heritage.go.kr/heri/html/HtmlPage.do?pg=/unesco/korInCulHeritage.jsp&pageNo=5_3_2_0#> accessed 1 December 2021.

42 UNESCO inscribed in 2008 on the Representative List of Intangible Cultural Heritage of Humanity: Decision 3.COM 1(originally proclaimed in 2001).

43 UNESCO inscribed in 2008 on the Representative List of Intangible Cultural Heritage of Humanity: Decision 3.COM 1 (originally proclaimed in 2003).

44 UNESCO inscribed in 2008 on the Representative List of Intangible Cultural Heritage of Humanity: Decision 3.COM 1 (originally proclaimed in 2005).

45 UNESCO inscribed in 2009 on the Representative List of Intangible Cultural Heritage of Humanity: Decision 4.COM 13.65.

46 UNESCO inscribed in 2009 on the Representative List of Intangible Cultural Heritage of Humanity: Decision 4.COM 13.67.

47 UNESCO inscribed in 2009 on the Representative List of Intangible Cultural Heritage of Humanity: Decision 4.COM 13.68.

48 UNESCO inscribed in 2009 on the Representative List of Intangible Cultural Heritage of Humanity: Decision 4.COM 13.66.

49 UNESCO inscribed in 2009 on the Representative List of Intangible Cultural Heritage of Humanity: Decision 4.COM 13.64.

Table 5.1 Criteria to designate the subject-matter of national intangible cultural heritage

Classification	*Factors*	*Method to evaluate factors*	*Remarks*
A. Transmittable value			
Historical characteristics (20 pts)	Duration of transmission (10 pts)	The number of years of transmission	Quantitative
	The level of credibility of historical grounds (10 pts)	The level of credibility of historical grounds such as artefacts, literature, oral statements	Qualitative
Academic features (15 pts)	The level of contribution to research on Korean culture (8 pts)	Its value as materials necessary to understand Korean culture	Qualitative
	Possibility to be used as materials for academic research (7 pts)	Possibility to be used as materials for academic research	Qualitative
Artistry and technical features (15 pts)	The level of aesthetics in form, contents, and expression (10 pts)	The level of aesthetics in form, contents, and expression	Qualitative
	The level of functionality (5 pts)	Functional availability and value	Qualitative
Representativeness (20 pts)	The level of singularity (10 pts)	The level of singularity (uniqueness)	Qualitative
	The extent to which it represents a Korean traditional culture (10 pts)	The extent to which it represents a Korean traditional culture	Qualitative
B. Environment for transmission			
Skill for transmission (50 pts)	Practice skill of the applied item (50 pts)	The level of practice skill of the applied item	Qualitative
	The level of comprehension of the applied item (10 pts)	The level of understanding of the history and contents of the applied item	Qualitative
Sustainability (10 pts)	Frequency and scope of performance of the item (5 pts)	Frequency and scope of performance of the applied item	Qualitative
	Viability of transmission of the subject of transmission (5 pts)	Viability of internal and external activities for transmission carried out by the subject of transmission	Qualitative

Public Notification of Cultural Heritage Administration (No 2019-149).

Table 5.2 Criteria to recognise a holder of intangible cultural heritage as a group holder of national intangible cultural heritage (unit: points)

Classification	*Factors*	*Method to evaluate factors*	*Remarks*
A. Ability for transmission (75 pts)			
Skill for transmission (50 pts)	Practice skill for the applicable item (40)	The level of practical skill of the applied item	Qualitative
	The level of understanding about the applied item (10 pts)	The level of understanding about the history and contents of the applied item	Qualitative
Activities for transmission (25 pts)	Durability of term during which a transmitting group has been operating (7 pts)	The term during which an incorporated, transmitting group has been operating	Quantitative
	The level of viability of transmitting activities within the transmitting group (8 pts)	Education for transmission within the transmitting group, period of meeting	Qualitative
	Record of transmitting activities (10 pts)	The record of transmitting activities such as performances, presentations, displays, and repair and restoration of cultural properties	Quantitative
B. Environment for transmission (20 pts)			
Infrastructure for transmission (10 pts)	The level of facilities of a transmitting group (3 pts)	The level of adequacy of essential facilities	Qualitative
	The level of equipment of a transmitting group (3 pts)	The level of the necessary equipment	Qualitative
	Human resources of a transmitting group (4 pts)	The required number of people in the group	Qualitative
Willingness to transmit (10 pts)	The holder's willingness to transmit his/her skill (10 pts)	The holder's willingness to transmit his/her skill and his/her future plan to transmit	Qualitative
The level of participation in transmitting activities (5 pts)			
Participation in transmitting activities (5 pts)	The level of participation in transmitting activities of the constituent members of a holder group (5 pts)	The level of participation in transmitting activities of the constituent members of a holder group	Qualitative

Public Notification of Cultural Heritage Administration (No 2019-149).

orchestra);[50] *Daemokjang* (traditional wooden architecture);[51] falconry (the living tradition of falconry);[52] *Jultagi* (tightrope walking);[53] *Taekkyeon* (a traditional Korean martial art);[54] weaving of *Mosi* (fine ramie) in the Hansan region;[55] *Arirang* (lyrical folk song in the Republic of Korea);[56] *Kimjang* (making and sharing kimchi in the Republic of Korea);[57] *Nongak* (community band music, dance, and rituals in the Republic of Korea);[58] *Juldarigi* (tug of war);[59] culture of *Jeju Haenyeo* (female divers);[60] *Ssirum/Ssireum* (traditional Korean wrestling);[61] and *Yeondeunghoe* (lantern lighting festival).[62]

Current industrial development has led to the gradual abandonment of agricultural activities to which some of forms of intangible cultural heritage, such as *Nongak*, are related. Moreover, the old generations familiar with agricultural industry have died. The Korean government vigorously tries to maintain cultural traditions, including intangible cultural heritage. However, the Korean government is not allowed to compel anyone to continue cultural traditions because of human rights.[63] In this context, intellectual property protection of intangible cultural heritage can give its holders an economic incentive to transmit and develop intangible cultural heritage in a creative way.

50 UNESCO inscribed in 2010 on the Representative List of Intangible Cultural Heritage of Humanity: Decision 5.COM 6.37.
51 UNESCO inscribed in 2010 on the Representative List of Intangible Cultural Heritage of Humanity: Decision 5.COM 6.36.
52 UNESCO inscribed in 2016 on the Representative List of Intangible Cultural Heritage of Humanity: Decision 11.COM 10.b.15. In 2010, the nomination for registration jointly consisted of 11 countries.
53 UNESCO inscribed in 2011 on the Representative List of Intangible Cultural Heritage of Humanity: Decision 6.COM 13.41.
54 UNESCO inscribed in 2011 on the Representative List of Intangible Cultural Heritage of Humanity: Decision 6.COM 13.44.
55 UNESCO inscribed in 2011 on the Representative List of Intangible Cultural Heritage of Humanity: Decision 6.COM 13.45.
56 UNESCO inscribed in 2012 on the Representative List of Intangible Cultural Heritage of Humanity: Decision 7.COM 11.27.
57 UNESCO inscribed in 2013 on the Representative List of Intangible Cultural Heritage of Humanity: Decision 8.COM 8.23.
58 UNESCO inscribed in 2014 on the Representative List of Intangible Cultural Heritage of Humanity: Decision 9.COM 10.36.
59 UNESCO inscribed in 2015 on the Representative List of Intangible Cultural Heritage of Humanity: Decision 10.COM 10.b.12. The nomination for registration jointly consisted of four countries: Cambodia, Philippines, Republic of Korea, and Viet Nam.
60 UNESCO inscribed in 2016 on the Representative List of Intangible Cultural Heritage of Humanity: Decision 11.COM 10.b.24.
61 UNESCO inscribed in 2018 on the Representative List of Intangible Cultural Heritage of Humanity: Decision 13.COM 10.b.41.
62 UNESCO inscribed in 2020 on the Representative List of Intangible Cultural Heritage of Humanity: Decision 15.COM 8.b.c.
63 Ingrida R Latoza, 'Amber Tears and Copyright Fears: The Inadequate Protection of Cultural Heritage in the United States' (2016) 15 *J Marshall Rev Intell Prop L* 543, 554–55.

Intellectual property protection of intangible cultural heritage

Legal sources

Article 49 of the Intangible Cultural Heritage Act, entitled Intellectual Property Protection of Intangible Cultural Heritage, provides that

> [t]he Administrator of the Cultural Heritage Administration shall protect [intangible cultural heritage] against acquisition of domestic and international patents, by such means as digitalizing the details and elements of the [intangible cultural heritage] transmitted and posting such details and elements on the website accredited under the Patent Cooperation Treaty, in order to prevent acquisition of domestic and international patents for the protection of such [intangible cultural heritage].

Furthermore, it also provides that

> [t]he Administrator of the Cultural Heritage Administration shall endeavour to create advanced knowledge or craftsmanship from [intangible cultural heritage], in order to facilitate the transmission of the [intangible cultural heritage] and shall take measures necessary to protect the [intellectual property] of successors, as provided for the Framework Act on Intellectual Property.

Patent protection of intangible cultural heritage

Article 2(1) of the Korean Patent Act defines *inventions* as 'highly advanced creation of technical ideas utilising the laws of nature'. Inventions are patentable when they meet the requirements of industrial application, novelty, and non-obviousness.[64] In other words, patents protect inventions, usually defined as any technical solution of a problem in any field of human activity which is new, involves an inventive step, and is industrially applicable. For example, the making and sharing process of *kimchi* cannot be protected by a patent because it does not meet novelty criteria. Inventions liable to contravene public order or morality or to jeopardise public health shall not be patentable. The duration of patent protection is 20 years from the date of the filing of the patent application, commencing upon registration of the patent right. As far as intangible cultural heritage is concerned with 'the protection of artistic designs, symbols, literature, or music', patent law is not applicable to those types of intangible cultural heritage since those types of works are not technological and thus not patentable subject-matter.[65]

Traditional knowledge of herbal or other oriental medicines can result in processes or medicines for curing human disease or other physical ailments.[66] For

64 Korean Patent Act, Article 29.
65 Paterson and Karjala (n 2) 645.
66 ibid.

instance, in the typical case in which a scientist came to know that a local group has found a certain plant effective in treating human disease, a pharmaceutical company can obtain a patent for a drug by extracting the active ingredient from the plant and creating an industrial process for producing the drug, and showing its effectiveness and safety.[67] Nothing in Korean patent law mandates sharing any of the profits with the source of the information that results in its discovery.[68] However, local groups can invalidate the patent based on the absence of novelty and non-obviousness.

A good illustration of patent invalidation due to lack of novelty may be Nestlé's *kimchi*-related case. In 1983, the Societé d'Assistance Technique pour Produits Nestlé SA applied for a patent on a process for producing vegetable juice through fermentation, similar to the process used to make *kimchi*, in 15 countries, including South Korea.[69] Its patent application was denied in South Korea because the patent application was similar to the process for making *kimchi* and thus did not meet the novelty requirement. However, except for its patent application in South Korea, patent applications for an identical process were granted in other countries. For instance, in the United States, the 'preparation of a flavoured solid vegetable and vegetable juice utilising hydrolysed protein'[70] was filed on 4 October 1983 and patented on 25 December 1984.[71] Patent law is territorial, and the United States did not take into account *foreign use* when assessing the novelty of the process. The reason why Nestlé obtained patents for the process in the other countries is that, in 1983, no official references (documentation) were available to prevent Nestlé from patenting the process of making vegetable juice through fermentation.[72]

Hence, to provide patent offices worldwide with official references documenting Korean traditional cultural food and foodways, thus preventing their misappropriation, the Intangible Cultural Heritage Act requires the Administrator of the Cultural Heritage Administration in South Korea to ensure the appropriate digitalisation and diffusion of such documentation. In other words, under the Intangible Cultural Heritage Act, the Administrator of the Cultural Heritage Administration in South Korea shall protect intangible cultural heritage against acquisition by domestic and international patents, by such means as digitalising the details and elements of the intangible cultural heritage transmitted, and posting such details

67 Rebecca S Eisenberg, 'Re-Examining the Role of Patents in Appropriating the Value of DNA Sequences (2000) 49 *Emory L J* 783, 785–786.

68 Paterson and Karjala (n 2) 645.

69 Hyun-cheol Kim, 'Web Site for Korean Recipes Launched' *The Korea Times* (28 July 2009) <http://www.koreatimes.co.kr/www/tech/2020/02/693_49220.html> accessed 8 December 2021.

70 Korean Intellectual Property Office, 'Introduction of Korean Traditional Knowledge Portal (KTKP)' (*Korean Intellectual Property Office*, March 2011) <https://www.wipo.int/edocs/mdocs/tk/en/wipo_tkdl_del_11/wipo_tkdl_del_11_ref_t9_4.pdf> accessed 8 December 2021.

71 United States Patent No 4,490,396 (25 December 1984).

72 Kim (n 69).

and elements on the website accredited under the Patent Cooperation Treaty.[73] In this regard, in order to protect intangible cultural heritage, the Administrator of the Cultural Heritage Administration shall take measures to prevent the acquisition of domestic and international patents of intangible cultural heritage.

The Korean government has established the Korea Traditional Food portal,[74] which is very pivotal for the Korea Food Research Institute (KFRI), to meet international standards on its promotion of Korean food and foodways. In 2009, the website was introduced by the KFRI through a year-long collaboration with the Korea Agency of Digital Opportunity and Promotion and the Korea Institute of Science and Technology.[75] Another significant website is the Korean Traditional Knowledge Portal.[76] This website was opened by the Korean Intellectual Property Office in December 2007. The website for traditional food and foodways in the Korean Traditional Knowledge Portal covers information on traditional food,

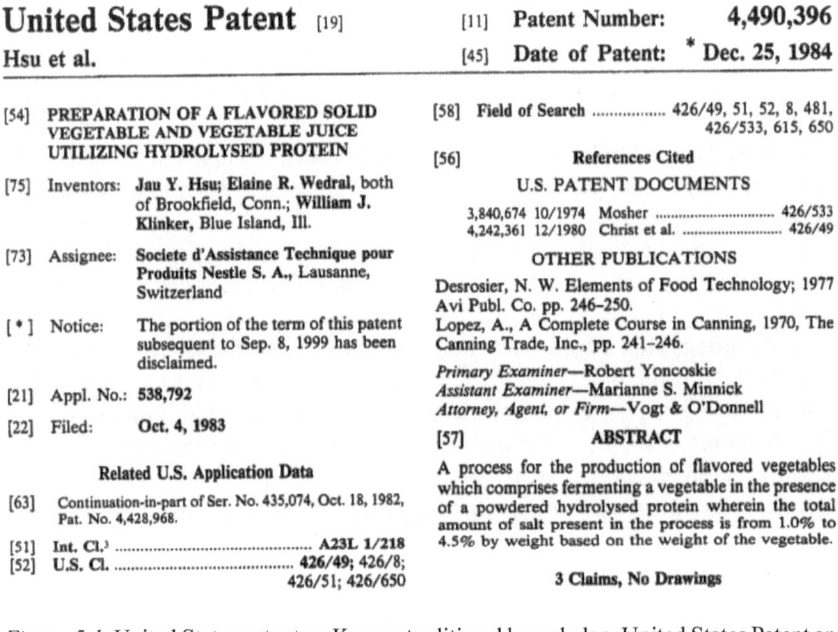

United States Patent [19]
Hsu et al.

[11] **Patent Number: 4,490,396**
[45] **Date of Patent: * Dec. 25, 1984**

[54] **PREPARATION OF A FLAVORED SOLID VEGETABLE AND VEGETABLE JUICE UTILIZING HYDROLYSED PROTEIN**

[75] Inventors: **Jau Y. Hsu; Elaine R. Wedral,** both of Brookfield, Conn.; **William J. Klinker,** Blue Island, Ill.

[73] Assignee: **Societe d'Assistance Technique pour Produits Nestle S. A.,** Lausanne, Switzerland

[*] Notice: The portion of the term of this patent subsequent to Sep. 8, 1999 has been disclaimed.

[21] Appl. No.: **538,792**

[22] Filed: **Oct. 4, 1983**

Related U.S. Application Data

[63] Continuation-in-part of Ser. No. 435,074, Oct. 18, 1982, Pat. No. 4,428,968.

[51] **Int. Cl.**[3] **A23L 1/218**
[52] **U.S. Cl.** **426/49; 426/8; 426/51; 426/650**
[58] **Field of Search** 426/49, 51, 52, 8, 481, 426/533, 615, 650

[56] **References Cited**

U.S. PATENT DOCUMENTS

3,840,674 10/1974 Mosher 426/533
4,242,361 12/1980 Christ et al. 426/49

OTHER PUBLICATIONS

Desrosier, N. W. Elements of Food Technology; 1977 Avi Publ. Co. pp. 246–250.
Lopez, A., A Complete Course in Canning, 1970, The Canning Trade, Inc., pp. 241–246.

Primary Examiner—Robert Yoncoskie
Assistant Examiner—Marianne S. Minnick
Attorney, Agent, or Firm—Vogt & O'Donnell

[57] **ABSTRACT**

A process for the production of flavored vegetables which comprises fermenting a vegetable in the presence of a powdered hydrolysed protein wherein the total amount of salt present in the process is from 1.0% to 4.5% by weight based on the weight of the vegetable.

3 Claims, No Drawings

Figure 5.1 United States patent on Korean traditional knowledge. United States Patent and Trademark Office, Preparation of a Flavored Solid Vegetable and Vegetable Juice Utilizing Hydrolysed Protein, United States Patent No 4,490,396.

73 Intangible Cultural Heritage Act, Article 49(1).
74 Korea Food Research Institute at <http://www.tradifood.net> accessed 8 December 2021.
75 Kim (n 69).
76 Korean Intellectual Property Office (1996) <http://www.koreantk.com> accessed 8 December 2021.

their recipes, and foodstuff.[77] By documenting traditional food and foodways in Korea, such initiatives aim at preventing applications for patenting such items domestically or overseas because they lack the novelty criteria.

Trade secret protection of intangible cultural heritage

According to Article 2 subparagraph 2 of the Korean Unfair Competition Prevention and Trade Secret, the term *trade secret* means information, including production methods, sale methods, or useful and technical or business information for business activity, that is not known publicly, is managed with secrecy, and has independent economic value. Therefore, in cases where information is secret, it is managed as a trade secret. A holder of intangible cultural heritage can develop a trade secret, e.g., the process of making a big gong (*jing*) is designated as intangible cultural heritage of Kyungsangnam-Do province.[78] In making the big gong, its master, Yong-Gu Lee, has applied modern technology instead of the traditional method of making the big gong.[79] In this regard, he may become a holder of the trade secret if the modern technology he has applied is kept secret.

The intrinsic features of the archetype of intangible cultural heritage cannot be protected as a trade secret. However, the extrinsic features of the intangible cultural heritage can be protected as a trade secret when they meet such requirements.

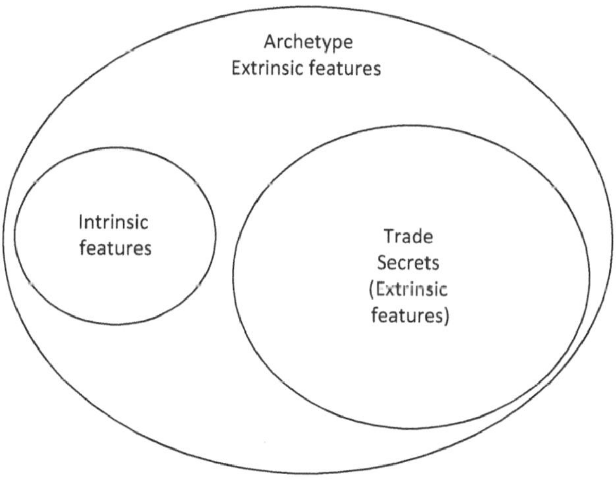

Figure 5.2 Archetype of intangible cultural heritage and trade secrets.

77 Lee (n 25) 565.

78 Kyungsangnam-Do province national intangible cultural heritage No 14.

79 Cultural Heritage Administration, 'Cultural Property Search' (Cultural Heritage Administration, 2000) http://www.heritage.go.kr/heri/cul/culSelectDetail.do?pageNo=1_1_1_1&ccbaCpno =2223800140000> accessed 8 December 2021.

Copyright protection of intangible cultural heritage

The global community has used copyright mechanisms to protect intangible cultural heritage.[80] This section discusses whether Korean copyright law is in line with the Korean intangible cultural heritage law. As a starting point, as intangible cultural heritage is passed from one generation to another, it is difficult to establish who contributes to the authorship unless it is attributable to one author. Moreover, copyright ownership vests initially in the author(s) of the copyrighted work.[81]

In some countries like the United States, for copyright protection to subsist, the work must be fixed in a tangible medium of expression.[82] Intangible cultural heritage refers to cultural traditions which are mostly oral and may have never been recorded in any tangible medium.[83] Yet, some oral traditions have been converted into and published in printed form by non-Indigenous and/or local groups' authors, which are afforded copyright protection.[84] For example, a photograph of an Indigenous person in traditional clothes affords copyright protection to the photographer but not the subject of the photograph.[85] A person who films or makes a documentary for intangible cultural heritage is the author of the film. Therefore, the holder/user of the intangible cultural heritage is neither the author of the photograph nor the film.

Article 2(1) of the Korean Copyright Act defines *work* as 'an original production that expresses an idea and an emotion of a human being'.[86] The term *author* refers to a person who makes an original production that expresses human ideas and emotions.[87] Therefore, expression of an author's ideas or emotions does not need to be fixed to a tangible medium for copyright protection to subsist, so an impromptu performance, a lecture, or dancing without any basic tangible material can be protected under the Korean Copyright Act. Article 18.4 (1) footnote 7 of the United States–Korea Free Trade Agreement (KORUS FTA) sets that 'The Parties reaffirm that it is a matter for each Party's law to prescribe that works and phonograms shall not be protected by copyright unless they have been fixed

80 Janet Blake, *Developing a New Standard-Setting Instrument for the Safeguard of the Intangible Cultural Heritage: Elements for Consideration* (UNESCO Publishing 2001) 18.

81 Gyooho Lee, *Understanding Intellectual Property, Pakyoungsa* (2020) (ISBN: 979-11-303-3706-7) 9-22; Korean Copyright Act, Article 2(2).

82 17 US Code § 102.

83 Paterson and Karjala (n 2) 639.

84 See 17 USC 103(b)(2000) prescribing that 'The copyright in a compilation or derivative work extends only to the material contributed by the author of such work, as distinguished from the pre-existing material employed in the work, and does not imply any exclusive right in the pre-existing material. The copyright in such work is independent of, and does not affect or enlarge the scope, duration, ownership, or subsistence of, any copyright protection in the pre-existing material'.

85 See *Kaplan v the Stock Market Photo Agency Inc.*, 133 F Supp2d 317, 323 (S.D.N.Y. 2001) holding that copyright in a photograph stems from the author's original conception of his subject, not the subject itself, and copyrightable elements include posing of the subjects, lighting, angle, selection of film and camera, and evoking the desired expression); cf. *Burrow-Giles Lithographic Co v Sarony* 111 US 53, 60 (1884) holding that a photograph of Oscar Wilde is an original work of art, the product of the plaintiff's [Sarony's] intellectual invention, of which the claimant is the author.

86 Korean Copyright Act, Article 2(1).

87 ibid Article 2(2).

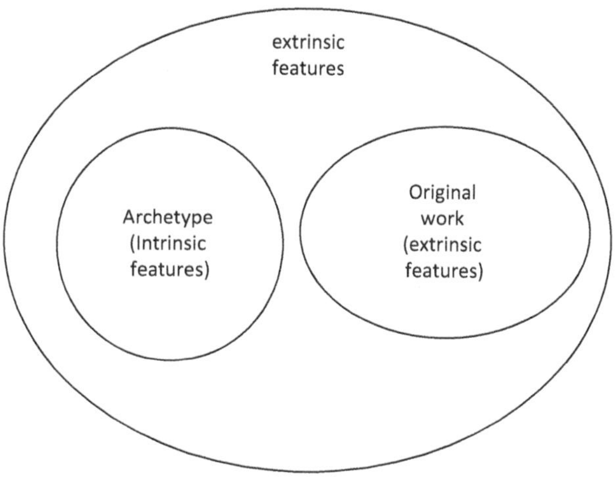

Figure 5.3 Copyrightable subject-matter of intangible cultural heritage.

in some material form'. Hence, this permits the Korean Copyright Act's stance, which does not require fixation to a tangible medium of expression for copyright protection.

An archetype of intangible cultural heritage cannot be protected by copyright law because it cannot be an original expression of an idea or emotion of an intangible cultural heritage holder. However, among the elements or features of intangible cultural heritage, its extrinsic elements or features are theoretically original and, thus, protectable by copyright law. This is because the extrinsic elements or features of intangible cultural heritage do not constitute the value of specific intangible cultural heritage. As the scope of the intrinsic features of intangible cultural heritage becomes narrower, its extrinsic ones are bigger, resulting in affording a greater copyrightable chance to a work of intangible cultural heritage holder(s). Nonetheless, the practice will often be that no one knows who took part in creating the original expressive aspect of intangible cultural heritage, and therefore, the absence of authorship and consequently ownership agreement among the joint authors makes reliance on a copyright approach difficult.[88] The owner of a copyright work is afforded protection for the limited time of the author's life plus 70 years, whereas intangible cultural heritage groups intend to preserve it indefinitely.[89] If each country as well as the international community fail to preserve the intangible cultural heritage of a local group indefinitely, the definitive loss throughout the world of languages, know-how, and customs can result in 'the progressive impoverishment of human society'.[90]

88 Susan Scafidi, *Intellectual Property and Cultural Products* (2001) 81 *B U L Rev* 793, 808.
89 Latoza (n 63) 554–555.
90 Federico Lenzerini, 'Intangible Cultural Heritage: The Living Culture of Peoples' (2011) 22(1) *EJIL* 101, 102.

Requirements under the Korean Copyright Act prevent it from being applied to intangible cultural heritage unless the intangible cultural heritage is just sufficiently altered to be afforded copyright protection. Copyright protection in Korea is linked to originality,[91] authorship,[92] and its term of duration.[93] In addition, the focus on economic incentives is another factor which precludes copyright law from being applied to intangible cultural heritage.[94] It should be noted that copyright law gives authors an economic incentive to create a copyrighted work whereas the main focus of the Intangible Cultural Heritage Act is to give intangible cultural heritage holders or intangible cultural heritage groups an incentive to preserve and promote intangible cultural heritage.[95]

Protection of intangible cultural heritage holders as performers

Intangible cultural heritage holders can be protected as performers. The term *performer* refers to

> a person who gives a stage performance by expressing works through acting, dancing, musical playing, singing, narrating, reciting or other artistic means or by expressing things other than works in a similar way, including a person who conducts, directs or supervises a stage performance.[96]

For example, a singer or a drummer of *Pansori* (also spelled p'ansori),[97] which is a Korean genre of musical storytelling performed by a vocalist and a drummer, can be protected as a performer under the current copyright law regime. However, collective management organisations do not appear to be efficient

91 Erin K Slattery, 'Preserving the United States' Intangible Cultural Heritage: An Evaluation of the 2003 UNESCO Convention of the Intangible Cultural Heritage as a Means to Overcome the Problems Posed by Intellectual Property Law' (2006) 16 *DePaul-LCA J Art &Ent L &Pol'y* 201, 231. Certain aspects of intangible cultural heritage such as rituals, songs, and stories have developed within a specific group over generations. For some groups, originality contradicts the mission of Indigenous people for example. Instead, accuracy and faithful transmissions are valued. See Latoza (n 63) 553.

92 Slattery (n 91) 232.

93 ibid 231.

94 Slattery (n 91) 231; Latoza (n 63) 553.

95 Rosemary Coombe, 'Fear, Hope, and Longing for the Future of Authorship and a Revitalized Public Domain in Global Regimes of Intellectual Property' (2003) 52 *DePaul L Rev* 1171.

96 Korean Copyright Act, Article 2(4).

97 '*Pansori* means that one singer tells a long story mixed with sori (singings), aniri (words), neoreumsae (gestures) to the beat of a drummer … presumed that pansori came into being at least before King Sukjong given the contents of Chunhyangga composed by Yu Jin-han in the 30th year of King Yeongjo of Joseon, or originated from Gwangdaesohakjihui seen in documents early in Joseon Dynasty, or dated back to Silla Era when pannoreum had been performed. Pansori is composed of slow and fast beats such as jinyangjo (adagio), jungmori, jungjungmori (moderato), *hwimori*, in accordance with situations'. Classification: Important (national) Intangible Cultural Heritage No 5.

for the protection of holders of intangible cultural heritage except for performers of traditional music, whose performances are collectively managed by the Federation of Korean Music Performers.[98] However, some intangible cultural heritages are not protectable under current Korean copyright law. A good illustration is *Akgijang* (making musical instruments),[99] which does not fall within the definition of a performer under the Copyright Act because it is a technique for making musical instruments or makers of musical instruments.

Performers' rights consist of moral rights and economic rights. Performers' moral rights are comprised of the right of paternity and the right of integrity. In regard to the right of paternity, a 'performer shall have the right to indicate his real name or pseudonym on the performance or reproduction of his performance'.[100] Those who intend to exploit a performance shall indicate the real name or pseudonym of the performer as it has been indicated insofar as there is no special declaration of intention by the performer.[101] If it is recognised as unavoidable in view of the character of the performance, and the purpose and form of exploitation, those who intend to exploit a performance do not need to indicate the real name or pseudonym of the performer.[102] A 'performer shall have the right to preserve the integrity of the content, form and title of his work'.[103] Moral rights of a performer shall belong exclusively to the performer.[104] A performer has economic rights such as the right of reproduction, right of distribution, right of rental, right of public performance, right of broadcasting, right of interactive transmission, right of remuneration to be paid by broadcasting organisations, right of remuneration to be paid by digital audio transmission organisations, and right of remuneration to be paid by persons doing public performances using commercial phonograms on which the performance of a performer is recorded. In the case of communal performers, that is, two or more performers performing 'jointly in a chorus, concert, or drama, etc., the rights of performers (excluding the performer's moral right of performers) … shall be exercised by a representative elected by the joint performers'.[105] Where such a representative is not elected, the conductor or director shall exercise the rights of the performers.[106] If the scope of a group who has performed intangible cultural heritage cannot be identified easily, its representative is expected to not be elected. As noted previously, sometimes is difficult to know who was involved in performing intangible cultural heritage. A good example is *Nong-Ak*

98 Federation of Korean Music Performers at <https://www.fkmp.kr/eng/> accessed 8 December 2021.
99 *Akgijang* (Classification: Important (national) Intangible Cultural Heritage No 42).
100 Korean Copyright Act, Article 66(1).
101 ibid Article 66(2).
102 ibid.
103 ibid Article 67.
104 ibid Article 68.
105 ibid Article 77(1).
106 ibid.

(Community Band Music, Dance, and Rituals in the Republic of Korea).[107] In this case, intangible cultural heritage local groups cannot exercise the rights of the performers because there is no conductor or director. In other words, intangible cultural heritage holders may be protectable under a neighbouring right system if they are easily identified and countable.

Performers' moral rights to a joint performance may not be exercised without the unanimous agreement of all the performers concerned. In such cases, each of the performers may not, in bad faith, prevent the agreement from being reached.[108] When it comes to joint performances of intangible cultural heritage holders, they need to consider the exercise of their moral rights to their joint performance. Potentially, joint performers may designate one of them as a representative in the exercise of their moral rights.[109] Limitations imposed on the representation, if any, shall not be effective against a *bona fide* third person.[110]

Trade mark protection of intangible cultural heritage

The makers of the traditional musical instruments (*Akgijang*) such as big gongs (*Jing*), drums (*Buk*), and small gongs (*KKwaenggwari*) can be holders of intangible cultural heritage. Usually, those musical instruments have no brand name and are advertised by the name of a holder of intangible cultural heritage and/or endorsed by the holder. Yet, they typically have no brand name because the holder of intangible cultural heritage is not financially capable of filing and maintaining a trade mark. In this regard, local governments enable its makers to use geographical indication (GI) such as GI certification marks[111] and GI collective marks.[112] Nonetheless, if the name of a holder of intangible cultural heritage becomes well-known, the Korean Unfair Competition Prevention and Trade Secret Protection Act can be used.

107 *Nong-Ak* originated from communal rites and rustic entertainments that promoted harmony as people gathered to pray for peace and prosperity; it has evolved into a representative performing art genre of Korea. *Nong-Ak* has been practiced for various purposes, such as appeasing gods, chasing evil spirits and seeking blessings, praying for a rich harvest in spring, celebrating the harvest in autumn festivals, and professional entertainment.

108 Korean Copyright Act, Articles 77(3) and 15(1). Article 77 (3) states that '[t]he provisions of Article 15 shall apply *mutatis mutandis* to the exercise of the moral rights of joint performers'.

109 ibid Articles 77(3) and 15(2).

110 ibid Articles 77(3) and 15(3).

111 Korean Trademark Act, Article 2(1) 4 notes that the term *geographical indication* refers to 'an indication used to identify goods produced, manufactured, or processed in a specific area in cases where a certain quality, reputation or other characteristic of goods has essentially originated from such specific area'. The term *geographical certification mark* means 'a certification mark with geographical indication used by a person who carries on the business of certifying the quality, origin, mode of production, or other characters of goods in order to certify whether the goods of a person who carries on the business of producing, manufacturing or processing goods satisfy specified geographical characters'. Korean Trademark Act, Article 2(1) 4-2.

112 Available for goods and not for services.

Geographical indications protection of intangible cultural heritage

Traditional foodways have frequently some bearing on GIs under the Agricultural and Fishery Quality Control Act.[113] GI rights do not aim to encourage innovation and individual originality by granting a monopoly for a limited period. Rather, they represent commonly used geographical names, establish permanent communal rights, and purport to protect 'old knowledge'.[114] It should be noted that GIs for goods used by the holder of intangible cultural heritage are relevant to the scope of the intrinsic features of intangible cultural heritage because GIs mandate the history of traditional foodways.

Conclusion

By examining the harmonisation between the Intangible Cultural Heritage Act and intellectual property laws, it seems that there are several legal challenges in terms of intangible cultural heritage and intellectual property. Those are, first, to promote the transparency of the process for the recognition and designation of holders of intangible cultural heritage; second, to clearly determine the scope of the terms, *transmission, and intrinsic features*; third, to strike a balance between intangible cultural heritage and intellectual property rights; and fourth, to preserve and promote transboundary intangible cultural heritage.

Traditional foodways such as *Kimjang* can be related to intangible cultural heritage such as traditional knowledge concerning Korean medicine, agriculture, fishery, and so on; traditional ways of life concerning food; social rituals; and/or traditional festivals. The transmission of the archetype of intangible cultural heritage is one of the pivotal factors for the Korean government to approve cultural heritage as intangible cultural heritage.[115] This is because the term *archetype* refers to intrinsic features constituting the value of specific intangible cultural heritage.[116]

Whether or not intangible cultural heritage maintains and transmits its archetype depends upon whether its intrinsic features constituting the value of specific

113 Agricultural and Fishery Quality Control Act, Act No 17618, revised on 8 December 2020, Article 2(1) 8 prescribes that 'The term "geographical indication" means, where the reputation, quality and other distinctive features of agricultural and fishery products or processed agricultural and fishery products referred to in subparagraph 13 fundamentally result from the geographical characteristics of a specific region, an indication describing that the relevant agricultural and fishery products or processed agricultural and fishery products have been produced, made or processed in the specific region'.

114 Graham Dutfield, 'Protecting Traditional Knowledge and Folklore: A Review of Progress in Diplomacy and Policy Formulation' (2003) United Nations Conference on Trade and Development-International Center for Trade and Sustainable Development Project on Intellectual Property Rights and Sustainable Development Issue Paper No 1, 23.

115 Lee, *Understanding Intellectual Property, Pakyoungsa* (n 81) 569.

116 Intangible Cultural Heritage Act, Article 2(2).

intangible cultural heritage have been identical over several generations.[117] The matter is that the current definition of intellectual property[118] seems to create tensions between the safeguarding and promotion of intangible cultural heritage and the protection of intellectual property holders. This is so because it appears to be inconsistent with the intellectual property protection of its holders as long as it maintains, transmits, and falls within its archetype.[119] However, to the extent to which the creations or creative activities of its holder(s) constitute its extrinsic features, the holder(s) can maintain and transmit its archetype and also be afforded intellectual property rights.[120] For instance, as far as the royal cuisine of the Chosun Dynasty[121] is concerned, how to make food and what to wear in the course of serving food are extrinsic features of the intangible cultural heritage.[122] The archetype of royal cuisine of the Chosun Dynasty is to maintain and transmit its foodways and the constitution of its food.[123] Therefore, it is very important to set up more clear-cut criteria to determine the scope of intrinsic features of intangible cultural heritage and to encourage its holders to create intellectual property and intellectual property rights in terms of its extrinsic features. In this regard, the criteria to determine the archetype of intangible cultural heritage are very important, so that the archetype of intangible cultural heritage constitutes the intrinsic features of the intangible cultural heritage.

In spite of efforts of the global community to adopt a proper mechanism to protect intangible cultural heritage under copyright law, and other intellectual property rights, an inventory system may be the only option available.[124] The 2003 Convention supports an inventory system to document intangible cultural heritage so as to preserve it.[125] Some problems with inventory systems are related to the inherent difficulty in creating them, value judgements to determine what is included on the list, and local groups' and Indigenous people's reluctance to participate in this project.[126] Among these difficulties, the biggest practical hurdle is that some local groups are hesitant to be inventoried due to their intent to maintain cultural secrecy.[127] Current industrial development has deviated from agricultural industry which some intangible cultural heritage is related to, and the old generations familiar with agricultural industry have died. These situations drive the Korean government to vigorously try to maintain cultural traditions, including

117 Lee, *Understanding Intellectual Property, Pakyoungsa* (n 81) 569.
118 Framework Act on Intellectual Property, Articles 3(1) and (3).
119 Lee, *Understanding Intellectual Property, Pakyoungsa* (n 81) 569.
120 ibid.
121 No 38 of National Intangible Cultural Property in Korea.
122 Lee, *Understanding Intellectual Property, Pakyoungsa* (n 81) 569.
123 ibid.
124 Slattery (n 91) 24.
125 ibid.
126 Latoza (n 63) 556.
127 Slattery (n 91) 245–250; Latoza (n 63) 556.

intangible cultural heritage. Furthermore, the Korean government is not allowed to compel anyone to continue cultural traditions due to human rights.[128]

While UNESCO serves an important role in providing model action plans, each nation can launch and develop its own plans to preserve and promote intangible cultural heritage. A worldwide escrow system can help an individual holder of intangible cultural heritage protect his/her trade secrets if they do not fall within the archetype of intangible cultural heritage. In this regard, it is proposed that the governmental agencies and civic groups in Korea should set up a code of legal ethics for the restoration of the performance of holders of intangible cultural heritage covering new technology such as artificial intelligence, 3D printing, or robots. The government-funded agencies and civic groups can contribute to this goal.[129] Another proposal is that the central government and/or government-funded agencies should encourage local governments to register GI certification marks for holders of intangible cultural heritage. Furthermore, the global federation of collective management organisations is necessary to internationally preserve and promote intangible cultural heritage.

References

Arezzo E, 'Struggling Around the "Natural" Divide: The Protection of Tangible and Intangible Indigenous Property' (2007) 25 *Cardozo Arts & Ent L J* 367

Blake J, *Developing a New Standard-Setting Instrument for the Safeguard of the Intangible Cultural Heritage: Elements for Consideration* (UNESCO Publishing, 2001)

Coombe R, 'Fear, Hope, and Longing for the Future of Authorship and A Revitalized Public Domain in Global Regimes of Intellectual Property' (2003) 52 *DePaul L Rev* 1171

Dutfield G, 'Protecting Traditional Knowledge and Folklore: A Review of Progress in Diplomacy and Policy Formulation, United Nations Conference on Trade and Development-International Center for Trade and Sustainable Development Project on Intellectual Property Rights and Sustainable Development' (2003) Issue Paper No 1

Eisenberg R, 'Re-Examining the Role of Patents in Appropriating the Value of DNA Sequences' (2000) 49 *Emory L J* 783

Kim H, 'Web Site for Korean Recipes Launched' *Korea Times* (July 28, 2009)

Latoza I, 'Amber Tears and Copyright Fears: The Inadequate Protection of Cultural Heritage in the United States' (2016) 15 *J Marshall Rev Intell Prop L* 8

Lee G, 'How to Protect Traditional Food and Foodways Effectively in Terms of Intangible Cultural Heritage and Intellectual Property Laws in the Republic of Korea' (2018) 24 *Int'l J Cult Prop* 543

——— 'Understanding Intellectual Property, Pakyoungsa' (2020) (ISBN: 979-11-303-3706-7) 9–22

Lenzerini F, 'Intangible Cultural Heritage: The Living Culture of Peoples' (2011) 22(1) *EJIL* 101

128 Latoza (n 63) 557.
129 ibid.

Marden E, 'The Neem Tree Patent: International Conflict over the Commodification of Life' (1999) 22 *B C Int'l Comp L Rev* 279

Paterson R and Karjala D, 'Looking Beyond Intellectual Property in Resolving Protection of the Intangible Cultural Heritage of Indigenous Peoples' (2003) 11 *Cardozo J Int'l & Comp L* 633

Pager S, 'Traditional Knowledge Rights and Wrongs' (2016) 20 *Va J L & Tech* 82

Roht-Arriaza N, 'Of Seeds and Shamans: The Appropriation of the Scientific and Technical Knowledge of Indigenous and Local Communities' (1996) 17 *Mich J Int'l L* 919

Yu P K, 'Cultural Relics, Intellectual Property, and Intangible Heritage' [2008] *Temple Law Review* 433

WIPO, 'The Protection of Traditional Cultural Expressions: Draft Articles' 28th session WIPO/GRTK/IC/28/6 (June 2, 2014)

——— 'Protection of Traditional Knowledge and Genetic Resources: A Bottom-up Approach to Development' (*WIPO Mag*, November–December 2003)

Scafidi S, 'Intellectual Property and Cultural Products' (2001) 81 *B UL Rev* 793

Slattery E, 'Preserving the United States' Intangible Cultural Heritage: An Evaluation of the 2003 UNESCO Convention of the Intangible Cultural Heritage as a Means to Overcome the Problems Posed by Intellectual Property Law' (2006) 16 *DePaul-LCA JATIP* 201

6 Cross-border safeguarding of intangible cultural heritage through geographical indications and EU collective marks

The issue

Benedetta Ubertazzi

Introduction

The process of globalisation facilitated by communication technologies has led to enhanced interaction between cultures. Yet, this process has raised the risk of the misappropriation of intangible cultural expressions all over the world. Misappropriations in this regard occur when heritage-practising communities consider individual members of the community, the state, tour operators, researchers, or other outside persons to have inappropriately obtained unjust reward through the exploitation of intangible cultural heritage. Misappropriations of intangible cultural heritage can consist in, among other things, wide-scale copying of traditional designs, motifs, symbols, and artworks for commercial gain without the knowledge or permission of communities. Misappropriation typically occurs in countries other than the state of origin of said culture and is therefore of a transnational nature.[1] The Convention for the Safeguarding of the Intangible Cultural Heritage (the 2003 Convention) was adopted in the UNESCO framework,[2]

1 Benedetta Ubertazzi, 'Territorial and Universal Protection of Intangible Cultural Heritage from Misappropriation' (2010) 8 *NZYIL* 69.

2 Janet Blake, *Commentary on the 2003 UNESCO Convention on the Safeguarding of the Intangible Cultural Heritage* (Institute of Art and Law 2006); Angélica Sola, '8 Quelques Réflexions à Propos de la Convention pour la Sauvegarde du Patrimoine Culturel Immaterial' in Tullio Socvazzi (ed), *Le Patrimoine Culturel del'humanité* (Martinus Nijhoff Publishers 2008) 487; Burra Srinivas, 'The UNESCO Convention for the Safeguarding of the Intangible Cultural Heritage' in Socvazzi (n 2) 529; Lauso Zagato, 'La Convenzione sulla Protezione del Patrimonio Culturale Intangibile' in Lauso Zagato (ed), *Le Identità Culturali nei Recenti Strumenti UNESCO, Un Approccio Nuovo alla Costruzione della Pace?* (CEDAM 2008); Toshiyuki Kono and Stefan Wrbka, 'General Report: Protection and Preservation of Cultural Heritage' in Toshiyuki Kono (ed), *The Impact of Uniform Laws on the Protection of Cultural Heritage and the Preservation of Cultural Heritage in the 21st Century* (Martinus Nijhoff Publishers 2010); Benedetta Ubertazzi, 'Su Alcuni Aspetti Problematici della Convenzione per la Salvaguardia del Patrimonio Intangibile' [2011] *Rivista di Diritto Internazionale* 777; Francesco Francioni, 'The Human Dimension of International Cultural Heritage

DOI: 10.4324/9781003345237-7

and aims at safeguarding intangible cultural heritage[3] domestically and internationally.

However, the 2003 Convention lacks rules on its safeguarding from transnational misappropriations. With the absence of these rules, state parties have adopted measures to safeguard cross-border intangible cultural heritage such as intellectual property rights protected geographical indications (GIs). This aligns with recent suggestions by the UNESCO Intergovernmental Committee for the Safeguarding of Intangible Cultural Heritage (Committee) that highlighted the high risk of intangible cultural heritage misappropriation and encouraged states parties to adopt collective intellectual property rights to mitigate this risk. Yet, since intellectual property rights are territorial and provide protection only in the country for which they are registered, implementing intellectual property rights to safeguard intangible cultural heritage from transnational misappropriation raises two interrelated problems. Therefore, this chapter will refer to national or regional legal frameworks providing examples of such international challenges.

Firstly, intellectual property rights on intangible cultural heritage must be *registered* not only in the country of origin, but also in each other state for which protection is required. For instance, states parties to the 2003 Convention that are non-EU member states register not only intellectual property rights in the country of origin of the relevant intangible cultural heritage (domestically), but also in the European Union (EU). The latter gives rise to unitary intellectual property rights, the effects of which cover the entire EU territory (Article 118 of the Treaty on the Functioning of the European Union (TFEU)).[4] Secondly, intellectual property rights must be *enforced* not only in the country of origin, but also in each state for which protection is required. For instance, states parties to the 2003 Convention that are non-EU member states, which have registered domestic GIs and EU GIs, must enforce these rights not only in their country of origin but also in every state of the entire EU territory to effectively protect their intangible cultural heritage from transnational misappropriations. In fact, unlike other EU unitary intellectual property rights, such as EU trade marks or designs, the cross-border enforcement

Law: An Introduction' (2011) 22(1) *Eur J Int'l Law* 9; Francesco Francioni, 'Public and Private in the International Protection of Global Cultural Goods' (2012) 23(3) *EJIL* 719; Tullio Scovazzi, Benedetta Ubertazzi and Lauso Zagato (eds), *Il Patrimonio Culturale Intangibile nelle sue Diverse Dimensioni* (Vol 71) (Giuffrè 2012); Lucas Lixinski, *Intangible Cultural Heritage in International Law* (OUP 2013).

3 Tullio Scovazzi, 'La Definizione di Patrimonio Culturale Intangibile' in Gaetano Golinelli et al., *Nuove Forme di Valorizzazione e Promozione delle Aree Rurali Italiane – Il Sistema* (UNESCO 2011). For an anthropological perspective, see Chiara Bortolotto, 'Introduzione. Il processo di Definizione del Concetto di "Patrimonio Culturale Immateriale". Elementi per una Riflessione' in Chiara Bortolotto (ed), *Il Patrimonio Immateriale Secondo l'UNESCO: Analisi e Prospettive* (Poligrafico dello Stato 2008).

4 The European Commission officially registers EU GIs and GIview is the database, which is developed and maintained by the European Union Intellectual Property Office (EUIPO). The EUIPO manages the registration of the EU trade mark and the registered EU design.

of EU GIs in transnational infringement cases is regulated individually by each EU member state.

While the relevant EU Regulations on unitary trade marks or designs determine, in a uniform way, the courts that are competent to adjudicate cross-border disputes, the Regulation on EU GIs considers only their domestic enforcement in purely national infringement cases but does not regulate the cross-border enforcement of GIs in transnational infringement situations. Therefore, by not including any rules on international jurisdiction and applicable law, it may need to be integrated by the EU Brussels system. This system includes an exclusive jurisdiction rule, which for intellectual property rights cannot be submitted to an international court competent to adjudicate a dispute in its entirety.[5] Thus, it obliges the interested parties first to register and second to defend. This leads to a multiplication of parallel proceedings, raising issues of conflicting judgments, inequalities between large multinational companies and small and medium-sized enterprises, and registration and litigation costs.

Intangible cultural heritage and intellectual property rights

The main purpose of the 2003 Convention is to safeguard intangible cultural heritage at an international and domestic level. States parties are obliged to submit periodic report progress on the implementation of the 2003 Convention to the Committee.[6] They are encouraged to cooperate by sharing information and expertise with other parties, to submit multinational safeguarding projects and nominations to the 2003 Convention's Lists,[7] and to apply for international assistance.[8]

Domestically, states must take the necessary safeguarding measures for intangible cultural heritage within their territory,[9] e.g., raising awareness to make intangible cultural heritage generally better known, ensuring appropriate access to it, encouraging respect and appreciation for intangible cultural heritage, and informing the public about the function of intangible cultural heritage in society and the importance of its safeguarding.[10] Furthermore, states parties should, with the help of public participation, identify, define, and categorise intangible cultural heritage within their territory[11] and should create a legal and administrative context to support the safeguarding of intangible cultural heritage.[12]

At the cross-border level, safeguarding measures are not included in the scope of the 2003 Convention, despite it highlighting the importance of safeguarding

5 Benedetta Ubertazzi, *Exclusive Jurisdiction in Intellectual Property* (Mohr Siebeck 2012).
6 UNESCO 2003 Convention for the Safeguarding of the Intangible Cultural Heritage (hereinafter the 2003 Convention), Article 29.
7 ibid Articles 16, 17 and 18.
8 ibid Article 19 onwards.
9 ibid Articles 11(a) and 15.
10 ibid Articles 1(b) and 13(d)ii.
11 ibid Articles 11 and 12.
12 ibid Article 13.

intangible cultural heritage, not only for the territorial state of origin, but also for the international community in its entirety.[13] Cases of intangible cultural heritage misappropriation typically occur in countries other than the state of origin of the specific intangible cultural heritage.[14] Therefore, measures aimed at safeguarding intangible cultural heritage in its country of origin and in other countries are needed; among these measures stand intellectual property rights. These latter require the identification of the physical author of the intellectual subject matter to be protected, and they are only granted for a limited duration. In contrast, for intangible cultural heritage, a single owner may not be ascertained; intangible cultural heritage is transmitted from generation to generation and usually is not incorporated into a physical form. For many years, this impeded the World Intellectual Property Organization (WIPO), the conference of the parties negotiating the Convention on Biological Diversity (CBD), and the World Trade Organization (WTO) from adopting treaties to extend intellectual property rights to folklore, traditional cultural expressions, and traditional knowledge.[15] Indeed, protection of these elements through *sui generis* intellectual property rights was recently introduced at the international level through the Nagoya Protocol to the CBD.[16]

The 2003 Convention establishes that nothing within it may be interpreted as 'b) affecting the rights and obligations of States Parties deriving from any international instrument relating to intellectual property rights'.[17] The inscription of intangible cultural heritage elements on the UNESCO Lists therefore does not impose the recognition of any corresponding intellectual property rights, nor a determination of ownership of those intellectual property rights; yet, they are extremely relevant to intangible cultural heritage. In fact, the Committee encourages states parties to adopt intellectual property rights as measures to mitigate

13 The 2003 Convention preamble, Articles 1, 5, 11–13, 17.3, and 23.1.

14 Ubertazzi, 'Territorial and Universal Protection of Intangible Cultural Heritage from Misappropriation' (n 1); Benedetta Ubertazzi, 'Non-Governmental Organizations and the 2013 Session of the UNESCO Intangible Cultural Heritage Committee' [2013] *Italian Y B Int'l L* 299.

15 Benedetta Ubertazzi, 'Una Nuova Condizione per L'iscrizione nelle Liste del Patrimonio Culturale Intangibile' [2012] *Rivista di Diritto Internazionale* 469; Antonietta Di Blasé, 'I Diritti di Proprietà Intellettuale Applicabili alla Cultura Indigena e Tradizionale' (2007) 23 *Comunicazioni e Studi* 511; Zagato (n 2) 60; Silke von Lewinski, *Indigenous Heritage and Intellectual Property: Genetic Resources, Traditional Knowledge and Folklore* (Kluwer Law International 2008); Toshiyuki Kono, 'Intangible Cultural Heritage and Intellectual Property: Communities, Cultural Diversity and Sustainable Development' in Toshiyuki Kono (ed), *Intangible Cultural Heritage and Intellectual Property: Communities, Cultural Diversity and Sustainable Development* (Intersentia 2009); Reto Hilty, *Rationales for the Legal Protection of Intangible Goods and Cultural Heritage* (Competition & Tax Law Research Paper No. 09-10, Max Planck Institute for Intellectual Property 2009) 833; Alexander Peukert, 'Individual Multiple and Collective Ownership of Intellectual Property Rights: Which Impact on Exclusivity?' in Annette Kur and Vytautas Mizaras (eds), *The Structure of Intellectual Property: Can One Size Fit All?* (Edward Elgar 2011); Scovazzi, 'La Definizione di Patrimonio Culturale Intangibile' (n 3) 311.

16 Kono and Wrbka (n 2) 205.

17 The 2003 Convention, Article 3.

the risk of over-commercialisation and misappropriation of intangible cultural heritage, considering their obligations to recognise, promote, and enhance the importance of intangible cultural heritage as a strategic resource for sustainable development. According to the Committee, intellectual property rights

> promote creativity, innovation and utilisation of intangible cultural heritage while ensuring that the bearers of such heritage, whether communities, groups or individuals, benefit from the protection of the moral and material interests resulting from the use or adaptation of that heritage.[18]

Additionally, intellectual property rights 'ensure that the rights of the communities, groups or individuals that create, bear and transmit their intangible cultural heritage are duly protected from misappropriation or abuse of their knowledge and skills'.[19] Thus, intellectual property rights at the international and domestic level mitigate the risks of over-commercialisation and misappropriation of intangible cultural heritage.

Over-commercialisation is an over-exploitation of natural resources with the aim of producing goods and services for unsustainable sale, bartering, or tourism.[20] Commercial activities are intrinsic to certain forms of intangible cultural heritage, such as handicrafts and other practices that create products for sale or barter. These elements are not excluded from consideration under the 2003 Convention unlike elements incompatible with human rights or sustainable development. Much intangible cultural heritage would not continue to be viable if there were no remuneration[21] for time and investments made in its practice and transmission.[22] Ensuring that communities benefit economically from practising their intangible cultural heritage can motivate them to continue doing so.

18 Intergovernmental Committee for The Safeguarding of The Intangible Cultural Heritage, Tenth session, Windhoek, Namibia, 30 November to 4 December 2015, Item 14.a of the Provisional Agenda: Draft amendments to the Operational Directives on safeguarding intangible cultural heritage and sustainable development, para 173. See Expert meeting on safeguarding intangible cultural heritage and sustainable development at the national level, Istanbul, Turkey, 29 September to 1 October 2014; Draft Operational Directives on 'Safeguarding intangible cultural heritage and sustainable development at the national level', para 3. See the current version of the Operational Directives for the implementation of the 2003 Convention, as amended (6.GA, 2016) paras 104 and 173.

19 ibid Intergovernmental Committee for the Safeguarding of The Intangible Cultural Heritage.

20 ibid. See also Operational Directives (2016) paras 116 and 117.

21 Intangible cultural heritage consists of knowledge, skills, and practices rather than products, yet the sale of the resulting products and services has often supported the continued practice and transmission thereof. For instance, the Khmer court supported the Royal Ballet of Cambodia, for over 1,000 years, remunerating the dancers and providing them with a space to train in the palace.

22 UNESCO Living Human Treasure systems encourage states to establish a national system to introduce forms of remuneration. The 2003 Convention, Article 2.3 places transmission among the safeguarding measures aimed at ensuring viability of heritage.

Commercialisation, however, should not lead to over-commercialisation.[23] A letter sent to the UNESCO Secretariat regarding the element listed as 'the Mediterranean Diet' raised concerns over such over-commercialisation. The element consisted of 'a set of skills, knowledge, practices and traditions ranging from the landscape to the table, including the crops, harvesting, fishing, conservation, processing, preparation and, particularly, consumption of food'.[24] It was criticised for having commercial aims, being against the spirit of the 2003 Convention; furthermore, the inscription of this element on the Representative List would have been in violation of the same Convention. However, a formal procedure for dealing with correspondence from civil society was absent at the time (introduced in 2012).[25] Thus, the letter was disregarded, and the element was inscribed on the Representative List in 2010.[26] Nonetheless, the Committee invited states parties to avoid commercial misappropriation of intangible cultural heritage and to use the Convention's emblem in commercial activities only in line with the relevant Convention's rules. Accordingly, firstly, the UNESCO Director-General shall expressly authorise any sale of goods or services bearing this emblem; then the Convention Secretariat, after consulting the state party that nominated the intangible cultural heritage element, shall conclude contractual arrangements with the private subjects interested in commercialising the element, ensuring a benefit sharing mechanism in favour of the intangible cultural heritage fund.[27] Another example of concerns of commercialisation were raised about the element of 'the Traditional production of the Kranjska klobasa' (Carniolan sausage). It was criticised for its commercial aims as 'the nomination focuses more on the product than on the skills related to its production or the social function of its consumption' by 'what appears to be an economically motivated interest group'.[28] The nomination was withdrawn.

Misappropriation is unjust benefit acquired in ways unacceptable to the intangible cultural heritage bearers through exploitation of communally held intangible cultural heritage.[29] The competent UNESCO national Commissions must notify the Paris Convention's contracting parties about the use of its emblem,[30] and shall have recourse to parties' domestic systems to prevent abusive use of said emblem, e.g., use falsely suggesting a connection with UNESCO and the

23 Operational Directives (2016) paras 116 and 117; Irene Calboli, *Of Markets, Culture, and Terroir: The Unique Economic and Culture-Related Benefits of Geographical Indications of Origin. Research Handbook on International Intellectual Property* (Edward Elgar Publishing 2014).

24 Decision of the Intergovernmental Committee (2010): 5.COM 6.41.

25 Intergovernmental Committee for the Safeguarding of the Intangible Cultural Heritage, Seventh session, Paris, France, 3 to 7 December 2012, 7.COM.

26 Decision of the Intergovernmental Committee: 5.COM 6.1 cit.

27 Decision of the Intergovernmental Committee: 5.COM CONF.202 and Operational Directives (2016) paras 140–143; Ubertazzi, 'Su Alcuni Aspetti Problematici della Convenzione per la Salvaguardia del Patrimonio Intangibile' (n 2).

28 Decision of the Intergovernmental Committee: 10.COM 10.b.28. File No 01022.

29 Operational Directives (2016) paras 116 and 117.

30 Paris Convention for the Protection of Industrial Property (1883), Article 6ter.

2003 Convention.[31] Parties shall provide the Secretariat with the names and addresses of their domestic authorities charged with managing the use of the emblem. At the national level, those requesting use of the emblem shall consult these authorities and await potential authorisation by the Secretariat. Although both the Secretariat and the national authorities cooperate to prevent domestic misuse, only the national authorities may initiate proceedings against unauthorised internal use. At the international level, the Director-General may monitor use of the emblem and initiate proceedings against abusive use.

Among the various intellectual property rights to be adopted by states as measures to mitigate the risk of over-commercialisation and misappropriation of intangible cultural heritage, those of a collective nature, including GIs, are particularly relevant.[32]

EU trade marks and geographical indications

A trade mark confers on a proprietor exclusive rights. The registered trade mark owner is entitled to prevent all third parties who do not have consent from using, in the course of trade and in the same territory, any identical or similar sign in relation to identical or similar goods or services if there exists a likelihood of confusion on the part of the public between the signs.[33]

At the international level, the Paris Convention and the Protocol Relating to the Madrid Agreement Concerning the International Registration of Marks (Madrid Protocol) regulate trade marks. International trade marks are governed by the 'territoriality principle', meaning that each trade mark is valid only in the jurisdiction where it has been registered. 'International' registration of trade marks gives rise to a 'bundle' of national trade marks. At the EU level, the EUTM Regulation regulates trade marks and applies throughout the territories of the member states of the EU, and a single registration offers protection in all member states. The EU trade mark system creates a unified intellectual property right as opposed to the bundle of national intellectual property rights created by the international trade mark system. It is for this reason that the chapter focuses on EU trade marks.

31 Operational Directives (2016) paras 145–150; Ubertazzi, 'Su Alcuni Aspetti Problematici della Convenzione per la Salvaguardia del Patrimonio Intangibile' (n 2).

32 Toshiyuki Kono, 'Geographical Indications and Intangible Cultural Heritage' in B Ubertazzi and E Muñiz Espada (eds), *Le Indicazioni di Qualità degli Alimenti. Diritto Internazionale ed Europeo* (Giuffré 2009); Rosemary Coombe and Nicole Aylwin, 'Bordering Diversity and Desire: Using Intellectual Property to Mark Place-Based Products' (2011) 43(9) (*Special issue of) Environment and Planning A: Society and Space New Borders of Consumption* 2027; Rosemary Coombe and Joseph Turcotte, 'Indigenous Cultural Heritage in Development and Trade: Perspectives from the Dynamics of Cultural Heritage Law and Policy' in Graber et al. (eds), *International Trade in Indigenous Cultural Heritage* (Edward Elgar 2012) 300; Rosemary Coombe and Nicole Aylwin, 'Marks Indicating Conditions of Origin in Rights-Based Sustainable Development' (2014) 47 *UC Davis L Rev* 753, 778.

33 Regulation (EU) 2017/1001 of the European Parliament and of the Council of 14 June 2017 on the European Union trade mark (hereinafter the EUTM Regulation). OJ L 154, 16.6.2017, Article 8.

Within the EU, there are three types of trade marks: individual, collective, and certification. An *individual trade mark* is any sign that distinguishes the goods or services of one undertaking from those of other undertakings.[34] Signs can consist of a wide range of expressions including words, designs, letters, numerals, colours, the shape or packaging of goods, or sounds. Furthermore, these signs must be capable of being represented in a manner which enables the competent authorities and the public to determine the clear and precise subject matter of the protection afforded to its proprietor.[35] Significantly, in the context of intangible cultural heritage protection, individual trade marks cannot designate the geographical origin of the goods or services they cover. *Collective marks* are used to denote the goods or services of a group of people, and include groups where membership rules and limitations on admission may apply.[36] They distinguish the goods or services of the members of an association (the proprietor of the collective mark) from those of other undertakings.[37] The main function is to guarantee and certify the origin, nature, or quality of products or services, which are under the constant control of the association that registers them. Finally, *certification marks* denote goods and services that meet specific criteria, such as using specific methods or materials. Any group can use the mark if the goods or services comply with specific criteria, the compliance with which is determined through an assessment process. Whilst an association itself can administer a collective mark, the owner of a certification mark (an independent actor) must administer it. The owner cannot sell goods or services bearing the certification mark but is responsible for assessing compliance with the criteria for goods and services which seek to use such a mark.

GIs are also important intellectual property rights employed to protect intangible cultural heritage. GIs are signs given different terms in national and international norms. They play a similar role to appellations of origin (AOs), in that both GIs and AOs highlight a qualitative link between the relevant product and its place of origin. The link with the place of origin is stronger for AOs, since the quality or characteristics of the product must result *exclusively* from their geographical origin: raw materials should be sourced in the place of origin, as should the processing of the product. In the case of GIs, a single criterion attributable to geographical origin is sufficient: the production of the raw materials and the development or processing of a GI product do not necessarily have to take place entirely in the defined geographical area. For the sake of simplicity, GIs and AOs will be referred to collectively as GIs, unless indicated differently.

The legal instruments and the protection available for GIs vary considerably from one country to another. A *sui generis* system providing for the registration of GIs exists in some states, e.g., Kenya, Nigeria, South Africa, Egypt, Mexico, Peru, Cuba, India, Pakistan, Mauritius, and Sri Lanka. The most advanced of these *sui*

34 EUTM Regulation, Article 4(a).
35 ibid Article 4(b).
36 Jeffrey Belson, *Certification and Collective Marks* (2nd edn, Edward Elgar 2017).
37 EUTM Regulation, Article 74(1).

generis systems is that of the EU, where GIs (as well as Protected Designations of Origin (hereinafter PDOs)[38] and Traditional Speciality Guaranteed (hereinafter TSGs))[39] are regulated by the EU Regulation No 1151/2012 (QS Regulation).[40] The registration of EU GIs gives rise to a unitary intellectual property right (overriding any national rules on domestic GIs) covering the entire EU territory (Article 118(2) TFEU).[41] The exhaustive nature of the QS Regulation distinguishes it from other EU Regulations on unitary EU intellectual property rights, e.g., the EUTM Regulation, the Regulation on Community Designs,[42] and the Regulation on Community Plant Variety Rights.[43] In fact, according to these Regulations, the interested parties may choose to register an EU trade mark according to the EU Regulation or a national trade mark based on the domestic legislation(s) in force in the member state(s) of registration.[44] In contrast, interested parties can only register their GIs in the EU, based on the QS Regulation, and can no longer register a national GI in a single member state.[45]

EU geographical indication vs collective trade marks vs certification trade marks

The QS Regulation provides for a far-reaching protection of EU GIs by, firstly, establishing that protected names under an EU GI system cannot become generic and cannot be declared invalid. Secondly, it allows the coexistence of an earlier trade mark with the relevant GIs, derogating from the 'priority principle', save when registration may mislead consumers.[46] Thirdly, by defining the infringement

38 An EU PDO serves to identify a product: (a) originating in a specific place, region, or, in exceptional cases, a country, (b) whose quality or characteristics are essentially or exclusively due to a particular geographical environment with its inherent natural and human factors, and (c) whose production entirely takes place in the defined geographical area (QS Regulation, Article 5(1)).

39 TSGs safeguard traditional methods of production and recipes (QS Regulation, Article 17).

40 Regulation (EU) No 1151/2012 of the European Parliament and of the Council of 21 November 2012 on quality schemes for agricultural products and foodstuffs. OJ L 343, 14.12.2012.

41 Benedetta Ubertazzi, 'sub art. 118 TFUE' in MC Baruffi and F Pocar (eds), *Commentario Breve ai Trattati dell'Unione europea* (2nd edn, CEDAM 2014).

42 Council Regulation (EC) No 6/2002 of 12 December 2001 on Community Designs. OJ L 3, 5.1.2002.

43 Council Regulation (EC) No 2100/94 of 27 July 1994 on the Community Plant Variety. OJ L 227, 1.9.1994.

44 Benedetta Ubertazzi, 'Diritto Privato Europeo' (*Diritto On-line, Treccani* 2014) <https://www.treccani.it/enciclopedia/diritto-privato-europeo-dir-u-e_(Diritto-on-line)/> accessed 14 December 2021.

45 Michael Blakeney, *The Protection of Geographical Indications: Law and Practice* (Edward Elgar Publishing 2014) 72–73; German Patent and Trade Mark Office (2016) Information on the Protection of Geographical Indications and Designations of Origins for Agricultural Products and Foodstuffs Pursuant to Council Regulation (EU) No 1151/2012. <https://www.dpma.de/docs/service/formulare_eng/marke_eng/w7729_1.pdf> accessed 18 December 2021.

46 QS Regulation, Articles 6.4 and 14.

of EU GIs in a broad sense,[47] it offers protection that is similar in scope to the protection afforded to reputed trade marks.[48]

In other states, such as the US and Australia, registration of a geographical name is prohibited, or regularly rejected. Since European immigrants had brought the names of GIs to the US and Australia, using them to promote their products in their new homes, these names became widely used and thus, represented a category of goods and services of the same type – becoming generic to consumers. However, GI names in those countries are protected through trade mark systems, e.g., certification or collective marks.[49] The use of trade marks, however, even though of a collective nature, does not provide for a protection as comprehensive as that offered by the *sui generis* GI systems. EU GI registrations protect from the use of translations, e.g., Parmesan in place of Parmigiano Reggiano; use of the name with de-localisers, e.g., German Parmigiano Reggiano; or expressions such as 'like' or 'style', e.g., like Parmigiano Reggiano. Additionally, EU GIs do not need a demonstration that a name is neither generic nor descriptive; and it cannot be cancelled for becoming generic and descriptive or for non-use, and does not need an effective use of the name on the markets of registration or a monitoring of these markets. In contrast, trade mark registration does not protect from translation; nor does it prevent the use of the name with de-localisers, or expressions such as 'like' or 'style'. Moreover, it requires demonstration that a name is neither generic nor descriptive; it can be cancelled for becoming generic and descriptive or for non-use. The latter requires GI producers, having registered their GIs as trade marks as a preventive measure, to effectively use the name in the various markets of registration and to monitor these markets.[50]

Concerning collective trade marks, firstly, quality standards of collective trade marks are fixed by regulatory governing use, which are acts of private autonomy. In contrast, in the case of EU GIs, the quality standards are attributable to the place of origin of the product and to the long-standing traditional knowledge developed

47 ibid Article 13.1.

48 ibid Article 13.1. See EUTM Regulation, Article 9.1(c).

49 Gianluca Contaldi, 'Il Conflitto tra Stati Uniti e Unione Europea sulla Portezione delle Indicazioni Geografiche' in Ubertazzi and Muñiz Espada (eds) (n 32) 27–35; see also Christine Haight Farley, 'The Protection of Geographical Indications in the Inter-American Convention' (2014) 6 (1) *The WIPO Journal: Analysis of Intellectual Property Issues* 68. For GI protection in the US see United States Patent and Trademark Office <https://www.uspto.gov/sites/default/files/web/offices/dcom/olia/globalip/pdf/gi_system.pdf> accessed 14 December 2021. For Australia, see Australian Government – IP Australia Website 'Geographical Indications' <https://www.ipaustralia.gov.au/trade-marks/understanding-trade-marks/types-trade-marks/certification-trade-mark/geographical> and <http://manuals.ipaustralia.gov.au/trademarks/Part_35_Certification_Trade_Marks/35.2_Certification_trade_marks_and_geographical_indications_(GIs).htm> accessed 14 December 2021.

50 Dev Saif Gangjee, 'Geographical Indications and Cultural Heritage' (2012) 4 *WIPO Journal* 92; Giulio Sironi, 'Conflitti tra Marchi e Indicazioni Comunitarie di Qualità' in Ubertazzi and Muñiz Espada (eds) (n 32); Irene Calboli, 'In Territorio Veritas: Bringing Geographical Coherence in the Definition of Geographical Indications of Origin under TRIPS' (2014) 6(1) *The WIPO Journal: Analysis of intellectual Property Issues* 58, 59, and 66.

by the local people, which are fixed in the relevant specifications. Secondly, in the case of collective trade marks, the consortium is the right holder. In contrast, EU GIs are owned and exercised collectively, and the consortium is not regarded as the owner but manager of the protected name. Thirdly, the collective mark owner is responsible for ensuring compliance with certain standards by its members. In contrast, in the case of EU GIs, specifications are subject to a monitoring system of official controls carried out either by public authorities or by private control bodies with objectivity and impartiality. Finally, collective marks may only be used by certain associations and legal persons governed by public law. In contrast, all producers who make their products in the place designated by such GI and whose products share the specification may use EU GIs. EU GIs are similar to certification marks, which are given only upon compliance with the defined standards but are not confined to membership. Certification marks may be used by anyone who can certify that their products meet established standards and are controlled by the registered entity, which is considered 'competent to certify' the products concerned.[51]

Since these legal instruments and the protection available for GIs at a national level vary considerably from state to state, harmonisation of domestic legislation on GIs around the world has become necessary.

Legislation, agreements, and the protection available for geographical indications

First, the Madrid Agreement for the Repression of False or Deceptive Indications of Source (1891) and the Paris Convention prohibit the use of false or deceptive indications of origin. However, they do not specify what amounts to a 'non-deceptive' origin of a product. Second, a string of agreements on GIs between EU and non-EU countries (1960s and 1970s),[52] the Stresa Convention on the Protection of Appellations of Origin and Names of Cheese (1951), and the Lisbon Agreement on the Protection of Appellation of Origin and their international registration (1958 revised in 2015) established a registration system for specific types of GIs. The latter implies that all states parties recognise and enforce the GIs listed on the registry in their respective territories according to the legislation of their country of origin. These treaties adopt the *country of origin* approach; accordingly, the legislation applies in all states parties. The agreements refused the *territoriality* approach, which provides for each country to recognise and enforce the relevant GI according to its proper legislation.[53] Third, within the WTO framework, the

51 ibid 95.

52 See the Additional Act of Stockholm of 14 July 1967 for Madrid Agreement for the Repression of False or Deceptive Indications of Source on Goods.

53 Carmen Otero Garcíca-Castrillón, 'Territorialidad y Estado de Origen en las Denominaciones de Origen, Indicaciones Geográficas y Especialidades Tradicionales Garantizadas' in B Ubertazzi and E Muñiz Espada (eds) (n 32); Peukert (n 15); Ubertazzi, *Exclusive Jurisdiction in Intellectual Property* (n 5); F Falconi, 'Chapter Twenty-One: Transnational Litigation on Infringement of Des-

Agreement on Trade-Related Aspects of Intellectual Property Rights (TRIPS) defines GIs as signs capable of identifying goods as originating from a specific place and of attributing to them specific quality, reputation, and other characteristics.[54] Furthermore, the TRIPS Agreement offers protection against misleading the public as to the origin of goods, according to its rules on unfair competition as well as those in which states parties shall refuse or invalidate misleading trade marks as to origin. The TRIPS Agreement establishes additional and absolute protection, independent of whether the public is misled, for GIs related to wines and spirits. However, the TRIPS Agreement is based on the *territoriality* approach, rather than *country of origin* approach, since it does not establish a GI register. Negotiations within the WTO framework on establishing a GI register and extending to any GIs the level of protection currently granted to wine and spirit GIs have come to a stand-still.[55] Fourth, in the last decade, a second generation of bilateral and multilateral agreements on GIs has adopted the *country of origin* approach. Some of these address specific matters, such as those on wine and spirits.[56] Others are based on the mutual recognition of specific GIs with a phasing out of other GIs, e.g., the European Union with Switzerland (2011)[57] and Georgia (2012).[58] Others include GIs in Economic Partnership Agreements,[59] in the Stabilisation and Association Agreement,[60] or in Free Trade Agreements (FTAs).[61] Finally, the Geneva Act of the Lisbon Agreement on Appellations of Origin and Geographical Indications was concluded in 2015 adopting the *country of origin* approach, like the Lisbon Agreement, but raising the standards of protection. The Lisbon Agreement applies to all categories of products and is based

---

ignations of Origin and Geographical Indications Protected under Regulation (EU) No 1151/2012' in Angela Lupone, Carola Ricci and Andrea Santini (eds), *The Right to Safe Food towards a Global Governance* (Giappichelli 2013).

54 Contaldi (n 49); Lupone, 'Il Dibattito sulle Indicazioni Geografiche nel Sistema Multilaterale degli Scambi: dal Doha Round dell'Organizzazione Mondiale del Commercio alla Protezione Trips Plus' in Ubertazzi and Muñiz Espada (eds) (n 32); Michael Blakeney, 'Geographical Indications: What Do They Indicate? (2014) 6(1) *The WIPO Journal: Analysis of Intellectual Property Issues* 50; Calboli, 'In Territorio Veritas: Bringing Geographical Coherence in the Definition of Geographical Indications of Origin under TRIPS' (n 50) 57–60; Blakeney, *The Protection of Geographical Indications: Law and Practice* (n 45) 57–60.

55 TRIPS Agreement has a coexistence of trade mark-based systems, GI *sui generis* systems, and the application of laws on commercial behaviour, e.g., unfair competition, passing off. Calboli, 'In Territorio Veritas: Bringing Geographical Coherence in the Definition of Geographical Indications of Origin under TRIPS' (n 50) 67; Haight Farley (n 49).

56 Examples: Australia (1994), Mexico (1997), South Africa (1999), Chile (2002), Canada (2003), and the US (2006).

57 OJ L 297.

58 OJ L 93.

59 OJ L 289.

60 Examples: the Republic of Albania, OJ L 107; the Republic of Serbia, OJ L 278; Bosnia Herzegovina, OJ L 164.

61 Examples: EU and the Republic of Korea, OJ L 127; the Swiss Confederation and the People's Republic of China of 6 July 2013 signed in Beijing, China.

on registration by the request of a party, preventing AOs from becoming generic and protecting them against usurpation and imitation. The Geneva Act extends the scope of the Lisbon Agreement to include GIs.[62]

While these legislations have gradually increased the level of protection available for GIs, they only provide for partial harmonisation, and countries across the globe continue to be divided on GIs protection. Countries against GIs, like the US and Australia, purport that GIs create exclusive rights to access markets, and hence trade barriers affecting competition in granting protection to related products that do not necessarily originate entirely from the GI's denominated region. Accordingly, GI protection has become an unjustified, anti-competitive subsidy, which has the potential to confuse or deceive consumers as to the origin of products. In response to this criticism, countries with *sui generis* GI systems emphasise that GIs create economic benefits, since they guarantee the quality, content, and reputation of products and services by identifying their true origin. Thus, GIs are an important tool for economic development, if they coherently identify a product's geographical origin.[63]

Sui generis

In favour of *sui generis* systems for GIs and the expansion of GI protection at the international and domestic level, a cultural heritage argument is being adopted.[64] GIs identify regional products made using traditional manufacturing techniques, embody a portion of local knowledge, and promote part of the cultural identity of the associated community. This may promote greater product diversity in an economy where products would otherwise be increasingly similar due to mass production techniques, the globalisation of trade, and the de-localisation of product manufacture.[65] Where GIs are not a feasible form of protection for intangible

62 Daniel Gervais, 'Irreconcilable Differences? The Geneva Act of the Lisbon Agreement and the Common Law' (2015) 53(2) *Houston L Rev* 339.

63 For a proposition to restrict GI protection and permit the use of GIs only on products entirely originating from the GI-denominated region, see Calboli, 'In Territorio Veritas: Bringing Geographical Coherence in the Definition of Geographical Indications of Origin under TRIPS' (n 50) 59.

64 Gangjee (n 50) 95.

65 According to the European Commission, 'GIs are key to EU and developing countries' cultural heritage, traditional methods of production and natural resources'. A European study into the multifunctional dimension of regional products reports that GIs have 'a high heritage dimension'. A growing number of developing states also follow the cultural heritage argument concerning GIs. Alan Matthews, 'Geographical indications (GIs) in the US-EU TTIP negotiations' (*CAP Reform*, 19 June 2014) <http://capreform.eu/geographical-indications-gis-in-the-us-eu-ttip-negotiations/> accessed 15 December 2021; Gangjee (n 50) 90; Calboli, 'In Territorio Veritas: Bringing Geographical Coherence in the Definition of Geographical Indications of Origin under TRIPS' (n 50) 24.

cultural heritage elements, alternative intellectual property rights, including trade marks, can be used.[66]

Those against the adoption of GIs and other intellectual property rights to promote and protect intangible cultural heritage purport that a cultural justification for intellectual property rights amounts to the disguise of economic protectionism with culture-related interests, thus oversimplifying the notion of culture. This imposes Western notions and ideologies of property on traditional knowledge that freeze intangible cultural heritage, which needs constant change to stay viable. In response to these criticisms, GI products should not be treated like other commodities in trade contexts: enhancing protectionism in relation to culture is necessary. The distinction between tradition and innovation is also at the core of GIs, since GIs facilitate the protection of their related product or services in a dynamic context, where natural changes may prompt product and service variations reflected in periodical variations to the GI specification.[67] For collective marks, one solution to the challenge posed by entities using 'culture' to justify economic protectionism has been the use of 'hybrid' trade marks, where the owner of the mark is a public institution.[68]

Notwithstanding criticisms of the applicability of intellectual property mechanisms for safeguarding culture, a range of intellectual property rights including GIs are in practice adopted by states to protect their culture. States parties to the 2003 Convention already register, within their territory, GIs on their intangible cultural heritage elements. For instance, the Republic of Korea: 'weaving of *Mosi* (fine ramie) in the Hansan region';[69] Turkey: 'Traditional Craftsmanship of Çini-making';[70] Morocco 'Argan, practices and know-how concerning the Argan Tree',[71] the latter locally registered as GI by the non-profit association l'AMIGHA.[72] Moreover, an application for an EU GI concerning 'Argane' is under examination by the European Commission.[73] Japan registered a GI for its

66 WIPO, 'Using Collective Marks and Certification Marks to Protect and Promote Culture' (*WIPO TK News Archive*, 7 April 2021) <https://www.wipo.int/tk/en/news/tk/2021/news_0007.html> accessed 14 December 2021.

67 QS Regulation, Article 53.2. If there is a major change, the modified product specification must be assessed according to the processes outlined in Articles 49 to 52, that is, the modified specification must be re-assessed from the beginning.

68 Example: the figurative mark registered for 'vetro artistico murano' (Murano Artistic Glass). The mark can be used only once special examination procedures have taken place and is safeguarded by the Promovetro Consortium together with the Veneto Region <http://www.regione.veneto.it/web/attivita-produttive/vetro-artistico-murano-inglese> accessed 14 December 2021.

69 Decision of the Intergovernmental Committee (2011): 6.COM 13.45.

70 Decision of the Intergovernmental Committee (2016): 11.COM 10.b.34.

71 Decision of the Intergovernmental Committee (2014): 9.COM 10.30.

72 According to the Nomination File for *Argan*, a GI 'gives argan women considerable added value in their work and encourages them to continue applying their traditional skills'.

73 File number PGI-MA-906.

territory for its intangible cultural heritage element 'Washoku, traditional dietary cultures of the Japanese, notably for the celebration of New Year'.[74]

EU PDOs have also been used by states to protect intangible cultural heritage, e.g., the community of Pantelleria's 'traditional agricultural practice of cultivating the *vite ad alberello*',[75] and the terms 'Pantelleria', 'Moscato di Pantelleria', and 'Passito di Pantelleria' have been registered as Italian 'Controlled Designations of Origin' and at EU level PDO. Another example is the Union of Khios Mastic Producers, in Greece, registering PDOs for Μαστίχα Χίου ('Masticha Chiou')[76] and Μαστιχέλαιο Χίου ('Mastichelaio Chiou').[77] Later, the cultural practice 'know-how of cultivating mastic on the island of Chios' was registered on the Representative List.[78]

For elements that do not have a territorial requirement, TSGs have offered an alternative. Inscribed on the Representative List of the Intangible Cultural Heritage of Humanity,[79] the 'Art of Neapolitan *Pizzaiuolo*' obtained a TSG in December 2009, after two associations representing the Pizzaiuolo community applied. In other instances, states have registered individual, collective, and certification trade marks not only for their respective territory where the intangible cultural heritage originates, but also for several other jurisdictions. For instance, Italy registered a collective mark domestically and internationally (over 30 countries) on its intangible cultural heritage element 'traditional violin craftsmanship in Cremona', which was inscribed on the Representative List.[80] A second example is the 'Mediterranean Diet'; as noted, this element was inscribed on the Representative list and later, acquired a figurative individual EU trade mark, with a denominative part 'we are what we eat MedDiet Mediterranean Diet'. Several public and private collective entities from many countries acted as applicants for the trade mark registration.

Aside geographical indication and trade marks

In Indonesia, 'Indonesian Batik' has been inscribed in the 2009 Representative List,[81] and domestically, registered for copyright and trade mark protection. Article 12(1)(i) of Law of the Republic of Indonesia No 19/2002 on Copyright stipulates that works protected 'in the field of science, arts and literature' include 'batik art', and Article 29(1)(d) sets up the term of protection for the life of the creator and an

74 Decision of the Intergovernmental Committee (2013): 8.COM 8.17.
75 Inscribed on the UNESCO Representative List of the Intangible Cultural Heritage of Humanity. Decision of the Intergovernmental Committee (2014): 9.COM 10.18.
76 File number PDO-GR-1558.
77 File number PDO-GR-1559.
78 Decision of the Intergovernmental Committee (2014): 9.COM 10.21.
79 Decision of the Intergovernmental Committee (2017): 12.COM 11.b.17.
80 Trade mark 'Cremona Liuteria' No 753373; Decision of the Intergovernmental Committee (2012): 7.COM 11.18.
81 Decision of the Intergovernmental Committee (2009): 4.COM 13.44.

additional 50 years after his or her death. Additionally, the Indonesian Department of Industry introduced the 'Batikmark' through its Ministerial Decree No 74/M IND/PER/9/2007. Under the Decree, only batik manufacturers who already sell their products under a registered trade mark can obtain a 'Batikmark' certification and the manufacturer's products must pass a series of tests conducted by the National Standardisation Agency.

Copyright has also served to protect intangible cultural heritage in several states. In Mauritius, the state has sought to safeguard the element 'Sega tambour of Rodrigues Island' by facilitating the protection afforded by conventional copyright to individual artists belonging to the community, for instance in case of adaptations or of derivative works based on the traditional knowledge. Mauritius has committed itself to providing funding 'to the Sega Tambour artists who participate in national and regional performances and will monitor the intellectual property rights associated with such performances, including copyright'.[82] The importance of copyright as a means of protection was noted in the nomination for 'Dikopelo folk music of Bakgatla ba Kgafela in Kgatleng District' from Botswana. The nomination file for this element states:

> There are several laws, policies and regulations that affect the enactment and transmission of the element. However, practitioners of Dikopelo are not well versed in these laws even though they affect their practice. The major law that affects the practice of Dikopelo is the Copyright and Neighbouring Rights Act, which regulates the use of rights holders' works. Three workshops are planned under the proposed Safeguarding Plan to capacitate Dikopelo practitioners on their rights relating to copyright and neighbouring rights issues.[83]

For yet other elements, the general value of intellectual property rights protection in achieving the goals of intangible cultural heritage safeguarding is acknowledged, e.g., 'Međimurska popevka, a folksong from Međimurje' (Croatia),[84] inscribed in the Representative List, stating that:

> for the communities that identified themselves with popevka it is of vital importance to raise awareness on the collective character of creativity, the corresponding intellectual rights in moral terms, and the importance of the free flow of ideas in the public domain.

Likewise, the nomination for 'Al Sadu, traditional weaving skills in the United Arab Emirates' made references to intellectual property rights stating that they 'should be enforced as part of heritage law to safeguard the element against

82 Decision of the Intergovernmental Committee (2017): 12.COM 11.b.22.
83 Decision of the Intergovernmental Committee (2017): 12.COM 11.a.1.
84 Decision of the Intergovernmental Committee (2018): 13.COM 10.b.9.

factory production'.[85] These case studies reveal that intellectual property rights can offer valuable protection for intangible cultural heritage elements, which is compatible with the 2003 Convention's aims.

Cross-border safeguarding of intangible cultural heritage through geographical indications and EU trade marks

Registration of the relevant intellectual property rights in the countries of origin or in other countries is not sufficiently effective to safeguard intangible cultural heritage in transnational misappropriation cases. Since intellectual property rights are territorial in nature, they only provide protection for the country of registration, and cannot safeguard the same intangible cultural heritage in other countries. This means that domestically registered intellectual property rights, like the GIs registered for the intangible cultural heritage element 'Weaving of Mosi', can only safeguard the element in the Republic of Korea and not abroad. Similarly, where parallel intellectual property rights have been registered on intangible cultural heritage elements, these provide protection for the countries of registration only. Therefore, the collective marks registered on 'Traditional violin craftsmanship in Cremona' provide protection in each of the countries where trade marks have been registered. Likewise, the EU GI that would protect the Moroccan element 'Argane' (if successful) would be enforceable in the whole EU territory.

Concerning parallel GIs, certification, and collective trade marks registered on the intangible cultural heritage elements of their respective states, their individual enforcement in each country of registration is costly and wholly ineffective. This is well represented by the following transnational cases concerning misappropriated elements that, despite not being inscribed or nominated to be inscribed on the UNESCO Intangible Cultural Heritage Lists, are nevertheless related to intangible traditions and culture, and therefore understood as being included in the category of intangible cultural heritage *lato sensu* intended.[86]

'Darjeeling Tea'

Examples of cases relating to the alleged misappropriation of intangible cultural heritage concern Indian 'Darjeeling Tea' in Germany, Israel, Norway, Sri Lanka, Japan, France, Russia, and the US. The Tea Board of India, the sole representative of tea producers in India, registered the sign 'Darjeeling Tea' as a GI and a certification mark in India and in other countries including the US, Canada, Japan, Egypt, and the United Kingdom.[87] The 'Darjeeling Tea' sign has offered

85 Decision of the Intergovernmental Committee (2011): 6.COM 8.21.

86 A first group of cases involves the appropriation of Māori intangible cultural heritage: in Lego toys in Denmark (2001), in Philip Morris cigarettes in Israel (2005–2006), and in a television advertisement by Fiat in Italy (2006). A second group of cases involves the misappropriation of traditional songs by rock groups.

87 See WIPO Global Brand Database.

distinctive characteristics of quality, flavours, and a global reputation for more than a century, due to it being cultivated, grown, and produced in the West Bengal district of Darjeeling over 2000 meters above sea level. Indian tea producers export significant quantities of their Darjeeling tea worldwide. Country-by-country enforcement of the GI and certification mark 'Darjeeling Tea' is carried out by the Tea Board of India, thus, filing opposition on several occasions. The following are some examples.

In Japan

First, the Tea Board of India filed an action of invalidation against a Japanese company 'over the registration of the Darjeeling logo, namely Darjeeling women serving tea/coffee/coca/soft drinks/fruit juice' in the Japanese Patent Office (JPO).[88] This action was successful: the JPO Appeal found the registration invalid for being contrary to public order and morality.

Second, the Tea Board of India opposed the application 'Divine Darjeeling' filed by another Japanese company. This action was partially successful: the action of invalidation was dismissed by the JPO Opposition Board on the ground that the trade mark 'Divine Darjeeling' was not misleading or descriptive of the quality of the goods; however, the revocation of the trade mark on the grounds of non-use succeeded, because the Japanese company did not prove use of the trade mark in Japan.

Third, the Tea Board of India brought an action of invalidation against a Japanese trade mark registration of 'Darjeeling tea' with a map of India by a Japanese company, claiming that the registration was contrary to public order and morality. This action was partially successful: it was rejected because

> the written English character 'Darjeeling tea' and the map of India for the goods of Darjeeling tea are used as an indication of the origin and quality of Darjeeling tea and will not harm the feelings of the Indian people.[89]

Yet, the revocation of the trade mark on the grounds of non-use succeeded because the Japanese company did not prove use of the trade mark in Japan.

In France

Despite Indian law protecting French GIs, there is no reciprocity for Indian GIs in France. Under French law, opposition to a trade mark application, where the trade mark is similar or identical to a GI, is prohibited if the goods in the class

88 SC Srivastava, 'Case Study 16: Protecting the Geographical Indication for Darjeeling Tea' (WTO) <https://www.wto.org/english/res_e/booksp_e/casestudies_e/case16_e.htm> accessed 14 December 2021.

89 Ibid.

for which the trade mark is registered are different to those of the GI. Therefore, despite the Tea Board of India protesting, 'Darjeeling' has been registered as a trade mark in respect of goods in several classes, amounting to misappropriation of the 'Darjeeling' GI.

In Russia and the US

The Tea Board of India filed an application against use of 'Darjeeling' by a Russian company. This application was objected to on the grounds of conflict with the same trade mark that had been registered earlier. However, the Russian Patent Office, that accepted the Tea Board of India's application, overruled the objection. The Tea Board of India filed an application for an unauthorised use by its licensee in the US of 'Darjeeling nouveau' relating to certain goods and services. This application was successful as it was found that confusion of the trade marks was likely.[90]

'Genuine Bavarian Beer' and 'Bayerisches Bier'

Bayerischer Brauerbund eV (Bavarian Brewery Association or BBA) registered 'Bavarian' and 'Bavaria'[91] and their German language equivalents as EU GIs and in several other jurisdictions. The Bavarian Brewery Association in Munich represents the interests of over 240 breweries located in Bavaria, Germany. The relevant GIs indicate that the beer originates in Bavaria and therefore possesses a quality, reputation, or other characteristic attributable to said origin.

Country-by-country enforcement of the GIs 'Genuine Bavarian Beer' and 'Bayerisches Bier' has been carried out by BAA against the Dutch brewer Bavaria NV (Bavaria co) in Germany, Italy, Spain, and Australia.[92] 'BAVARIA HOLLAND BEER' was registered by Bavaria with German priority from April 1995 and Italian priority from October 1995.

In Germany

BBA successfully challenged Bavaria co's trade mark.[93] After referring some legal questions to the Court of Justice of the European Union (CJEU), the German Federal Court referred the case back to Oberlandesgericht München (OLG Munich).[94] In 2012, OLG Munich determined that national German trade mark law protected the term 'Bayerisches Bier' in the period before it was registered

90 *Tea Board of India v the Republic of Tea, Inc.*, 80 USPQ2d 1881.

91 As such or together with specific wordings, e.g., 'Genuine Bavarian Beer & Device'.

92 Roland Knaak, 'Geographical Indications and Their Relationship with Trade Marks in EU Law' (2015) 46(7) *IIC* 843.

93 Blakeney, *The Protection of Geographical Indications: Law and Practice* (n 45) 125.

94 BGH 2011 *Bayerisches Bier II*, I ZR 69/04.

for protection internationally.[95] OLG Munich's ruling held that no further appeals were available to Bavaria co, but they have since filed an appeal against this denial of leave to appeal.[96]

In Italy

Bavaria co registered their figurative trade mark in 1971, whereas the EU GI 'Bayerisches Bier' was not registered by BBA until 2001.[97] In 2011, the Court of Appeal of Torino referred the question of the interaction between this GI and the 'BAVARIA' trade mark to the CJEU.[98] It was concluded that a *bona fide*, prior registration of a trade mark, which did not mislead as to the origin of the goods, could not take advantage of the reputation of a later GI.[99] Therefore, the Court of Appeal held that the Bavaria co trade mark was valid and legitimately used, which the Court of Cassation later upheld.[100]

In Spain

In 2009, the Spanish Supreme Court upheld the Provincial Court of Madrid's 2004 judgment against Verband Bayerischer Ausfurbrave Reien, EV.[101] It was concluded that (1) in Spanish, 'Bavaria' is not meaningful enough to evoke a sufficiently intense and precise connection with Bavaria the territory, thus generating the belief that 'Bavaria' beer originates from there; and (2) the two parties' trade marks are visually, aurally, and conceptually different enough to prevent confusion between them.[102]

In Australia

The BBA filed an opposition against Bavaria co registering a trade mark for beer that includes the word 'Bavaria', three references to Holland, and a few non-word elements. This opposition was rejected, and the trade mark was registered since it

95 OLG 2021 *Bavaria Holland Beer II*, 29 U 5084/03.

96 Yvonne Draheim and Maria Luce Piattelli, 'Coexistence of "Bavaria Holland Beer" Trademark and the Geographical Indication "Bayerisches Bier" in Europe?' (*Hogan Lovells Intellectual Property Newsletter*, January 2021) <https://ehoganlovells.com/rv/ff0002a46b098796b39f049238438135bab66c77/p=4> accessed 14 December 2021; Robert Börner, 'Germany (Munich) – Bavarian Beer Battle (almost) Over?' (*News Bavarian.Me*, 25 April, 2013) <news4.bavarian.me/germany-munich-bavarian-beer-battle-almost-over-8027/> accessed 14 December 2021.

97 Knaak (n 92).

98 Court of Appeal of Turin, *Bavaria NV v Bavaria Italia*, No 299/07.

99 C-478/07 *Budějovický Budvar, národní podnik v Rudolf Ammersin GmbH* ECLI:EU:C:2009:521. Draheim and Piattelli (n 96).

100 Italian Court of Cassation 20 September 2012, *Bayerischer Brauerbund v Ufficio Italiano Brevetti e Marchi*, No 15958.

101 STS 2009, *Verband Bayerischer Ausfurbrave Reien v Bavaria, N.V.*, No 397/2009.

102 Knaak (n 92).

was not substantially the same or deceptively similar to the BBA GIs, and therefore did not deceive or cause confusion. The Federal Court of Australia concluded that the trade mark 'Bavaria' was inherently adapted to distinguish Bavaria co's beer from that of the Bavarian Brewery Association.[103]

As these examples show, intellectual property rights registered in various countries are currently enforced in each of those countries. In particular, such a country-by-country enforcement of the relevant parallel intellectual property rights obliges the intellectual property owners to defend as many proceedings as there are registered according to a mosaic approach. This approach leads to a multiplication of parallel proceedings, raising the risk of conflicting judgments and the costs of litigation, and generating inequalities between big multinational companies and medium and small sized enterprises. Intangible cultural heritage bearers then may not be prepared to adopt such an approach: namely to register and enforce intellectual property rights not only in their domestic country but also in all other states for the territories in which they require their intangible cultural heritage to be protected. To effectively safeguard intangible cultural heritage, not just in the country of origin but also in other countries, intellectual property rights should be enforced in a single judicial proceeding (one country), consolidating the relevant multinational litigation proceedings. This consolidation could be achieved by applying private international law rules.

Conclusion

To safeguard intangible cultural heritage, the 2003 Convention was adopted aiming at safeguarding intangible cultural heritage both at the domestic and at the international level, but lacking rules on transnational misappropriation cases. To safeguard intangible cultural heritage across borders, states parties have adopted intellectual property rights. Yet, domestic registrations of such rights cannot safeguard intangible cultural heritage globally. Unless intellectual property rights are registered in the country of origin and are recognised and enforced abroad based on specific bilateral or multilateral treaties, or fall within a unitary EU system, intellectual property rights must not only be registered in their country of origin, but also in other jurisdictions. There are tensions between transboundary intangible cultural heritage, boundary-based legal frameworks, and cross-border misappropriation. Therefore, few states parties have registered intellectual property rights in their respective territories, and other countries. Yet, parallel GIs registered in many jurisdictions must currently be enforced in each country of registration. The mosaic approach is followed in the case of EU GIs since the QS Regulation does not establish a system of cross-border enforcement of GIs.

103 Federal Court of Australia 30 April 2009, *Bavaria NV v Bayerischer Brauerbund eV*, No 428.

References

Blake J, *Commentary on the UNESCO 2003 Convention on the Safeguarding of the Intangible Cultural Heritage* (Institute of Art and Law 2006)

Blakeney M, *The Protection of Geographical Indications: Law and Practice* (Edward Elgar Publishing 2014a)

——— 'Geographical Indications: What Do They Indicate?' (2014b) 6(1) *The WIPO Journal: Analysis of Intellectual Property Issues* 50

Bortolotto C, 'Il Processo di Definizione del Concetto di "Patrimonio Culturale Immateriale": Elementi per una Riflessione' in C Bortolotto (ed), *Il Patrimonio Immateriale Secondo l'UNESCO: Analisi e Prospettive* (Poligrafico dello Stato 2008)

Börner R, 'Germany (Munich) – Bavarian Beer Battle (almost) Over?' (*News Bavarian. Me*, 25 April, 2013) <news4.bavarian.me/germany-munich-bavarian-beer-battle-almost-over-8027/> accessed 14 December 2021.

Calboli I, 'In Territorio Veritas: Bringing Geographical Coherence in the Definition of Geographical Indications of Origin under TRIPS' (2014a) 6(1) *The WIPO Journal: Analysis of intellectual Property Issues* 58

——— *Of Markets, Culture, and Terroir: The Unique Economic and Culture-Related Benefits of Geographical Indications of Origin. Research Handbook on International Intellectual Property*. (Edward Elgar Publishing 2014b)

Contaldi G, 'Il Conflitto tra Stati Uniti e Unione Europea sulla Portezione delle Indicazioni Geografiche' in B Ubertazzi and E Muñiz Espada (eds), *Le Indicazioni di Qualità degli Alimenti* (Giuffrè 2009)

Coombe R and Aylwin N, 'Bordering Diversity and Desire: Using Intellectual Property to Mark Place-based Products' (2011) 43(9) *Special Issue of Environment and Planning A: Society and Space New Borders of Consumption* 2027

——— 'Marks Indicating Conditions of Origin in Rights-Based Sustainable Development' (2014) 47 *UC Davis L Rev* 753

Coombe R and Turcotte J, 'Indigenous Cultural Heritage in Development and Trade: Perspectives from the Dynamics of Cultural Heritage Law and Policy' in Graber et al. (eds), *International Trade in Indigenous Cultural Heritage* (Edward Elgar Publishing 2012)

Draheim Y and Piattelli M, 'Coexistence of "Bavaria Holland Beer" Trademark and the Geographical Indication "Bayerisches Bier" in Europe?' (*Hogan Lovells Intellectual Property Newsletter*, January 2021) <https://ehoganlovells.com/rv/ff0002a46b098796b39f049238438135bab66c77/p=4> accessed 14 December 2021

Falconi F, 'Chapter Twenty-One: Transnational Litigation on Infringement of Designations of Origin and Geographical Indications Protected under Regulation (EU) No 1151/2012' in A Lupone, C Ricci and A Santini (eds), *The Right to Safe Food Towards a Global Governance* (Giappichelli 2013)

Francioni F, 'The Human Dimension of International Cultural Heritage Law: An Introduction' (2011) 22(1) *Eur J Int'l Law* 9

——— 'Public and Private in the International Protection of Global Cultural Goods' (2012) 23(3) *EJIL* 719

Gangjee D, 'Geographical Indications and Cultural Heritage' (2012) 4 *WIPO Journal* 92

Gervais D, 'Irreconcilable Differences? The Geneva Act of the Lisbon Agreement and the Common Law' (2015) 53(2) *Houston L Rev* 339

Garcíca Castrillón C, 'Territorialidad y Estado de Origen en las Denominaciones de Origen, Indicaciones Geográficas y Especialidades Tradicionales Garantizadas' in B

Ubertazzi and E Muñiz Espada (eds), *Le Indicazioni di Qualità degli Alimenti* (Giuffrè 2009)

Haight Farley C 'The Protection of Geographical Indications in the Inter-American Convention' (2014) 6(1) *The WIPO Journal: Analysis of intellectual Property Issues* 68

Hilty R, *Rationales for the Legal Protection of Intangible Goods and Cultural Heritage* (Competition & Tax Law Research Paper No. 09–10, Max Planck Institute for Intellectual Property 2009)

Knaak R, 'Geographical Indications and Their Relationship with Trade Marks in EU Law' (2015) 46(7) *IIC* 843

Kono T, 'Geographical Indications and Intangible Cultural Heritage' in B Ubertazzi and E Muñiz Espada (eds), *Le Indicazioni di Qualità degli Alimenti* (Giuffrè 2009a)

——— 'Intangible Cultural Heritage and Intellectual Property: Communities, Cultural Diversity and Sustainable Development' in T Kono (ed), *Intangible Cultural Heritage and Intellectual Property: Communities, Cultural Diversity and Sustainable Development* (Intersentia 2009b)

Kono T and Wrbka S, 'General Report: Protection and Preservation of Cultural Heritage' in T Kono (ed), *The Impact of Uniform Laws on the Protection of Cultural Heritage and the Preservation of Cultural Heritage in the 21st Century* (Martinus Nijhoff Publishers 2010)

Lixinski L, *Intangible Cultural Heritage in International Law* (OUP 2013)

Lupone A, 'Il Dibattito sulle Indicazioni Geografiche nel Distema Multilaterale degli Scambi: dal Doha Round dell'Organizzazione Mondiale del Commercio alla Protezione Trips Plus' in B Ubertazzi and E Muñiz Espada (eds), *Le Indicazioni di Qualità degli Alimenti* (Giuffrè 2009)

Matthews A, 'Geographical Indications (GIs) in the US-EU TTIP Negotiations' (*CAP Reform*, 19 June 2014) <http://capreform.eu/geographical-indications-gis-in-the-us-eu-ttip-negotiations/> accessed 15 December 2021

Peukert A, 'Individual Multiple and Collective Ownership of Intellectual Property Rights: Which Impact on Exclusivity?' in A Kur and V Mizaras (eds), *The Structure of Intellectual Property. Can One Size Fit All?* (Edward Elgar Publisher 2011)

Scovazzi T, 'La Definizione di Patrimonio Culturale Intangibile' in G Golinelli et al. (eds), *Nuove Forme di Valorizzazione e Promozione delle Aree Rurali Italiane - Il Sistema* (UNESCO 2011)

Scovazzi T et al., *Il Patrimonio Culturale Intangibile nelle sue Diverse Dimensioni* (Giuffrè 2012)

Sironi G et al., 'Conflitti tra Marchi e Indicazioni Comunitarie di Qualità' in B Ubertazzi and E Muñiz Espada (eds), *Le Indicazioni di Qualità degli Alimenti* (Giuffrè 2009)

Sola A, 'Quelques Réflexions à Propos de la Convention pour la Sauvegarde du Patrimoine Culturel Immaterial' in J Nafziger and T Scovazzi (eds), *Le Patrimoine Culturel del'humanité* (Martinus Nijhoff Publishers 2018)

Srivastava S C, 'Case Study 16: Protecting the Geographical Indication for Darjeeling Tea' (WTO) <https://www.wto.org/english/res_e/booksp_e/casestudies_e/case16_e.htm> accessed 14 December 2021

Srinivas B, 'The UNESCO Convention for the Safeguarding of the Intangible Cultural Heritage' in J Nafziger et al. (eds), *Le patrimoine culturel del'humanité* (Martinus Nijhoff Publishers 2008)

Ubertazzi B, 'Territorial and Universal Protection of Intangible Cultural Heritage from Misappropriation' (2010) 8 *NZYIL* 69

——— 'Su Alcuni Aspetti Problematici della Convenzione per la Salvaguardia del Patrimonio Intangibile' [2011] *Rivista di Diritto Internazionale* 777

——— *Exclusive Jurisdiction in Intellectual Property* (Mohr Siebeck 2012a)

——— 'Una Nuova Condizione per L'iscrizione nelle Liste del Patrimonio Culturale Intangibile' [2012b] *Rivista di Diritto Internazionale* 469

——— 'Non-Governmental Organizations and the 2013 Session of the UNESCO Intangible Cultural Heritage Committee' [2013] *Italian Y B Int'l L* 299

——— 'Diritto Privato Europeo' (*Diritto On-line, Treccani* 2014) <https://www.treccani.it/enciclopedia/diritto-privato-europeo-dir-u-e_(Diritto-on-line)/> accessed 14 December 2021

——— 'sub art. 118 TFUE' in M C Baruffi and F Pocar (eds), *Commentario Breve ai Trattati dell'Unione europea* (2nd edn, CEDAM 2014)

Ubertazzi B and Muñiz Espada E (eds), *Le Indicazioni di Qualità degli Alimenti* (Giuffrè 2009)

von Lewinski S, *Indigenous Heritage and Intellectual Property: Genetic Resources, Traditional Knowledge and Folklore* (Kluwer Law International 2008)

Zagato L, 'La Convenzione sulla Protezione del Patrimonio Culturale Intangibile' in Lauso Zagato (ed), *Le Identità Culturali nei Recenti Dtrumenti UNESCO, Un Approccio Nuovo alla Costruzione della Pace?* (CEDAM 2008)

7 Colombian/Panamanian *molas*

Coping with the challenges posed in protecting and commercialising transboundary intangible cultural heritage

Florelia Vallejo-Trujillo[1]

Introduction

Like many countries in Latin America, Colombia is a multi-ethnic and pluricultural nation. Its Multicultural Public Policy Proposal for the Protection of Knowledge Systems Associated with Biodiversity states that, in this country, Indigenous and local communities are comprised of Indigenous peoples, afro-descendants (afro-Colombians in general, raizales, and palenqueros), the 'rom' people (Romany people), and peasants.[2] The last census, in 2018, by the National Administrative Department of Statistics (Departamento Administrativo Nacional de Estadística – DANE), found that 1,905,617 Colombians identify themselves as Indigenous, which is 4.4% of the country's entire population.[3] It was also found that Indigenous persons are grouped into 115 different Indigenous peoples,[4] with approximately 35% of them living in the border areas.[5]

1 Professor of Law, University of Tolima School of Law (Ibagué, Colombia), Council Member of the Departmental Cultural Heritage Council of Tolima. Prof Vallejo-Trujillo is a qualified lawyer by the National University of Colombia, holds an LLM in Intellectual Property Law from the University Externado of Colombia, an MSc in Law from the National University of Colombia, and a PhD from the University of Nottingham, UK.

This chapter is one of the outcomes of the study 'Alternativas para la protección del Patrimonio Cultural Inmaterial mediante el Derecho de Propiedad Intelectual' developed by the Research Group in Law of the University of Tolima.

2 Marcela Jiménez Larrarte, *Propuesta de Política Pública Pluricultural para la Protección de los Sistemas de Conocimiento Asociado a la Biodiversidad en Colombia* (Ministerio de Ambiente 2013) 14, 18–21.

3 Nevertheless, note that the peoples living in self-isolation, such as the Jurumi, Passe, and the Yury people, were not part of the census. DANE, *Población Indígena de Colombia* (Resultados del Censo Nacional de Población y Vivienda 2018, 16 September 2019) <https://www.dane.gov.co/index.php/estadisticas-por-tema/demografia-y-poblacion/grupos-etnicos/informacion-tecnica> accessed 2 December 2021.

4 ibid.

5 This is an estimated figure, given the lack of updated information. Dirección de Desarrollo Territorial Sostenible, Subdirección de Ordenamiento y Desarrollo Territorial, *Aspectos Básicos Grupo Étnico Indígenas* (Departamento Nacional de Planeación, República de Colombia 2010)

DOI: 10.4324/9781003345237-8

Sharing border areas facilitates the exchange of knowledge, resources, culture, and traditions for peoples living in more than one country. For instance, the Awá, Shuar, Wounan, Pasto, Kofan, Siona, and Secoya peoples live along the borders of Ecuador and Colombia; the Kichwa people live in a transboundary situation between Colombia, Ecuador, and Peru; the Tikuna people live both in Colombia and Brazil; the Embera and Kuna people are found in Colombia and Panama; and the Wayúu people live around the frontiers of Colombia and Venezuela.[6] Such an exchange of knowledge and culture creates great challenges for governments when the protection, preservation, safeguarding, and management of transboundary traditional knowledge and traditional cultural expressions, which are part of their intangible cultural heritage, are sought.

These challenges are far greater when the countries in which the Indigenous peoples live experience social crises as in the case of Colombia, a country with an internal armed conflict that has lasted more than 50 years. The peoples living within the Colombian territory are recognised as victims of the country's internal armed conflict. Circumstances such as these affect many Indigenous populations around the globe and, therefore, should not be overlooked in the analysis addressing the protection of traditional knowledge, traditional cultural expression, and intangible cultural heritage.

The above-mentioned circumstances are the main cause for asserting that the logical basis of the law, when considered in the abstract, could fail when it is applied in concrete contexts. In that regard, López extensively exposed the limitations of the interpretation and application of abstract legal concepts in specific contexts.[7] For that reason, although case studies may be less attractive due to the specific character of the subject to be dealt with, the fact that the theory of law can only be checked through its practical implementation should not be ignored. On this aspect is where the case study presented may positively contribute to the field. The experience presented reflects on the management and protection of transboundary traditional cultural expressions and intangible cultural heritage through the lens of the challenges that the Kuna people may face in the creation, protection, and commercialisation of their *molas* in Panama and Colombia, with particular attention on the Colombian internal armed conflict as a factor affecting Indigenous peoples' self-determination and capability to respond to these challenges. To this end, the chapter describes the protection of traditional cultural expressions in Colombia and the Kuna socio-political context, and explains the creation of *molas* in a cultural context and their commodification in Colombia

14 <https://colaboracion.dnp.gov.co/CDT/Desarrollo%20Territorial/Aspectos%20b%C3%A1sicos%20grupo%20%C3%A9tnico%20ind%C3%ADgena.pdf> accessed 2 December 2021.

6 Andrés David Álvarez Castrillón, *La Nación Gunadule en el contexto binacional Colombia-Panamá: configuración, manejo y luchas por el territorio sagrado* (Tesis de grado presentada como requisito para optar al título de Magister en Estudios Urbano Regionales, Facultad de Arquitectura, Universidad Nacional de Colombia, Sede Medellín. Medellín, 2016) 15.

7 Diego López, *Teoría Impura del Derecho: Transformación de la cultura jurídica latinoamericana* (Universidad de los Andes LEGIS, Universidad Nacional de Colombia 2004).

and Panama, as, by observing such a commodification, it is possible to understand some of the existing challenges for management and protection. In doing this, the common elements found in some successful experiences of traditional cultural expressions commodification are identified, to evaluate the possibility of implementing, in this context, some of the existing proposals for the protection and management of intellectual property rights in transboundary situations. Thus, the intent of this chapter is not to propose another solution for the management of intellectual property rights in transboundary situations; it rather seeks to contribute by reviewing some proposals in the specific context of the Kuna people. Therefore, the chapter contributes to comprehending this problem from a more pragmatic approach by means of examining the use of national laws by establishing a net of cooperatives to produce and sell *molas*.

Traditional cultural expressions protection in Colombia

Article 187.2 of the Law 23 of 1982, on Copyright, establishes that 'works of folklore and traditional works by unknown authors' belong to the public domain. Because of this, it is understood that traditional cultural expressions belong to the public domain. Traditional cultural expressions are, therefore, not protected by the copyright law, and it seems that in the short and medium terms no initiatives will be made for the creation of a *sui generis* law based on intellectual property rights to that end. Therefore, in Colombia the protection of traditional cultural expression has evolved in association with the development of international regulations created for the conservation and safeguarding of tangible and/or intangible cultural heritage.

In addition to the different international instruments that on this matter have been ratified by the government,[8] the Colombian Political Constitution contains a set of Articles that could be considered as a complete framework for the protection of culture within the country.[9] This framework imposes the State's obligation to promote, protect, safeguard, and publicise Colombian 'National Cultural Heritage'.

The constitutional status framed in such a way has been developed in Colombia by a special regime for the protection of (i) objects declared of 'cultural interest', and (ii) cultural objects included in the 'Representative List of Intangible Cultural Heritage' (hereinafter the representative list). Among others, this regime comprises the Laws 397 of 1997 and 1185 of 2008, and the Decrees 1080 of 2015 and 2358 of 2019. Accordingly, those types of objects will be declared of national cultural interest by the Ministry of Culture prior to approval from the

8 Some of these instruments are the Convention for the Protection of Cultural Property in the Event of Armed Conflict of 1954, the Convention Concerning the Protection of the World Cultural and Natural Heritage of 1972, and the Convention for the Safeguarding of the Intangible Cultural Heritage of 2003.

9 According to the Constitutional Judgements C-224 of 2016 and C-082 of 2020, such a framework comprises Articles 7, 8, 63, 70, and 72 of the Political Constitution of 1991.

National Council for Culture. The different administrative regions of the country can also declare of regional cultural interest such objects, prior to approval from the Departmental Cultural Heritage Council or the District Cultural Heritage Council, as the case may be. The competent authority will define whether such a declaration also needs the formulation of a 'Special Plan for Management and Protection' and if any objects entering the representative list require the elaboration and application of a 'Special Plan of Safeguarding'.

The entry of objects in the representative list has different features than their declaration of cultural interest. This is of special interest when the protection of traditional cultural expressions is sought, because the Decree 1080 of 2015 establishes that (i) no private person can have property rights over the 'manifestations'[10] belonging to the national cultural heritage (Article 2.5.1.5); and (ii) that 'traditions and techniques associated with the production of handicrafts' fall into the scope of what is considered to be intangible cultural heritage (Article 2.5.1.2.8 numeral 6). Based on these regulations, it would be expected that after a handicraft enters into the representative list, the peoples producing it should gain a little more control over its production and commercialisation. However, at the moment, the inclusion in this list has only served to enable the formulation and implementation of public policies and projects for the safeguarding of the handicraft technique.[11] This may not be the ideal level of protection expected, but despite that, it gives the opportunity to Indigenous peoples to push local and national authorities to include the safeguarding, promotion, and preservation of their artisanal techniques in public policies, and to participate in the programmes specially designed for Indigenous peoples.

Kuna socio-political context

Kuna people (also known as Gunadule, Tule, Guna, Cuna, Cuna Cuna, Tacarcuna, and Cerracuna) are some of the original inhabitants of America who still preserve some of their traditions. It is believed that the different names they are known by are linked to a certain extent to the word 'Tacarcuna', which designates an ancestral hill that plays an important role in their creation myths.[12] Although historical and anthropological findings suggest that they are originally from the Darién region of Colombia, nowadays, as a result of various processes of migration, most of them live in the San Blas Shire and the low part of the Bayano river in Panama.[13]

10 This is the legal term used to refer to intangible cultural expressions that form part of the national intangible cultural heritage (Decree 1080 of 2015, Article 2.5.1.2).

11 These projects are developed by the Government through Artesanías de Colombia.

12 Ministerio del Interior, *Pueblo Tule o Cuna* (República de Colombia 2012) 1 <https://www.mininterior.gov.co/sites/default/files/upload/SIIC/PueblosIndigenas/pueblo_tule_o_cuna.pdf> accessed 10 December 2021.

13 Ministerio de Cultura, *Tule (Kuna), la gente por amor por la palabra*, Ministerio de Cultura (República de Colombia 2010) 1, 3–4 <https://www.mincultura.gov.co/areas/poblaciones/noticias

The Panama separation from Colombia in 1903 was determinant for the Kuna people, because the division of the territory that used to be a single unit also represented their division into Panamanian and Colombian Kuna. Thus, although the Panamanian 1903 Constitution did not mention Indigenous peoples whatsoever, once Panama reached some stability, the Kuna people were forced to acquire the nation's identity, and in 1912 an Act was created to oblige them to integrate into the country's predominant culture. This provoked the 1925 rebellion for the Panamanian Kuna people and the creation of the Tule Republic, which would not last more than two days,[14] and which reaffirmed the *mola* as a symbol of their people and of resistance, as stated by Howe.[15] Nevertheless, the 1925 rebellion led to a constitutional reform in Panama, and to a Law recognising special districts for the Indigenous people. One of these is the San Blas Shire that was established by the Second Law of 1938, later named Kuna Yala District by the Law 99 of 1998, and finally named Gunayala by the Fundamental Law of Gunayala of 2013.[16] The Panamanian Fundamental Law recognises Kuna's collective personality for the exercise of rights in their own territory, for the creation of their own political institutions, and for the establishment of their own government. Although Panamanian Kuna people call themselves Gunayala, in this text they are referred to as Kuna.

Although the situation of Colombian Kuna is different from that of their people living in Panama, they have had recognised special rights in the Colombian Political Constitution. Among them are the recognition of the legal system principle of respect and protection of peoples' ethnic and cultural diversity, the protection of their traditional practices of the production and use of their natural resources,[17] and the collective exercise of individual constitutional rights.[18] Additionally, the ethnic minorities recognised under the Colombian government can exercise judicial and administrative functions within their territorial boundaries, for which a 'Special Jurisdiction' has been established. However, for the exercise of this right, they are required to achieve acknowledgement as 'Indigenous' by the national competent authority. Such a recognition also gives them the right to have a territory in the form of 'Indigenous reservations'.[19]

/Documents/Caracterizaci%C3%B3n%20del%20Pueblo%20Tule%20(Kuna).pdf> accessed 2 December 2021.

14 Miguel Bartolomé and Alicia Barabas, 'Recursos culturales y autonomía étnica. La democracia participativa de los Kuna de Panamá' (1998) 8(16) *Alteridades* 159, 162.

15 James Howe, 'La Revolución Dule: una revolución indígena del siglo XX' (2016) 56 *Boletín del Museo del Oro* 205, 206 <https://publicaciones.banrepcultural.org/index.php/bmo/article/view/7945/8338> accessed 2 December 2021.

16 Ley Fundamental de Gunayala of September 2013 <https://www.gunayala.org.pa/Ley%20Fundamenta.Gunayala.pdf> accessed 2 December 2021.

17 Florelia Vallejo-Trujillo 'Fundamentos Constitucionales para la Protección del Conocimiento Tradicional' (2007) 18 *Pensamiento Jurídico* 147.

18 Constitutional Court, Cases T-380 of 1993 and SU-039 of 1997.

19 See for example, Decision T-001 of 2019. See also Esther Sánchez Botero, *Justicia y Pueblos Indígenas de Colombia* (Universidad Nacional de Colombia 1998) 121.

As a result of such a complex condition for Indigenous peoples in Colombia, and despite the constitutional apparatus protecting these peoples' rights, self-determination, and traditions, the available mechanisms for their self-development are still incipient in their practicality and effectivity. To this situation should be added the incidence of the armed conflict as will be described in later on in this chapter. The question to highlight here is the different histories that the same people have experienced on one or the other side of the border, making the transboundary situation a problem that cannot be solved merely by legal mechanisms.

Molas: a cosmogonic thought

Molas are probably the most distinctive cultural element that characterises the Kuna people. They are made by Kuna women using colourful pieces of fabric which they sew in geometric patterns to create compositions that represent their vision of the world on subjects such as myths, the creation of the world, traditional customs, and the nature of the region. The Kuna women preserve the tradition of wearing *molas* by sewing them to their shirts. For that reason, they pass on the knowledge about their production from one generation to the next generation, from mothers to daughters. At the beginning, the 'language'[20] of *molas* was painted on the woman's bodies and on the bark of trees for protection against wild animals. It is unknown the moment when fabrics started to be used. However, Marks recognises the influence of conquerors in the Kuna's understanding of the use of fabric to produce *molas*.[21]

Although there are no differences between the *molas* produced by the Kuna peoples living in Colombia and Panama, the socio-political differences of these countries have had an impact on their legal protection and the recognised rights of Indigenous peoples. Such differences could be better appreciated by observing the way *molas* are commercialised, and the legal options that Kuna people have for their management and protection in each of these countries. For these reasons, the following sections offer a short and general view of the different ways in which *molas* are commercialised both in Colombia and Panama. Suffice to say for now that the evident development of Panamanian laws on the matter and the possibility of the Kuna people to organise and therefore commercialise their product more effectively and legally, shows how the social context of peace opened the field to improve the conditions.

20 This is how Kuna refer to the *mola* designs.

21 Diana Marks, *The Evolution of the Kuna Mola: From Cultural Authentication to Cultural Survival* (A thesis submitted in fulfilment of the requirements for the degree of Doctor of Philosophy, School of Fashion and Textiles College of Design and Social Context, RMIT University, August 2012) in Lorena Lozada Álvarez, *Las Capas Comerciales de la Mola en el Mercado Artesanal de Bogotá* (Trabajo presentado para optar al título de Antropología, Escuela de Ciencias Humanas, Universidad del Rosario, Bogotá 2018) 22 <https://repository.urosario.edu.co/handle/10336/19797> accessed 2 December 2021.

Commodification of *molas* in Colombia and Panama

Colombia

Lozada explains that the lack of commercial channels and knowledge of the Spanish language, and the geographic location of Kunas, have pushed them to sell their *molas* to intermediaries at reduced prices.[22] These intermediaries may be of two types: distributors and matchmakers.

Distributors or 'moleros' are retailers who buy *molas* from Kuna living in Colombia and Panama. Due to the small number of Kuna remaining in Colombia, they are unable to produce the amount of product the market requires; consequently, after buying all the *molas* they can find from Colombian Kuna, the moleros travel to Panama.

This practice is well known by the Panamanian authorities, who have prohibited it, alleging loss of money and information. In an attempt to discourage this practice, in 2000 'The Code of Use of Collective Right "*Mola* Kuna Panama"' was created which establishes that *molas* are a collective property belonging to the whole Kuna people and not to each one of the individuals that comprise the people. Nevertheless, Colombian traders are still able to buy *molas* from Panamanian Kuna.

Matchmakers, the second type of intermediaries, are independent entrepreneurs who usually buy *molas* from traders. However, evidence shows that once their companies get bigger, they buy *molas* directly from Kuna.[23] In addition to the intermediaries, some associations of artisans are emerging as a third party in the Colombian *mola* market. This is the case of Asoimola. So far, the creation of associations of Indigenous peoples for the commercialisation of their traditional cultural expressions has been done with government support through 'Artesanías de Colombia' (Crafts of Colombia). Importantly, intellectual property rights are used by Artesanías de Colombia as a tool that helps the strengthening of artisans' capabilities and promotes the matching of the supply and demand. In that regard, the seal of quality 'Hecho a Mano' (handmade),[24] some collective trade marks, and some designations of origin[25] have been obtained in Colombia by such associations.

22 For example, Kuna used to sell to intermediaries *molas* of 30 × 30 cm for between 23,000 and 30,000 Colombian pesos, which later are sold for about 200,000 Colombian pesos. ibid 27–28.

23 'Mola Sasa' is an example of a company that has grown and keeps buying directly from Indigenous communities, see <https://molasasa.com/> accessed 2 December 2021.

24 ICONTEC, *Certificación Sello Hecho a mano* (ICONTEC) <https://www.icontec.org/eval_conformidad/%E2%80%8Bcertificacion-sello-hecho-a-mano/> accessed 2 December 2021.

25 This is the case of, for example, the black pottery from the Chamba and Chipuelo municipalities in the department of Tolima <https://artesaniasdecolombia.com.co/PortalAC/Contenido/ListaTag.jsf?tag=%20denominaci%C3%B3n%20de%20origen> accessed 2 December 2021.

Panama

The context of the Kuna people in Panama shows the existence of a growing economy in which *molas* play an important role. Information on their commodification can be found reporting that a path for a future market started to open up during the 1960s. The interest in *molas* resulted in the expansion of their selling to local stores and tourists in Panama City. By 1968 the 'Cooperativa de Productores de *Molas'* ('cooperative for producers of *molas'*, hereinafter the Cooperative) was formally established, and by 1969 it had its own store. However, the Cooperative did not result from a Kuna initiative, but from a sewing school that was under the direction of the US Peace Corps.[26] Under the Cooperative function, members share assets, profits, and risks. For the production, women retrieve fabrics from the cooperatives and return them transformed into *molas*. Once they are received, the Cooperative tags each *mola*, and records it with the price of each sale.[27] In principle, this scheme allows better control over production, helps women receive a much higher price per *mola* than they would receive through an intermediary, and ensures an equal distribution of profits among members. As in Colombia, intermediaries have a place in the commodification of *molas* in Panama. Nonetheless, a major portion of the market is under Cooperative control.

As the demand for *molas* increases, replicas and imitations appeared. In response, with the support of the national government and the WIPO, Kunas registered 'GaluDugbis', a collective trade mark created for guaranteeing their authenticity to consumers. In addition, *molas* are protected under the Panamanian Law 20 of 2000, a *sui generis* law to protect the collective rights of Indigenous peoples (including traditional knowledge and traditional cultural expressions). Nevertheless, national protection does not prevent imitation and unauthorised trade in different jurisdictions.

Differences between Colombian and Panamanian protection of traditional cultural expression through the trade of *molas*

As mentioned before, the legal differences in the management and protection of traditional cultural expressions in Colombia and Panama can be better appreciated by observing the alternatives Kuna have for the commodification of their *molas*. First of all, the fact that in Colombia no law protects traditional cultural expressions allows the existence of a market in which anyone can legally (though not necessarily fairly) commercialise *molas*. On the contrary, on the Panama side there are specific laws and a code of conduct stating that the market for *molas* must remain under the Kuna's control. The advantages of this situation are evident: intellectual property rights granted to Indigenous peoples, the possibility to have greater control over the selling of *molas*, the consequent higher revenues

26 Lynn Stephen, 'Culture as a Resource: Four Cases of Self-Managed Indigenous Craft Production in Latin America. Economic Development and Cultural Change' (1991) 40(1) *EDCC* 101, 113.

27 ibid 114.

from sales, and better distribution of the profits among community members. The absence of this kind of law in Colombia also means the need for Colombian Kuna to conduct a long process for the recognition of their traditional cultural expressions as a part of the National Cultural Heritage. However, within the intangible cultural heritage frame, protection is only granted against unauthorised copying and reproduction, as can be appreciated in the 'Sombrero Vueltiao' (the upside-down hat) case.[28] Table 7.1 contains the existent Colombian and Panamanian legal frame for the protection of traditional cultural expressions. The problems that these different approaches protecting traditional cultural expressions bring within the context of a transboundary situation, and the options Kunas may have, are noted below.

Common elements in some successful experiences of commodification of traditional cultural expressions

In addition to the protection and preservation of traditional knowledge and traditional cultural expression, there is interest in the commodification of objects based on such goods, as well as concerns about the possible negative effects that this could bring for Indigenous peoples. Given the importance of the commodification of *molas* for the Kuna economy and the fact that this is an issue heightening division between Colombian and Panamanian Kuna, this section reviews some experiences of traditional cultural expressions considered as successful, with the aim of identifying useful elements that may help to cope with such a challenge. Stephen reports the experiences of the Otavelefios from Ecuador, the Nahua and the Zapotec from Mexico, and the Kuna from Panama as successful cases of 'community-controlled craft production'. The common elements she identifies are, first, the existence and preservation of community land as basic support for the Indigenous people's way of life; second, the specialised production of goods for exchange and commercial experience which is of another type than created during the colonial period;[29] and third, the maintenance of traditional institutions responsible for social and cultural reproduction, providing the basis for community self-management.[30] Specifically on the Panamanian Kuna's experience, Stephen states that the use

28 In Colombia, protection against imitation of a traditional cultural expressions is given. For example, the 'Sombrero Vueltiao' (the upside-down hat), belonging to the culture of the Zenú people. In this case, through Resolution 439 of 2013, the Superintendence of Industry and Commerce (SIC) ordered to suspend the production and commercialisation of all hats imitating the sombrero vueltiao and impose a fine on the offenders. The action was based on three legal precedents: first, the sombrero vueltiao recognition as symbol of national identity by the Law 908 of 2004; second, the declaration of 'Tejeduría Zenú' (Zenú weaving) as a protected appellation of origin by the Resolution 71097 of 2011 of the SIC; and third, the register of the collective trade mark 'Sombrero Vueltiao' granted by Resolution 70661 of 2011 of the SIC.

29 Stephen (n 26) 108-115.

30 ibid 124, 125.

Table 7.1 Colombian and Panamanian laws on the protection and management of traditional cultural expressions

Colombia	*Panama*
Constitutional[a] framework recognising fundamental rights of Indigenous and local communities (Articles 7, 8, 10, 63, 68, 70, and 72 of the Political Constitution of 1991). It also recognises: • That the protection of the Indigenous peoples' fundamental rights might be sought through the constitutional action of 'tutela' (Article 86). • A Special Indigenous Jurisdiction that confers political, administrative, and jurisdictional powers to the Indigenous communities to implement their customs within their territories around the country (Article 246). • Collective property on their territories (Article 329).	**Constitutional** framework recognises Indigenous cultural identity, with a mention of their material, social, and spiritual values (Articles 76, 77, 83), provides protection for Indigenous languages (Article 84), and establishes the creation of an institution for the study, dissemination, preservation, and promotion of such values (Article 86).
Laws on intangible cultural heritage Law 397 of 1997 General Law of Culture. Law 1185 of 2008 by way of which Law 397, 1997 is amended and **added**, and other provisions are decreed. This law: • **States the recognition** and protection of the Indigenous peoples' intangible cultural heritage to preserve, enrich, and disseminate it as well as their identity (Articles 4, 11.1.1, and 11-1). • Creates the procedure for the institutional protection of intangible cultural heritage (Article 8).	**Law recognising collective rights of the Kuna people** Fundamental Law of Gunayala of 2013, recognising Kuna': • Collective personality for the exercise of rights in their own territory (principles 3 and 4, Articles 5, 9, 12, 17, 24, and 84). • Right to protect, preserve, and recover their culture (Articles 15, 22). • Collective intellectual property ownership of *molas* and their innovations (Article 92).

(*Continued*)

Table 7.1 (Continued)

Colombia	*Panama*
Law 23 of 1982 on Copyright Recognises that 'folklore and traditional works from unknown authors' (Article 187.2) belong to the public domain.	***Sui generis* Law** recognising intellectual property rights of Indigenous and local communities over their traditional knowledge and traditional cultural expression. Law 20 of 2000, on the Special Intellectual Property Regime Governing the Collective Rights of Indigenous Peoples for the Protection and Defence of their Cultural Identity and their Traditional Knowledge and Enacting Other Provisions. This law seeks the protection of collective intellectual property rights and the traditional knowledge of Panamanian Indigenous peoples over their creations, by means of establishing: • Legal recognition and protection of the collective intellectual property rights of Indigenous peoples over their immaterial creations and culture (Articles, 1, 5, and 6). • The creation of a special register system (Articles 1, 4, 7, 8, and 9). • A legal impediment for third parties to obtain intellectual property rights over Indigenous peoples' cultural elements (Article 2). • The cultural objects under this law (Article 3). • The promotion of Indigenous arts and handicrafts (Articles 10-14) and their right to use and commercialise their cultural manifestations according to their customary law and traditions (Article 15). • A set of punishable acts related to the unauthorised commercialisation, distribution, and imitation of Indigenous peoples' cultural elements (Articles 17-23). The Code of Use of Collective Right '*Mola* Kuna Panama' of 2000 which, despite its voluntary nature, is an instrument complementing the application of the Laws mentioned above.

[a] The Constitute Project provides access to the texts of the related documents. See Zachary Elkins, Tom Ginsburg and James Melton, 'Constitute Project' (2013) <https://www.constituteproject.org/> accessed 2 December 2021.

of a cooperative network for the direct sale of *molas* to tourists and foreign middlemen who sell them abroad is the key element that makes this a successful experience of culture commodification.[31]

For Chennells, the San-Hoodia is another case of success, due to the achievement of an agreement with a private party[32] and the involvement of a third party for the implementation of a 'media and research contract'[33] and for the training of the San leaders in its use.[34] Although this case does not relate to traditional cultural expressions or traditional knowledge, it shares similarities with the characteristics identified by Stephen: the Kuna and San people received external support to develop their commodification strategies. The Panamanian *Mola* Cooperative originated from a sewing school that was under the direction of a Peace Corps volunteer, and the San people were assisted by the Working Group of Indigenous Minorities in Southern Africa (WIMSA) for the implementation of the contracts used within the agreement made for the 'access and benefit-sharing' of their traditional knowledge associated to the use of the hoodia plant.

From the study of Chennells and others, a causal link can be observed between the level of communal institutions and the benefits obtained by Indigenous peoples when external aid is received. This study compares the development of the same project in two different Indigenous peoples, one in Mexico and the other in Peru, to conclude that the better results found in Peru were related to the robustness of their communal institutions.[35] The Mayan communities in Chiapas were less organised, as there were hardly any Indigenous political organisations authorised to represent and speak on behalf of the communities in relation to local and national natural resources[36] and, seemingly, the opposite contributed to the more successful development of 'prior informed consent' in the Peruvian case.[37] This way, one could agree with Stephen in that self-management and successful entrepreneurship are linked to an internal reinforcement of local cultural identity,[38] and 'can result in locally controlled capital accumulation and cultural self-defence'.[39]

31 ibid 108.

32 Roger Chennells, 'Putting Intellectual Property Rights into Practice: Experiences from the San' in Rachel Wynberg, Doris Shroeder and Roger Chennells (eds) *Indigenous Peoples, Consent and Benefit Sharing. Lessons from the San-Hoodia Case* (Springer 2009) 225.

33 ibid.

34 ibid 220.

35 Roger Chennells, Victoria Haraseb, and Mathambo Ngakaeaja, 'Speaking for the San: Challenges for Representative Institutions' in Wynberg, Shroeder and Chennells (eds) (n 32) 166, 167.

36 Joshua P Rosenthal, 'Politics, Culture and Governance in the Development of Prior Informed Consent in Indigenous Communities' (2006) 47(1) *Current Anthropology* 119; Chennells, Haraseb, and Ngakaeaja (n 35) 166.

37 Chennells, Haraseb, and Ngakaeaja (n 35) 166, 167.

38 Stephen (n 26) 101.

39 ibid 125.

The Colombian armed conflict: an element affecting traditional cultural expressions protection due to negative impacts on Indigenous peoples' lives

The first question that may rise if Colombian and Panamanian Kuna's actual situations are compared is, why they have not developed equally? After all, they are one single people. Probably, the different answers to this question will be linked to their fragmentation after the independence of Panama and may also be related to the many sociological, political, and economic conditions that characterise each country. Among all the possible causes that could be identified, the Colombian internal war seems to be determinant, as it has caused a constant internal forced displacement which has had a major negative effect for the Indigenous population, the Darien and Urabá regions being particularly affected.[40] Aside from the social trauma this can cause,[41] the constant situation of displacement[42] and the potential risks for social leaders' lives (Indigenous leaders, farmers, and trade unions)[43] prevent Indigenous peoples from remaining in the same territory for long periods of time. A situation of constant displacement might affect Indigenous peoples' capacity to develop and strengthen their community-based organisations, which, as explained in the previous section, are deemed to be critical for capacity building, both among the members of these peoples and between the peoples and external parties. Due to the weak or non-existent community organisations, Indigenous peoples seem to have more difficulties in reaching decisions and finding the legitimate channels for discussion and communication with external organisations, institutions, and individuals. Under these conditions it is reasonable that the actions and strategies for the protection and commercialisation of *molas* in Colombia have been carried out with the necessary support of the government. It

40 The Ombudsman Office states that forced displacement of the population continues to be the most evident manifestation of systematic violation of international humanitarian law by armed actors, and that Indigenous peoples are one of the most affected and vulnerable populations. Defensoría del Pueblo, *Informe Defensorial sobre el Desplazamiento Forzado por la Violencia en Colombia* (República de Colombia 2001) 2, 5 <https://www.defensoria.gov.co/es/public/Informesdefensoriales/765/El-Desplazamiento-Forzado-por-la-Violencia-en-Colombia-desplazamiento-forzado-en-Colombia-Informes-defensoriales---Conflicto-Armado-Informes-defensoriales---Derecho-Internacional-Humanitario-Informes-defensoriales---Desplazados.htm> accessed 2 December 2021.

41 On social trauma experienced by Indigenous peoples, e.g., Sousan Abadian 'From Wasteland to Homeland: Trauma and the Renewal of Indigenous Peoples and Their Communities' (PhD thesis, Harvard University, Cambridge, MA, 1999) in Chennells, Haraseb and Ngakaeaja (n 35) 170, 171.

42 The 'Single Register of Victims' (Registro Único de Víctimas – RUV) of the national government reports that between 1985 and the 31 December 2019 a total estimated of more than 8 million people were displaced as a result of the internal armed conflict, <https://www.unidadvictimas.gov.co/es/victimas-en-el-exterior/mas-de-un-millon-y-medio-de-victimas-de-desplazamiento-en-colombia-han> accessed 2 December 2021.

43 According to the 'Instituto de Estudios para el Desarrollo y la Paz' – Indepaz (Research Institute for Development and Peace), during the year 2020 in Colombia 310 social leaders were assassinated <http://www.indepaz.org.co/lideres/> accessed 2 December 2021.

is not yet possible for these communities to act independently, not because of the lack of socio-political maturity but because of the unstable conditions for the consolidation of proper autonomic institutions that must be developed by the Kuna people. The paradox is evident; the Colombian war weakens the communities, the government has to intervene, and the impact of such intervention probably reproduces communities' dependence on external support for their own processes, in this case, the protection and commodification of *molas*, that, otherwise, would develop with a more horizontal relationship with governments as in Panama.

Some alternatives for the Kuna in Colombia

Contexts of violence may have many different consequences. The previous section pointed out the way in which Indigenous peoples may be directly affected by the Colombian internal armed conflict. Some other factors may create, in addition, indirect effects. Governmental lack of capacity to develop and implement 'positive and defensive' measures for traditional knowledge and traditional cultural expressions' protection and management is, amongst other factors, probably the most important.

Currently, the Colombian government's focus of attention (in addition to the COVID-19 pandemic response) is the implementation of the Colombia-FARC peace agreement. As can be logically deduced, in a situation such as this, other social needs have not been included in the political agenda. Nonetheless, some advances have been made. For instance, a process for designing the outlines of a public policy for the development of a traditional knowledge inventory has been established.[44] There is also the support provided by Artesanías de Colombia for the commercialisation of Indigenous peoples' traditional cultural expressions. Thus, possible mechanisms may be identified to improve Indigenous peoples' conditions within a framework of armed conflict, governmental difficulties, and commodification of cultural expressions. Because the Kuna people live in Colombia and Panama, the development and application of any of those measures have an additional implication, they should be sought within a transboundary context. The evident difficulty this brings is that laws have their scope limited to the territory of the country they belong to. For this reason, despite the existence of proposals supporting the use of national laws to take legal action in national courts based on immaterial rights,[45] authors such as Oberthür and Rosendal, and

44 See Mincultura, 'Política de Patrimonio Cultural Inmaterial' <http://patrimonio.mincultura.gov.co/patrimonio/Paginas/POL%c3%8dTICA-DEL-PATRIMONIO-CULTURAL-INMATERIAL-.aspx> accessed 2 December 2021.

45 See for example Christine Godt, 'Enforcement of Benefit-Sharing Duties in User Countries' in Evanson Kamau, and Gerd Winter (eds), *Genetic Resources, Traditional Knowledge and the Law: Solutions for Access & Benefit Sharing* (Earthscan 2009) 432; Hiroji Isozaki, 'Enforcement of ABS Agreements in User States' in Evanson Kamau and Gerd Winter (eds), *Genetic Resources, Traditional Knowledge and the Law: Solutions for Access & Benefit Sharing* (Earthscan 2009) 441.

Tvedt have pointed out the difficulties derived from the inadequate incorporation of core elements into national legal systems,[46] and the failure to enact compatible legislations in provider and user countries.[47] In the case of the Kuna, on the one hand Panama protects Indigenous peoples' 'cultural elements' and 'traditional artistic expressions'[48] through the Law 20 of 2000 and the Executive Decree 12 of 2001; on the other hand, Colombia has no special laws for that purpose and traditional cultural expressions protection is provided in connection with intangible cultural heritage regulations. Although protection against unauthorised copying and reproduction can be obtained in Colombia, the incompatibility between the laws of these countries results in the need for Panamanian Kuna to initiate completely new actions of a different kind when the protection of their rights is sought in Colombia. Such processes could take years, notwithstanding the issues related to the territoriality of the intellectual property right involved. For that reason, finding a bilateral solution seems very appropriate, as Cabrera and López suggested for access and benefit-sharing.[49]

Bilateral approaches have also been a subject of study, where three main approaches can be identified: first, the implementation of a full-fledged intergovernmental organisation based on a binding international treaty; second, a non-governmental organisation built upon existing institutions; and third, a contractual framework between willing governments.[50] However, it is unclear whether Colombia and Panama would ever enter into negotiations of any kind within a context as described above, and it is also uncertain whether they could reach an agreement. Despite the opportunities that achieving an agreement on this matter may offer, this seems unlikely to happen in the near future. An option that would create the first steps towards reaching a bilateral agreement would be opening branch offices of the Panamanian cooperative in Colombia. This strategy should be accompanied by the registration of the cooperative's trade mark in this country.

46 Sebastian Oberthür and G Kristin Rosendal, 'Global Governance of Genetic Resources: Background and Analytical Framework' in Sebastian Oberthür and G Kristin Rosendal (eds), *Global Governance of Genetic Resources: Access and Benefit Sharing after the Nagoya Protocol* (Routledge 2014) 6; Morten Walløe Tvedt, 'Beyond Nagoya: Towards a Legally Functional System of Access and Benefit Sharing' in Sebastian Oberthür and G Kristin Rosendal (eds), *Global Governance of Genetic Resources: Access and Benefit Sharing after the Nagoya Protocol* (Routledge 2014) 158–159.

47 Tvedt (n 46) 158, 161–163.

48 Own translation of the Spanish terms 'elementos culturales' and 'expresiones artísticas tradicionales' used in Panama's Article 1 of the Law 20 of 2000.

49 Jorge Cabrera Medaglia and Cristian López Silva, 'Addressing the Problems of Access: Protecting Sources, while Giving Users Certainty' (IUCN Environmental Policy and Law, Paper No. 67/1 2007) 65.

50 Tom Dedeurwaerdere et al., 'Governing Global Scientific Research Commons under the Nagoya Protocol' in Elisa Morgera, Matthias Buck and Elsa Tsioumani (eds), *The 2010 Nagoya Protocol on Access and Benefit-Sharing in Perspective: Implications for International Law and Implementation Challenges* (Legal Studies on Access and Benefit-sharing, v. 1, BRILL Nijhoff 2012) 402–403.

Alternatively, the use of an appellation of origin (AO) may be explored, as handicrafts could be included in addition to agricultural products.[51] The benefits of its use have been acknowledged by authors such as Covarrubia. She has found that its use has the potential to improve the community economy, preserving traditional cultural expressions and protecting biodiversity.[52] Additionally, the intellectual property system should be open to the possibility that AO can be transboundary when identifying a product (either agricultural or a handicraft) produced by peoples whose existence has shared the territory of two or more countries. However, this would require the development of an agreement between countries, despite cases in which geographical and cultural conditions (for instance the traditions of a particular community such as the Kuna people) are the same between two or more countries.[53]

Article 132 of Panama's Law 35 of 1996 on Industrial Property protects AO related to the geographical indication (from a country, a region, or a locality) which serves to designate a product that has its origin in that part of the geography. Such a denomination refers to the quality or characteristics that are determined exclusively by the geography, human and natural factors included.[54] The protection is related to ban on the use of such appellations if they do not correspond to the country, region, or locality. It is also interesting that the Panamanian Law 20 of 2000 on intellectual property related to the collective rights of Indigenous peoples forbids, in its Article 2, the use of peoples' 'customs, traditions, beliefs, spirituality, religion, worldview, expressions of folklore, artistic expressions, traditional knowledge and all other traditional forms of expression' for intellectual property purposes unless there is an authorisation for such use or the use or protection via intellectual property has been requested directly by the Indigenous peoples.[55]

Nevertheless, to date there is no information about an AO applied in a transboundary situation. Within the WTO forum, the protection of wines and spirits has moved forward towards a proposal for multilateral registration, yet no agreement

51 Some examples can be appreciated on the web page of the Colombian Superintendence of Industry and Commerce at <https://www.sic.gov.co/productos-con-denominacion-de-origen> accessed 2 December 2021.

52 Patricia Covarrubia, 'Geographical Indications of Traditional Handicrafts: A Cultural Element in a Predominantly Economic Activity' (2019) 50 *IIC* 441. See Dev S Gangjee 'Geographical Indications and Cultural Rights: The Intangible Cultural Heritage Connection?' in Christophe Geiger (ed), *Research Handbook on Human Rights and Intellectual Property* (Edward Elgar Publishing 2015) 545–559.

53 It is possible to develop a shared agreement on the protection of these appellation of origin in transboundary situations. See Irina Kiryushina and Andrey Serebryakov, 'Legal Protection of Cross-Border Use of Intellectual Property' (2019) 4(22) *Religación* 279–285.

54 Law No 35 of May 10, 1996 which dictates provisions on industrial property, https://wipolex.wipo.int/en/legislation/details/3387 accessed 2 December 2021.

55 Law No 20 of June 26, 2000, concerning the Special System for the Collective Intellectual Property Rights of Indigenous Peoples, for the Protection and Defense of their Cultural Identity and Traditional Knowledge (2000) <https://wipolex.wipo.int/en/text/188986> accessed 2 December 2021.

has been reached. By the same token, the proposal for the extension of the 'higher level of protection' recognised in Article 22 of the TRIPS Agreement, but only for wines and spirits has not reach an agreement either. Given these difficulties in reaching an international agreement, it would be necessary to negotiate an agreement between both countries, Colombia and Panama, to protect AOs for the Kuna people. However, if no agreement is reached, there is still the possibility for each country to obtain an AO to protect *molas*, as with 'pisco' through a bi-national AO conferred to Chile and Peru. Thus, there are signs on the horizon for such an initiative.

As in fact the intellectual property system seems to be insufficient for the purposes of transboundary situations such as the Kuna people, the judicial system of enforcement should be surpassed for a system of association in which the organisations in both countries can work out possible ways to protect and appropriate their own process while the countries reach a bilateral agreement eventually. Such an association could mean common registration of the AO in both countries under a common understanding that the conditions for such AO are in fact shared on both sides of the border, and the registration of common trade marks. The chain for the commercialisation and distribution and the communities' self-appropriation could be improved with the support of each country's organisation such as *Artesanías de Colombia* and the Panamanian Kuna's Cooperative.

For now, the better option Kuna seem to have is the use of their national laws on protection of the Collective Intellectual Property Rights (in Panama) and the traditional cultural expressions under the intangible cultural heritage law (in Colombia) and the register of an AO in Colombia and Panama, complemented using the unfair competition law. Ideally, Panamanian and Colombian Kuna should both work together in order to achieve the protection of *molas* and, maybe, to create closer ties that give them the opportunity to develop together.

Conclusion

The management and protection of traditional knowledge and traditional cultural expressions in transboundary situations can be one of the major challenges that neighbouring countries have, perhaps because, despite legal initiatives such as the global multilateral benefit-sharing mechanism proposed in Article 10 of the Nagoya Protocol, the countries have not yet been able to reach an agreement with some level of internationalisation for the management of transboundary situations. Consequently, responses should be sought through national laws. Thus, in this case, unless a bilateral agreement between Colombia and Panama exists, the national laws of each of these countries must be applied within their territories for the protection and commodification of *molas*, with the limitations and obstacles this may have. For instance, *molas* are protected in Colombia as an intangible cultural heritage and in Panama as a traditional cultural expression within the intellectual property frame.

The Colombian internal armed conflict is a factor adding further challenges to this case. On the one hand Indigenous peoples' needs are outside of the country's political agenda and, on the other hand, the displacement suffered by Indigenous peoples as a direct effect of the war has caused for them a low level of development of their community-based organisations. Because of this, unlike their Panamanian counterparts, now, Colombian Kuna will need more support for the protection and management of their traditional cultural expressions. Additionally, the lack of organisation of the Colombian *mola* market is perceived by Panamanian Kuna as a factor of risk for theirs, which increases division among this people.

In this context, proposals such as developing a bilateral agreement or obtaining a single AO to protect *molas* in both countries do not appear feasible in the short or middle terms. The use of national laws seems the best option for Kuna for the protection and management of *molas*, and traditional cultural expressions and intangible cultural heritage in general, as well as the use of intellectual property rights to obtain more comprehensive protection of these goods, such as trade marks and an AO for each country.

References

Abadian S, 'From Wasteland to Homeland: Trauma and the Renewal of Indigenous Peoples and their Communities' (PhD thesis, Harvard University 1999)

Álvarez A D, *La Nación Gunadule en el contexto binacional Colombia-Panamá: configuración, manejo y luchas por el territorio sagrado* (Tesis de grado presentada como requisito para optar al título de Magister en Estudios Urbano Regionales, Facultad de Arquitectura, Universidad Nacional de Colombia, Sede Medellín 2016)

Bartolomé M and Barabas A, 'Recursos culturales y autonomía étnica. La democracia participativa de los Kuna de Panamá' (1998) 8(16) *Alteridades* 159

Cabrera J and López C, 'Addressing the Problems of Access: Protecting sources, while giving users certainty' (IUCN Environmental Policy and Law, Paper No. 67/1 2007)

Covarrubia P, 'Geographical Indications of Traditional Handicrafts: A Cultural Element in a Predominantly Economic Activity' (2019) 50 *IIC* 441

Chennells R, 'Putting Intellectual Property Rights into Practice: Experiences from the San' in R Wynberg, D Shroeder and R Chennells (eds), *Indigenous Peoples, Consent and Benefit Sharing: Lessons from the San-Hoodia Case* (Springer 2009)

Chennells R, Haraseb V and Ngakaeaja M 'Speaking for the San: Challenges for Representative Institutions' in R Wynberg, D Shroeder and R Chennells (eds) *Indigenous Peoples, Consent and Benefit Sharing. Lessons from the San-Hoodia Case* (Springer 2009)

DANE, *Población Indígena de Colombia* (Resultados del Censo Nacional de Población y Vivienda 2018 Septiembre 16 de 2019)

Defensoría del Pueblo, *Informe Defensorial sobre el Desplazamiento Forzado por la Violencia en Colombia* (República de Colombia 2001)

Dedeurwaerdere T et al., 'Governing Global Scientific Research Commons under the Nagoya Protocol (ch 13)' in E Morgera, M Buck and E Tsioumani (eds), *The 2010 Nagoya Protocol on Access and Benefit-Sharing in Perspective: Implications for International Law and Implementation Challenges* (Legal Studies on Access and Benefit-sharing, v. 1, BRILL Nijhoff 2012)

Dirección de Desarrollo Territorial Sostenible, Subdirección de Ordenamiento y Desarrollo Territorial, *Aspectos Básicos Grupo Étnico Indígenas* (Departamento Nacional de Planeación, República de Colombia 2010)

Elkins Z, Ginsburg T and Melton J, 'Constitute Project' (2013) <https://www.constituteproject.org/>

Gangjee D S, 'Geographical Indications and Cultural Rights: The Intangible Cultural Heritage Connection?' in C Geiger (ed), *Research Handbook on Human Rights and Intellectual Property* (Edward Elgar Publishing 2015)

Godt C, 'Enforcement of Benefit-Sharing Duties in User Countries' in E Kamau and G Winter (eds), *Genetic Resources, Traditional Knowledge and the Law: Solutions for Access & Benefit Sharing* (Earthscan 2009)

Howe J, 'La Revolución Dule: una revolución indígena del siglo XX' (2016) 56 *Boletín del Museo del Oro* 205

ICONTEC, *Certificación Sello Hecho a mano* (ICONTEC) <https://www.icontec.org/eval_conformidad/%E2%80%8Bcertificacion-sello-hecho-a-mano/>

Isozaki H, 'Enforcement of ABS Agreements in User States' in E Kamau and G Winter (eds), *Genetic Resources, Traditional Knowledge and the Law: Solutions for Access & Benefit Sharing* (Earthscan 2009)

Jiménez M, *Propuesta de Política Pública Pluricultural para la Protección de los Sistemas de Conocimiento Asociado a la Biodiversidad en Colombia* (Ministerio de Ambiente 2013)

Kiryushina I and Serebryakov A, 'Legal protection of cross-border use of intellectual property' (2019) 4(22) *Religación* 279

López D, *Teoría Impura del Derecho: Transformación de la cultura jurídica latinoamericana* (Universidad de los Andes LEGIS, Universidad Nacional de Colombia 2004)

Lozada L, *Las Capas Comerciales de la Mola en el Mercado Artesanal de Bogotá* (Trabajo presentado para optar al título de Antropología, Escuela de Ciencias Humanas, Universidad del Rosario 2018)

Marks D, *The Evolution of the Kuna Mola: From Cultural Authentication to Cultural Survival* (A thesis submitted in fulfilment of the requirements for the degree of Doctor of Philosophy, School of Fashion and Textiles College of Design and Social Context, RMIT University, August 2012) in Lozada L, *Las Capas Comerciales de la Mola en el Mercado Artesanal de Bogotá* (Trabajo presentado para optar al título de Antropología, Escuela de Ciencias Humanas, Universidad del Rosario 2018)

Ministerio de Cultura, *Tule (Kuna), la gente por amor por la palabra* (Ministerio de Cultura, República de Colombia 2010)

Ministerio del Interior, *Pueblo Tule o Cuna* (República de Colombia 2012)

Oberthür S and Rosendal G K, 'Global Governance of Genetic Resources: Background and Analytical Framework' in S Oberthür and G K Rosendal (eds), *Global Governance of Genetic Resources: Access and Benefit Sharing after the Nagoya Protocol* (Routledge 2014)

Rosenthal J P, 'Politics, Culture and Governance in the Development of Prior Informed Consent in Indigenous Communities' (2006) 47(1) *Current Anthropol* 119

Ruiz M, 'The Legal Protection of Widely Shared and Dispersed Traditional Knowledge' in D F Robinson, A Abdel-Latif and P Roffe (eds), *Protecting Traditional Knowledge: The WIPO Intergovernmental Committee on Intellectual Property and Genetic Resources, Traditional Knowledge and Folklore* (Routledge 2017)

Sánchez B E, *Justicia y Pueblos Indígenas de Colombia* (Universidad Nacional de Colombia 1998)

Stephen L, 'Culture as a Resource: Four Cases of Self-Managed Indigenous Craft Production in Latin America: Economic Development and Cultural Change' (1991) 40(1) *EDCC* 101

Tvedt M W, 'Beyond Nagoya: Towards a Legally Functional System of Access and Benefit Sharing' in S Oberthür and G K Rosendal (eds), *Global Governance of Genetic Resources: Access and Benefit Sharing after the Nagoya Protocol* (Routledge 2014)

Vallejo-Trujillo F, 'Fundamentos Constitucionales para la Protección del Conocimiento Tradicional' (2007) 18 *Pensamiento Jurídico* 147

8 The '*Pisco* War'

A Chilean-Peruvian conflict at the crossroads of an intellectual property regime and intangible cultural heritage

Bernardo Alarcón Porflidtt

Introduction

Pisco, a grape spirit produced in the Andean region in South America, presents a case study of conflict over the transboundary use of geographical indications regarding intangible cultural heritage practice. People in both Peru and Chile claim that *pisco* is a part of the identity and heritage of their traditional *pisco*-making communities. Some of these communities are located across the border and others are very distant from each other. Geographical indications have been registered in both countries in an attempt to legally protect the use of the name *pisco*, sparking a '*Pisco* War'.

In this chapter, the 'geographical indication' term is used in a broad sense – including denomination of origin – taking as a starting point the definition given by the Trade-Related Aspects of Intellectual Property Rights (TRIPS) Agreement of the World Trade Organization (WTO), as stated in Article 22.1:

> Geographical indications are, for the purposes of this Agreement, indications which identify a good as originating in the territory of a Member, or a region or locality in that territory, where a given quality, reputation or other characteristics of the good is essentially attributable to its geographical origin.

The TRIPS Agreement does not oblige member states of the WTO to recognise an exclusive right concerning geographical indications, thus enabling global harmonisation. Rather, it obliges member states to establish legal means so that interested parties can prevent the misuse of geographical indications or denomination of origin in a product. This may be done through trade mark law rather than under original and specific (*sui generis*) geographical indications laws.[1] This has been the case since the late 1990s. This lack of global harmonisation of geographical indications has increased the controversy over *pisco* ownership in the intellectual

1 Graham Dutfield, 'Intellectual Property Tools for Products Based on Biocultural Heritage: A Legal Review of Geographical Indications, Trademarks and Protection from Unfair Competition' (International Institute for Environment and Development 2011) 14.

DOI: 10.4324/9781003345237-9

property arena. Subsequently, the Chilean and Peruvian governments have tried to secure international protection for their national registered geographical indications through different legal strategies. Chile, on the one hand, has signed trade agreements where Chilean *pisco* is recognised as a geographical indication, but these also accept the existence of Peruvian *pisco*. On the other hand, Peru has designed a public policy that claims *pisco* is an exclusively Peruvian product, without accepting the coexistence of the right to protect the name of homologous Chilean products.

Although there seems to be a strong commercial possibility to conduct a *pisco* joint market exercise, both countries have chosen not to. Instead, they have engaged in a '*Pisco* War', which is political in nature. That is why this chapter provides an overview of the '*Pisco* War', with an emphasis on each party's positioning. It critically examines the legal tools that Peru and Chile have used in attempting to protect their interests and/or solve the conflict. The chapter is organised into three main sections: first, it provides an overview of the evolution of the *pisco* conflict itself. Second, the focus shifts onto the legal strategies that each country has developed, including processes and institutions that have mediated in this controversy. Third, it proposes using intangible cultural heritage analysis to differentiate both varieties of *pisco*. Registering opposing geographical indications in Peru and Chile will not address controversies around *pisco* and may even exacerbate them. To find a solution to the '*Pisco* War', a broad approach is needed that includes a cultural perspective.

The '*Pisco* War': comparing positions from Chile and Peru

Pisco is a high-quality *moscato* brandy that represents an important cultural tradition in Chile and Peru linked to the geographical environment and human factors. Mitchell and Terry state

> Pisco's origins coincide with Spanish colonization. The viceroyalty of Peru included both modern Chile and Peru. Grapes brought from Europe and originally meant for general consumption and wine production found a second use in Pisco production when the Spanish crown prohibited wine exports that would compete with Spain's domestic industry.[2]

It follows that the Chilean and Peruvian varieties of the brandy would have originated from a common historical context and seem to have been produced before the current national borders were put in place which dates to 1929.[3] The so-called '*Pisco* War' is a commercial dispute between Chile and Peru. There is a

2 Jerry T Mitchell and William C Terry, 'Contesting Pisco: Chile, Peru, and the Politics of Trade' (2011) 101 *Geogr Rev* 518, 524.
3 See Pablo Lacoste et al., 'A Bi-National Appellation of Origin: Pisco in Chile and Peru' (2013) 73 *Chil J Agric Res* 424.

disagreement over the intellectual property rights, namely the geographical indications, which both states have registered the use of the name, which is linked to the origin, creation, and process of this liquor. In Chile, *pisco*'s denomination of origin was enforced by the 1931 Decree No 181, which delimited the production area;[4] while in Peru, the 1946 Ministerial Resolution No 1.206 officially defined that the name *pisco* would be followed by the name of the place where the product was obtained, prepared, and distilled.

The Peruvian state argues that the term *pisco* was misappropriated by Chile, as the word is indeed found in a Peruvian port of the same name. The Port of Pisco (200 km south of Lima) was used for the transport of products, this being the reason why the name began to be associated with this brandy, often made in the valley of *Ica*, a little further south.[5] One might infer that the Peruvian *moscato* brandy is the only variety that deserves this denomination, being incompatible with the Chilean version. The Chilean state, on the other hand, contends that this liquor was also produced during the colonial period in the Northern Chilean regions of *Coquimbo* and *Huasco*. Besides, the Chilean position goes that the Peruvian Port of Pisco was only a packaging and trade centre, and not the actual place of origin.[6]

Mitchell and Terry point out 'tensions over the rights to own [rights to the name] Pisco simmered throughout the twentieth century each country's systems of production began to mature'.[7] At present, Peru's position excludes the use of the name *pisco* by any other country 'on the grounds that the products are distinct—Chile's being just another "aguardiente" and Peru's as the original'.[8] Chile's position, instead, is to share the name and work with Peru on a joint strategy to promote the brandy within international markets.

The '*Pisco* War' saw a resurgence during the negotiation of different international trade agreements in the early 2000s, in particular, those that established the protection of the *pisco* name through specific clauses in favour of Chile. However, these international agreements also recognised an exception in Peru's favour as a holder of rights over this denomination. The international acceptance of both Peruvian and Chilean *pisco* is coherent with the TRIPS Agreement regulations that set minimum standards for intellectual property protection. Part II, Section 3: Geographical Indications of the TRIPS Agreement, establishes the rules on geographical indication, which does not oblige members to recognise an exclusive right, but rather to establish the legal means for interested parties to prevent the misuse of a geographical indication or denomination of origin in a product. Therefore, the owner of a particular geographical indication – either a state,

4 Article 2 rules that 'The name Pisco is exclusively reserved for spirits that come from the distillation of grape produced within the [*Copiapó, Huasco, La Serena, Elqui*] regions'.

5 Pablo Lacoste et al., 'Pisco Denomination of Origin in Chile: Some National and International Matters' (2014) 32 *IDESIA* 47.

6 Hernán F Cortés Olivares, 'El Origen, Producción y Comercio del Pisco Chileno 1546–1931' (2005) 2 *Revista Universum* 42.

7 Mitchell and Terry (n 2) 528.

8 ibid 529.

community, company, or individual – must ask for protection in all the countries where a right holder is interested in having a protected geographical indication. Those countries will determine, according to their own legal procedures, whether a geographical indication will be protected.

As Peru and Chile have taken different positions regarding the '*Pisco* War', the next section will explore both stances, paying attention to national legislations and trade agreements signed by Chile and Peru.

The Chilean approach

Although Chile has accepted the international coexistence of Chilean and Peruvian *pisco*, at a national level the country has regulated the production of this brandy in some detail. The Production, Elaboration and Marketing of Ethyl Alcohol, Alcoholic Beverages and Vinegars Act[9] lays down rules to establish viticultural zones and denomination of origin for wines and other liquors in certain areas of the country. Article 28 of this Act establishes that the name *pisco* is reserved for the brandy that is produced and bottled in the Northern regions of *Coquimbo* and *Huasco*, which is made by distillation from the grape varieties that grow in such regions. Therefore, the special characteristics of *pisco* come from the place where it is produced and its natural ingredients.

In 2005, the Industrial Property Act[10] added geographical indication as an official category of protection within the scope of the intellectual property legal framework. Accordingly, a geographical indication involves a product originating in either the whole of Chile or a specific region or locality, when the product's quality, reputation, or another characteristic is attributable to its geographical origin. The Industrial Property Act also takes into consideration natural and/or human factors that may influence the production of the good. The geographical indication, as an independent category of protection, was part of the harmonisation of national regulations with the requirements of the TRIPS Agreement.

All the technical aspects for the making of *pisco* are set out in the Ministry of Agriculture Decree,[11] which enforces its denomination of origin regulating the use, conditions, and characteristics that must be respected during the elaboration, bottling, and packing of the product. This decree recognises 13 *pisco* grape varieties,[12] which are divided into 4 groups:[13] (1) varieties introduced by the Spaniards during the colonial period; (2) creole (local) grapes born from the natural crossbreeding

9 Act No 18.455 (1985).

10 Act No 19.039 (2005), Articles 92–105.

11 Decree No 521 (2000).

12 The so-called '*pisco* grapes' that are listed are: *Moscatel de Alejandría* or *Italia*, *Moscatel Rosada* or *Pastilla*, *Torontel*, *Moscatel de Austria*, *Pedro Jiménez*, *Moscatel Blanca* o *Temprana*, *Chasselas Musque Vrai*, *Moscatel Amarilla*, *Moscato de Canelli*, *Moscatel de Frontignan*, *Moscatel de Hamburgo*, *Moscatel Negra* y *Muscat Orange*.

13 Philippo Pszczólkowski and Pablo Lacoste, 'Native Varieties, an Opportunity for Chilean Pisco' (2016) 48 *Revista de la Facultad de Ciencias Agrarias* 239.

of Spanish grapes; (3) varieties incorporated after 1850 using French grapes; and (4) other European varieties. At present, 85.7% of Chilean *pisco* is produced using creole grape varieties and 14% using the Spanish one (*Moscatel Alexandria*).[14] Therefore, most of the Chilean grape varieties to make *pisco* encompass particular creole grape varieties derived from the natural and continuous crossbreeding of European grapes.

At the international level, Chile has used bilateral or multilateral free trade agreements as a strategy to obtain the protection of Chilean *pisco*. For example, the United States-Chile Free Trade Agreement, signed in 2003, rules that each country shall provide the legal means to identify and protect geographical indications;[15] among them is 'Pisco Chileno', which is produced only in Chile as a distinctive product.[16] Another example is an agreement signed between the European Union and Chile,[17] which rules in Annex VI that *pisco* is a protected designation for spirit drinks originating in Chile. However, in a joint declaration, the European Union clarified that 'The Community will recognise the denomination of origin Pisco for the exclusive use of products originating in Chile. This shall in no way prejudice the rights that the Community may recognise in addition to Chile, exclusively to Peru'.[18] Other international trade agreements follow the same protection.[19] This admits homonymous geographical indications, namely Chilean *pisco* and Peruvian *pisco*, which are spelt and pronounced alike, 'but which identify products originating in different places, usually in different countries'.[20] Therefore, the rights of Chile over the geographical indication

14 ibid 249.

15 Article 17.4 Geographical Indications:

> 1. Geographical indications, for the purposes of this Article, are indications which identify a good as originating in the territory of a Party, or a region or locality in that territory, where a given quality, reputation, or other characteristics of the good is essentially attributable to its geographical origin. Any sign or combination of signs (such as words, including geographical and personal names, letters, numerals, figurative elements, and colours), in any form whatsoever, shall be eligible for protection or recognition as a geographical indication.

16 Section E – Other Measures, Article 3.15: Distinctive Products:

> 2. The United States shall recognize *Pisco Chileno* (Chilean Pisco), *Pajarete*, and *Vino Asoleado*, which is authorized in Chile to be produced only in Chile, as distinctive products of Chile. Accordingly, the United States shall not permit the sale of any product as *Pisco Chileno* (Chilean Pisco), *Pajarete*, or *Vino Asoleado*, unless it has been manufactured in Chile in accordance with the laws and regulations of Chile governing the manufacture of *Pisco*, *Pajarete*, and *Vino Asoleado*.

17 Agreement establishing an association between the European Union and Chile [2002] OJ L352/3.

18 ibid.

19 Other examples of trade agreements that recognise Chilean *pisco* are: China-Chile Free Trade Agreement (2006) Annex 2b; Mexico-Chile Free Trade Agreement (1999) Annex 15-24; Canada-Chile Free Trade Agreement Annex C-11; Australia-Chile Free Trade Agreement (2009), Article 3.12.

20 WIPO, 'Frequently Asked Questions: Geographical Indications' (WIPO About IP) <https://www.wipo.int/geo_indications/en/faq_geographicalindications.html> accessed 2 December 2021.

pisco are accepted by the European Commission without affecting those of Peru. Identifying homonymous geographical indications guarantees consumer protection and avoids unfair competition, and in the process persuades *pisco* producers to specify on the labels the differences between one geographical indication and another.

This is the position that Chile has taken during the '*Pisco* War'. It has ensured that different trade agreements recognise Chilean *pisco* as a geographical indication, without excluding or denying the existence of Peruvian *pisco* as a homonymous product.

Peruvian approach[21]

Unlike Chile, the Peruvian state does not acknowledge any *pisco* but Peru's. All the public policies on the subject aim at the protection of Peruvian *pisco* as exclusive, wherein the *pisco* denomination of origin ownership corresponds to the Peruvian state. The National Institute of Culture Resolution No 179 (1988) declares the *pisco* appellation of origin as a 'cultural heritage of the Peruvian Nation' because the name *pisco* originates in the *Quechua* language, which relates to one of Peru's aboriginal peoples. In 2017, this resolution became an Act.[22] In addition, Peru declared that *pisco* is a subject that, being of national interest, the country should promote and disseminate, and that the Executive Power should use all possible means to secure international recognition of *pisco* as exclusively Peruvian.[23] For instance, India recognised the Peruvian geographical indication for pisco in 2005.[24] Public policies thus highlight the political importance of the *pisco* geographical indication to the Peruvian state. The Industrial Property Act regulates the DO in Peru.[25] It states that this name should be used to designate a product originating from a region or geographical place within the country whose qualities or characteristics are unique or derive from natural and human factors linked to that place (i.e., cultures, traditions, and/or resources).

21 Information obtained from the Peruvian bill No 1596-2016 called 'Pisco Designation of Origin as Cultural Heritage of the Nation'.

22 Act No 30.639 (2017).

23 Act No 30.460 (2016).

24 Intellectual Property India, Geographical Indications Registry, Geographical Indication No 43, Certificate No 118 (2005). On 29 September 2005, the Embassy of Peru applied for the registration of the geographical indication '*pisco*' without placing the word 'Peruvian' before the name *pisco*. The registration was accepted and published in the Indian Gl Journal, No 13 on 1 August 2006. However, oppositions were filed with regard to this registration. On 29 November 2018, in the cases number OA/1/2010/GI/CHN and OA/2/2010/GI/CHN, the Intellectual Property Appellate Board (IPAB) of India ruled that the mark '*pisco*' is eligible for registration by itself, and consequently, oppositions filed were dismissed. On the other hand, on 3 June 2020, the *Asociacion De Productores de Pisco A. G.* filed an application to register 'Chilean *pisco*' as a geographical indication. This application is currently on pre-examination status.

25 Legislative Decree No 823 (1996).

The Production and Marketing of Beverage National Alcoholic Act[26] provides the current definition of *pisco*.[27] It declares that *pisco* is a Peruvian DO applicable to products obtained from the distillation resulting from the fermentation of ripe grapes, elaborated on the coast of the departments of *Lima*, *Ica*, *Arequipa*, *Moquegua*, and *Locumba*, and the *Sama* and *Caplina* valleys of the department of Tacna. Peruvian *pisco* is made from two colonial grape varieties, namely *País* and *Muscatel de Alexandria*, and other creole varieties.[28] At this point, it becomes evident that the production processes of Chilean and Peruvian *pisco* differ in location, but also in grape varieties. Although both brandies have in common the use of *Muscatel de Alexandria and Torontel* grapes, all the other grapes currently used are varieties that resulted from local crossbreeding in Chile and Peru respectively. It is not yet known when these creole (local) *pisco* varieties were born. Crossbreeding could have started between the 18th and 19th centuries[29] before the border was clearly set in 1929.[30]

Moreover, Peru is a member of the Andean Community of Nations.[31] Decision No 486 rules the concepts of DO and geographical indication in similar terms to those of the Lisbon Agreement, establishing the mechanisms for both categories to be protected in the Andean countries. The Decision sets out special provisions for 'well-known' names, which can be protected beyond the bounds of speciality and territoriality.[32] In respect to this Andean Community Decision, Peru affirms that the DO *pisco* is classified as a well-known[33] name among a wide range of

26 Act No 26.426 (1994). This Act makes into law a Supreme Decree 001-ICTI / IND (January 1991). All the other technical aspects of pisco are regulated in the Technical Standard No 211.001/2006.

27 Definition based on the Institute for Industrial Technological Research and Technical Standards (ITINTEC).

28 *Quebranta, Mollar, Albilla, Torontel, Negra Criolla, Corriente* y *Uvina.*

29 Pszczółkowski and Lacoste (n 13) 245.

30 The Treaty of Lima was signed on 3 June 1929. This treaty delimited the current borders between Chile and Peru.

31 The Andean Community of Nations is a regional, economic, and political organization. The active members are Bolivia, Colombia, Ecuador, and Peru. The Cartagena Agreement created it on 29 May 1969. The Decision No 486 approved the 'Common Regime on Industrial Property', in September 2000.

32 Administrative Decision No 13880 (2017) INDECOPI.

33 The Decision No 486 regulates well-known distinctive signs in the Title XIII. Article 228 states that

> In order to determine the notoriety of a distinctive sign, due regard shall be had to the following factors among others:
>
> (b) the duration, extent and geographical scope of its use inside or outside any member country;
>
> (c) the duration, extent and geographical scope of the publicity accorded to it inside or outside any member country, including the advertising and display of the goods or services, the establishment or the activity to which it is applied, at fairs, exhibitions or other events;
>
> (d) The value of any investment made to promote it, or to promote the establishment, activity, goods or services to which it is applied.

consumers, not only those who consume *pisco* but also among general Peruvian consumers. The well-known status of (Peruvian) *pisco* among consumers sets up legal protection and recognition for the name within all four member countries of the Andean Community, as established in one of the latest rulings by the Court of Justice of the Andean Community.[34] As a result, within the Andean Community countries, Peruvian *pisco* should benefit from the same exclusive protection as within Peru.

At a supranational level, Peru submitted a formal request to register *pisco* DO at the International Bureau of the World Intellectual Property Organization (WIPO) following the Lisbon Agreement provisions.[35] The requested protection applies to 'a liquor of grape, obtained by distilling fresh must of recently fermented grapes under traditional methods established in the production areas previously recognised and classified as such in the normative rules contained in the Peruvian Technical Standard 211-011:2002'. This request was accepted and published. However, the Lisbon Agreement has a limited scope as only 30 countries have signed it. Chile is one of the countries that has not signed and thus, has followed the strategy of obtaining 'Chilean Pisco' geographical indication recognition through trade agreements, which have been successfully negotiated since the mid-1990s. That is why, even though some countries are part of the Lisbon Agreement, they have actually refused Peru's registration request based on previous commercial agreements with Chile.[36] The European participating countries in the Lisbon Agreement[37] have partially refused the Peruvian request due to a previous association agreement[38] between the European Union and Chile. This association agreement recognises *pisco* as a protected designation for spirit drinks from Chile, and determines that protecting *pisco* 'for products originating in Peru does not hinder the use of such denomination for products originating in Chile'.[39]

A good example that reflects the Chilean and Peruvian position in the '*Pisco* War' at a European level was the case O/079/20 argued in the Intellectual Property Office of the United Kingdom.[40] The applicant, a Chilean private society, applied

34 Court of Justice of the Andean Community, Case No 50-IP-2017.

35 Apellation of Origin 865 Pisco (19/05/2005).

36 Mexico (*Declaración de Denegación de Protección en virtud del artículo 5.3 del Arreglo de Lisboa*, October 2006); Costa Rica (*Denegación de Protección en virtud del artículo 5.3 del Arreglo de Lisboa*, July 2006) totally refused the inscription in favour of Peru based on the signing of previous commercial agreements with Chile.

37 Czech Republic, France, Italy, Hungary, Slovakia, Portugal, and Bulgaria.

38 Council Decision of 18 November 2002 on the signature and provisional application of certain provisions of an Agreement establishing an association between the European Union and Chile [2002] OJ L352/1.

39 Commission Regulation (EU) No 1065/2013 of 30 October 2013 amending Annex III to Regulation (EC) No 110/2008 of the European Parliament and of the Council on the definition, description, presentation, labelling, and protection of geographical indications of spirit drinks [2013] OJ L289/48.

40 Trade mark decision [2020] BL No O/079/20.

to register a trade mark under the Class 33 goods (Alcoholic beverage: *Pisco*). The Peruvian Institute opposed this application for the Defence of Competition and Protection of Intellectual Property (*INDECOPI*). It claimed that registering this trade mark would be deceiving to the public in regard to the geographical origin of the good, as the products had not been processed in Pisco, the Peruvian town and region that the opponent describes as famous for its fruit spirits.[41] The opponent claimed that the mark is protected in England and Wales under the 'extended form' of passing off.[42][43] The applicant, however, reaffirmed Chile's position regarding the '*Pisco* War', claiming that *pisco* is widely recognised as the national drink of both Peru and Chile and that the EU has adopted legal provisions permitting the sale of goods originating from both Peruvian and Chilean producers under the registered name *pisco*.[44] The Intellectual Property Office illustrated this dispute very clearly by asserting that the issue is not whether the European Union has protected the Chilean geographical indication against misuse in the EU, but whether the EU protection of the Peruvian geographical indication applies to using *pisco* in the EU for goods covered by the Chilean geographical indication. However, Intellectual Property Office decided that 'it does not'.[45] Concerning deceiving the public, the Intellectual Property Office stated that the relevant consumer association of the term *pisco* with Peru is also far from made.[46] Accordingly, the Intellectual Property Office accepted the trade mark registration for the Chilean company,[47] using the coexistence principle;[48] in other words, weakening Peru's position.

The Trade Promotion Agreement signed by Peru and the United States further limited the ability of Peru to make a sole claim to the name *pisco*.[49] Annexe 1.3

41 ibid para 3.
42 ibid para 5.
43 Passing off protects trade marks and reputation of businesses against unfair competition when a business deceives the public into believing their goods are those of another competitor. Therefore, the 'unfair' business benefits from the reputation that another competitor legitimately built. The principles of passing off were summed up in *Reckitt & Colman Products Ltd v Borden Inc* [1990] R.P.C. 341, para 406. It requires three elements to be proven: (1) it must establish goodwill or reputation attached to the goods or services in the mind of the purchasing public. It is recognised by the public as distinctive specifically of the 'affected business'. (2) It must demonstrate a misrepresentation by the 'unfair business' to the public (whether or not intentional) leading or likely to lead the public to believe that goods or services offered are the goods or services of the 'affected business'. (3) It must demonstrate that the 'affected business' suffers or is likely to suffer damage due to the erroneous belief engendered by the 'unfair business' misrepresentation.
44 Trade mark decision [2020] BL No O/079/20 para 6.
45 ibid para 36.
46 ibid para 46.
47 ibid para 47.
48 The coexistence principle allows that two different business use a similar or identical trade mark to market a product or service, in this case the name *pisco*, without unfairly interfering with others' businesses. Therefore, both parties recognise the right of the other to exist together in the market. In this case, the coexistence is based on the geographical origin of the product.
49 The United States-Peru Free Trade Agreement (TPA 2009).

under the title 'Country-Specific Definitions' reads that the United States shall recognise 'Pisco Perú' as a distinctive product of Peru.[50] According to Mitchell and William, 'Peru's [Trade Promotion Agreement] with the United States bears no language specific to Pisco, the implication being that Peru recognised Chile's prior established partial claim to Pisco in its own FTA [Free Trade Agreement]'.[51] The Peruvian state made an implicit acceptance that the geographical indication that belongs to that country is '*pisco* Perú' and not solely *pisco* as historically claimed.

For Peru, the '*Pisco* War' evolved into a nationalistic issue rather than a juridical discussion, with *pisco* itself being elevated into a state affair. On the other hand, the Chilean approach has based its defence on a commercial nature rather than a state policy.[52] It would seem that at the international level, the '*Pisco* War' has been legally resolved by recognising the coexistence of legal rights to use the same name for these brandy varieties. This guarantees accurate consumer information and keeps them informed by persuading *pisco* producers to specify the origin of the *pisco* on the labels.

The geographical indication is an effective legal mechanism in certifying a product's good reputation, assuring homogeneous quality and informing consumers. However, an interesting new Peruvian strategy arose to link *pisco* with local cultural practices, highlighting the relevance of the product to cultural identity. This strategy will be discussed in the following section.

Cultural heritage related to *pisco*

Although the protection of a geographical indication may include the recognition of a production method that incorporates cultural expressions, the '*Pisco* War' has been focused on the geographical origin of the product rather than a cultural approach to differentiate Chilean and Peruvian *pisco*. Strategically, Peru policy is now covering this approach; the Ministry of Culture submitted a request[53] to enter the UNESCO World Heritage List. The country seeks the 'Wineries and Vineyards for traditional Pisco Production' acknowledgement because *pisco* has a longstanding tradition and is part of a deeply rooted identity in Peru, whose production has historically involved social, economic, and cultural aspects of the

50 ibid Annex 1.3, Section E: Other Measures, Article 2.12 (2).

51 Mitchell and Terry (n 2) 528.

52 A private entity arose in 2003 to protect the interests of Chilean *pisco* producers. The Chilean Pisco Producer Association is a trade union organisation that represents producers and *pisco* companies that are protected under the Chilean geographical indication *pisco*.

53 UNESCO Tentative List, request submitted by the Peruvian Ministry of Culture on 5 August 2019 based on criteria ii and iv: (ii) to exhibit an important interchange of human values, over a span of time or within a cultural area of the world, on developments in architecture or technology, monumental arts, town-planning, or landscape design; (iv) to be an outstanding example of a type of building, architectural, or technological ensemble or landscape which illustrates (a) significant stage(s) in human history, <https://whc.unesco.org/en/tentativelists/state=pe> accessed 2 December 2021.

aforementioned *pisco*-producing regions from the late 16th century onwards.[54] *Pisco*, as the argument goes, is linked to specific manifestations of culture that inspire a feeling of identity and belonging.[55]

> Wineries testify to various aspects of traditional culture in today's communities linked to the production of wines and Piscos, which show strong elements of continuity from the viceroyalty and republican past in the field of agricultural technologies and pre-industrial production, the knowledge associated with Pisco making and handcrafted work for producing vessels, repairing and maintaining equipment, etc., as well as in the gastronomy, customs, festivities and traditions related to Pisco production, among other aspects.

Peru's request is framed within a cultural heritage approach to its architectural-typological-productive process. It presented evidence of the technology historically used to produce *pisco*, which involves traditional utensils and pottery that are not necessarily found elsewhere.[56] Dutfield points out that 'Chilean and Peruvian Pisco differ in terms of definition, grape type, alcoholic content, and (obviously) designated growing area, and this does not make cooperation between the two countries at all easy'.[57] Consequently, a geographical indication debate drawing exclusively on technical aspects of the respective legal frameworks, such as this, a cultural heritage approach could help to broaden the analysis as to include a sociocultural context.

The underlying principles of geographical indication protection are the defence of consumers against deception when products are attributed qualities that they do not have and the defence of local producers from unfair competition; a cultural heritage approach seeks to promote local development and the acknowledgement of local cultural practices. Therefore, the focus of the attention is different from geographical indication protection. A cultural heritage approach highlights the social bonds and participation between those who have jointly made – within their geographic area and community – goods such as *pisco*.

Acknowledging the cultural heritage differences between Chilean and Peruvian *pisco* can greatly contribute to resolving the conflict behind the '*Pisco* War'. The cultural approach is a useful conceptual framework to distinguish broader processes, ownership, and applicability of the regulation in cases of blurry boundaries such as Chilean and Peruvian *pisco*. Rinallo and Pitardi suggest two dimensions to differentiate more clearly a geographical indication in conflict: geographical

54 UNESCO Tentative List, request submitted by the Peruvian Ministry of Culture on 5 August 2019, 'Justification of Outstanding Universal Value' at <https://whc.unesco.org/en/tentativelists/state=pe> accessed 2 December 2021.

55 ibid.

56 ibid 8.

57 Graham Dutfield (n 1) 30.

area and production methods.[58] Establishing a geographical area defines the territory of origin of the product, which is a basic prerequisite to obtain a geographical indication protection. For *pisco*, these are Chile's *Coquimbo* and *Huasco* regions and Peru's departments of *Lima, Ica, Arequipa, Moquegua*, and *Locumba* as well as the valleys of *Sama* and *Caplina* in the department of *Tacna*. On the other hand, identifying the production methods specifies traditional expertise, which derives from carrying out a production process in a certain way across time. The specific production method of Peruvian *pisco* is explained as follows:[59]

> The particular production process of Pisco, which differs notoriously from the production of wine and other beverages derived from the total or partial alcoholic fermentation of grape must, is based on the must extraction and fermentation and its subsequent distillation through the use of falcas and/or stills, a process that required a specific infrastructure adapted to soil conditions, climate, availability of materials to produce presses, stills, falcas, jars, jugs, ovens, etc., of which there are numerous examples from the 17th, 18th and 19th centuries in the producing regions, many of which are still in use.

The *pisco* production method has been shaped by its cultural heritage and passed down through generations using it, and as such, it captures the history and idiosyncrasy of a distinct Peruvian region. This Peruvian cultural heritage has evolved historically from the common past with Chile – from the 19th century to an independent one after the border was set in 1929. During the 20th century, separate national law-making processes started to strengthen their respective national identities regarding *pisco*. Each state regulated *pisco* production in such a way that could protect and strengthen its own cultural identity, helping to reach a product differentiation between these two countries. This production method, regulated in detail by law, upholds the cultural knowledge around *pisco*.

Generally, the production method of *pisco* can be understood as both a 'culture of production' and a 'culture of identity'.[60] The former is the process of method creation of *pisco*-making as such that becomes a technique that is being protected. This aspect is more objective in nature and is already included in the respective Peruvian and Chilean *pisco* technical standards of production (i.e., grape varieties, temperature, distillation, age). The latter is somehow representative of a national/regional cultural value associated with group identity, which is more subjective in nature as it relates to cultural practices around *pisco* (i.e., gastronomy, customs, festivities, and traditions). This 'culture of identity' has been mobilised by state actions, such as the registration and international promotion of the geographi-

58 Diego Rinallo and Valentina Pitardi, 'Open Conflict as Differentiation Strategy in Geographical Indications: The Bitto Rebels Case' (2019) 121 *Brit Food J* 3102.

59 UNESCO Tentative List (n 54).

60 Tomer Broude, 'Taking Trade and Culture Seriously: Geographical Indications and Cultural Protection in WTO Law' (2005) 26 *U Pa J Int'l Econ L* 623.

cal indication. Broude states that 'these dimensions should help us better understand the cultural basis of the arguments for increased geographical indication protection for food and wine products'.[61] This suggests that both aspects together, the 'culture of production' and the 'culture of identity', should be highlighted by Peru and Chile to differentiate their respective brandies.

The cultural approach followed by Peru, which could also be used by Chile, emphasises the association between *pisco* production and its traditional cultural expression – things that, while relating to *pisco* production, have symbolic value.[62] Kamperman affirms that

> the protection of cultural diversity, as market differentiation, even in purely economic terms, increases consumer welfare. Its abilities to engender collective stakeholdership, the connection to a certain place or locality, and differentiating characteristics, make GIs eminently suitable to play a role in the protection, not only of a market in traditional cultural expressions (TCEs), but also of TCEs and cultural diversity itself.[63]

Differentiating *pisco* based on cultural identity linked to transmission of the knowledge and skills for making the brandy within specific areas may provide more commercial benefit than legal protection of the name of the final product. Information about the cultural basis for the differentiation of Chilean and Peruvian *pisco* could be included in the labelling, conveying a message about cultural uniqueness and giving meaning to the name protected under the geographical indication.

If *pisco*-producing culture is highlighted in marketing messages, then Chilean and Peruvian brandies could have a greater product differentiation in the market. Differentiation in the market helps, first, to improve consumer perception about *pisco*, and second, to reaffirm the cultural identity of the community involved in the *pisco* production. This can promote economic and social advancement in the context where increased cultural diversity has displaced the, once dominant, nationalist model. When not protected, products are easily homogenised by the market, or as Ubertazzi puts it, 'products would otherwise be increasingly similar

61 ibid 642.

62 The consideration of the *pisco* production as a cultural expression is aligned with Article 2(1) of the UNESCO Convention for the Safeguarding of the Intangible Cultural Heritage, which adopts a broad definition of intangible cultural heritage, emphasising the practices, representations, expressions, knowledge, skills – as well as the instruments, objects, artefacts, and cultural spaces associated therewith – that communities, groups, and, in some cases, individuals recognise as part of their cultural heritage.

63 Anselm Kamperman Sanders, 'Incentives for and Protection of Cultural Expression: Art, Trade and Geographical Indications' (2010) 13 *J World Intellect Prop* 81, 82.

due to mass production techniques, the globalisation of trade and the de-localisation of product manufacture'.[64]

Conclusion

The '*Pisco* War' between Chile and Peru is a political dispute with a clear nationalist-political tone, as well as an international conflict of a purely legal-commercial nature, and both aspects seem often to coexist. Chile and Peru have embarked on a political dispute over the 'historical' or 'original' rights that each country claims to have over *pisco* geographical indication. However, from a legal point of view, this 'war' has been partially solved in some trade agreements in key markets, such as the EU and the US, by using the homonymous geographical indication, allowing the coexistence of Peruvian and Chilean *pisco*. The homonymous geographical indication solution has been used in different international trade agreements based on the recognition that Chilean and Peruvian *pisco* have differences in terms of grape varieties, processing method, and, of course, origin.

Currently, the Chilean and Peruvian *pisco* industries are internationally in a rather marginal position compared to other spirits. Thus, a joint strategy to promote and position *pisco* may be sought to compete with other internationally recognised spirits such as tequila or whiskey. Even recognising a cultural heritage differentiation between the different kinds of Chilean and Peruvian *pisco* could work under a common commercial strategy. A commercial alliance, mainly in the distribution and sale processes, constitutes a strategic decision that may be considered to obtain greater benefits in foreign markets.

Even though for the time being a joint commercial strategy to promote *pisco* internationally seems unlikely, each country (and producers in areas with a specific culture of production) might want to focus on a cultural heritage approach. The cultural dimension of such an approach strengthens not only social linkages between local producers assuring product quality through a defined method of production but also the uniqueness that Chile and Peru have sought separately in respect of the '*Pisco* War'. The intangible cultural heritage approach can be fruitfully used to differentiate homonymous products such as *pisco* in the market, especially in cases where transboundary conflicts over the use of geographical indication protection, whether political or legal in origin, cannot be resolved.

References

Broude T, 'Taking Trade and Culture Seriously: Geographical Indications and Cultural Protection in WTO Law' (2005) 26 *Pa J Int'l Econ L* 623

Cortés H, '*El Origen, Producción y Comercio del Pisco Chileno* 1546–1931' (2005) 2 *Revista Universum* 42

64 Benedetta Ubertazzi, 'EU Geographical Indications and Intangible Cultural Heritage' (2017) 48 *IIC* 562, 567.

Dutfield G, *Intellectual Property Tools for Products Based on Biocultural Heritage. A Legal Review of Geographical Indications, Trademarks and Protection from Unfair Competition* (International Institute for Environment and Development 2011)

Kamperman Sandres A, 'Incentives for and Protection of Cultural Expression: Art, Trade and Geographical Indications' (2010) 13 *J World Intellect Prop* 81

Lacoste P et al., 'A Bi-National Appellation of Origin: Pisco in Chile and Peru' (2013) 73 *Chil J Agric Res* 424

Lacoste P et al., 'Pisco Denomination of Origin in Chile: Some National and International Matters' (2014) 32 *IDESIA* 47

Mitchell J and William T, 'Contesting Pisco: Chile, Peru, and the Politics of Trade' (2011) 101 *Geogr Rev* 518

Pszczólkowski P and Lacoste P, 'Native Varieties, an Opportunity for Chilean Pisco' (2016) 48 *Revista de la Facultad de Ciencias Agrarias* 239

Rinallo D and Pitardi V, 'Open Conflict as Differentiation Strategy in Geographical Indications: the Bitto Rebels Case' (2019) 121 *Brit Food J* 3102

Ubertazzi B, 'EU Geographical Indications and Intangible Cultural Heritage' (2017) 48 *IIC* 562

WIPO, 'Frequently Asked Questions: Geographical Indications' (WIPO About IP) <https://www.wipo.int/geo_indications/en/faq_geographicalindications.html>

9 Cross-border safeguarding of intangible cultural heritage through geographical indications and EU collective marks

Consolidation of litigation through private international law

Benedetta Ubertazzi

Introduction

Unlike transnational disputes concerning intellectual property rights, those regarding European Union (EU) geographical indications and trade marks do not fall into the exclusive jurisdiction rule of the Brussels system. Country by country enforcement of the relevant geographical indication is not imposed by any (international or) EU norm, while the relevant court in EU trade mark disputes is determined according to Regulation (EU) 2017/100[1] (hereinafter the EUTM Regulation), which provides competent courts whose judgment applies throughout the EU. Therefore, consolidation of the relevant litigation can occur, with the advantage of avoiding conflicting judgments and high litigation costs. This would be in line with recent international academic proposals, among which is that of the International Law Association Committee on Intellectual Property and Private International Law.

Consolidation of international intellectual property rights litigation provides one solution to the boundary-based limitations of geographical indication and trade marks for safeguarding intangible cultural heritage in transnational misappropriation cases. A second solution is the use of intellectual property rights as part of a 'broad positive strategy' for safeguarding intangible cultural heritage, with the aim of enhancing the reputation of and encouraging respect for the heritage in question. In turn, this enhanced reputation and respect may result in fewer cross-border misappropriations.

1 Regulation (EU) 2017/1001 of the European Parliament and of the Council of 14 June 2017 on the European Union trade mark (codification) (Text with EEA relevance) (2017) OJ L 154/1.

DOI: 10.4324/9781003345237-10

Consolidation of litigation through private international law

Private international law applies in transnational cases to determine which court is competent to adjudicate them and according to which law. Regarding cross-border geographical indication and trade mark cases, for instance, private international law norms may grant jurisdiction to a single court, allowing for a consolidation of the relevant multi-state legal proceedings. In addition, private international law norms may designate the law of the country of origin as the applicable law, allowing the competent court to apply one law to solve the multi-state litigation proceedings.

Among the private international law norms that grant international jurisdiction to the court of just one of the various states involved are the relevant EU private international law norms. Even though the EU Regulation No 1151/2012 (hereinafter QS Regulation)[2] is exhaustive, it does not prevent the application of national laws because it must still be integrated. In fact, with particular regard to geographical indication infringement, the QS Regulation establishes that EU member states 'shall take appropriate administrative and judicial steps to prevent or stop the unlawful use of geographical indications ... that are produced or marketed in that Member State'.[3] Thus, the QS Regulation takes into account domestic enforcement of geographical indications in purely national infringement cases. However, the QS Regulation does not establish any provision related to the cross-border enforcement of geographical indications in transnational infringement situations. In particular, unlike all other Regulations on unitary intellectual property rights, the QS Regulation does not include any rules on international jurisdiction and applicable law and therefore needs to be integrated. Concerning applicable law, the QS Regulation is integrated by the aforementioned international treaties on geographical indications that determine the application of the law of the state of origin (*lex originis*) to issues such as the geographical indication's existence, ownership, infringement, and remedies. In contrast, for disputes related to intellectual property rights other than geographical indications, the law of the state for which the protection is requested (*lex loci protectionis*) applies under the EU Rome II Regulation.[4] With regard to international jurisdiction, the QS Regulation is integrated by the EU Brussels system, as well as by the Lugano

2 Regulation (EU) No 1151/2012 of the European Parliament and of the Council of 21 November 2012 on quality schemes for agricultural products and foodstuffs. OJ L 343, 14.12.2012.

3 QS Regulation, Article 13.3.

4 Regulation (EC) No 864/2007 of 11 July 2007 on the Applicable Law to Non-Contractual Obligations [Rome II], Article 8. See the Court of Justice of the European Union (CJEU) C-478/07 *Budějovický Budvar, národní podnik v Rudolf Ammersin GmbH* ECLI:EU:C:2009:521, para 79: the 'mechanism' for the protection of geographical indications *lato sensu* intended 'is distinguished by the fact, derogating from the principle of territoriality, that the protection conferred is determined by the law of the Member State of origin and by factual circumstances and perceptions in that State'. See also C-3/91 *Exportur SA v LOR SA and Confiserie du Tech*, paras 12, 13, and 38 ECLI:EU:C:1992:420.

Convention.[5] The Brussels system internationalises cross-border intellectual property rights litigation, concentrating adjudication of disputes before a single judicial authority even in cases of multi-state infringement and reducing the risks of conflicting judgments and the inequalities between different players. In fact, it is true that this system establishes an exclusive jurisdiction rule,[6] according to which international jurisdiction, in cases of legal proceedings concerning registration or validity of patents, trade marks, designs, and other registered intellectual property rights, lies exclusively with the courts of the member state of deposit or registration. This exclusive jurisdiction rule requires proceedings related to the registration or validity of intellectual property rights to be brought before each country of registration. However, the Brussels system limits the scope of the (exclusive) jurisdiction of the courts of the state granting the intellectual property rights to disputes that imply changes in the administrative acts of registration (i.e., validity of registered intellectual property right claims). In contrast, the same system allows other courts, such as those at the defendant's domicile or at the place of the illegal action, to adjudicate other multi-state parallel intellectual property right disputes, which could be consolidated before a single competent court. In addition, the Brussels system's exclusive jurisdiction rule may be applicable to an invalidation of a trade mark registered in breach of a geographical indication under Article 14.1 of the QS Regulation, but it does not apply to claims concerning only geographical indications. In fact, exclusive jurisdiction requires that the registration took place at the national level, whereas the geographical indications registration under the QS Regulation takes place at the EU level. Furthermore, geographical indications cannot become generic or declared invalid and therefore, disputes related to geographical indications cannot concern their validity and do not fall into the exclusive jurisdiction rules, which address validity only. Thus, as long as the relevant cross-border intellectual property rights disputes, in particular those concerning geographical indications, do not fall under the exclusive jurisdiction rule, the Brussels system allows for their consolidation before a single competent court.

Consolidation is also feasible with regard to cross-border enforcement cases related to EU trade marks. The key provisions regulating jurisdiction for EU trade marks are set out in the EUTM. Article 125 of the Regulation provides competent courts capable of providing a judgment that will apply throughout the EU, without

5 Convention on Jurisdiction and the Recognition and Enforcement of Judgments in Civil and Commercial Matters in Lugano of 30 October 2007, OJ L 339/3 (Lugano Convention).

6 Convention on Jurisdiction and the Enforcement of Judgments in Civil and Commercial Matters of 27 September 1968, signed in Brussels (Brussels Convention), then Regulation (EC) No 44/2001 on jurisdiction and the recognition and enforcement of judgments in civil and commercial matters of 22 December 2000, signed in Brussels (Brussels I Regulation) (Brussels, December 2000), and now Regulation (EU) No 1215/2012 of the European Parliament and of the Council on jurisdiction and the recognition and enforcement of judgments in civil and commercial matters (recast) of 12 December 2012, signed in Brussels (Brussels I Regulation Recast), Article 22.4.

the need for litigation in each member state.[7] Article 124 sets out the scope of the EUTM Regulation, stating that the Regulation applies to disputes relating to 'infringement actions',[8] 'actions for declaration of non-infringement',[9] and 'acts occurring after the date of publication of an EU trade mark application, where those acts would, after publication of the registration of the trade mark, be prohibited by virtue of that publication'.[10] Article 124(d) also states that 'counterclaims for revocation or for a declaration of invalidity of the EU trade mark'[11] fall within the scope of the EUTM Regulation. As a result of this, declarations of invalidity as a defence are within the scope of Article 124 of the EUTM Regulation, but validity principally raised is not.

As *lex specialis*, all provisions of the EUTM Regulation prevail over those of the Brussels system. Consequently, even though a declaration of invalidity principally raised falls outside of the scope of the EUTM Regulation as set out by Article 124, other principles contained in the EUTM Regulation apply to such a dispute rather than the Brussels system. Paragraph 32 of the EUTM Regulation's preamble states that

> It is essential that decisions regarding the validity and infringement of EU trade marks have effect and cover the entire area of the Union, as this is the only way of preventing inconsistent decisions on the part of the courts and the Office and of ensuring that the unitary character of EU trade marks is not undermined. The provisions of Regulation (EU) No 1215/2012 of the European Parliament and of the Council[12] should apply to all actions at law

7 Article 125.1 provides that where the defendant is domiciled (or, if not domiciled, has an establishment) in a member state, proceedings should be brought in the place of domicile (or establishment). Article 125.2 provides that where 'the defendant is neither domiciled nor has an establishment in a Member State', but the claimant is either domiciled or has an establishment in a member state, proceedings should be brought in the place of domicile (or establishment). Where neither the defendant nor the claimant is domiciled or established in any member state, Article 125.3 states that 'proceedings shall be brought in the courts of the Member State where the Office has its seat'. 'The Office' here refers to the European Union Intellectual Property Office (EUIPO), meaning that where this provision applies, proceedings will be heard in Spain (as EUIPO is based in Alicante). Consolidation is also feasible before the court that is chosen as that having jurisdiction by the parties expressly or tacitly (Article 125.4). Additionally, proceedings within the scope of the EUTM Regulation, except for actions for a declaration of non-infringement of an EU trade mark, may also be brought in the courts of the member state in which the act of infringement has been committed or threatened, or in which an act referred to in Article 11(2) has been committed (Article 125.5).

8 This also applies to 'actions in respect of threatened infringement relating to EU trade marks' under EUTM Regulation, Article 124 (a).

9 ibid Article 124(b).

10 ibid Article 11(2).

11 ibid Article 124(d).

12 Regulation (EU) No 1215/2012 of the European Parliament and of the Council of 12 December 2012 on jurisdiction and the recognition and enforcement of judgments in civil and commercial matters. OJ L 351, 20.12.2012, 1.

relating to EU trade marks, save where this Regulation derogates from those rules.

As such, the EUTM Regulation provides for consolidation of litigation before a single court in all EU trade mark disputes and the exclusive jurisdiction rule of the Brussels system does not apply.

In sum, transnational disputes concerning EU geographical indications and EU trade marks can be consolidated, with the advantage of avoiding conflicting judgments and high litigation costs. This is in line with recent international academic proposals that, to promote consolidation of cross-border intellectual property right litigation even further, are limiting the scope of exclusive jurisdiction rules. These proposals serve as a model for future negotiations of an international agreement on intellectual property and private international law, as well as for amendments to the Brussels system.

These discussions resulted in the adoption of four sets of principles, namely the ALI Principles;[13] the CLIP Principles;[14] the Transparency Proposal;[15] and the Joint Japanese-Korean Proposal[16] (hereinafter the four sets of principles). All four sets of principles apply to trade marks. Only the CLIP Principles explicitly cover geographical indications, by being applied *mutatis mutandis* to geographical indications.[17] However, it is submitted that the four sets of principles are applicable without reservation to the protection of geographical indications under the condition that this protection can be qualified as an exclusive right. This condition is certainly met under the QS Regulation since Article 4(b) expressly characterises geographical indications as (EU unitary) intellectual property rights.[18]

In November 2010, the International Law Association (ILA) instituted a committee on 'Intellectual Property and Private International Law', which, since its creation, has been working intensively to examine the current state of affairs on the protection of intellectual property in the transnational sphere. Building upon the four sets of principles, the ILA's Committee has finished its work with the adoption and publication of the 'Kyoto Guidelines on Intellectual Property and

13 The American Law Institute, *Intellectual Property: Principles Governing Jurisdiction, Choice of Law and Judgments in Transnational Disputes* (American Law Institute Publishers 2008).

14 European Max Planck Group, *Conflict of Laws in Intellectual Property, The CLIP Principles and Commentary* (OUP 2013).

15 Jürgen Basedow, Toshiyuki Kono and Axel Metzger, *Intellectual Property in the Global Arena* (Mohr Siebeck 2010).

16 Waseda University Global COE Project (2010) *Commentary on Principles of Private International Law on Intellectual Property Rights: Joint Proposal Drafted by Members of the Private International Law Association of Korea and Japan* (Waseda University Global COE Project October 14, 2021) <win-cls.sakura.ne.jp/pdf/28/08.pdf> accessed 17 December 2021.

17 European Max Planck Group (n 14), Article 1:101, para 3(a).

18 F Falconi, 'Chapter Twenty-One: Transnational Litigation on Infringement of Designations of Origin and Geographical Indications Protected under Regulation (EU) No 1151/2012' in Angela Lupone, Carola Ricci and Andrea Santini (eds), *The Right to Safe Food Towards a Global Governance* (Giappichelli 2013).

Private International Law'.[19] The scope of the Guidelines includes geographical indications and trade marks.[20] The Guidelines provide soft-law principles on the private international law aspects of intellectual property, which may guide the interpretation and reform of national and international legislation,[21] and may serve as a model for future international agreements promoting a more efficient adjudication of transnational intellectual property disputes. All four sets of principles and the ILA Guidelines allow for the consolidation of multinational geographical indication and trade mark-related claims, limiting the scope of exclusive jurisdiction rules. This is based on general jurisdiction norms on, first, overcoming exclusive jurisdiction in cases related to validity issues incidentally raised; second, establishing that those issues can be brought before a court of a state other than that of registration, provided that the judgment on validity would have *inter partes* effect; and third, allowing for the adjudication of a geographical indication or trade mark multi-state infringement in its entirety by a single court.

A 'broad positive approach' to intellectual property rights

Through this book, it is noticeable that there exist cases where intellectual property rights can offer valuable protection for intangible cultural heritage elements that are fully compatible with the 2003 Convention for the Safeguarding of the Intangible Cultural Heritage (the 2003 Convention). However, it has also addressed a limitation of intellectual property rights as safeguarding mechanisms: namely, that registration of the relevant intellectual property rights in the countries of origin, or even in other countries, is not sufficient to effectively safeguard intangible cultural heritage in transnational misappropriation cases. This chapter therefore sets out systemic solution to this problem: the consolidation of multinational geographical indication and trade mark-related claims, limiting the scope of exclusive jurisdiction rules in private international law. A second solution is set out: the use, by heritage-bearing communities, groups, and individuals, of intellectual property rights as part of a 'broad positive strategy' for safeguarding intangible cultural heritage.

In many instances, it can be challenging for communities, groups, and individuals to enforce intellectual property rights in court to protect their intangible cultural heritage, particularly in transnational cases. One solution to this is the use of a broader 'positive approach' to safeguard intangible cultural heritage. This

19 The Kyoto Guidelines have been approved by the plenary of the ILA 79th Biennial Conference, held (online) in Kyoto on 13 December 2020.

20 In the current provisional draft, the first guideline on 'scope' emphasises that '1. These Guidelines apply to civil and commercial matters involving intellectual property rights which are connected to more than one country. 2. "Intellectual property right" means … trademark, geographical indication and similar rights'.

21 Toshiyuki Kono, Pedro de Miguel Asensio and Axel Metzger, 'ILA "Kyoto Guidelines on Intellectual Property and Private International Law" Published with Comments' (*Conflict of Laws.net*, 14 April 2021) <https://conflictoflaws.net/2021/ila-kyoto-guidelines-on-intellectual-property-and-private-international-law-published-with-comments/> accessed 17 December 2021.

approach ‘consists of what can be described as semi-legal protection, namely, taking extrajudicial measures in order to settle the dispute out-of-court’.[22] This positive approach therefore encompasses the use of intellectual property rights alongside other legal and marketing safeguarding tools to protect intangible cultural heritage without enforcing legal rights in court. The purpose of this approach is to enhance the reputation[23] of and encourage respect for the heritage in question. In turn, this may create a virtuous circle, with the enhanced reputation of and respect for the intangible cultural heritage (both within and across borders) resulting in non-community members and the general public being more aware of the intangible cultural heritage, leading to fewer misappropriations and therefore resulting in greater safeguarding for the heritage in question.

Addressing this positive approach from the framework of the 2003 Convention, the use of intellectual property rights as safeguarding mechanisms according to such an approach is entirely consistent with the Operational Directives for the Implementation of the Convention for the Safeguarding of the Intangible Cultural Heritage (Operational Directives). The Operational Directives encourage

> the application of intellectual property rights, privacy rights and any other appropriate forms of legal protection, to ensure that the rights of the communities, groups and individuals that create, bear and transmit their intangible cultural heritage are duly protected when raising awareness about their heritage or engaging in commercial activities.[24]

Intellectual property rights are legal rights that are enforceable in court. One of the purposes of intellectual property rights is to ‘enable people to earn recognition or financial benefit from what they invent or create’.[25] Recognition is therefore a concept that is central to intellectual property rights. Moreover, it is a concept that also allows intellectual property rights to provide out of court transnational protection to intangible cultural heritage. For example, trade marks

> are any sign capable of distinguishing the goods or services of one enterprise from that of another … whether the sign is composed of letters, numerals or figurative elements if it is capable of distinguishing the product or service it could amount to a trade mark.[26]

22 Benedetta Ubertazzi, ‘Territorial and Universal Protection of Intangible Cultural Heritage from Misappropriation’ (2010) 8 *NZYIL* 69, 79.

23 Which may be defined as ‘the status and respect given to the heritage (and the bearer community), linked to its value and meaning to the community’.

24 Operational Directives (2018), paras 104, 173(b).

25 WIPO, ‘What is Intellectual Property?’ (WIPO About IP) <www.wipo.int/about-ip/en/> accessed 17 December 2021.

26 Tamara Nanayakkara, ‘Role of Intellectual Property in Enhancing the Competitiveness of the Tourism Industry’ (Small and Medium-sized Enterprises Division, WIPO) 4 <https://www.wipo.int/export/sites/www/sme/en/tourism/tourism_ip.pdf> accessed 17 December 2021.

Thus, a trade mark may safeguard intangible cultural heritage by distinguishing heritage goods and services from the goods and services of other enterprises. In distinguishing goods and services, a trade mark may in turn become synonymous with the reputation of those goods and services. Geographical indications may also enhance the reputation of heritage goods, since a geographical indication 'is a sign used on goods that have a specific geographical origin and possess qualities, reputation or characteristics that are essentially attributable to that origin'.[27] Even out of court, therefore, intellectual property rights such as geographical indications and trade marks may safeguard intangible cultural heritage by enhancing its reputation. As reputation is not rigidly constrained by borders, reputation can therefore be an important means of transnational safeguarding of intangible cultural heritage. Practical examples of using intellectual property rights as safeguarding mechanisms that enhance the reputation of intangible cultural heritage may be found in the work of the Heritage-Sensitive Intellectual Property and Marketing Strategies Project (HIPAMS), which worked with communities in India to develop '"heritage-sensitive" intellectual property protection strategies [that] can give communities greater control over the commercialisation of their heritage while contributing to its safeguarding and ongoing viability'.[28]

In practice, many measures may be used to complement intellectual property rights as part of a positive approach to cross-border intangible cultural heritage safeguarding. Among the transboundary measures that overcome borders and succeed in offering cross-border protection of intangible cultural heritage, this chapter will predominantly focus on case studies in which the author has been directly involved. Two measures that communities, groups, and individuals may use to try to safeguard their intangible cultural heritage element against cross-border misappropriation are codes of ethics, and 'cease and desist' letters. Cease and desist letters can be sent by communities to misappropriators in an effort to make them 'cease and desist' from the act of misappropriation. One practical example of this is the case of the misappropriation of the *Ritual ceremony of the Voladores* by the Mexican company Cerveceria Moctezuma and Heineken (its Dutch parent company).[29] In this case, the intangible cultural heritage practising community sent a 'cease and desist' letter to both the Mexican and Dutch companies.[30] This letter emphasised that the ceremony at stake has been considered to be intangible

27 ibid.

28 Heritage-Sensitive Intellectual Property and Marketing Strategies (HIPMAS India) Project at <https://hipamsindia.org/> accessed 17 December 2021.

29 In June 2021, a further example of misappropriation relating to the *Ceremonial Ritual de los Voladores* occurred when the company 'Moneyman' misused the image of the *Ceremonial Ritual de los Voladores* in an advertisement, offending, discriminating, devaluing, and ridiculing the ceremony. J Francisco De Anda Corral, 'Secretaría de Cultura defiende el Ritual de los Voladores' *El Economista* (Mexico, 28 June 2021).

30 desInformémonos, 'Voladores de Papantla Denuncian que la Cervecera Cuauhtémoc-Moctezuma Profana su Ceremonia Ritual' (*desInformémonos*, 31 March 2017) <https://desinformemonos.org/voladores-papantla-denuncian-la-cervecera-cuauhtemoc-moctezuma-profana-ceremonia-ritual/> accessed 17 December 2021.

cultural heritage by UNESCO since its registration on the Representative List of the Intangible Cultural Heritage of Humanity by Mexico in 2009.[31] The objective of the ceremony is to express profound respect for nature and the spiritual universe, and the use of images alluding to the ceremony by Cerveceria Moctezuma and Heineken was contrary to the cultural and spiritual values that the *Ritual ceremony of the Voladores* represents. Such misuse of the traditions was understood by the community, as indicated in their letter, as trivialising their cultural expressions and violating the protection given by UNESCO and its status of intangible cultural heritage.[32] In the letter, the community required the beer companies to immediately cease their misappropriations and indemnify community representatives.[33] The letter based the community's petition on the relevant Mexican law on *sui generis* copyright, as well as on other international human rights instruments. Despite this letter and the strong reaction of support for the community against the beer companies that the misappropriation originated, these companies did not behave in the expected manner and perpetrated their infringement.

'Cease and desist' letters on their own are not always successful, as the case of the *Ritual ceremony of the Voladores* indicates. This is explained by the fact that 'cease and desist' letters typically invoke the misappropriation of first, conventional or *sui generis* intellectual property rights, second, cultural rights, and third, ethical principles associated with cultural rights. Yet, misappropriators may think that with regard to these claims legally binding enforcement mechanisms are typically lacking. For conventional intellectual property rights, misappropriators may interpret them as either not protecting traditional intellectual creations or as protecting them only in the country of origin rather than in that where the misappropriation occurs. For cultural rights and the human right to culture, misappropriators may interpret them as not enforceable under the intangible cultural heritage because there is no enforcement mechanism related to the cross-border safeguarding of the right to intangible cultural heritage.[34] As for codes of ethics associated with cultural rights, misappropriators may think that those codes are just guidelines that bind only the community members and those who voluntarily adhere to them.

With particular regard to ethical codes, in 2015 the Intergovernmental Committee endorsed 12 ethical principles[35] for safeguarding intangible cultural

31 ibid.

32 Zósimo Camacho, 'Voladores de Papantla Acusan "Daño Moral" de Cervecería Cuauhtémoc-Moctezuma' (*Contralínea*, 30 March 2017) <contralinea.com.mx/archivo-revista/2017/03/30/voladores-de-papantla-acusan-dano-moral-de-cerveceria-cuauhtemoc-moctezuma/> accessed 17 July 2021.

33 ibid.

34 The recommendation of the Mexican National Commission on human rights, characterising misappropriations of culture as human rights violations, enforceable before courts, is particularly significant in this context. If this recommendation is implemented, 'cease and desist' letters would be able to invoke cultural rights and pursue them in court, which may make such letters a more effective tool to counter misappropriation.

35 For a full list of the 12 Principles, see UNESCO, 'Ethics and Intangible Cultural Heritage' Decision of the Intergovernmental Committee: 10.COM 15.a. <https://ich.unesco.org/en/ethics-and-ich-00866> accessed 17 December 2021.

heritage.[36] These principles 'represent a set of overarching aspirational principles' and 'are intended to serve as a basis for the development of specific codes of ethics … adapted to local and sectoral conditions'.[37] One context in which codes of ethics have been used by communities to safeguard their cultural heritage is that of arts festivals, where ethical guidelines and protocols have been used to advise visitors and members of the media about the need to respect intangible cultural heritage. Protocols can ensure proper attribution to intangible cultural heritage bearers and achieve respect for the eventual sacred character of a performance. Such protocols might request the audience to 'please exercise courtesy and sensitivity when taking photographs: seek the permission of the subjects' or may state 'no use, adaptation or commercialisation of intangible cultural heritage without the prior informed consent of traditional custodians'.

The second example involves the Chhau community and it has cross-border implications for two reasons. First, because Zee5 is an 'online video streaming Over The Top (OTT) platform'[38] and can be accessed across international borders. Second, because following the misappropriation, the Chhau community worked alongside the HIPAMS Project, which is composed of an international, multi-disciplinary team, to develop a Chhau Dance Code.[39] This Code contains a number of principles that are embedded in Indian law, such as the right of attribution for performers, and a number that emanate from general human rights norms, such as the right to culture. The purpose of this Code is to lay out the hopes and expectations of the members of the Chhau dance community in their dealings with these different groups who draw on and often profit from their dance. The Chhau Dance Code will be distributed among these groups generally, and each time that the Chhau dancers interact with one of these groups for a particular project or event, the organisers will individually be given a copy of this Code. The aim is that through this process, first, respect will be shown for the Chhau dancers and their intangible heritage, and second, they will be given due acknowledgement and remuneration to ensure that their heritage continues into the future.

From a legal perspective, codes of ethics are characterised as guidelines. Guidelines function in much the same way as contracts; they are binding on those who voluntarily accept to be bound by them. Thus, they can only be partially enforced since in legal terms 'guidelines, no matter how good they are, are just guidelines. They are seldom legally enforced and they often only apply within a certain context'.[40] The partially enforceable nature of codes of ethics (and codes

36 ibid.

37 ibid.

38 Zee5 at <https://www.zee5.com/global/aboutus> accessed 17 December 2021.

39 The HIPAMS Chhau Dance Code, along with the Baul Fakiri Art Code, the Patachitra Art Code, and the Chhau Mask Art Code are available at http://hipamsindia.org/research-output/code-of-ethics/ accessed 17 December 2021.

40 Tunon Håkan, Marie Kvarnström and Henrik Lerner, 'Ethical Codes of Conduct for Research Related to Indigenous Peoples and Local Communities–Core Principles, Challenges and Opportu-

of conduct) is evident in the examples of such codes provided by UNESCO.[41] One such example states that 'codes that are not complied with *can* also have legal implications for code adherents and others who voluntarily accept to follow them.[42] Ultimately, ethical guidelines and protocols and 'cease and desist' letters can provide a degree of safeguarding against misappropriation for intangible cultural heritage. However, as ethical guidelines and protocols only apply to those who agree to be bound by them and 'cease and desist' letters are not in themselves legally binding, they leave misappropriators with the power to choose whether to carry out or continue their misappropriation.

One other mechanism that may complement intellectual property rights, as part of a positive approach to the transnational safeguarding of intangible cultural heritage, which can affect the choice made by misappropriators (particularly when they misappropriate for commercial gain) are campaigns by consumers, such as boycotting. In one case of cultural appropriation, in which the author was not directly involved, consumer campaigns successfully led to the misappropriator publicly acknowledging and seeking to rectify their misappropriation. In this case, Papercut Patterns, a New Zealand company of pattern creators, labelled a new pattern of jackets as 'Kochi Kimono'. The pattern of the jacket labelled as 'Kochi Kimono' 'was a square-cut short jacket, with optional side ties'.[43] Influenced by the creation and advertisement of 'Kochi Kimono' jackets on social media, the Instagram followers of Papercut Patterns, specifically, inexpert seamstresses, started creating their own patterns for jackets and shared their results on the social media Instagram, with the Instagram hashtag Kochikimono, that is, '#Kochikimono', comprising the name of a traditional Japanese dress, 'Kimono'. An Instagram hashtag is a hyperlink that aims to label and categorise content; it is suggested to be a 'powerful marketing and branding tool … helping you be discovered among one billion (and 25 million businesses) on Instagram'.[44] Indeed it is an effective way to get more 'views' on Instagram's posts. Kimono is considered the national dress of Japan, with loose long sleeves and typically

nities' in Anna-Lill Drugge (ed), *Ethics in Indigenous Research, Past Experiences – Future Challenges* (Vaartoe/Centre for Sami Research (CeSam) 2016) 76.

41 UNESCO, 'Examples of Code of Ethics and Professional Codes of Conduct' (UNESCO) <https://ich.unesco.org/en/examples-of-codes-of-ethics-00868> accessed 17 December 2021.

42 See Government of Canada Office of Consumer Affairs, Industry Canada, and the Regulatory Affairs Division, Treasury Board Secretariat. Ottawa, ON: Distribution Services Communications Branch, 'Voluntary Codes: A Guide for Their Development and Use' <https://ich.unesco.org/doc/src/Example_guidance_document-Canada-EN.pdf> accessed 17 December 2021. Italics by the author.

43 Calla Wahlquist, 'Stitch-up: Online Sewing Community at War over Cultural Appropriation' *The Guardian* (London, 1 June 2019) <https://www.theguardian.com/lifeandstyle/2019/jun/01/stitch-up-online-sewing-community-at-war-over-cultural-appropriation> accessed 17 December 2021.

44 Annie Crawford, 'The Ultimate Guide to Instagram Hashtags' (Adobe Creative Cloud Express by Adobe, 20 February 2020) <https://www.adobe.com/express/learn/blog/the-ultimate-guide-to-instagram-hashtags-in-2020> accessed 16 December 2021.

tied with a sash.[45] This popularity of tagging a particular design of jackets as '#kochikimono' continued for 18 months until Helen Kim, an Asian-American woman, pointed out that labelling any design of jacket as 'Kimono', a name of a Japanese traditional dress, 'without any connection beyond a certain boxiness about the sleeves to the traditional Japanese dress, was cultural appropriation'.[46] There was much debate on the topic of cultural appropriation on social media regarding 'Kimono' as well as an interview with Helen Kim, who initiated the awareness of the cultural significance of the design of traditional Japanese dress, 'Kimono', through a leading newspaper company, the *Guardian*.[47] Following this awareness campaign on social media as well as print media, Papercut Patterns, the New Zealand company of pattern creators, promised to rename the pattern of the jacket in question to 'kochi' and also publicly thanked everyone 'who let [them] know the mistake [they] made in giving one of [their] patterns a culturally sensitive name'.[48] This was therefore a clear case of cross-border misappropriation, with a New Zealand company appropriating the national dress of Japan. This case study also reflects the power of consumer campaigns to act as transboundary measures that overcome borders and succeed in offering cross-border protection for intangible cultural heritage.

A further extrajudicial approach that can be employed alongside intellectual property rights to prevent transnational misappropriation of intangible cultural heritage is the use of policy briefs. 'A policy brief is a concise summary of a particular issue, the policy options to deal with it, and some recommendations on the best option' and is 'aimed at government policymakers and others who are interested in formulating or influencing policy'.[49] Policy briefs, therefore, provide communities with the opportunity to engage with policy-makers and play an active role in identifying how existing policy frameworks can be adapted to better safeguard cultural heritage.[50] Such briefs may therefore address the challenges of transnational misappropriations of intangible cultural heritage and may encourage policy-makers to adopt specific measures that may help to enhance the cross-border protection of intangible cultural heritage.

In sum, the purpose of a 'broad positive approach' to intellectual property rights as safeguarding mechanisms is to view intellectual property rights as one among many complementary extrajudicial safeguarding mechanisms that enhance

45 BBC, 'Kim Kardashian West's Kimono Underwear Meets Japanese Backlash' *BBC News* (27 June 2019) <www.bbc.com/news/world-asia-48767678> accessed 20 December 2021.

46 Wahlquist (n 43).

47 ibid.

48 ibid.

49 Agriculture and Economic Development Analysis Division, 'Food Security Communications Toolkit' (Food and Agriculture Organization of the United Nations) 141 <https://www.fao.org/3/i2195e/i2195e.pdf> accessed 17 December 2021.

50 As an example, HIPAMS is currently developing a policy brief alongside communities in India in relation to the Ministry of Culture, Government of India's June 2015 initiative to set up a National Mission on the intangible cultural heritage of India.

the reputation of and encourage respect for the heritage in question. Extrajudicial mechanisms like codes of ethics (which impose ethical behavioural requirements on those who are party to them) and 'cease and desist' letters (which seek to inform parties that are misappropriating cultural heritage about their misappropriation while also inducing the misappropriating party to 'cease and desist' their practices) can be used alongside intellectual property rights as part of a positive approach. Consumer campaigns and policy briefs can provide further out of court mechanisms that complement intellectual property rights in combatting transnational misappropriation by enhancing the reputation of and encouraging respect for intangible cultural heritage.

Conclusion

The 2003 Convention for the Safeguarding of the Intangible Cultural Heritage aims to safeguard intangible cultural heritage but does not regulate transnational misappropriation. Therefore, to safeguard cross-border intangible cultural heritage some intellectual property rights tools are used, e.g., geographical indication and trade marks. Yet, intellectual property is territorial and must be registered and enforced in each country where misappropriation occurs but with the limitation that it does not regulate cross-border enforcement in transnational infringement cases. Because of this, one may think to bring the Brussels system, but it is not feasible for intellectual property rights due to its territoriality approach. Consequently, the Brussels system's exclusive jurisdiction rule does not apply to claims concerning geographical indications. In fact, exclusive jurisdiction requires that the registration took place at the national level, whereas the geographical indications registration under the QS Regulation takes place at the EU level. In addition, geographical indications cannot become generic or be declared invalid, and therefore disputes related to geographical indications cannot concern their validity and do not fall into the exclusive jurisdiction rules, which address validity only. In the case of EU trade marks, the EUTM Regulation provides that the judgment of one jurisdiction can be enforced throughout the EU. The exclusive jurisdiction rule can apply only when a matter is outside the scope of the Regulation (i.e., when validity is principally raised), and even when this rule applies it also allows the judgment of a single court to apply in all member states.

Thus, country-by-country enforcement within the EU of the geographical indication or trade mark at stake is not imposed by any (international or) EU norm, while the relevant court in EU trade mark disputes is determined according to the EUTM Regulation, which provides competent courts whose judgment applies throughout the EU. Therefore, consolidation of the relevant litigation before a single competent court can occur, with the advantage of avoiding conflicting judgments and high litigation costs. This would be in line with recent international academic discussions that, to promote consolidation of cross-border intellectual property rights litigation even further, are limiting the scope of exclusive jurisdiction rules, and in particular that of the ILA Committee on Intellectual Property and Private International Law. Such consolidation of international intellectual property rights litigation provides one solution to the limitations of geographical indications and trade marks for safeguarding intangible cultural heritage in transnational misappropriation cases.

A second solution is proposed by the use of intellectual property rights as part of a 'broad positive strategy' for safeguarding intangible cultural heritage. This positive approach encompasses the use of intellectual property rights alongside other legal and marketing safeguarding tools, with the aim of enhancing the reputation of and encouraging respect for the heritage in question. In turn, this may create a virtuous circle, with the enhanced reputation of and respect for intangible cultural heritage resulting in non-community members and the public being more aware of the intangible cultural heritage, leading to fewer misappropriations and, therefore, resulting in greater safeguarding for the heritage in question.

It can be hoped that the combination of consolidation of international intellectual property rights litigation, together with the use of intellectual property rights as part of a 'positive approach' to enhance the reputation of and encourage respect for intangible cultural heritage may together be effective mechanisms for safeguarding intangible cultural heritage against misappropriations on the international stage.

References

Agriculture and Economic Development Analysis Division, *Food Security Communications Toolkit* (Food and Agriculture Organization of the United Nations) 141 <https://www.fao.org/3/i2195e/i2195e.pdf> accessed 17 December 2021

Basedow J, Kono T and Metzger A, *Intellectual Property in the Global Arena* (Mohr Siebeck 2010)

BBC, 'Kim Kardashian West's Kimono Underwear Meets Japanese Backlash' *BBC News* (27 June 2019) <www.bbc.com/news/world-asia-48767678> accessed 20 December 2021

Camacho Z, 'Voladores de Papantla Acusan "Daño Moral" de Cervecería Cuauhtémoc-Moctezuma' (Contralínea, 30 March 2017) <contralinea.com.mx/archivo-revista/2017/03/30/voladores-de-papantla-acusan-dano-moral-de-cerveceria-cuauhtemoc-moctezuma/> accessed 17 December 2021

Crawford A, 'The Ultimate Guide to Instagram Hashtags' (Adobe Creative Cloud Express by Adobe, 20 February 2020) <https://www.adobe.com/express/learn/blog/the-ultimate-guide-to-instagram-hashtags-in-2020> accessed 17 December 2021

De Anda Corral JF, 'Secretaría de Cultura defiende el Ritual de los Voladores' *El Economista* (Mexico, 28 June 2021)

desInformémonos, 'Voladores de Papantla Denuncian que la Cervecera Cuauhtémoc-Moctezuma Profana su Ceremonia Ritual' (*desInformémonos*, 31 March 2017) <https://desinformemonos.org/voladores-papantla-denuncian-la-cervecera-cuauhtemoc-moctezuma-profana-ceremonia-ritual/> accessed 17 December 2021

European Max Planck Group, *Conflict of Laws in Intellectual Property, The CLIP Principles and Commentary* (OUP 2013)

Falconi F, 'Chapter Twenty-One: Transnational Litigation on Infringement of Designations of Origin and Geographical Indications Protected Under Regulation (EU) No 1151/2012' in A Lupone, C Ricci and A Santini (eds), *The Right to Safe Food Towards a Global Governance* (Giappichelli 2013)

Government of Canada Office of Consumer Affairs, Industry Canada, and the Regulatory Affairs Division, Treasury Board Secretariat, *Voluntary Codes: A Guide for their Development and Use* (Distribution Services Communications Branch) <https://ich.unesco.org/doc/src/Example_guidance_document-Canada-EN.pdf> accessed 17 December 2021

Håkan T, Kvarnström M and Lerner H, 'Ethical Codes of Conduct for Research Related to Indigenous Peoples and Local Communities–core Principles, Challenges and Opportunities' in A Drugge (ed), *Ethics in Indigenous Research, Past Experiences - Future Challenges* (Vaartoe/Centre for Sami Research (CeSam) 2016)

Heritage-sensitive Intellectual Property & Marketing Strategies (HIPMAS India) Project at <https://hipamsindia.org/> accessed 17 December 2021

Kono T, Asensio P and Metzger A, 'ILA "Kyoto Guidelines on Intellectual Property and Private International Law" Published with Comments' (*Conflict of Laws.net*, 14 April 2021)

Nanayakkara T, 'Role of Intellectual Property in Enhancing the Competitiveness of the Tourism Industry' (Small and Medium-sized Enterprises Division, WIPO) 4 <https://www.wipo.int/export/sites/www/sme/en/tourism/tourism_ip.pdf> accessed 17 December 2021

The American Law Institute, *Intellectual Property: Principles Governing Jurisdiction, Choice of law and Judgments in Transnational Disputes* (American Law Institute Publishers 2008)

Ubertazzi B, 'Territorial and Universal Protection of Intangible Cultural Heritage from Misappropriation (2010) 8 *NZYIL* 69

UNESCO, 'Ethics and Intangible Cultural Heritage' Decision of the Intergovernmental Committee: 10.COM 15.a. <https://ich.unesco.org/en/ethics-and-ich-00866> accessed 17 December 2021

UNESCO, 'Examples of code of Ethics and Professional Codes of Conduct' (UNESCO) <https://ich.unesco.org/en/examples-of-codes-of-ethics-00868> accessed 17 December 2021

Wahlquist C, 'Stitch-up: Online sewing Community at War Over Cultural Appropriation' *The Guardian* (London 1 June 2019) <https://www.theguardian.com/lifeandstyle/2019/jun/01/stitch-up-online-sewing-community-at-war-over-cultural-appropriation> accessed 17 December 2021

Waseda University Global COE Project, *Commentary on Principles of Private International Law on Intellectual Property Rights: Joint Proposal Drafted by Members of the Private International Law Association of Korea and Japan* (Waseda University Global COE Project, 2010, 14 October 2021)

WIPO, 'What is Intellectual Property?' (WIPO About IP) <www.wipo.int/about-ip/en/> accessed 17 December 2021

Zee5 at <https://www.zee5.com/global/aboutus> accessed 17 December 2021

10 Codes and protocols

Protecting transboundary traditional medical knowledge in Southern Africa[1]

Pamela Andanda

Introduction

Traditional medical knowledge has been described by the World Health Organization (WHO), the World Intellectual Property Organization (WIPO) and the World Trade Organization (WTO) trilateral study as:

> the content or substance of traditional knowledge, skills and learning, with specific application to human health, wellness and healing. It may apply to traditional medicines as such, or to knowledge systems relating to medical treatment (such as healing massage or yoga postures).[2]

This definition, which shows that 'traditional medical knowledge' is a type of 'traditional knowledge', is adopted in this chapter; these terms are used interchangeably in the following discussions. Holders who are recognised as beneficiaries of traditional medical knowledge may be Indigenous peoples and/or Indigenous/traditional/local communities; individuals, families, or nations and even national entities.[3] Another common term is that of 'protection', which means the prevention of unauthorised use of materials by third parties.[4] However, WIPO acknowledges that the meaning of the term depends on the context. In the intellectual property context, it means using intellectual property 'tools and principles to prevent unauthorised or inappropriate uses of [traditional knowledge]'.[5] Accordingly, traditional medical knowledge has mostly been protected against misappropriation

1 An earlier version of this paper was presented at the 4th Biennial conference of the Association of Critical Heritage Studies (ACHS) held in Zhejiang University, Hangzhou, China, from 1 to 6 September 2018. I would like to thank Kimberley Majongwe for providing much needed research assistance in preparing the paper.

2 WHO, WIPO and WTO, *Promoting Access to Medical Technologies and Innovation: Intersections between Public Health, Intellectual Property and Trade* (World Trade Organization 2013) 90.

3 See Article 2 – Beneficiaries of Protection in IGC-GRTKF Secretariat 2013, 9.

4 WIPO, *Overview of Activities and Outcomes of the Intergovernmental Committee*, WIPO IGC, 11th session, Agenda Item 10, WIPO Doc WIPO/GRTKF/IC/11/9 Annex (Geneva 25, 2007).

5 WIPO, *Intellectual Property and Genetic Resources, Traditional Knowledge and Traditional Cultural Expressions* (WIPO 2015) 20.

DOI: 10.4324/9781003345237-11

by unauthorised third parties through the intellectual property rights regime.[6] This regime focuses more on economic benefits and does not safeguard the traditional medical knowledge as anticipated by the UNESCO 2003 Convention for the Safeguarding of the Intangible Cultural Heritage (the 2003 Convention). 'Safeguarding' goes beyond protection in terms of monetary value and 'prevention' of misappropriation in so far as it ensures the 'protection' of cultural integrity and the realisation of the human right to self-determination.[7] Safeguarding, in this sense, is critical since traditional medical knowledge is used as 'a means of maintaining and developing group identity rather than pursuing private economic benefit'.[8] WIPO acknowledges that protection differs from safeguarding, which is aimed at ensuring that traditional knowledge does not disappear, is not degraded, and is properly maintained and promoted.[9] Safeguarding ensures respect for cultural heritage, which is an element of respect for human dignity.[10]

The transboundary protection of traditional medical knowledge is important because, as Silberman observes, 'we live in a time of movement, diaspora, cultural displacement, and the creation of new cultural forms that profoundly alter the traditional heritage concepts of coherent national narratives'.[11] Deacon discerns that transboundary protection is particularly relevant in Africa since the national borders cut across culturally similar communities ever since colonial administrations who negotiated many borders never considered local settlement patterns. This leads to situations where traditional knowledge can be infringed by third parties across national borders.[12] For instance, the San community in Southern Africa is spread across geographical boundaries sharing traditional medical knowledge, which has been misappropriated by herbal medicines companies beyond Southern Africa. WIPO acknowledges that traditional knowledge may be dispersed across communities and jurisdictions, hence its call for member states' transboundary cooperation.[13] An emerging trend is that traditional knowledge right holders are

6 Pamela Andanda and Hojjat Khademi, 'Protecting Traditional Medicine Knowledge through the Intellectual Property Regime Based on the Experience of Iran and South Africa' in Caroline B Ncube and Elmien du Plessis (eds), *Indigenous Knowledge & Intellectual Property: Contemporary Studies in Law and Applied Research Series* (Juta 2016) 48–73.

7 Brendan Tobin, 'The Role of Customary Law in Access and Benefit-Sharing and Traditional Knowledge Governance: Perspectives from Andean and Pacific Island Countries' (WIPO and United Nations University 2008).

8 Chika A Ezeanya, 'Contending Issues of Intellectual Property Rights Protection and Indigenous Knowledge of Pharmacology in Africa South of the Sahara' (2013) 6(5) *JPAS* 24, 38.

9 WIPO, *Intellectual Property and Genetic Resources, Traditional Knowledge and Traditional Cultural Expressions* (n 5) 21.

10 Janet Blake, 'Taking a Human Rights Approach to Cultural Heritage Protection' (2011) 4 (2) *Heritage & Society* 199.

11 Neil A Silberman, 'Heritage Interpretation and Human Rights: Documenting Diversity, Expressing Identity, or Establishing Universal Principles?' (2012) 18(3) *Int J Her Stu* 245, 253.

12 Harriet Deacon, 'Transboundary Knowledge and Regional Cooperation in the Protection of Traditional Knowledge in Kenya' (2017) 12(3) *JIPLP* 226.

13 WIPO, 'The Protection of Traditional Knowledge: Draft Articles' WIPO/GRTKF/IC/40/18, Article 16 (WIPO 2019).

attempting to protect and safeguard knowledge and practices that are embedded in the traditional medical knowledge through protocols and codes.

The central argument in this chapter is that community codes and protocols, which are viewed as a suitable bridge between the communities' customary law and positive law regimes,[14] can be used to effectively safeguard transboundary traditional medical knowledge. While it can be argued that legal pluralism should ideally unify customary and positive laws, this is not the case in the context of traditional medical knowledge since the application of customary law depends on the respective countries' political economy.[15] This position emerges from the assumptions of the existence of two parallel legal systems comprising customary law and state legal systems thus blurring the practice of legal pluralism in Africa.[16] For example, in the South African context, Rautenbach argues that the South African legal system still symbolises a society that remains splintered along cultural and religious lines.[17] In the *Alexkor* case, which dealt with customary law interest in land, the constitutional court stated that customary law must be seen as an integral part of South African law.[18] However, such recognition is not sufficient to embed customary law into the current legal framework that governs traditional medical knowledge. Frankel observes that traditional medical knowledge is place-based in terms of origin and the manner in which the knowledge is developed and used.[19] Transboundary protection relates to how traditional knowledge should be protected in places other than where the knowledge originates.[20] This level of protection is difficult to guarantee if the application of legal pluralism depends on the political economy of the respective countries and is subject to customary law satisfying the constitutional conformity test.[21]

Furthermore, the extent to which the communities' codes and protocols can be used strategically to protect transboundary traditional medical knowledge ensuring that the communities' heritage is safeguarded is examined. The limited focus on Southern Africa is justified by the fact that the San communities are dispersed

14 Tobin (n 7).

15 Berihun A Gebeye, 'Decoding Legal Pluralism in Africa' (2017) 49(2) *J Leg Plur Unoff* 228, 233.

16 ibid.

17 Christa Rautenbach, 'Deep Legal Pluralism in South Africa: Judicial Accommodation of Non-State Law' (2010) 42(60) *J Leg Plur Unoff* 143, 144.

18 *Alexkor Ltd and Another v Richtersveld Community and Others* 2004 (5) SA 460 (CC) para 51.

19 Susy Frankel, 'The Challenges of Cross-Border Protection of Traditional Knowledge' in Daniel F Robinson, Ahmed Abdel-Latif and Pedro Roffe (eds), *Protecting Traditional Knowledge: The WIPO Intergovernmental Committee on Intellectual Property and Genetic Resources, Traditional Knowledge and Folklore* (Routledge 2017) 325.

20 ibid.

21 Section 39 (3) of the South African Constitution recognises rights under customary law, to the extent that they are consistent with the Bill of Rights. This recognition of customary law evinces the 'repugnancy test' that was applied in colonial Africa; see Gebeye (n 15) 241. Gebeye confirms 'that the post-colonial legal system recognises customary laws in limited circumstances subject to constitutional conformity'.

across South Africa, Botswana, Namibia, Angola, Zambia, and Zimbabwe.[22] The national boundaries considered in this discussion are limited to the first three countries, which have similar community governance structures through the establishment of a regional San network called the Working Group of Indigenous Minorities in Southern Africa (WIMSA).[23] This network coordinates a democratically elected San Council in these three countries and has attempted to assist the San to unite across national boundaries.[24] The second part of the chapter provides the context of the San community's traditional medical knowledge; then, it considers the nature of traditional medical knowledge and the mechanisms that have been used to protect and safeguard it. The effectiveness of protecting transboundary traditional medical knowledge through the intellectual property law regime, as one of the mechanisms in Southern Africa, is critically analysed. The emerging use of community codes and protocols in Southern Africa to protect and safeguard transboundary traditional medical knowledge is discussed. The San community's code is highlighted as an example that can guide other communities in developing similar codes. This is followed by an evaluation of the effectiveness of such community codes and protocols in ensuring the protection and safeguarding of traditional medical knowledge.

The nature of traditional medical knowledge and mechanisms that have been used to protect and safeguard it

The nature of traditional medical knowledge is such that it consists of 'ethnobotanical knowledge on plant and genetic resources as well as folkloristic oral traditions that deal with medicinal applications of these resources'.[25] African traditional medical knowledge is strongly based on oral tradition and theories that consider human beings to be 'inseparable from their social, natural, spiritual and cosmic environment'.[26] Some components of traditional medical knowledge require secrecy and initiation into a particular group before information can be disclosed.[27] These undisclosed aspects imply that some traditional medical knowledge is non-disclosed[28] or uncodified. Another key feature of traditional knowledge in Africa is that the right holders view the knowledge to have a communal

22 Rachel Wynberg and Roger Chennells, 'Green Diamonds of South Africa: An Overview of the San-*Hoodia* Case' in Rachel Wynberg, Doris Schroeder and Roger Chennells (eds), *Indigenous Peoples, Consent and Benefit Sharing: Lessons from the San Hoodia Case* (Springer 2009) 91.

23 Roger Chennells, Victoria Haraseb and Mathambo Ngakaeaja, 'Speaking for the San: Challenges for Representative Institutions' in Wynberg, Schroeder and Chennells (eds) (n 22) 166.

24 Wynberg, Schroeder and Chennells (n 22) 93.

25 Sita Reddy, 'Making Heritage Legible: Who Owns Traditional Medical Knowledge?' (2006) 13(2) *Int J Cult Prop* 167.

26 UNESCO International Bioethics Committee (IBC), *Report of the IBC on Traditional Medicine Systems and their Ethical Implication* (IBC 2013) 2, 5.

27 Ezeanya (n 8) 35.

28 In terms of the Traditional Medicine Team of the World Health Organization, un-codified traditional medical knowledge is distinguishable from codified traditional medical knowledge, which falls within the public domain. See WIPO, *Glossary of Key Terms* (WIPO/GRTKF/IC/22/INF/8).

value and can be placed in the public domain without the intention of making profits.[29] In terms of knowledge governance, the utilisation of traditional medical knowledge has to be collectively authorised by the right holders and the use must be within what is culturally acceptable.[30]

Traditional medical knowledge is an example of intangible cultural heritage.[31] The features of traditional medical knowledge effectively create a link between intellectual property rights and intangible cultural heritage. This link has led traditional knowledge holding communities to call for an approach that responds to their distinct customary laws and worldviews.[32] Accordingly, any mechanism that is used to protect traditional medical knowledge must acknowledge the relevance of the common laws and culture of the affected communities that have rights in the traditional medical knowledge.[33]

Competition and tensions may arise when traditional medical knowledge holders in different countries, not only in Africa but other regions of the world, such as South East Asia, lay claim to the same or similar cultural heritage for the commercialisation of traditional medical knowledge.[34] Competitors mostly rely on a mixture of cultural property claims and intellectual property rights.[35] Therefore, this part discusses two commonly used protective mechanisms, namely protection under the intellectual property regime and the emerging use of community protocols and codes in Southern Africa to protect transboundary traditional medical knowledge. The need to protect and safeguard traditional medical knowledge has become urgent due to moves in different jurisdictions to integrate it into the national health systems thus raising fears of possible misappropriation.[36]

The San and their traditional medical knowledge in hoodia

The San community has been using a plant called *hoodia gordonii*, which grows in Southern Africa, for its appetite suppressant qualities;[37] the plant has been

29 Lorreta Feris, 'Protecting Traditional Knowledge in Africa: Considering African Approaches' (2004) 4(2) *Afr Hum Rights Law J* 242, 243.

30 Ezeanya (n 8) 35.

31 Federico Lenzerini, 'Intangible Cultural Heritage: The Living Culture of Peoples' (2011) 22(1) *Eur J Int Law* 101.

32 Krystyna Swiderska, 'Protecting Traditional Knowledge: A Holistic Approach Based on Customary Laws and Bio-Cultural Heritage' in K N Ninan (ed), *Conserving and Valuing Ecosystem Services and Biodiversity: Economic and Institutional Challenges* (Earthscan 2009) 332.

33 Pamela Andanda, 'Striking a Balance between Intellectual Property Protection of Traditional Knowledge, Cultural Preservation and Access to Knowledge' (2012) 17 *J Intellect Pro Rights* 549, 550.

34 Christoph Antons and Lisa Rogers, 'Cultural and Intellectual Property in Cross-Border Disputes over Intangible Cultural Heritage' in Christoph Antons and William Logan (eds), *Intellectual Property, Cultural Property and Intangible Cultural Heritage* (Routledge 2018) 69.

35 ibid 70.

36 WHO, WIPO and WTO (n 2) 91.

37 Roger Chennells, 'Traditional Knowledge and Benefit Sharing after the Nagoya Protocol: Three Cases from South Africa' (2013) 9(2) *J Environ Law* 163, 169.

known by the San people for generations for its healing properties.[38] The South African Council for Science and Industrial Research (CSIR) was guided by the San's traditional knowledge to these qualities of *hoodia* in their research, which led to the CSIR patenting the *hoodia* molecule as an appetite suppressor in 1996.[39] Empirical evidence collected by Foster in her interactions with the San community reveals different views about *hoodia* as held by the CSIR and the San community. The San consider *hoodia* 'as a natural plant connected to the history and identity of San cultures … quite different from the understanding of CSIR and its commercial partners who viewed hoodia as patented molecules divorced from the San histories and heritage'.[40]

The patent was challenged by the San in 2001 on the basis of the San's traditional knowledge, and this compelled the CSIR to acknowledge the San as the knowledge holders.[41] The challenge was a political strategy developed after WIMSA authorised the South African San Council and their lawyer to address the issue of the *hoodia* patent.[42] This strategy entailed a choice between challenging the validity of the patent in court and demanding benefit sharing from the CSIR.[43] The San Council opted for a benefit sharing agreement, bringing them financial benefits. The case had gained public attention after international media reports accused the CSIR of biopiracy thus putting pressure on them to agree to a benefit sharing agreement. In March 2003 the San and CSIR scientists signed a benefit sharing agreement in which the CSIR scientists agreed to share revenue from the joint development between CSIR and global partners Pfizer (USA) and Phytopharm (UK) with the San from Southern Africa. No other communities had claimed rights over traditional knowledge of *hoodia*.[44] However, the signing of a benefit sharing agreement with the San led to inter-community mistrust and resentment from the Nama Indigenous community from Namibia as they were excluded from the *hoodia* benefit sharing agreement between the Southern African San community and the CSIR.[45] This illustrates the challenge of protecting shared or widely disseminated traditional knowledge as in this case the knowledge is shared

38 Laura A Foster, *Reinventing Hoodia: Peoples, Plants, and Patents in South Africa* (University of Washington Press 2017) 3.

39 Chennells, 'Traditional Knowledge and Benefit Sharing after the Nagoya Protocol: Three Cases from South Africa' (n 37); Foster (n 38).

40 Foster (n 38) 50.

41 Chennells, 'Traditional Knowledge and Benefit Sharing after the Nagoya Protocol: Three Cases from South Africa' (n 37) 169.

42 Foster (n 38) 55.

43 ibid.

44 Chennells, 'Traditional Knowledge and Benefit Sharing after the Nagoya Protocol: Three Cases from South Africa' (n 37) 169.

45 Harry Jonas, Kabir Bavikatte and Holly Shrumm, 'Community Protocols and Access and Benefit Sharing' (2010) 12(3) *Asian Biotechnol Dev Rev* 49, 55.

among the San and Nama communities, yet the latter community was excluded from the benefit sharing agreement.[46] A subsequent agreement rectified this.[47]

Apart from the patenting of the *hoodia* molecule by CSIR, *hoodia* had drawn attention from herbal supplement companies that harvested and sold dried *hoodia*, marketed as weight loss products, using images of the San people without their consent.[48] After the CSIR and its partners disclosed the plans of using *hoodia* as an anti-obesity drug, companies from the USA and South Africa started selling dried *hoodia* as a weight control supplement.[49] The South African San Council negotiated a second agreement with the *hoodia* growers in South Africa to supply the plant to the supplement industry.[50] Foster provides a detailed discussion of how *hoodia* was reinvented through *inter alia* patent ownership, pharmaceutical research, and contractual benefit sharing.[51]

Protecting traditional medical knowledge through the intellectual property regime

The 2003 Convention recognises an overlap between intellectual property rights and intangible cultural heritage. Accordingly, Article 3 states that nothing in the Convention affects intellectual property rights. Antons and Rogers observe the remit of WIPO to ensure the protection of intangible cultural heritage is similar to UNESCO's objectives to safeguard intangible cultural heritage under the 2003 Convention.[52] However, the similarities do not lead to an easy relationship between safeguarding and protecting traditional medical knowledge.

Although the limitations of using the intellectual property regime to protect traditional knowledge are well-known,[53] intellectual property rights still remain 'the principal mechanism for protecting and enforcing control over information, and no discussion on protecting knowledge, traditional or scientific, can disregard their significance'.[54] In acknowledgement of the intellectual property regime's limitations, various reforms have been initiated under the leadership of the WIPO

46 ibid.

47 Chennells, 'Traditional Knowledge and Benefit Sharing after the Nagoya Protocol: Three Cases from South Africa' (n 37).

48 Foster (n 38) 4.

49 ibid.

50 ibid 5.

51 ibid, chapters 2 and 3.

52 Antons and Rogers (n 34) 72.

53 Emeka Polycarp Amechi, 'Traditional Knowledge Relating to Medical Uses of Plants and the Patent Regime in South Africa: Whither the Traditional Healers?' (2015) 27 *SAMLJ* 58; Andanda (n 33); Roger Chennells, 'Putting Intellectual Property Rights into Practice: Experience from the San' in Wynberg, Schroeder and Chennells (eds) (n 22); the Center for International Environmental Law (CIEL), *The Gap between Indigenous Peoples' Demands and WIPO's Framework on Traditional Knowledge* (CIEL 2007); Feris (n 29).

54 Yusuf Daya and Nick Vink, 'Protecting Traditional Ethno-Botanical Knowledge in South Africa through the Intellectual Property Regime' (2006) 45(3) *Agrekon* 319, 325–326.

Intergovernmental Committee on Intellectual Property, Traditional Knowledge and Folklore (IGC) and other international institutions. In the meantime, the intellectual property regime has been used in Southern Africa and other regions to protect traditional medical knowledge against misappropriation.

Legal frameworks for protecting traditional knowledge in the three countries

Regional frameworks: two regional *sui generis* frameworks that are worth mentioning are the Swakopmund Protocol on the protection of traditional knowledge and expressions of folklore[55] and the African Model Law for the protection of the rights of local communities.[56] The Protocol offers broad protection of traditional knowledge and includes a dispute resolution mechanism through the African Regional Intellectual Property Organization (ARIPO). It is applicable to Namibia and Botswana as members of ARIPO who have signed the Protocol; it is not applicable to South Africa since it is not a member. The Protocol sets normative regional standards, and member states have their national laws to protect traditional knowledge. Section 2.1 of the Protocol defines customary laws and practices as laws, norms, and practices of local and traditional communities recognised by contracting states. Member states are free to determine the application of customary law thus leaving customary law subject to the constitutional 'conformity test'. Sections 5.2 and 5.3 provide for the maintenance of registers or other records, where appropriate, in the interest of transparency and without compromising the status of undisclosed traditional knowledge. Transboundary protection is covered under section 5.4, which provides that 'where two or more communities in the same or different countries share the same traditional knowledge, the relevant national competent authority' will register it and retain relevant records. The other framework is the Model Law that aims to guide African countries in developing their national laws to ensure the conservation, evaluation, and sustainable use of biological resources. Part IV of the Model Law recognises community rights over their biological resources and requires their informed consent when the resources are used.

National frameworks that govern traditional medical knowledge: in line with the African Model Law, the three countries have relevant provisions in their intellectual property laws to protect traditional knowledge. Section 115 of Botswana's Industrial Property Act provides for the registration of both undisclosed and disclosed traditional knowledge. In the case of disclosed traditional knowledge, section 115(1)(b) notes that it should not be commercially or industrially exploited in Botswana. This essentially excludes components of disclosed

55 ARIPO, 2010. The Protocol entered into force on 11 May 2015 and was amended on 6 December 2016.

56 OAU, African model legislation for the protection of the rights of local communities, farmers, and breeders, and for the regulation of access to biological resources, 2000.

traditional medical knowledge from protection if the holders have exploited it commercially in the process of rendering healing services. Registered undisclosed traditional knowledge is protected under section 121(4) of the Act. Secrecy can be problematic in the context of traditional medical knowledge because it hampers scrutiny on the safety and efficacy of the products that are used for healing.[57] It is also contrary to the goal of safeguarding traditional medical knowledge, which is achieved by encouraging positive collaboration with the bearers of traditional medical knowledge to protect its cultural significance while ensuring its sustainability.[58] The Namibian Industrial Property Act (Act 1 of 2012), section 12(1)(c) provides that traditional knowledge, 'which originated at a date prior to the priority date of the relevant invention' forms part of prior art. Actually, the three countries treat documented traditional knowledge as prior art. Regarding the principle of 'prior informed consent', the Botswana Industrial Property Act, section 127(1) notes that any intellectual property rights granted are unenforceable against third parties 'until the written consent of the local community owning the traditional knowledge is obtained'. South Africa incorporated the principle in its Patent Act (Amendment Act 20 of 2005)[59] as applicants for patent registration must disclose 'whether or not the invention for which protection is claimed is based on or derived from an Indigenous biological resource, genetic resource, or traditional knowledge or use'.[60] Consequently, the registrar can demand proof of applicants' title or authority to make use of such resources.[61] South Africa has also enacted the Intellectual Property Laws Amendment Act, to protect traditional knowledge through the intellectual property regime.[62] This entails changing the substantive intellectual property law statutes to accommodate the holistic nature of traditional knowledge. This approach has been criticised for being too ambitious,[63] and achieved at a high price for taxpayers and Indigenous communities.[64]

Intersections between safeguarding intangible cultural heritage and protecting traditional medical knowledge through the intellectual property regime

Traditional medical knowledge is one of the most difficult categories of intangible cultural heritage to regulate due to the need to respond to diverse legal instruments

57 Valentina Vadi, 'Intangible Heritage: Traditional Medicine and Knowledge Governance' (2007) 2(10) *JIPLP* 682, 688.

58 Alex Riordan and John Schofield, 'Beyond Biomedicine: Traditional Medicine as Cultural Heritage' (2015) 21(3) *Int J Herit Stud* 280, 292.

59 See ss 30(3A) and 30(3B).

60 ibid s 30(3A).

61 ibid.

62 Number 28 of 2013 (hereinafter IPLA).

63 Andanda and Khademi (n 6).

64 Andre van der Merwe, 'South and Southern Africa—Recent Developments in the Legal Protection of Traditional Knowledge and Traditional Cultural Expressions' (2014) 9(1) *JIPLP* 411.

and ethical codes such as 'bioresources and folkloristic healing, trade discussions and biodiversity conservation, botanical knowledge and Indigenous rights'.[65] This section focuses on how the case study countries used the intellectual property regime to protect traditional medical knowledge and how this relates to safeguarding intangible cultural heritage as anticipated by the 2003 Convention, in which Articles 11 and 12 encourage signatory nations to create inventories and databases of traditional knowledge.[66]

Two mechanisms that have been used within the intellectual property regime are positive protection and defensive protection. Positive protection entails granting rights 'that empower communities to promote their [traditional knowledge]'.[67] Traditional knowledge-related inventions have been patented by traditional knowledge holders or co-owned by them.[68] Trade secrets have also been used for positive protection in case of undisclosed information.[69] Secrecy, however, is not a viable option for protecting because the components which the traditional medical knowledge holders seek to protect such as 'formulations, compositions; appropriate dosage; Particular forms of administration; Procedures and rituals applied as part of the healing processes' may have already been disclosed.[70] Section 115 of the Botswana Industrial Property Act protects both undisclosed and disclosed traditional knowledge. Defensive protection, on the other hand, entails the use of certain strategies to ensure that third parties do not have access to intellectual property tools in circumstances that would be prejudicial to the interests of traditional knowledge holders.[71] Strategies that have been used for defensive protection are the establishment of databases that can serve as prior art defence against applications for the registration of patents, secrecy, and disclosure and prior consent requirements before patents can be granted.[72]

Defensive and positive mechanisms of protecting traditional knowledge have shortcomings. Documentation risks putting traditional medical knowledge in the public domain, revealing secret traditional medical knowledge[73] and facilitating unauthorised use by third parties.[74] Kuruk confirms that companies that use natural ingredients in manufacturing cosmetics acquire information on traditional use

65 Reddy (n 25) 162.
66 ibid 166.
67 WIPO, 'The Protection of Traditional Knowledge: Draft Articles' (n 13).
68 Chennells, 'Putting Intellectual Property Rights into Practice: Experience from the San' (n 53) 225.
69 Lee-Ann Tong, 'Protecting Traditional Knowledge: Does Secrecy Offer a Solution?' (2010) 13(4) *Potchefstroomse Elektroniese Regsblad* 159.
70 Esther Kibuka-Sebitosi, 'Protecting Indigenous Knowledge and the Rights and Interests of Indigenous Medicine Practitioners in Africa: Law, Leadership and Governance' (2008) 7(1) *IAJIKS* 77.
71 WIPO, 'The Protection of Traditional Knowledge: Draft Articles' (n 13) 22.
72 Nagoya Protocol, Article 6(2). An example is the Indian Traditional Knowledge Digital Library.
73 Ryan Abbott, *Documenting Traditional Medical Knowledge* (WIPO 2014).
74 Susette Biber-Klemm et al., 'Flanking Policies in National and International Law' in Susette Biber-Klemm and Thomas Cottier (eds), *Rights to Plant Genetic Resources and Traditional Knowledge: Basic Issues and Perspectives* (CABI 2016) 239.

and scientific validity from *inter alia* databases and intermediary suppliers.[75] The mechanisms are also premised on the concept of individual ownership, which is alien to the rights in traditional medical knowledge that are collective in nature and cannot be exclusively owned by an individual. Even in circumstances where ownership vests in national states and communities, this may exclude communities that may not be located within the same state. Moreover, documentation entails converting traditional medical knowledge into medical information, which 'opens itself to information's unique properties, such as its essential homelessness or the fact that it can simultaneously reside in several places, and thus to increasing claims and counterclaims of ownership'.[76] Reddy observes that 'states and communities are stronger players than ever before in successful ownership disputes over [traditional medical knowledge]'.[77] Certainly, there has been cultural resistance in attempting to allocate ownership of traditional medical knowledge to individuals. This mostly lies in the fact that traditional medical knowledge can consist of two components: traditional knowledge in respect of which confidentiality is maintained among different communities, and shared traditional knowledge, which is already in the public domain.[78]

The following challenges of protecting traditional knowledge which arise from the first component are well documented.[79] First, if the communities decide to share the traditional knowledge, negotiating with each or all the communities may be practically impossible. Second, certain expertise and capacity, required for contractual negotiations to define the terms of sharing traditional knowledge, may be lacking. Third, where the communities are not closely integrated, the confidential knowledge may be divulged by chance or on purpose. Fourth, a question remains whether or not *ad hoc* tools that are developed by the national authorities such as the registration of confidential traditional knowledge can be used to challenge novelty and inventiveness. With regard to the second component of traditional knowledge, what is in the public domain cannot strictly be protected subject to some limitations on its use.[80] The limitations can be used as defensive measures or tools to prevent misappropriation. These are the registration of traditional knowledge and the application of the principle of domain *public payant*, which is applied in relation to copyright works in the public domain by requiring payment of a fee to the state for the subsequent use of works, crafts, and arts.

Making provisions within the intellectual property regime to protect traditional knowledge in the three countries is yet to achieve the intended purpose of curbing the misappropriation of traditional knowledge. The countries continue to contend

75 Paul Kuruk, *Traditional Knowledge, Genetic Resources, Customary Laws and Intellectual Property: A Global Primer* (Edward Elgar 2020).

76 Reddy (n 25) 165.

77 ibid 167.

78 Manuel Ruiz Muller, 'The Legal Protection of Widely Shared and Dispersed Traditional Knowledge' in Robinson, Abdel-Latif and Roffe (eds) (n 19) 128–129.

79 ibid 128–129.

80 ibid 130.

with misappropriation even after the amendment of their laws to incorporate the principle of 'prior informed consent' into the intellectual property regime.[81] This is because the amendments target local users while foreign user countries or companies are left 'to decide for themselves whether to apply source-country laws'[82] since the protection of intellectual property is territorial. The incorporation of the principle of 'prior informed consent' into the intellectual property regime had been advocated by a group of developing countries who proposed the amendment to the Agreement on Trade-Related Aspects of Intellectual Property Rights (TRIPS) to include Article 29bis, which would oblige applicants to disclose, in their patent applications, the source of origin of biological resources and traditional knowledge used in inventions.[83] The Conference of the Parties to the Convention on Biological Diversity has supported the disclosure proposal by calling upon states to 'encourage disclosure of the country of origin of genetic resources in applications for intellectual property rights'.[84] The proposal has however been opposed by developed countries like the USA and Japan, since they consider it to be burdensome and possibly destabilising the patent registration system.[85]

The use of contract law to govern the relations between intellectual property rights holders and traditional medical knowledge holding communities

The San community started using contractual agreements to govern the sharing of their traditional knowledge after theirs was patented and commercialised without their knowledge.[86] The advantages of using contract law are that it is identical in all countries and is based upon natural justice.[87] The latter makes contracts relevant for protecting the human rights of the traditional knowledge holders. Contracts are mostly used to govern 'prior informed consent' and 'benefit sharing' between third-party users and traditional knowledge holders. Yet, contracts have two major limitations: first, they can only function where there is a legal framework that regulates access to traditional knowledge. If it is non-existent,

81 Melissa Lewis, 'Access and Benefit-Sharing in the Wake of CBD COP10: The Nagoya Protocol and Its Potential Implications for South Africa' (2010) 17(2) *SAJELP* 69.

82 Morten Walloe and Tomme Young, 'Beyond Access: Exploring Implementation of the Fair and Equitable Sharing Commitment in the CBD' [2007] *IUCN Environmental Policy and Law Paper* No 67/2, 31.

83 WT/GC/W/564/Rev.2; TN/C/W/41/Rev.2; IP/C/W/474 (5 July 2006); the Delegation of Paraguay requested to be added to the list of co-sponsors document, see WT/GC/W/564/Rev.2/Add.5; TN/C/W/41/Rev.2/Add.5 IP/C/W/474/Add.5 (24 July 2007); see also communication by the ACP Group and the African Group (TN/C/W/59). No progress has been made in discussing this proposal.

84 COP 6, Decision VI/ 24.

85 Emanuela Arezzo, 'Struggling around the "Natural" Divide: The Protection of Tangible and Intangible Indigenous Property' (2007) 25(367) *Cardozo Arts & Ent L J* 381–382.

86 Chennells, 'Putting Intellectual Property Rights into Practice: Experience from the San' (n 53) 224.

87 ibid.

standard term contracts are typically used, and these can only be enforced by the parties to the contract thus excluding successors of the community members who entered the contract.[88] Second, contracts assume equality of bargaining power to negotiate fair terms. Feris observes that where there is no legal framework to regulate access to traditional knowledge the communities may not have such power.[89] Codes and protocols can be used to overcome some of the limitations of contracts.

A notable effect of the use of contracts is the review of non-profit intention when sharing traditional medical knowledge. The change has occurred in a globalised context due to exploitative practices where users of traditional medical knowledge such as research institutions, biotechnological companies, and pharmaceutical companies access the knowledge for profit purposes to the exclusion of other parties.[90] The experience of exploitation and misappropriation of the San communities' traditional medical knowledge has led them to review the non-profit intention when sharing their traditional medical knowledge with researchers and other organisations and insisting on benefit sharing through contractual agreements that govern the intellectual property rights which are derived from their knowledge.[91] This is the main reason why traditional medical knowledge holders have contested the concept of 'public domain' as understood in the intellectual property context as 'elements of [intellectual property] that are ineligible for private ownership and the contents of which any member of the public is legally entitled to use'.[92]

Community codes and protocols

Blake's insightful observation that cultural heritage theory and law as well as intellectual property law are 'based on premises that are inappropriate for Indigenous heritage' provides a good basis for discussing the communities' attempts to find more suitable mechanisms for safeguarding their rights.[93] The concept of 'safeguarding' is used in the sense defined in Article 2 of the 2003 Convention.

> measures aimed at ensuring the viability of the intangible cultural heritage, including the identification, documentation, research, *preservation*, protection, promotion, enhancement, transmission, particularly through formal and nonformal education, as well as the *revitalisation of the various aspects of such heritage.*
>
> [emphasis added]

88 Feris (n 29) 250.
89 ibid.
90 ibid 243.
91 Chennells, 'Putting Intellectual Property Rights into Practice: Experience from the San' (n 53).
92 WIPO, 'The Protection of Traditional Knowledge: Draft Articles' (n 13).
93 Blake (n 10) 212.

The criteria for the recognition of intangible cultural heritage under the convention are that the heritage must be compatible with international human rights instruments, exhibit the need for mutual respect between communities, and be sustainable.[94] The 2003 Convention defines intangible cultural heritage as 'the practices, representations, expressions, knowledge, skills – as well as the instruments, objects, artefacts and cultural spaces associated therewith – that communities, groups and, in some cases, individuals recognise as part of their cultural heritage'.[95] The nature of traditional medical knowledge qualifies as intangible cultural heritage under the description found in its Article 2, para 2(d), that is, 'knowledge and practices concerning nature and the universe'. Intangible cultural heritage is equated to living heritage in the national policy on South African living heritage, which 'means cultural expressions and practices that form *a body of knowledge* and provide for continuity, dynamism, and meaning of social life to generations of people as individuals, social groups, and communities' [emphasis added].[96] The draft policy obliges the state to ensure that 'people contribute innovatively to industries (in areas such as medicine) ... using [Indigenous knowledge systems] for innovation'.[97] This resonates with the definition of intangible cultural heritage in the 2003 Convention.

Some of the means used under the 2003 Convention are the inventorying of traditional practices[98] and the establishment of centres for documentation.[99] These are state-driven and provide limited opportunities for the traditional knowledge holding communities to be actively involved in safeguarding their rights.[100] To ensure that customary practices governing access to heritage are respected, as required by the 2003 Convention and the Swakopmund Protocol, traditional knowledge holding communities must be actively involved in the documentation process. Failure to do so may risk making the secret aspects of the knowledge public, which is damaging[101] since such knowledge is usually transmitted through 'subtle and exclusive socio-cultural practices carried out by selected members in a community'.[102] Removing the knowledge from its original context contradicts the intention of safeguarding it. The 2003 Convention has however played a role in ensuring the participation of communities, groups, and, where appropriate, individuals in the management of intangible cultural heritage.[103] This provides an

94 Article 2(1); Richard Kurin, 'Safeguarding Intangible Cultural Heritage in the 2003 UNESCO Convention: A Critical Appraisal' (2004) 56(1–2) no 221–222 *Museum International* 66, 70.

95 Article 2, para 1.

96 The national policy on South African living heritage, 2009.

97 ibid para 1.3.5.

98 Article 12.

99 Article 13.

100 Blake (n 10) 230.

101 Riordan and Schofield (n 58) 283.

102 Susan Keitumetse, 'UNESCO 2003 Convention on Intangible Heritage: Practical Implications for Heritage Management Approaches in Africa' (2006) 61(184) *South African Archaeological Bulletin* 166, 169.

103 Article 15.

important link between initiatives under the 2003 Convention and the use of community protocols and codes.

The challenges of ensuring the transboundary protection of traditional medical knowledge through the intellectual property regime have led traditional medical knowledge holding communities to resort to using community protocols and codes to ensure that third parties are bound by the communities' customary laws and practices. Protocols are rules and procedures that 'regulate conduct and interactions within … communities, with outsiders, and with the territories and areas on which they depend'.[104] Codes typically 'represent a consensus among persons engaged in a particular specialised occupation about proper conduct in performing their function'.[105] Although codes are usually developed by professional bodies that are involved in heritage management, communities also develop codes to govern the use of traditional medical knowledge.

The emerging use of community protocols and codes in Southern Africa to protect and safeguard transboundary traditional medical knowledge

The use of community protocols as a tool is provided for by Article 12 of the Nagoya Protocol, which requires parties to 'take into consideration Indigenous and local communities' customary laws, community protocols and procedures' in implementing their obligations. The text was inserted into the Nagoya Protocol as a result of the lobbying by the non-governmental organisation Natural Justice and the African group.[106] Traditional medical knowledge holders have indeed stated their preference that in the protection of their rights, customary law should be used as a starting point rather than intellectual property law.[107] This preference is protected under Article 15 of the United Nations' International Covenant on Economic, Social and Cultural Rights,[108] which requires states to take into account Indigenous peoples' preferences in adopting measures to protect their scientific, literary, and artistic productions. Although the legal status of customary law is determined at the national level, it derives from the obligations under

104 Krystyna Swiderska et al., 'Community Protocols and Free, Prior Informed Consent – Overview and Lessons Learnt' in Krystyna Swiderska et al. (eds), *Biodiversity and Culture: Exploring Community Protocols, Rights and Consent, Participatory Learning and Action* 65 (IIED 2012) 25, 26 <http://pubs.iied.org/pdfs/ 14618IIED.pdf> accessed 1 December 2021.

105 P J O'Keefe, 'Codes of Ethics: Form and Function in Cultural Heritage Management' (1998) 7(1) *Int J Cult Prop* 32, 33.

106 Natalia Aguilar Delgado, 'Community Protocols as Tools for Resisting Exclusion in Global Environmental Governance' (2016) 56(4) *RAE-Revista de Administração de Empresas* 395, 398.

107 WIPO, *Intellectual Property Needs and Expectations of Traditional Knowledge Holders: WIPO Report on Fact-Finding Missions on Intellectual Property and Traditional Knowledge* (WIPO 2001) 57.

108 International Covenant on Economic, Social and Cultural Rights, General Comment No 17. See also United Nations Declaration on the Rights of Indigenous Peoples, Article 11.

international law.[109] The African Union has included compliance with Article 12 of the Nagoya Protocol in its practical guidelines on 'access and benefit sharing'[110] applicable to traditional knowledge associated with genetic resources.

Protocols have three functions:[111] first, they clarify the nature, scope, and form of protecting traditional knowledge that is considered appropriate by the Indigenous people and local communities. Second, they ensure compliance with international human rights law, which requires the participation and consultation of traditional knowledge holders. Third, they secure more effective consideration of customary law thus increasing the legitimacy of law-making. These functions confirm that protocols can be used as tools to 'bridge the gap between the customary laws and institutions of communities … and national or international frameworks for management of natural resources'.[112]

Biocultural protocols

One of the options which can be used to protect shared traditional knowledge is the use of community protocols that are inclusive.[113] Biocultural protocols are instruments that are developed by communities in a participatory manner and are based on their customary laws, national and international laws.[114] They are commonly used in Southern Africa and other regions to protect and safeguard traditional medical knowledge. In South Africa, the Bushbuckridge/Kakula healers developed their biocultural protocol in 2009.[115] It contains the healers' biocultural values, details of traditional knowledge, and information for those who would like to access the traditional knowledge.[116] The biocultural protocol has been supplemented with a code of ethics developed with the support of Natural Justice.[117] The protocol and code have been instrumental in helping the healers to ensure standardised practices, and gain government recognition and partnership with South African conservation agencies to curb the illegal overharvesting of medicinal

109 Tobin (n 7) 201.

110 AU practical guidelines <http://www.absinitiative.info/fileadmin/media/Knowledge_Center/Pulications/African_Union_Guidelines/AU_Practical_Guidelines_On_ABS_-_20150215.pdf> accessed 1 December 2021.

111 Tobin (n 7) 208.

112 Deutsche Gesellschaft für Internationale Zusammenarbeit (GIZ), *Biocultural Community Protocols* (GIZ 2013).

113 Muller (n 78) 133; Jonas, Bavikatte and Shrumm (n 45) 62.

114 Jonas, Bavikatte and Shrumm (n 45) 102, 109.

115 Natural Justice, *2011–2012 Annual Report*, 8 <https://naturaljustice.org/wp-content/uploads/2015/09/2011-2012-Annual-Report.pdf> accessed 1 December 2021.

116 Sibuye R, Uys MT, Cocchiaro G and Lorenzen J 'The Bushbuckridge BCP: Traditional Health Practitioners Organise for ABS in South Africa' in Swiderska et al. (eds) (n 104) 105.

117 ibid.

plants.[118] Natural Justice is also working with the San Support Organization in Namibia to develop biocultural protocols.[119]

Since protocols embody the traditional holding communities' values and cultural practices, which have been recognised and incorporated into the intellectual property regimes of some of the case study countries, they offer practical solutions to the problems noted. For example, Botswana's Industrial Property Act provides for rights over collectively owned traditional knowledge to be exercised and enjoyed collectively in accordance with cultural practices.[120] It also makes provision for communities from Botswana and other countries to register their traditional knowledge in Botswana and in the other countries.[121] These provisions, which are in line with the Swakopmund Protocol,[122] effectively make it possible to protect transboundary traditional medical knowledge in accordance with the communities' cultural values thus ensuring both protection and preservation of the intangible cultural heritage. The protocol requires traditional knowledge to be recorded subject to, *inter alia*, the needs and aspirations of the traditional knowledge holders concerned.[123] It also specifies that the recording 'shall not compromise the status of hitherto undisclosed traditional knowledge or the interests of holders of traditional knowledge in relation to undisclosed elements of their knowledge'.[124]

The San Code of ethics

The approach widely used to develop community biocultural protocols is engagement. The unique feature of the San Code is that the community was an equal partner in the process of developing the code and played a leading role in the process. The TRUST project co-created the values on which the code is based, and the San community through South African San Institute (SASI) was an equal partner in the project.[125] The values are respect, honesty, justice and fairness, care, and the following of due process. While the code was developed in the context of genomic research, its requirement can be applied to traditional medical knowledge.

The code[126] was prepared in response to previous research activities in which researchers investigated the communities' lifestyles, language, and rock art in a

118 Natural Justice, *2011–2012 Annual Report* (n 115) 8.
119 ibid 9.
120 s117 (2).
121 s117 (4).
122 ARIPO (n 55).
123 s5.2.
124 s5.3.
125 TRUST project, <http://trust-project.eu/> accessed 13 January 2021.
126 South African San Institute, *San Community's Code* (2017) <http://trust-project.eu/wp-content/uploads/2017/03/San-Code-of-RESEARCH-Ethics-Booklet-final.pdf> accessed 1 December 2021.

manner that the San community considered disrespectful.[127] Although the code is not legally binding, it is a prerequisite to collaborating with or accessing any information from the community. The code prescribes a number of requirements that researchers must comply with, namely collective consent, joint development of the research design and methodology, early determination of potential benefits, and commitment to pre-publication consultation and post-publication feedback to the community.[128]

The code is used in conjunction with a media and research contract to ensure that the intellectual property of the San community, including traditional knowledge and other heritage components, is controlled and protected.[129] Signing a contract effectively makes the code legally binding on the parties and can be enforced in court.[130] Additionally, a contract ensures the safeguarding of traditional medical knowledge since signatories undertake to respect the culture, dignity, and wishes of the San.[131]

The effectiveness of community codes and protocols in protecting and safeguarding traditional medical knowledge

Three important attributes can be highlighted as markers of the effectiveness of the community-based approaches that have been used to protect transboundary traditional medical knowledge in this chapter: first, the ability to create a sense of belonging among geographically dispersed communities. Second, the ability to bridge the gaps between customary and legal management of biocultural heritage. These gaps are evident from the challenges of protecting traditional medical knowledge through the intellectual property regime, which can be addressed if, as suggested by Bannister and Nicholas, different stakeholders move beyond mere consultation to collaborative, community-based approaches to decision-making in heritage management.[132] Third, the ability to protect the undisclosed spiritual components of traditional medical knowledge. Biocultural protocols were precisely added to the 'access and benefit sharing' regimes of the Nagoya Protocol to ensure that such spiritual values of the communities are respected and safeguarded.[133]

127 Ewen Callaway, 'South Africa's San People Issue Ethics Code to Scientists' (2017) 543(7646) *Nature* 475.

128 South African San Institute (n 126); Roger Chennells and Andries Steenkamp, 'International Genomics Research Involving the San People' in Doris Schroeder et al. (eds), *Ethics Dumping. Case Studies from North-South Research Collaborations* (Springer 2018) 21.

129 WIMSA Media and Research Contract (General Purpose) of the San of Southern Africa, approved by the WIMSA Annual General Assembly on 28 November 2001, 4.

130 O'Keefe (n 105) 37.

131 WIMSA Media and Research Contract (n 129) para 2.2.

132 Kelly Bannister and George Nicholas, 'Irony as Inspiration: From Academic Research to Community Action in Protecting Biocultural Landscape' (2015) 4(1) *Langscape* 62, 67.

133 Natural Justice, Biocultural Community Protocols <https://naturaljustice.org/wp-content/uploads/2013/08/Brief-intro-BCP.pdf> accessed 1 December 2021.

Safeguarding entails going beyond the limited scope of protection that is accorded by the intellectual property regime. It involves protecting the cultural integrity and realisation of the human right to self-determination of the traditional knowledge holding communities.[134] Consequently, there is a difference between the limited protection under the intellectual property regime and the more holistic protection that includes safeguarding, which the traditional knowledge holding communities' own legal regimes provide for. The communities' legal regimes safeguard 'the cultural, spiritual and social significance of the traditional knowledge'.[135] Traditional medical knowledge may be affected by the listing of a site as a world heritage site. Nonetheless, traditional systems can mitigate potential negative effects by promoting sustainable use of cultural and natural resources while safeguarding the qualities and values of the site.[136]

There is significant evidence of the positive impact that using community protocols and codes has had on the transboundary protection and safeguarding of traditional medical knowledge. For instance, the Bushbuckbridge biocultural protocol has successfully 'fostered a sense of identity amongst dispersed healers' and reassured conservation authorities that local healers are not overharvesting medicinal plants thus gaining access to restricted areas, and the healers have signed an 'access and benefit sharing' agreement with a commercial company.[137] The biocultural protocol makes it easier to set the rules of engagement with third parties and addresses the issue of the exclusion of communities from decision-making in heritage management.

Biocultural protocols and codes of ethics have also been used by communities to effectively bridge the gaps between customary management of their biocultural heritage and external management through positive laws.[138] The Bushbuckbridge community has, however, indicated that they are yet to enter into any benefit sharing agreements relating to the use of their traditional medical knowledge; a relationship of distrust still exists between them and external researchers who access their knowledge.[139] Such shortcomings of biocultural protocols can be addressed through codes of ethics. Although the San Code is relatively new and it is too early to assess its effectiveness, the global acclaim of its launch testifies to the fact that stakeholders easily identify with the global values on which it is premised.[140] While community protocols emphasise customary and national laws that have territorial limits, the global values that are enshrined in the San Code are likely

134 Tobin (n 7) 209.

135 ibid.

136 Albino Jopela, 'Reorienting Heritage Management in Southern Africa: Lessons from Traditional Custodianship of Rock Art Sites in Central Mozambique' in Webber Ndoro, Shadreck Chirikure, Janette Deacon (eds), *Managing Heritage in Africa: Who Cares?* (Routledge 2019).

137 Swiderska et al. (n 104) 36.

138 Jonas, Bavikatte and Shrumm (n 45) 63.

139 ibid 65.

140 Callaway (n 127).

to have a global reach thus being more effective in safeguarding transboundary traditional medical knowledge beyond Southern Africa.

The combination of biocultural protocols and codes of ethics that are developed by community members essentially leads to a fusion of law and ethics. This fusion is important for protecting transboundary traditional medical knowledge; this is evident in the incorporation of the principle of 'prior informed consent' into the intellectual property law regime since the principle has its origins in bioethics.[141] To elaborate, a parallel can be drawn between this combination in protecting traditional medical knowledge and the influence of ethical engagement in archaeology where managing issues relating to tangible heritage has led to 'engaged archaeology', a term aptly described by Soderland and Lilley as 'equitable decolonised collaboration between archaeologists or heritage specialists and local, Indigenous, or other descendent communities'.[142] Southern African communities will likely experience better levels of engagement with third parties who access and use their traditional medical knowledge since the terms of engagement are clarified in the biocultural protocols and codes of ethics thus not left to the exclusive domain of the intellectual property regime.

Protecting non-commercial spiritual values in traditional medical knowledge can also be achieved through biocultural protocols and codes of ethics. Evidently, biocultural protocols are made part of the process of granting access to natural resources and procuring 'prior and informed consent' from the communities.[143] Since the latter is incorporated into the intellectual property regime of the case study countries, making biocultural protocols part of the process increases their effectiveness in protecting traditional medical knowledge. The biocultural protocols and codes are effective because they are based on the communities' customary laws and they are integrated into the 'access and benefit sharing' regime.

Conclusion

The discussions in this chapter have shown that communities are using codes and protocols to ensure that their rights in traditional medical knowledge are protected and safeguarded. Although these mechanisms have limitations, these can be overcome through the use of contracts that communities enter into with third parties and by integrating them into the 'access and benefit sharing' as well as the intellectual property regimes thus making codes and protocols legally binding. Using codes and protocols essentially contributes to creating a sense of belonging among geographically dispersed communities, bridging the gaps between customary and

141 Krishna Ravi Srinivas, 'Protecting Traditional Knowledge Holders' Interests and Preventing Misappropriation—Traditional Knowledge Commons and Biocultural Protocols: Necessary but Not Sufficient?' (2012) 19 *Int J Cult Prop* 401.

142 Hilary A Soderland and Ian A Lilley, 'The Fusion of Law and Ethics in Cultural Heritage Management: The 21st Century Confronts Archaeology' (2015) 40(5) *J Field Archaeol* 508, 510.

143 Srinivas (n 141) 413.

legal management of biocultural heritage, and protecting non-commercial spiritual values in traditional medical knowledge.

The community-based approaches also show that ownership of traditional medical knowledge is not in itself negative since, as Reddy observes, if used well it can emancipate the communities.[144] The use of biocultural protocols and codes can further enhance the incorporation of the principle of 'prior and informed consent' into the intellectual property regimes of the case study countries since they have the added advantage of ensuring the safeguarding of traditional medical knowledge. Indeed, protocols bring the value of a plurality of approaches in heritage management and conservation of biodiversity. As observed by Jonas and others, biocultural protocols 'are contributing to a paradigm shift in conservation law, policy, and practice towards the recognition of and support for the right to diversity through legal and conservation pluralism'.[145]

References

Abbott R, *Documenting Traditional Medical Knowledge* (WIPO 2014)

Amechi E P, 'Traditional Knowledge Relating to Medical Uses of Plants and the Patent Regime in South Africa: Whither the Traditional Healers?' (2015) 27 *SAMLJ* 58

Andanda P, 'Striking a Balance between Intellectual Property Protection of Traditional Knowledge, Cultural Preservation and Access to Knowledge' (2012) 17 *J Intellect Pro Rights* 549

Andanda P and Khademi H, 'Protecting Traditional Medicine Knowledge Through the Intellectual Property Regime Based on the Experience of Iran and South Africa' in C Ncube and E du Plessis (eds), *Indigenous Knowledge & Intellectual Property: Contemporary Studies in Law and Applied Research series* (Juta 2016)

Antons C and Rogers L, 'Cultural and Intellectual Property in Cross-Border Disputes Over Intangible Cultural Heritage' in C Antons and W Logan (eds), *Intellectual Property, Cultural Property and Intangible Cultural Heritage* (Routledge 2018)

Arezzo E, 'Struggling Around the "Natural" Divide: The Protection of Tangible and Intangible Indigenous Property (2007) 25(367) *Cardozo Arts & Ent L J* 381

Bannister K and Nicholas G, 'Irony as Inspiration: From Academic Research to Community Action in Protecting Biocultural Landscape' (2015) 4(1) *Langscape* 62

Biber-Klemm S et al., 'Flanking Policies in National and International Law' in S Biber-Klemm and T Cottier (eds), *Rights to Plant Genetic Resources and Traditional Knowledge: Basic Issues and Perspectives* (CABI 2016)

Blake J, 'Taking a Human Rights Approach to Cultural Heritage Protection' (2011) 4(2) *Heritage & Society* 199

Callaway E, 'South Africa's San People Issue Ethics Code to Scientists' (2017) 543(7646) *Nature* 475

Chennells R, 'Putting Intellectual Property Rights into Practice: Experience from the San' in R Wynberg, D Schroeder and R Chennells (eds), *Indigenous Peoples, Consent and Benefit Sharing: Lessons from the San Hoodia Case* (Springer 2009)

144 Reddy (n 25) 181.

145 Jonas, Bavikatte and Shrumm (n 45) 112.

——— 'Traditional Knowledge and Benefit Sharing After the Nagoya Protocol: Three Cases from South Africa' (2013) 9(2) *J Environ Law* 163

Chennells R, Haraseb V and Ngakaeaja M, 'Speaking for the San: Challenges for Representative Institutions' in R Wynberg, D Schroeder and R Chennells (eds), *Indigenous Peoples, Consent and Benefit Sharing: Lessons from the San Hoodia Case* (Springer 2009)

Chennells R and Steenkamp A, 'International Genomics Research Involving the San People' in D Schroeder et al. (eds), *Ethics Dumping: Case Studies from North-South Research Collaborations* (Springer 2018)

Daya Y and Vink N, 'Protecting Traditional Ethno-Botanical Knowledge in South Africa through the IPregime' (2006) 45(3) *Agrekon* 319

Deacon H, 'Transboundary Knowledge and Regional Cooperation in the Protection of Traditional Knowledge in Kenya' (2017) 12(3) *JIPLP* 226

Delgado A N, 'Community Protocols as Tools for Resisting Exclusion in Global Environmental Governance' (2016) 56(4) *RAE-Revista de Administração de Empresas* 395

Deutsche Gesellschaft für Internationale Zusammenarbeit (GIZ), *Biocultural Community Protocols* (GIZ 2013)

Ezeanya A C, 'Contending Issues of Intellectual Property Rights Protection and Indigenous Knowledge of Pharmacology in Africa South of the Sahara' (2013) 6(5) *JPAS* 24

Feris L, 'Protecting Traditional Knowledge in Africa: Considering African Approaches' (2004) 4(2) *Afr Hum Rights Law* 242

Foster L, *Reinventing Hoodia: Peoples, Plants, and Patents in South Africa* (University of Washington Press 2017)

Frankel S, 'The Challenges of Cross-Border Protection of Traditional Knowledge' in F D Robinson, A Abdel-Latif and P Roffe (eds), *Protecting Traditional Knowledge: The WIPO Intergovernmental Committee on Intellectual Property and Genetic Resources, Traditional Knowledge and Folklore* (Routledge 2017)

Gebeye A B, 'Decoding Legal Pluralism in Africa' (2017) 49(2) *J Leg Plur Unoff* 228

Jonas H, Bavikatte K and Shrumm H, 'Community Protocols and Access and Benefit Sharing' (2010) 12(3) *Asian Biotechnol Dev Rev* 49

Jopela A, 'Reorienting Heritage Management in Southern Africa: Lessons from Traditional Custodianship of Rock Art Sites in Central Mozambique' in W Ndoro, S Chirikure and J Deacon (eds), *Managing Heritage in Africa: Who Cares?* (Routledge 2019)

Keitumetse S, 'UNESCO 2003 Convention on Intangible Heritage: Practical Implications for Heritage Management Approaches in Africa' (2006) 61(184) *South African Archaeological Bulletin* 166

Kibuka-Sebitosi E, 'Protecting Indigenous Knowledge and the Rights and Interests of Indigenous Medicine Practitioners in Africa: Law, Leadership and Governance' (2008) 7(1) *IAJIKS* 77

Kurin R, 'Safeguarding Intangible Cultural Heritage in the 2003 UNESCO Convention: A Critical Appraisal' (2004) 56(1–2) *Museum International* 221–222

Kuruk P, *Traditional Knowledge, Genetic Resources, Customary Laws and Intellectual Property: A Global Primer* (Edward Elgar 2020)

Lenzerini F, 'Intangible Cultural Heritage: The Living Culture of Peoples' (2011) 22(1) *Eur J Int Law* 101

Lewis M, 'Access and Benefit-Sharing in the Wake of CBD COP10: The Nagoya Protocol and its Potential Implications for South Africa' (2010) 17(2) *SAJELP* 69

Muller M R, 'The Legal Protection of Widely Shared and Dispersed Traditional Knowledge' in D F Robinson, A Abdel-Latif and P Roffe (eds), *Protecting Traditional*

Knowledge: The WIPO Intergovernmental Committee on Intellectual Property and Genetic Resources, Traditional Knowledge and Folklore (Routledge 2017)

O'Keefe P J, 'Codes of Ethics: Form and Function in Cultural Heritage Management' (1998) 7(1) *Int J Cult Prop* 32

Rautenbach C, 'Deep Legal Pluralism in South Africa: Judicial Accommodation of Non-State Law' (2010) 42(60) *J Leg Plur Unoff* 143

Reddy S, 'Making Heritage Legible: Who Owns Traditional Medical Knowledge?' (2006) 13 *Int J Cult Prop* 167

Riordan A and Schofield J, 'Beyond Biomedicine: Traditional Medicine as Cultural Heritage' (2015) 21(3) *Int J Herit Stud* 280

Silberman A N, 'Heritage Interpretation and Human Rights: Documenting Diversity, Expressing Identity, or Establishing Universal Principles?' (2012) 18(3) *Int J Her Stu* 245

Soderland H and Lilley I A, 'The Fusion of Law and Ethics in Cultural Heritage Management: The 21st Century Confronts Archaeology' (2015) 40(5) *J Field Archaeol* 508

Srinivas K R, 'Protecting Traditional Knowledge Holders' Interests and Preventing Misappropriation – Traditional Knowledge Commons and Biocultural Protocols: Necessary but Not Sufficient?' (2012) 19 *Int J Cult Prop* 401

Swiderska K, 'Protecting Traditional Knowledge: A Holistic Approach based on Customary Laws and Bio-cultural Heritage' in N K Ninan (ed), *Conserving and Valuing Ecosystem Services and Biodiversity: Economic and institutional challenges* (Earthscan 2009)

Swiderska K et al., 'Community Protocols and Free, Prior Informed Consent – Overview and Lessons Learnt' in K Swiderska et al. (ed), *Biodiversity and Culture: Exploring Community Protocols, Rights and Consent, Participatory Learning and Action 65* (IIED 2012)

Tobin B, *The Role of Customary Law in Access and Benefit-Sharing and Traditional Knowledge Governance: Perspectives from Andean and Pacific Island Countries* (WIPO and United Nation University 2013)

Tong L, 'Protecting Traditional Knowledge: Does Secrecy Offer a Solution?' (2010) 13(4) *Potchefstroomse Elektroniese Regsblad* 159

UNESCO International Bioethics Committee (IBC), *Report of the IBC on Traditional Medicine Systems and their Ethical Implication* (IBC 2013)

Vadi V, 'Intangible Heritage: Traditional Medicine and Knowledge Governance' (2007) 2(10) *JIPLP* 682

van der Merwe A, 'South and Southern Africa – Recent Developments in the Legal Protection of Traditional Knowledge and Traditional Cultural Expressions' (2014) 9(1) *JIPLP* 411

Walloe M and Young T, 'Beyond Access: Exploring Implementation of the Fair and Equitable Sharing Commitment in the CBD' ([2007]) *IUCN Environmental Policy and Law Paper* No 67/2

WHO, WIPO & WTO, *Promoting Access to Medical Technologies and Innovation: Intersections between Public Health, Intellectual Property and Trade* (World Trade Organization 2013)

WIPO, *Intellectual Property and Genetic Resources, Traditional Knowledge and Traditional Cultural Expressions* (WIPO 2015)

——— 'The Protection of Traditional Knowledge: Draft Articles' WIPO/GRTKF/IC/40/18 (WIPO 2019)

——— 'Intellectual Property Needs and Expectations of Traditional Knowledge Holders: WIPO Report on Fact-Finding Missions on Intellectual Property and Traditional Knowledge' (WIPO 2001)

Wynberg R and Chennells R, 'Green Diamonds of South Africa: An Overview of the San-Hoodia Case' in R Wynberg, D Schroeder and R Chennells (eds), *Indigenous Peoples, Consent and Benefit Sharing: Lessons from the San Hoodia Case* (Springer 2009)

11 Knitting a future for the Aymara's weavers

The Andean project[1]

Patricia Covarrubia

Introduction

In September 2009, UNESCO supported the project to safeguard the intangible cultural heritage of the Aymara communities of Bolivia, Chile, and Peru, which, at the time, was seen and promoted as exemplary.[2] The five-year project aimed to identify and prepare a catalogue of the Aymara's traditional knowledge, to consolidate the language in efforts to maintain practice and transmission, to promote and disseminate the Aymara's oral and musical expressions, and to support traditional knowledge on the production of textile arts and traditional agricultural techniques. Based on this, the chapter will establish if the project has been successful and if the principles given by the Convention 2003 have been followed. Subsequently, the chapter seeks to determine if intellectual property rights in this transboundary cultural heritage are helpful or detrimental to the Aymara people and their traditional knowledge.

A vast literature covers the protection of traditional knowledge holders' interest and the prevention of misappropriation. The extent to which the principles and legislation that exist (both by the World Intellectual Property Organization (WIPO) and by UNESCO) deal with the expectations of the community will be explored. Protecting and promoting Indigenous peoples' traditional knowledge, in this case shared by neighbouring countries, also requires finding the interconnection with a broader aspect that sustains such traditional knowledge. Debates and controversies around the intellectual property system aside, this chapter considers the challenge that may arise when intellectual property protection of traditional knowledge becomes a legal reality at a national level, as could be the case of the textile arts created by the skilled Aymara weavers, a long-standing tradition.

1 An earlier version of this paper was presented at the 4th Biennial conference of the Association of Critical Heritage Studies (ACHS) held in Zhejiang University, Hangzhou, China, from 1 to 6 September 2018. This research was supported by the Dennison Research Grant (University of Buckingham). The author would like to thank an anonymous reviewer for helpful comments on an earlier draft of this chapter.

2 UNESCO Register of Best Safeguarding Practices, 2009. Decision of the Intergovernmental Committee: 4.COM 15B.

DOI: 10.4324/9781003345237-12

The first section of the chapter provides the background of the project and examines its aims, praises and flaws, including the narrative of the Aymara people, followed by research questions. Next, an evaluation of the principles of the UNESCO 2003 Convention for the Safeguarding of the Intangible Cultural Heritage and its links with intellectual property legislation is offered, especially to what degree the principles/legislation that does exist may benefit communities. This aids in highlighting ways in which there is a feasible possibility of having a mechanism for transboundary cooperation on the protection, promotion, and enhancement of the Aymara's intellectual property rights when traditional knowledge is shared across national borders and thus if the project registered at UNESCO safeguards the Aymara's traditional knowledge.

The UNESCO 2003 Convention for the Safeguarding of the Intangible Cultural Heritage and the Aymara's involvement in the Andean project

The intangible cultural heritage of the Aymara communities was selected, along with two other projects,[3] as 'best practice programmes, projects and activities' for the Register of Good Safeguarding Practices (Representative List). UNESCO noted the programmes, projects, and activities to be 'exemplary' for they portrayed the principles and objectives of the 2003 Convention.

The Regional Centre for the Safeguarding of the Intangible Cultural Heritage of Latin America (CRESPIAL)[4] coordinated and provided assistance to the Aymara community. The UNESCO Committee requested the Secretariat to promote the safeguarding of the intangible cultural heritage of Aymara communities in Bolivia, Chile, and Peru.[5] The Aymara's project was seen as an example of sub-regional cooperation (Andean Region) among local communities, governmental bodies, and NGOs. The Aymara communities' intangible cultural heritage is found in several countries, and the sub-regional project aimed to 'develop safeguarding measures to ensure the viability of the oral expressions, and music and traditional knowledge (textile arts and agricultural technologies) of the Aymara communities of Bolivia, Chile and Peru'.[6] The Subsidiary Body noted that although countries are free to apply on their own even though an 'element' is practised in other places too, the Convention encourages cooperation between states to address instances of shared heritage.[7] The Aymara communities' joint

3 Decision of the Intergovernmental Committee: 4.COM 15B.

4 CRESPIAL was created under the auspices of UNESCO as a Category 2 Centre. Sixteen Latin American countries are members.

5 Proposal MUL-00299 – Plurinational State of Bolivia, Chile, Peru; Decision 4.COM 15.B.

6 Decision of the Intergovernmental Committee: 4.COM 15B.

7 UNESCO Subsidiary Body for the Examination of Nominations to the Representatives List of the Intangible Cultural Heritage of Humanity, Report by the Rapporteur, Fourth session Abu Dhabi, United Arab Emirates 28 September to 2 October 2009, para 34. See Sarah Sargent, '"Fractured Resemblances": Contested Multinational Heritage and Soft Power' (2020) 27 *Int J Cult Prop* 97.

application seems a good example of fulfilling such aspirations due to potentially having a mechanism for transboundary cooperation on the protection, promotion, and enhancement of traditional knowledge and traditional cultural expressions shared across national borders.

Research theory and research questions

The project of the Aymara communities, supported by UNESCO and advertised as exemplary, is examined, aiming to evaluate what has happened since the registration, what events took place, and how they have safeguarded the Aymara's traditional knowledge and traditional cultural expressions. The primary question is whether the project has achieved the 2003 Convention's objectives; the overarching idea being to evaluate the degree to which the principles/legislation that exist may deal with the expectations of the Aymara communities and, accordingly, have or could have helped in the development of the project, and acknowledge if intellectual property rights in this transboundary cultural heritage could be of assistance or a deterrent. This case study is a starting point for a better understanding of how heritage is valued, preserved, politicised, mobilised, financed, planned, and/or destroyed in transboundary situations.

The Aymara people

The Aymara is an Indigenous nation in the Andes highlands region and the second-largest Indigenous linguistic group of South America.[8] Their social identification is called *ayllu* (community) consisting of several extended kinships. They usually live in small villages, sitting between neighbouring countries, yet the Aymara people identify themselves as one people,[9] speaking a common language.[10] A decline in the population is noticeable as the community is abandoned for most of the year due to seeking earnings in large towns. They continue to suffer from socio-political marginalisation and discrimination and claim to be in danger of extinction.[11] They still raise their voice for their right to self-determination,[12] the

8 Rafael E Núñez and Carlos Cornejo, 'Facing the Sunrise: Cultural Worldview Underlying Intrinsic-Based Encoding of Absolute Frames of Reference in Aymara' (2012) 36 *Cognitive Science* 965; Encyclopedia Britannica.

9 Tomas Alarcón, 'Ayllu, the Basic Social Unit of the Aymara People' (2001) 14 *St Thomas L Rev* 449.

10 Harold Osborne, *Indians of the Andes: Aymaras and Quechuas* (Routledge 2013) 11.

11 Alarcón, 'Ayllu, the Basic Social Unit of the Aymara People'. As an example of this, see Front Line Defenders, 'Aymara Leader Sentenced to Seven Years in Prison' (*Front Line Defenders*, 7 July 2017) <https://www.frontlinedefenders.org/en/case/aymara-community-leaders-trial#case-update-id-6015> accessed 2 December 2021.

12 Silvia Rivera Cusicanqui, *Oprimidos pero no Vencidos: Lluchas del Campesinado Aymara y Qhechwa, 1900–1980* (Aruwiyiri, Editorial del Taller de Historia Oral Andino (THOA) 2003).

latter to be understood as a broad concept which refers to the 'economic, social and cultural development of a people'.[13]

The main economic activity is agriculture, the cultivation of crops like potatoes, quinoa, and barley, and herding llama and alpaca.[14] The Aymara are known for excellent knitting and weaving skills,[15] producing textiles and weaving accessories made of wool from llamas and alpacas. They produce many utilitarian products like *aguayos* to carry babies and the *chuspa*, used by men for carrying coca leaves. The weaving skills lead to the creation of tangible works and in the case of the Aymara's textile arts, the intangible cultural heritage which are the skills, is converted into the tangible cultural heritage, and so, they 'dependent' on each other.[16] Suitably, Lixinski refers to dependent intangible cultural expressions as cultural expressions incorporating the process, skills, and beliefs, which leads to creating a 'physical' work. Expressions incorporated into tangible objects represent the relationship of a people with its cultural heritage.[17]

The project: background and merits

The project was aimed at, first, identifying and preparing a catalogue of the Aymara's traditional knowledge; second, consolidating the language in efforts to maintain practice and transmission; third, promoting and disseminating the Aymara's oral and musical expressions; and fourth, supporting traditional knowledge on the production of textile arts and traditional agricultural techniques.[18] Textile arts will be the focus.

Before UNESCO's decision, Bolivia, Chile, and Peru received from UNESCO US$7,500 for preparatory assistance in elaborating the proposal.[19] CRESPIAL coordinated and provided the Aymara assistance and continues to be the responsible centre in driving this project. However, participation at the international level is a moot point; on one hand, the implementation of the Convention does not provide spaces to communities as experts replace them.[20] On the other hand, it is claimed that they must be excluded due to lacking the required expertise.[21]

13 Christoph B Graber, 'Aboriginal Self-Determination vs the Propertisation of Traditional Culture' (2009) 13 *Aust Indig Law Rev* 18, 26.
14 Núñez and Cornejo (n 8) 965.
15 Their weaving skills are so precise that it was put forward by a medical team as an alternative solution for an occlusive device. See Alexandra Heath, Alexander Javois and Franz Freudenthal, 'Weaving Indigenous Textile Art into Cardiac Devices' (2018) 319 *Jama* 966.
16 Lucas Lixinski, 'Selecting Heritage: The Interplay of Art, Politics and Identity' (2011) 22 *Eur J Int Law* 81, 83.
17 ibid, 83.
18 Decision of the Intergovernmental Committee: 4.COM 15B. 4.COM 15.B.
19 UNESCO Decision 4.COM 1 BUR 1, 17 December 2008, contract number 4500057894.
20 Doc. ITH/08/2.EXT. COM/CONF.201/INF.4, of 12 Feb. 2008. Annex 1. See Lixinski (n 16) 81, 96.
21 Lixinski (n 16) 96–97.

Attributable to these contradicting views, a set of operational directives were approved providing stronger forms of community involvement.[22]

The successful application reflected the principles and objectives of the 2003 Convention,[23] embracing safeguarding, awareness-raising, and international cooperation.[24] The Aymara's project seemed effective due to the 'systematic and logical action plan'; it was clearly 'measurable and assessable' and seemed appropriate to the needs of Bolivia, Chile, and Peru.[25] Moreover, the submitted documentation contained the 'consent' form of the Aymara communities, a vital factor and essential aspect that must be submitted within the documentation determining the community involvement in the overall safeguarding process. Although the meaning of 'free, prior, and informed consent' is debated in some forums,[26] UNESCO and its Subsidiary Body assert that communities' consent might take many forms, and it is neither possible nor necessary to define a specific format for expressing consent.[27] For instance, UNESCO's 'ICH-02 nomination form', used for nominations and proposals, notes that a particular format is not required but documentation is necessary.[28] In the Aymara's project, the documentation submitted had declarations of local NGOs regarding the Aymara communities' willingness to take part in the project. In the submission, all parties attested their willingness to share their experiences in the 'dissemination of best practices'.[29] This is welcomed and commended as many developing countries have similar conditions where traditional knowledge and traditional cultural expressions come from a people but are divided by geographical borders. Yet, the Committee strongly

22 Two years after the project was recognised, the parties were not successful in the request made to UNESCO international financial assistance. It was denied on the grounds of lack of elaboration on the active participation by the Aymara communities and how they were to be involved in the claimed financial application; in addition, it noticed that 'recording' and 'documentation' were not enough for the transmission and viability of traditional knowledge and traditional cultural expressions and further safeguard measures were needed. See Decision of the Intergovernmental Committee: 6.COM 10.1 (number 5).

23 Article 1, Scientific United Nations Educational and Cultural Organization, *Convention for the Safeguarding of the Intangible Cultural Heritage* (UNESCO 2003).

24 Decision of the Intergovernmental Committee: 4.COM 15B.

25 ibid.

26 There is a lack of agreement on what 'free, prior informed consent' means. The World Bank and the International Monetary Fund have their own interpretations. There are also different interpretations across the Articles of the United Nations Declaration on the Rights of Indigenous Peoples. Finally, the Hague 2010 Report and the Sofia 2012 Report from the International Law Association provide a balanced discussion and good interpretation. See Sarah Sargent, 'The Contested Meaning of Free, Prior and Informed Consent in International Financial Law and Indigenous Rights' in Valentina Vadi and Bruno de Witte (eds), *Culture and International Economic Law* (Routledge 2015) 87, 89.

27 This approach is followed by UNESCO in the Inscription on the Urgent Safeguarding List, and the Inscription on the Representative List.

28 Representative List of the Intangible Cultural Heritage of Humanity Instructions for Completing Form ICH-02, checklist of required technical conditions for a nomination to be considered complete, supporting evidence (point 6).

29 Decision of the Intergovernmental Committee: 4.COM 15D.

recommended Bolivia, Chile, and Peru to 'fully' include the Aymara communities by emphasising their 'empowerment'; to reinforce their capacities, encouraging the revitalisation and traditional transmission of their traditional knowledge and traditional cultural expressions, and to promote a 'sustainable future-oriented development'.[30] For instance, the Committee recalled that the aim of 'recording' and 'documentation' is to 'ensure the feasibility of the intangible cultural heritage concerned which needs to be complemented by *other* suitable safeguarding measures'.[31] Ten years later, the only phase completed is the 'recording' and 'documentation' of oral and musical expressions: therefore *other* suitable measures are still required. The latter has resulted in, first, three 'traditional music' discs of the Aymara communities of Bolivia, Chile, and Peru, one for each country containing 20 songs; and second, three 'oral tradition' discs of the Aymara communities of Bolivia, Chile, and Peru complemented by an introductory text and three essays, one for each country.[32] The material was published by CRESPIAL and sponsored by the Bolivian Minister of Culture, the Chilean National Council of Art and Culture, and the Peruvian Ministry of Culture.[33] While this was a five-year project, CRESPIAL notes that it is still 'ongoing'.

Equivalent to the CRESPIAL engagement, the Aymara communities keep working for their recognition and remain active in the safeguarding of their traditional knowledge. In 2017, the Bolivian Minister of Culture promoted the participation of young people in schools for the oral transmission of national heritage to collect heritage knowledge. This resulted in around 46 oral histories being rescued and published in two books (Spanish and Aymara respectively).[34] This campaign was repeated in 2018. Parallel to this, the Chilean Cultural Council recognised artisans.[35] However, these safeguarding practices are outside the main project and defeat the 'best practice' of sub-regional cooperation. Nevertheless, one cannot ignore the fact that these stand-alone projects consolidate the Aymara language, maintaining their traditional knowledge practice and transmission.

CRESPIAL continues to promote intangible cultural heritage by running different projects; for instance, a call or competition for 'photo and video to safeguard intangible cultural heritage' seeking to finance photographic and audio-visual projects of social initiative linked to the safeguarding of the intangible cultural

30 ibid.

31 Decision of the Intergovernmental Committee: 4.COM 15B.

32 CRESPIAL, 'Proyectos en Desarrollo – Aymara' (CRESPIAL org) <http://crespial.org/proyectos-desarrollo/> accessed 2 December 2021.

33 UNESCO, 'Musica Aymara – Chile, Bolivia, Peru' (UNESCO org Multimedia 2012) <http://www.unesco.org/archives/multimedia/document-4323> accessed 2 December 2021.

34 CRESPIAL, 'Impulsan participación de jóvenes para la transmisión oral del patrimonio nacional – BOLIVIA' (*CRESPIAL org*, 21 September 2018) <http://crespial.org/impulsan-participacion-de-jovenes-para-la-transmision-oral-del-patrimonio-nacional-bolivia/> accessed 2 December 2021.

35 CRESPIAL, 'Consejo de la Cultura Reconoce a Siete Artesanos de Pueblos Originarios con el Sello de Artesanía Indígena – CHILE' (*CRESPIAL org*, 09 December 2017) <http://crespial.org/consejo-de-la-cultura-reconoce-a-siete-artesanos-de-pueblos-originarios-con-el-sello-de-artesania-indigena-chile/> accessed 2 December 2021.

heritage of Latin America.[36] Still, no safeguard measures on Aymara's traditional knowledge textile arts have been developed. The difficulty is that a UNESCO declaration seems to be a political commitment towards states based on good faith.[37]

The 2003 Convention and the WIPO: purpose and rights

The Aymara's project focuses strongly on the importance of preserving the language as a flawless transmission of their intangible cultural heritage.[38] The project looks at safeguarding measures relating to 'the viability of oral expressions, music and traditional knowledge (textile arts and agricultural technologies)' by promoting these in primary schools and teacher-training programmes, and by launching contests. The project appears to comply with Article 1 of the 2003 Convention referring to safeguarding intangible cultural heritage, ensuring respect for the people concerned, raising awareness, and providing international cooperation and assistance. All of these safeguarding measures are fulfilled via awareness and educational programmes rather than the legal protection of traditional knowledge. Suitably, Hafstein states that heritage lists intend to 'channel funds and attention to the task of safeguarding', providing a people and their culture better visibility.[39] In this respect, the Aymara's project has not obtained further funds.

Concerning legal protection, either *positive* (acquiring intellectual property rights or *sui generis*) or *defensive* (preventing unfair exploitation), the WIPO was created to promote and protect intellectual property, and synergies between WIPO's purpose and UNESCO's objectives are visible. These do not necessarily need to merge, but the final goal should be a combination of the two. Evidently, it is better to produce a combined total effect than the sum of their separate effects. Twarog notes that while traditional knowledge is a 'multi-faceted issue', focusing on just one and ignoring the others, risks creating a solution.[40] Consequently, the link with intellectual property is that the 2003 Convention has been criticised for not creating a system of legal guarantees, bringing intellectual property into this scenario may serve this purpose.[41] This is not to suggest that intellectual property rights or a sui generis right is the best way forward, nor that intellectual property meets all the Aymara communities' needs; the reality is that any legal system proposed to protect traditional knowledge ought to accommodate their cultural

36 CRESPIAL, 'Programa de Incentivos' (*CRESPIAL org*) <http://crespial.org/programa-incentivos/> accessed 2 December 2021.

37 No normative action is needed. See Mike Robinson and David Picard, *Tourism, Culture and Sustainable Development* (UNESCO 2006) 58.

38 Lixinski (n 16) 81, 83.

39 In the early discussion of the UNESCO Intangible Heritage List, China noted that the UNESCO World Heritage List is a great source of 'publicity'. See Valdimar Tr Hafstein, 'Intangible Heritage as a List: From Masterpieces to Representation' in Laurajane Smith and Natsuko Akagawa (eds), *Intangible Heritage* (Routledge 2009) 93–94, 103.

40 Sophia Twarog and Promila Kapoor (eds), *Preserving, Protecting, and Promoting Traditional Knowledge: National Actions and International Dimensions* (UNCTA 2004).

41 Lixinski (n 16) 81.

identity, and their *cosmovisión*, i.e., their holistic perspective.[42] The proposal is that intellectual property tools such as a collective mark, certification mark, or a geographical indication could be used strategically to decrease illegal use of their traditional cultural expressions.

Because there is no international agreement or international minimum standard on how traditional knowledge or traditional cultural expressions should be protected, this creates a problem for the Aymara's textile arts. Several Indigenous peoples' declarations continually call for traditional knowledge protection,[43] and since 2000, the WIPO Intergovernmental Committee on Intellectual Property and Genetic Resources, Traditional Knowledge and Folklore continues negotiations to finalise an agreement on international legal instruments for the protection of traditional knowledge, traditional cultural expressions, and genetic resources.[44] While the Indigenous peoples' voice focuses on normative claims, the aim is towards the effect that they have.[45] Even though the 'preservation, conservation and safeguarding' of traditional knowledge and traditional cultural expressions are not covered by intellectual property protection[46] there are tools in the intellectual property system that safeguard, by 'protect[ing] from loss, harm or damage'.[47] National intellectual property systems or *sui generis* laws that protect traditional knowledge (hard law but with no extra-territorial effect) exist in some jurisdictions. In Latin America, there is the regional Andean Community Decision 391 (Bolivia, Colombia, Ecuador, and Peru);[48] Chile's Law No 19.253; Panama's Law 2000;[49] and Brazil's Provisional Measure No 2186-16 of 2001[50] among others.

42 For the survival of Indigenous peoples and communities it is paramount to protect their cultural identity; thus, no need to separate the work or expertise that different fields bring to it. See Yvonne Donders, 'A Right to Cultural Identity in UNESCO' in Francesco Francioni and Martin Scheinin (eds), *Cultural Human Rights* (Martinus Nijhoff Publishers 2008).

43 Michael Blakeney, 'The Pacific Solution: The European Union's Intellectual Property Rights Activism in Australia's and New Zealand's Sphere of Influence' in Peter Drahos and Susy Frankel (eds), *Indigenous Peoples' Innovation Intellectual Property Pathways to Development* (ANU Press 2012).

44 Back in September 2000, Latin American countries submitted a document calling for the creation of a standing committee, which could internationally define and recognise methods for the protection of intellectual property rights in traditional knowledge. See WIPO Doc WO/GA/26/9 (200) annex I, 10.

45 Daniel Gervais, 'The Pacific Solution: The European Union's Intellectual Property Rights Activism in Australia's and New Zealand's Sphere of Influence' in Peter Drahos and Susy Frankel (eds) (n 43) 141.

46 WIPO, *Protect and Promote Your Culture: A Practical Guide to Intellectual Property for Indigenous Peoples and Local Communities* (WIPO 2017) 11.

47 *Concise Oxford English Dictionary* (12th edn, OUP 2011).

48 Regulating Bioprospecting and Protecting Indigenous Peoples' Knowledge.

49 Regulating Collective Rights of Indigenous Peoples for the Protection and Defence of Their Cultural Identity and Their Traditional Knowledge.

50 Regulating Access to the Genetic Heritage, Protection of and Access to Associated Traditional Knowledge.

These legislative examples are rewarding and give their people legitimacy that is denied in political fora,[51] but there are not many cases reported.

Existing legal tools such as contracts, licenses, or registers can accommodate traditional knowledge,[52] and some have been protected using the intellectual property system. The objective of protecting traditional knowledge in Latin America is about control, compensation, recognition of collective rights over traditional knowledge, prevention and decrease of misuse or illegal use, and maintaining and preserving traditional knowledge.[53] The case of the textile arts created by the skilled Aymara weavers engaging in commercial activities is threatened by the impact of culture in the business world,[54] and by traditional skills disappearing, depriving the communities of a source of income.[55] UNESCO provides a window for intangible cultural heritage via awareness and educational programmes, but they are not enough to stop the copying and mass production by outsiders. In practice, the spirit of any convention does not go far if it is not effective. Although the Operational Directives for the implementation of the 2018 Conventions[56] encourage countries to protect the rights of communities by using intellectual property, without 'political will'[57] conventions and guidelines will not become operational.[58]

Recognising 'genuine' traditional cultural expressions

Searching for 'Aymara' in the national intellectual property offices of the three countries returned no results. The Aymara communities have not yet used any

51 Lixinski (n 16) 81, 96.

52 Robert K Paterson and Dennis S Karjala, 'Looking beyond Intellectual Property in Resolving Protection of the Intangible Cultural Heritage of Indigenous Peoples' (2003) *Cardozo J Int'l & Comp L* 635.

53 Manuel Ruiz Muller, *Regulating Bioprospecting and Protecting Indigenous Peoples' Knowledge in the Andean Community: Decision 391 and Its Overall Impacts in the Region* (Protecting and Promoting Traditional Knowledge: Systems, National Experiences and International Dimensions, 2000) (UNCTAD 2000); Manuel Ruiz Muller, 'The Protection of Traditional Knowledge in Latin America' (Peruvian Society for Environmental Law, Jamaica, March 2008); see also Silke Von Lewinski, 'The Protection of Folklore' (2003) 11 *Cardozo J Int'l & Comp L* 747, 763.

54 François Rivière, *Investing in Cultural Diversity and Intercultural Dialogue*, vol 2 (UNESCO 2009) chapter 6.

55 Graham Dutfield, *Harnessing Traditional Knowledge and Genetic Resources for Local Development and Trade* (2005) Draft paper presented at the International Seminar on Intellectual Property and Development Organized by WIPO jointly with UNCTAD, UNIDO, WHO and WTO (2005) 11.

56 Operational Directives for the implementation of the Conventions (2018) 104.

57 Cécile Duvelle, 'We Need to Make Synergies between the Conventions: This Is the Next Step for UNESCO…' (2017) 2017 *Santander Art and Cult Law Rev* 21, 23.

58 Agreeing with Dutfield, positive protection is not enough when traditional knowledge has fallen into the public domain. There is a need for compensation. See Graham Dutfield, 'Legal and Economic Aspects of Traditional Knowledge' in Keith Eugene Maskus and Jerome H Reichman (eds), *International Public Goods and Transfer of Technology under a Globalized Intellectual Property Regime* (CUP 2005) 514.

intellectual property rights regarding the protection of textile arts as other communities have done in Latin America, e.g., the Ecuadorian toquilla straw hat inscribed in 2012 on the UNESCO Representative List of the Intangible Cultural Heritage of Humanity,[59] and registered as *Montecristi*, a national denomination of origin which is a type of geographical indication. Both registrations have provided tools to keep the weavers in business. Carrera asserts that sales have increased, but also, valuable to safeguarding and preserving, schools teaching the art of weaving have become popular among the younger generation.[60] Consequently, organisations are providing clean water, medical care, and trade workshops and paying a sales commission to weavers, enhancing communities – giving pride and making them visible to governments' agendas. Robinson and Picard recognise that safeguarding heritage from being forgotten or threatened generates 'collective identity'.[61] Nevertheless, neither an inscription at UNESCO nor a legal entitlement granting intellectual property should be seen as the end of a project. Safeguarding is a never-ending plan of action.[62]

A registered UNESCO project is a starting point for several action points in which local governments and societies play a role. The window provided by UNESCO permits global society to become aware of the intrinsic value of traditional knowledge and traditional cultural expressions, but what follows? Popular online marketplaces such as Amazon or Etsy reveal hundreds of 'genuine' and 'original traditional cultural expressions', but there is nothing to guarantee that these are 'genuine' pieces or that royalties are benefiting the stakeholders and if so, in an equitable way. Consequently, communities are harmed by not obtaining profits[63] (due to misappropriation), and traditional cultural expressions lose intrinsic value (by appropriation) which goes farther than deprivation of an economic benefit.[64] Tools such as collective marks, certification marks, and geographical indications may provide parties national legal recognition, that is, positive defence, and a defensive protection tool. In the case of a geographical indication, specifically, a denomination of origin, it may guarantee that the entire chain is certified, from the farming or herding stage to the marketing of the finished product. The value-chain includes the production attributes, having a system of control, standards, and obtaining visibility via branding.[65] However, these tools are

59 Decision of the Intergovernmental Committee: 7.COM 11.12.

60 GL Carrera, 'Denominaciones de Origen en el Ecuador. Consorcios de Origen' (paper presented in Bogotá, Colombia, 11 December 2013, sponsored by the Ecuadorian National Intellectual Property Office and Artesanías de Colombia).

61 Robinson and Picard (n 37) 57.

62 'Montecristi' continues to run campaigns, e.g., in 2020 the national Ecuadorian Intellectual Property Office streamed a limited series 'Montecristi: Fabrics of Origin'.

63 Robert K Paterson and Dennis S Karjala, 'Looking beyond Intellectual Property in Resolving Protection of the Intangible Cultural Heritage of Indigenous Peoples' (2003) 11 *Cardozo J Int'l & Comp L* 633, 637.

64 See further ibid, 658.

65 Davide Petenella, 'Sustainable Management of Wild Collected Products for GIs' (OriGin Webinar) 12 November 2020, Zurich.

regulated nationally and do not have legal extra-territorial enforcement. Ideally, conscious buyers buy the product with confidence and are pleased that there is a recognition of and a benefit to communities by seeing labels of origin such as a collective mark, certification mark, or geographical indication. An example is the label 'Fair Trade' that aims to bring greater social justice to small farmers. This started as an alternative trading mechanism and now has brought to society a moral, economy and ethics attitude. However, while consumers value ethical aspects and create an emotional link with a product, one cannot be romantic. By using a measurable 'research model' a team based in Belgium asserts that actually, the most important attribute when buying a product is the brand, and the 'Fair Trade' label is the third attribute.[66] While ethicality appears not to be the number one reason for buying a product, consumers' buying behaviour does have a positive mind-set towards it but not as much as we would like to think.[67]

Zografos provides examples of how best to use intellectual property in the marketplace, preventing misappropriation and contributing to the safeguarding of traditional cultural expressions.[68] In Latin America, there are various examples: 'Autentico Pemon' (Venezuela) as a certification mark promoting Indigenous handicraft; from Colombia's cultural heritage and registered denomination of origins there are the 'Artesanías de Guacamayas'[69] for handicraft products, a tradition inherited from the pre-Columbian *Lache* culture; 'Tejedurias Wayuu'[70] made by the women from the *Wayuu* tribe; 'Sombrero Zenú', a hat made by the Zenú Indigenous Reservation; and the handicraft women from Goiabeira (Brazil) organised themselves into an association and applied successfully to the National Heritage Institute for the recognition of their pottery craft which originated from the *Tupi-Guarani* and *Una*, both ancient Indigenous cultures, and passed from mother to daughter,[71] and later registered as an Indicação de Procedência (a type of geographical indication). From the Colombian examples, we gather that Wayuu and Zenú do not refer to a territory, which is common to geographical indication names indicating geographical origin, *terroir*. The selected denomination of origins refers to the name of a people and is based on, as a crucial factor, the human knowledge, their traditional knowledge. The Aymara communities may use the latter examples, as they are residents in several countries, potentially using an 'Aymara weavers' label. Jurisprudence on geographical indications refers to this as indirect geographical indication; Petenella calls it a typological origin product

66 Patrick De Pelsmacker, Liesbeth Driesen and Glenn Rayp, 'Do Consumers Care about Ethics? Willingness to Pay for Fair-Trade Coffee' (2005) 39 *J Consum Aff* 363.

67 ibid.

68 Daphne Zografos Johnsson, 'The Branding of Traditional Cultural Expressions: To Whose Benefit?' in Peter Drahos and Susy Frankel (eds) (n 43) 147.

69 Resolución 30000 de 19 junio de 2009.

70 Resolución 71098 de 07 de diciembre de 2011.

71 Elizabeth Ferreira da Silva and Patrícia Pereira Peralta, 'Collective Marks and Geographical Indications: Competitive Strategy of Differentiation and Appropriation of Intangible Heritage' (2011) 16 *J Intellect Prop Rights* 246.

which is named after special areas, like national parks, e.g., Potato Park of Peru, and Indigenous communities, e.g., Tejedurías Wayuu.[72]

Generally, the international intellectual property debate links geographical indications to traditional knowledge due to its indefinite term of protection, the collective interest, the relationship with the land, and the knowledge that comes from the land.[73] Traditional cultural expressions cannot be given only a label of cultural originality but also an intellectual property label signposting their origin and its differentiation from other products; legal protection can also be obtained, making those that engage in cross-cultural appropriations and misappropriation weak defendants. The consequence of this intellectual property label goes farther than a mere assertion of originality; it provides an assertion and exclusionary right of self-determination and a principle of respect, dignity, and cultural integrity.[74]

Intellectual property: you have been warned. Checklist

Intellectual property is *territorial*, meaning that it will be protected in the national territory it was registered in and prevents the registration and marketing of the same name by third parties in that national territory. Yet, the enforceability of intellectual property rights is always a problem.[75] Bolivia, Chile, and Peru recognise handicrafts as denominations of origin, which recognises the crucial role and the qualitative link brought by both natural and human factors. This means that all producers, manufacturers, or weavers operating within the delimited geographical area, including those who were not among those who initially applied for recognition, shall have the right to use the denomination of origin if they comply with the provisions governing its use. However, a technical map is submitted for geographical indications, and in the Aymara case, it covers three countries. Intellectual property is a national law, so to what extent would this be a valid application? The national application will need to indicate the specific national/regional map when the Aymara communities are localised. Consequently, three applications in the three countries are needed, as there cannot be a joint application as the communities belong to different jurisdictions. Even so, when products cross borders and trade among these countries, a legitimate 'Aymara textile' product will be taken as a fake because it is not a 'national' one. This indeed seems a reason to dismiss this intellectual property tool. How can it be overcome? For instance, the

72 Davide Petenella, 'Sustainable Management of Wild Collected Products for GIs' (OriGin Webinar) 12 November 2020, Zurich.

73 Susy Frankel, 'The Mismatch of Geographical Indications and Innovative Traditional Knowledge' (2011) 29 *Prometheus* 253.

74 In this section the word 'authenticity' is avoided. The Intangible Cultural Heritage Convention rejects 'authenticity' as a criterion for heritage identification, while the intellectual property system defends authenticity (recognised as something original or new). Therefore, the word 'genuine' is preferable.

75 Sophia Twarog and Promila Kapoor, *Protecting and Promoting Traditional Knowledge: Systems, National Experiences and International Dimensions* (UN 2004) 65.

EU geographical indication regime granted 'Pisco' to Peru, without hindering the use of 'Pisco' from Chile, which is also a recognised geographical indication in the EU. This is also the case in Thailand.[76] Essentially, a country may allow the registration of a geographical indication but preserve the right of another country to use that same geographical indication. This will work for the Aymara communities' transboundary traditional cultural expressions. Remarkably, the Geneva Act of the Lisbon Agreement sets up the possibility of registering transboundary geographical indications. Article 5(4) allows contracting parties to the Act to file a joint application in cases where the product comes from a transboundary geographical area, yet the issue is that the countries must be contracting parties, and in the present case, only Peru has signed it.

Another warning is that in some Latin American countries, the geographical indication system is *controlled* by the government or owned by the state, e.g., Mexico. Others do not expressly confer a property right on the geographical indication but designate a party (an individual or an association) entitled to 'use' the geographical indication, e.g., Bolivia, Peru, Argentina.[77] An indirect effect of UNESCO's objective is to empower communities, and entitling a government can be seen as undesirable by a people still battling for their recognition. Smiths remarks on the crucial link between heritage and identity and the importance of controlling heritage to manage such identity.[78] Graber and Lai agreed that Indigenous knowledge assets may enhance socio-economic development but only as long as they are controlled by them (per UNDRIP).[79] In any case, the granting of an intellectual property registration can be seen as given by a government authority with discretionary power to make decisions over heritage.[80] Additionally, in a transboundary matter, they will be controlled by different national bodies, which must agree on their standards, processes, tools, etc., before submitting to their national body. Any changes and amendments must be coordinated with the Aymara communities in the three countries.

Management can be an issue. The basic function of collective and certification marks, as well as geographical indications, is the information function, but they cannot escape the *managerial role* that they play. The latter sees the introduction of rules, standards, and inspections, which consequently, may interfere in the organisations that are structured around them.[81] Organisation, policies, and

76 Patricia Covarrubia, 'Chile vs Peru: The Battle over "Pisco" Continues' (*IPTango*, 02 October 2019) <https://iptango.blogspot.com/2019/10/chile-vs-peru-battle-over-pisco.html> accessed 2 December 2021.

77 Patricia Covarrubia, 'Protection of Non-Agricultural GIs: A Window on What Is Happening in Latin America' (2016) 38(3) *EIPR* 129.

78 Laurajane Smiths, *The Uses of Heritage* (Routledge 2006).

79 The 2016 American Declaration on the Rights of Indigenous Peoples (ADRIP) AG/RES. 2888 (XLVI-O/16) is also applicable to the region under analysis in this chapter.

80 Graber (n 13) 22.

81 Marina Dantas de Figueiredo, 'The Effects of Safeguarding on Ways to Organize, Produce and Reproduce Intangible Cultural Heritage' (2015) 13 *PASOS Revista de Turismo y Patrimonio Cultural* 1037.

technical documents have not only legal consequences but also economic ones, which is detrimental due to Indigenous peoples and communities having limited resources. Moreover, policies of safeguarding intangible heritage obstruct 'the action of individuals that can produce and reproduce cultural assets' and commodified cultural identities.[82] A people divided by a geographical border can be seen as a difficult task to manage. Organisation for collective marks and geographical indications and, consequently, a well-organised group of producers are necessary.[83] Indigenous peoples, communities, and small farmers are usually isolated from each other, and in the Aymara case, geographical and political borders separate them. Yet, CRESPIAL can continue with the coordination and assistance of the Aymara communities as it successfully did with the UNESCO application.

Caution is needed with the boom of *tourism* when linked to heritage; indeed, there is a connection between tourism and national heritage with potential economic benefits.[84] For instance, in Colombia, the 'Artesanías de Colombia', which is the institution in charge of the development and promotion of handicrafts, is attached to the Ministry of Commerce, Trade and Tourism.[85] Economic development might affect the production of the craft by introducing production at an industrial scale, which may modify the specific context of this form of craft, the human factor;[86] additionally, tourism does not necessarily spread economic fruits equally.[87] This brings us to a matter widely covered by scholars, the effect of modernisation and commercialisation. The extensively covered debate aside, it is relevant to evaluate what the UNESCO Subsidiary Body has noted on this.

Concerning the *modernisation* of production methods, it is not taken to be an a priori disqualifying factor. While each case is studied on its own merits, modernisation does not impinge if first, the human factor continues to be a key element,[88] and second, if it properly respects the objectives of the communities concerned.[89] To expect Indigenous peoples and communities to continue using traditional techniques may have repercussions occasioning a low subsistence, and consequently could place an enormous burden on them.[90] Equally, by accommodating

82 ibid.

83 Frankel (n 73).

84 Figueiredo (n 81).

85 Patricia Covarrubia, 'Colombia: Intellectual Property and Aboriginal Handicraft' in Sarah Sargent and Jo Samanta (eds), *Indigenous Rights Changes and Challenges for the 21st Century* (University of Buckingham Press 2016) 76.

86 Figueiredo (n 81).

87 While tourism can have positive economic benefits connected to employment and other incomes, there are also threats posed by this industry. See Marie-Theres Albert et al., *Community Development through World Heritage* (UNESCO 2012) 50, 52; Robinson and Picard (n 37) 9.

88 See Johnsson (n 68) 157.

89 Decision of the Intergovernmental Committee: 4.COM 15B.

90 Graham Dutfield, *Developing and Implementing National Systems for Protecting Traditional Knowledge: A Review of Experiences in Selected Developing Countries* (UNCTAD 2000) 144.

new technology, natural resources could be overexploited.[91] They have a right to develop following their expectations, and UNESCO notes the need to respect the communities' wishes. In agreement with Gervais, the issue with changes to traditional products is to do with who decides if they are needed and 'on what basis';[92] control must remain with the community.

Commercialisation is not an a priori disqualifying factor either. Certainly, traditional cultural expressions play a vital role for some communities if they rely on them for their economic development. Nevertheless, excessive commercialisation could distort traditional cultural expressions;[93] one should avoid converting culture into a commodity.[94] It does not mean that traditional cultural expressions should not be commercialised, because culture entails, aside from 'art and heritage', 'ways of life',[95] including economic sustainable development for communities. Processes ought to remain under the control of the communities.[96] Coombe and Aylwin discuss the case of 'Chulucanas' (pottery, Peru),[97] where changes in the production process were introduced due to the national intellectual property office establishing a partnership with international exports to meet the orders.[98] By deleting the 'human factor', noted by the Sub Body as a key element, the economic success may mean the deterioration of the cultural value of the traditional cultural expression. Therefore, it is crucial to reemphasise the fact that changes and amendments must be coordinated with the communities.

Finally, traditional knowledge *evolves* and many claim that the intellectual property system is *static* due to fixation at the time of registration. The intellectual property tools mentioned for the potential protection of Aymara's textiles permit slight amendments to the records. This is observed in Champagne, which has grown from its traditional roots.[99] While quality control systems appear to inhibit innovations,[100] geographical indications take into consideration the ever-changing nature of the environment as much as the human factor, modernisation, and the like. Blakeney asserts that geographical indication protects the indication as well

91 Rudi Colloredo-Mansfeld, 'Work, Cultural Resources, and Community Commodities in the Global Economy' (2011) 32 *Anthropol Work Rev* 51.

92 Gervais (n 45) 134.

93 Decision of the Intergovernmental Committee: 4.COM 15B.

94 The UNESCO Convention on the Protection and Promotion of the Diversity of Cultural Expressions.

95 Christiaan De Beukelaer, Miikka Pyykkönen and JP Singh, *Globalization, Culture, and Development: The UNESCO Convention on Cultural Diversity* (Springer 2015) 19.

96 Decision of the Intergovernmental Committee: 4.COM 15B.

97 Resolution No 011517 – 2006/OSD-INDECOPI. The national and international applications note the use of hand paddles and stone polishing. Coombe and Aylwin claim that machines and ceramic moulds have replaced these. See Rosemary J Coombe and Nicole Aylwin, 'Bordering Diversity and Desire: Using Intellectual Property to Mark Place-Based Products' (2011) 43 *Environment and Planning A: Economy and Space* 2027, 2035.

98 ibid 2034–2035.

99 Frankel (n 73) 253.

100 Justin Hughes, 'Champagne, Feta, and Bourbon: The Spirited Debate about Geographical Indications' (2006) 58 *Hastings Law J* 299.

as the innovations that stand behind it.[101] This goes in line with the Subsidiary Body recognising that intangible cultural heritage might change in time and space adapting to the needs of contemporary life.[102] The intellectual property system provides both positive and defensive protection, but it does not protect traditional knowledge as such; it protects against third parties using their names, logos, identification, etc. It is not the perfect system either for Indigenous peoples or communities or for society;[103] and even if ideal legal systems exist, they are run by human beings and can be corrupted or abused.

In this case study, intellectual property might indirectly help in the preservation of customs and skills, which is crucial to traditional knowledge interests and economic benefits from it as in the *Montecristi* example. The use of a geographical indication, which has been linked to rural development, may be compatible with many forms of Indigenous innovation and production. However, benefits should not be measured by economic success, but by how a community has enhanced its day-to-day life, including maintaining well-being and having a sustainable local ecosystem.[104] By this reflection, the synergies between the 2003 Convention and the intellectual property system are noticeable.

Moving forward

Under the United Nations Conference on Trade and Development (UNCTA) Bolivia, Chile, and Peru are regarded as 'developing economies'.[105] The business sector of many developing countries is considered to have an extensive informal sector and is therefore difficult to collect data from.[106] The handicraft sector is made mostly of micro-small businesses with no sophisticated workforce and is developed with the local culture. To promote community-based development, measures such as national mapping of traditional knowledge, access to finances, technical assistance, and encouraging the formation of producers' associations must be present.[107] UNESCO registration and shared intellectual property tools play a role, but other measures must be in place for safeguarding.

Intellectual property protection of traditional cultural expressions might work for some, and a case-by-case evaluation is needed. By studying other traditional

101 Michael Blakeley, 'The Pacific Solution: The European Union's Intellectual Property Rights Activism in Australia's and New Zealand's Sphere of Influence' in P Drahos and S Frankel (eds) (n 43) 185.

102 The Subsidiary Body Decision 4.COM 15.B.

103 Generally, heated debate exists in the intellectual property system, e.g., patents on pharma products and the right to health.

104 Dutfield (n 90) 142.

105 United Nations Conference on Trade and Development, 'UNCTAD Handbook of Statistics 2019' (UNCTAD, 10 December 2019).

106 Noëlla Richard, *Handicrafts and Employment Generation for the Poorest Youth and Women* (UNESCO 2007).

107 Twarog and Kapoor, *Protecting and Promoting Traditional Knowledge: Systems, National Experiences and International Dimensions* (UNCTAD 2004) 67.

cultural expressions in Latin America, Bolivia, Chile, and Peru should evaluate whether it may work for the Aymara communities. The emphasis is to assess both successful and unsuccessful cases and to examine legislation, projects, and incentives that are feasible to achieve. The WIPO provides guidelines for developing national legislations for the protection of traditional knowledge and traditional cultural expressions based on the Pacific Model Law 2002,[108] which provide a strategy to check if an intellectual property tool can meet the needs of the Aymara communities. Seeking appropriate directions, the following are some of the questions that the Aymara communities need to reflect upon: what is the subject matter of protection? Equally, what type of protection is needed to safeguard and preserve their traditional cultural expressions? What are the criteria for protection, and the scope of such protection, including limitation to such rights? This is under the understanding that traditional knowledge as such is not protected however intellectual property indirectly contributes to preserving knowledge, protecting reputation,[109] and providing positive and defensive protection. Moreover, it may help with collective organisation, and subsequently, what would be the formalities for protection and how will rights be enforced? Who are the beneficiaries of protection and how will they be managed? Communities should reflect on these questions and in this case, how the regional protection in neighbouring countries should be addressed.

Conclusion

Transboundary cooperation on the protection, promotion, and enhancement of Aymara's textiles in shared heritage should not only be seen as a challenge but can potentially be seen as an opportunity to start collaborations and secure relationships among separated communities (separated by force or by a border). Certainly, organising communities might help to enhance them as this brings social unity. UNESCO's registration of the Aymara's project can be a starting point to collect data. Previous examples can help communities to generate sets of best practices while others can be used to anticipate possible pitfalls. Yet, a multi-stakeholder dialogue is crucial in trying to reach a common and clear understanding of what is pursued. There are difficulties such as not trusting external parties or governments, mainly if the authority to license the use of the traditional knowledge does not rely on the same community. Matters of lack of awareness of local innovation capabilities, technical matters, and external and economic assistance must be resolved.[110] Additionally, the challenge of division, due to

108 WIPO, 'Guidelines for Developing National Legislation for the Protection of Traditional Knowledge and Expressions of Culture Based on the Pacific Model Law 2002', Secretariat of the Pacific Community (WIPO 2006).

109 Johnsson (n 68) 158.

110 The Peruvian Intellectual Property Office runs campaigns covering the free application for collective marks for small enterprises. The Ecuadorian counterpart runs plans where national geographical indications do not pay any fee for their registration.

geographical borders, is a burden, but will not impinge when there is a willingness from the community and the government. While a conclusion to the main question, whether UNESCO's registration has enhanced Aymara's traditional knowledge, cannot be answered simply, perhaps the five-year deadline was not realistic; it is important to be open-minded about intellectual property (yet wary) and understand that this is a tool that provides economic protection which can be used for 'preservation', 'safeguarding', and 'promotion' in line with UNESCO's objective.

Although the world awaits international development for the legal protection of traditional knowledge, the UNESCO registration of the Aymara project can be used by the countries to fulfil many aims. A good part of the project was the first step: coordinating the communities, NGOs, and GOs was successfully tested by CRESPIAL when applying to UNESCO. Yet, we as individuals play an important role in the safeguarding of traditional cultural expressions and need to build greater awareness; we must be self-reflective as consumers and then, together, we can knit a future for the Aymara weavers.

References

Alarcón T, 'Ayllu, the Basic Social Unit of the Aymara People' (2001) 14 *St Thomas L Rev* 449

Albert M-T et al., *Community Development Through World Heritage* (UNESCO 2012)

Blakeney M, 'The Pacific Solution: The European Union's Intellectual Property Rights Activism in Australia's and New Zealand's Sphere of Influence' in P Drahos and S Frankel (eds), *Indigenous Peoples' Innovation Intellectual Property Pathways to Development* (ANU Press 2012)

Colloredo-Mansfeld R, 'Work, Cultural Resources, and Community Commodities in the Global Economy' (2011) 32 *Anthropol of Work Rev* 51

Coombe R J and Aylwin N, 'Bordering Diversity and Desire: Using Intellectual Property to Mark Place-Based Products' (2011) 43 *Environment and Planning A: Economy and Space* 2027

Covarrubia P, 'Colombia: Intellectual Property and Aboriginal Handicraft' in S Sargent and J Samanta (eds), *Indigenous Rights Changes and Challenges for the 21st century* (University of Buckingham Press 2016a)

——— 'Protection of Non-Agricultural GIs: A Window on What is Happening in Latin America' (2016b) 38(3) *EIPR* 129

——— 'Chile vs Peru: The Battle Over "Pisco" Continues' (*IPTango*, 2 October 2019)

Cusicanqui S R, *Oprimidos pero no Vencidos: Luchas del Campesinado Aymara y Qhechwa, 1900–1980* (Aruwiyiri, Editorial del Taller de Historia Oral Andino (THOA 2003))

da Silva E F and Peralta P P, 'Collective Marks and Geographical Indications-Competitive Strategy of Differentiation and Appropriation of Intangible Heritage' (2011) 16 *J Intellect Prop Rights* 246

De Beukelaer C, Pyykkönen M and Singh J, *Globalization, Culture, and Development: The UNESCO Convention on Cultural Diversity* (Springer 2015)

De Pelsmacker P, Driesen L and Rayp G, 'Do Consumers Care About Ethics? Willingness to Pay for Fair-Trade Coffee' (2005) 39 *J Consum Aff* 363

Donders Y, 'A Right to Cultural Identity in UNESCO' in F Francioni and M Scheinin (eds), *Cultural Human Rights* (Martinus Nijhoff Publishers 2008)

Drahos P and Frankel S, *Indigenous Peoples' Innovation: Intellectual Property Pathways to Development* (ANU Press 2012)

Dutfield G, *Developing and Implementing National Systems for Protecting Traditional Knowledge: A Review of Experiences in Selected Developing Countries* (UNCTAD 2000)

——— *Harnessing Traditional Knowledge and Genetic Resources for Local Development and Trade* (2005) Draft paper presented at the International Seminar on Intellectual Property and Development Organized by WIPO jointly with UNCTAD, UNIDO, WHO and WTO (2005a)

——— 'Legal and economic aspects of traditional knowledge' in K E Maskus and J Reichman (eds), *International Public Goods and Transfer of Technology under a Globalized Intellectual Property Regime* (CUP 2005b)

Duvelle C, 'We Need to Make Synergies between the Conventions. This is the Next Step for UNESCO…' (2017) 2017 *Santander Art and Cult Law Rev* 21

Figueiredo M D, 'The Effects of Safeguarding on Ways to Organize, Produce and Reproduce Intangible Cultural Heritage' (2015) 13 *PASOS Revista de Turismo y Patrimonio Cultural* 1037

Frankel S, 'The Mismatch of Geographical Indications and Innovative Traditional Knowledge' (2011) 29 *Prometheus* 253

Graber C B, 'Aboriginal Self-Determination vs the Propertisation of Traditional Culture' (2009) 13 *Aust Indig Law Rev* 18

Hafstein V T, 'Intangible Heritage as a List: from Masterpieces to Representation' in L Smith and N Akagawa (eds), *Intangible Heritage* (Routledge 2009)

Heath A, Javois A and Freudenthal F, 'Weaving Indigenous Textile Art Into Cardiac Devices' (2018) 319 *Jama* 966

Hughes J, 'Champagne, Feta, and Bourbon: The Spirited Debate About Geographical Indications' (2006) 58 *Hastings Law J* 299

Johnsson D Z, 'The Branding of Traditional Cultural Expressions: To Whose Benefit?' in P Drahos and S Frankel (eds), *Indigenous Peoples' Innovation: Intellectual Property Pathways to Development* (ANU Press 2012)

Lixinski L, 'Selecting Heritage: The Interplay of Art, Politics and Identity' (2011) 22 *Eur J Int Law* 81

Muller M R, *Regulating Bioprospecting and Protecting Indigenous Peoples' Knowledge in the Andean Community: Decision 391 and its Overall Impacts in the Region* (Protecting and Promoting Traditional Knowledge: Systems, National Experiences and International Dimensions, 2000)

Núñez R E and Cornejo C, 'Facing the Sunrise: Cultural Worldview Underlying Intrinsic-Based Encoding of Absolute Frames of Reference in Aymara' (2012) 36 *Cognitive Science* 965

Osborne H, *Indians of the Andes: Aymaras and Quechuas* (Routledge 2013)

Paterson R K and Karjala D S, 'Looking Beyond Intellectual Property in Resolving Protection of the Intangible Cultural Heritage of Indigenous Peoples' (2003) 11 *Cardozo J Int'l & Comp L* 633

Richard N, *Handicrafts and Employment Generation for the Poorest Youth and Women* (UNESCO 2007)

Rivière F, *Investing in Cultural Diversity and Intercultural Dialogue, vol 2* (UNESCO 2009)

Robinson M and Picard D, *Tourism, Culture and Sustainable Development* (UNESCO 2006)

Sargent S, 'The Contested Meaning of Free, Prior and Informed Consent in International Financial Law and Indigenous Rights' in V Vadi and B de Witte (eds), *Culture and International Economic Law* (Routledge 2005)

Twarog S and Kapoor P, *Protecting and Promoting Traditional Knowledge: Systems, National Experiences and International Dimensions* (UN 2004)

United Nations Educational Scientific and Cultural Organization, *Convention for the Safeguarding of the Intangible Cultural Heritage* (UNESCO 2003)

Von Lewinski S, 'The Protection of Folklore' (2003) 11 *Cardozo J Int'l & Comp L* 747

WIPO, *Guidelines for Developing National Legislation for the Protection of Traditional Knowledge and Expressions of Culture based on the Pacific Model Law 2002, Secretariat of the Pacific Community* (WIPO 2006)

——— *Protect and Promote Your Culture: A Practical Guide to Intellectual Property for Indigenous Peoples and Local Communities* (WIPO 2017)

Index

Note: Page numbers in *italics* indicate figures, **bold** indicates tables, and 'n' refers to footnotes.